Jazz Anecdotes

JAZZ

Anecdotes Second Time Around

BILL CROW

OXFORD
UNIVERSITY PRESS
2005

OXFORD
UNIVERSITY PRESS

Oxford University Press, Inc., publishes works that further
Oxford University's objective of excellence
in research, scholarship, and education.

Oxford New York
Auckland   Cape Town   Dar es Salaam   Hong Kong   Karachi
Kuala Lumpur   Madrid   Melbourne   Mexico City   Nairobi
New Delhi   Shanghai   Taipei   Toronto

With offices in
Argentina   Austria   Brazil   Chile   Czech Republic   France   Greece
Guatemala   Hungary   Italy   Japan   Poland   Portugal   Singapore
South Korea   Switzerland   Thailand   Turkey   Ukraine   Vietnam

First published by Oxford University Press, Inc., 1990, 2005
198 Madison Avenue, New York, New York 10016
www.oup.com

First issued as an Oxford University Press Paperback, 1991, 2005

Oxford is a registered trademark of Oxford University Press

Library of Congress Cataloging-in-Publication Data
Crow, Bill
Jazz anecdotes / Bill Crow.—2nd time around
p. cm.
Includes bibliographical references (p.) and index.
ISBN-13: 978-0-19-518795-3 (pbk.: alk. paper)

1. Jazz—Anecdotes
I. Title.
ML3506.C76 2005
781.65—dc22   2005012877

9 8 7 6 5
Printed in the United States of America

For Aileen

Preface to the New Edition

The original edition of *Jazz Anecdotes* was published in 1990, and the paperback edition seems to have become a minor classic in the jazz world. I keep meeting people who tell me the special place it occupies in their libraries, bedrooms, bathrooms, schoolrooms. One jazz educator told me, "Your books are required reading in all my classes. They give my students a real taste of what it means to be a jazz musician."

Sheldon Meyer, the now retired senior editor at Oxford University Press, was the one who originally encouraged me to assemble this book on the strength of my column of musicians' anecdotes called "The Band Room" which still runs every month in *Allegro*, the official publication of Local 802, American Federation of Musicians. I have been writing that column since 1983, and still manage to find enough musician stories to fill a page every month. In the fourteen years since *Jazz Anecdotes* was published, stories have continued to accumulate in my files. Linda Robbins, my editor at Oxford, suggested a revised edition of this book with some of that material added. I've selected a number of the anecdotes I like best. They're sprinkled throughout the book in the appropriate chapters. I hope this edition of *Jazz Anecdotes* continues to provide those who love jazz with entertainment and possibly some insight.

Those interested in my "Band Room" columns can find them at the Local 802 website, www.local802afm.org. And my own personal stories are still available in the Oxford paperback *From Birdland to Broadway*.

Bill Crow
November 2004

Preface

Jazz musicians are bound together by a rich and colorful history that lives in the music itself, remembered, created and re-created. In addition, we have stories about ourselves, stretching back to the beginnings of the music, that are told and retold; legends and laughter that remind us of who we are and where we are from.

Most jazz musicians are good laughers. If you want to play jazz for a living you either learn to laugh or you cry a lot. We don't laugh all the time; we have our low moments just like the rest of the world. But the pleasure of getting together to play the music we love seems to bring out our good humor.

As a bass player, I can expect to be asked with some regularity, "Don't you wish you played the piccolo?" The questioner's tone implies that he has thought of a humorous comment on the plight of someone who plays an instrument of such an inconvenient size. But that's not a joke that makes musicians laugh. The size of a bass is appropriate to the wonderful sound it produces and is not considered a handicap by bass players. If I wanted to play the piccolo, I'd play one.

Musical jokes from outside the profession rarely tickle the funnybones of musicians. Our own jokes arise from exaggerating the realities of our lives. Like:

"How late does the band play?"
"About half a beat behind the drummer." Or,

"What's the difference between a bass and a cello?"
"A bass burns longer." Or,

"How can a jazz musician wind up with a million dollars?"
"Start out with two million." Or,

"What sort of people hang around musicians?"
"Drummers."

(There are some longer musicians' jokes in Chapter 43.)

The anecdotes we tell about each other seem to be the ones we like the best. They remind us of our individuality and our human nature. There is a wonderful variety of subjects: bandstand stories, road stories, jam-session stories, bandleader stories, tales about innocence and venality, serendipity and catastrophe. And there are at least as many stories about Benny Goodman as there are ex-sidemen from his band. As an appetizer, here is a sampling of anecdotes from some of the categories delineated in the following chapters:

When Teddy Napoleon was playing piano with Gene Krupa's band, his sister Josephine was the vocalist, and Sid Caesar, later to become the famous comedian, was playing saxophone. They were driving through New Jersey to a gig in Pennsylvania and were stopped by a cop for speeding. Teddy was driving, and Gene was sitting next to him. Josephine was in the back seat with Sid Caesar. When the cop saw Teddy's license he said,
    "Napoleon?" and Sid began to laugh.
    The cop said, "What are you laughing at?"
    Sid said, "He's Napoleon and I'm Caesar!"
    The cop frowned at him.
    "Caesar and Napoleon, eh?" He looked at the girl in the back seat. "And I supposed you're Josephine?"
    "Yeah, how did you know?" ♪

John Glasel once played a gig with Willie "The Lion" Smith. During a break Smith began talking about astrology, and John said he didn't believe in it. Smith assured him it was very important, especially in one's love life.
    "Take me," he said. "I'm a Sagittarius, my wife is Sagittarius, and my chick is Sagittarius!" ♪

When New Orleans bass player Montudie Garland arrived in London on a concert tour, the English road manager, conscious of Garland's advanced age, inquired, "May I help you up to your room?" Garland replied, "Oh, thanks, man, but I'm okay. I got my chick with me." His "chick" was seventy-eight years old. ↬

In 1950, after Count Basie had broken up his big band, he put together a small group with Clark Terry, Buddy DeFranco, Bob Graf, Jimmy Lewis, and Gus Johnson. They worked a month at the Brass Rail in Chicago, where everyone was surprised that Freddie Green was not with the group. Green had been an important member of Basie's famous "All American Rhythm Section" during fourteen prewar years with the big band. When the sextet met in New York for their next gig, there was Green with his guitar. Clark Terry remembered the dialogue between Basie and Green, whose nickname was "Pepper":

"Say, Pep, *you're* not on this gig, are you?"

"You're workin', aren't you?" said Freddie. "After I gave you the best years of my life, you think you're going to leave me now?"

The sextet became a septet. Freddie remained as the anchor of the rhythm section when Basie reorganized his big band about a year later, and he stayed there for another thirty-five years. ↬

Russ Savakus and his wife Arlene came to New York in the early 1950s and found a house in Sunnyside, Queens. Russ used to take his bass to Bob Dorough's studio on the Upper West Side where there were nightly jam sessions. He got to know a lot of musicians there.

Late one night he got a call at home from a musician who was finishing an out of town engagement. He wanted Russ to do a job with him in New York on the next evening and also wanted him to find a piano player. Russ knew there would be someone at Dorough's, but Bob had no phone at the studio. Russ and Arlene jumped into their car and hurried toward Manhattan.

Afraid he might get there too late to find a pianist, Russ stepped on the gas pedal pretty hard. As they were crossing the Queensborough Bridge, he saw the flashing red light of a police car behind him.

"Hold your stomach!" he told Arlene as he pulled over. "I'll say you're having a miscarriage and we're rushing you to the hospital!"

Doubtfully, Arlene agreed. The cop looked in the window and growled, "All right, what's the hurry?"

Russ shouted desperately, "I've gotta get a piano player!" ♩

Joe Lopes was having a little difficulty at a New York City bank. He hadn't filled out a form correctly, and the lady who pointed out the error made an impatient remark that Joe took as a reflection on his intelligence.

"Hey," Joe bristled, "if you're so smart, what's a C-seventh?"

"C, E, G, B-flat," she replied. ♩

Trumpeter Johnny Best saw a sign at the bar of a Holiday Inn where the Bob Crosby band was staying: HAPPY HOUR—ALL YOU CAN DRINK FOR A DOLLAR. Johnny told the bartender,

"Give me two dollars' worth." ♩

One night as Gene Quill was leaving the bandstand at Birdland, a young self-appointed critic accosted him.

"All you're doing is playing just like Charlie Parker," he accused. Gene held out his saxophone.

"Here," he said, "*you* play just like Charlie Parker!" ♩

Patti Bown once played a record date with blues singer Jimmy Rushing ("Mr. Five by Five") and walked him out to a cab afterwards.

"He took up the whole back seat," said Patti.

Otto Preminger, who had just come out of the same building, stopped to watch Jimmy squeeze himself into the cab and couldn't resist commenting.

"You're the shortest, fattest man I've ever seen!" he said through the cab window.

Rushing smiled up at him and replied, "And you're the tallest, baldest man *I've* ever seen!" ♩

Bobby Hackett was known for never saying anything bad about anyone. When a friend insisted that he make some comment on Adolf Hitler, he though he had him. Bobby said,

"Well, he was the best in his field." ♩

George Wettling was driving back to New York through the Holland Tunnel early one morning after a gig in New Jersey. Finding no other cars in the Tunnel at that hour, he stepped down a little too hard on the gas. His speed attracted the attention of one of the Tunnel guards, who phoned ahead to the toll booth, where George was flagged down by a Port Authority cop.

"What's the big idea?" barked the cop. "You were doing sixty through the Tunnel!" George smiled apologetically.

"Gee, officer, I saw a sign in there that said 'Keep 45 feet apart' and I was just trying to catch up with the guy in front of me!" ♩

Al Klink was being interviewed by a radio disk jockey who was interested in Al's tenure on the Glenn Miller band.

"That band was never really considered one of the swing bands, was it?" asked the interviewer.

"We were all too scared to swing," Al replied.

After years of hearing Miller's hits revived ad nauseam, Al commented, "Glenn should have lived, and the music should have died." ♩

In his early days in Chicago, Bud Freeman knew an alto player named Bill Doler. Bud and Bill lived near Lincoln Park, and on the way home from work at four in the morning they often dropped in at the nearby Ohio Inn for a drink and a bite to eat. One morning Doler, fairly well oiled, thought it would be a good idea if they took some peanuts over to the Lincoln Park Zoo to feed the bears. Bud went along and watched with trepidation as Bill held some peanuts on his open hand between the bars of the polar bear's cage. The bear ate the nuts delicately, hardly touching his hand.

When Doler tried the same thing with the female grizzly in the next cage she clawed at his hand, slitting three of his fingers open. Horrified, Bud hurried him to a nearby hospital. The wounds took several weeks to heal.

Doler brooded a lot about the ungrateful bear, especially when he was drinking. One night he went home, got a five-iron from his golf bag and headed for the zoo. He yelled at the grizzly until it came near his side of the cage, then reached through the bars with the golf club and belted her on the head. Later, he told Bud, "As she was going down, I noticed she had a guilty look on her face." ↱

Anecdotes, arising from an oral tradition, have their own rules. A good story will often acquire modifications and improvements as it is retold. If the teller can't remember a particular detail he needs to move the story along, he will invent one and half believe in its veracity as he invents it, because it fits the situation. Things that happen to one person will sometimes be attributed to someone else who seems a more appropriate protagonist.

Once a good story enters the lore of the jazz world, it takes on a life of its own. A good example is the famous story about Red Kelly and the dog. Red, a large, good-natured bass player from the Pacific Northwest, was with the Woody Herman band in the 1950s. The widely repeated legend about him goes like this:

Red was invited to a party at the home of a wealthy patron of the arts. The liquor was flowing freely, and Red accepted most of the drinks that were offered. Toward the end of the evening he fumbled his way upstairs in search of a bathroom. As he made his way through an unlighted bedroom toward the bathroom door, he collided with a small writing desk, spilling a bottle of ink on the white rug. His clumsy attempts to mop up the spill only made things worse. He finally bolted from the room, leaving behind a horrible blot and several inky footprints. He fled the house, hurried home, and collapsed unconscious into his bed.

He awoke the next day and remembered the mess he had made at the party. Remorseful, he returned to the scene of the crime, intending to offer to have the rug cleaned. A maid answered the door and showed him into a small sitting room where she asked him to wait while she called the lady of the house. As Red dropped into an easy chair he heard a small yip beneath him. He leaped up and discovered his hostess's tiny dog, its neck broken. Completely unnerved, he hid the corpse under the lid of the grand piano and made a second escape, never to return. ↱

This story has been passed back and forth by musicians for thirty years. One or two writers have told their versions of the story in books and magazine articles, attributing it to Red Kelly. In 1980, novelist Tom Robbins borrowed it for *Still Life with Woodpecker*, ascribing the event to his redheaded outlaw bomber, Bernard Mickey Wrangle.

While preparing this book, I called Red Kelly at his home in Tacoma, Washington, and asked him for the year and location of the famous dog sitting on. He said:

The truth about that story is, I was on my way to work in Seattle one night with a trombone player named Mike Hobi, and he told me this story that he'd read someplace about the guy and the dog. I latched onto it, because I just loved it, and I started telling it to people. I guess because of my erratic behavior, people said, "Oh, you're just telling a story about yourself." I said, "No, it ain't me." But they just would say, "Ah, bullshit." Finally you just tell the story, and everybody assumes it's you. Total strangers would come up and say, "Are you the guy that sat on the dog?"

After years of going through this, it got to where I had finally re-signed myself, where I didn't even deny any complicity in it at all. People would come up to me in Florida or someplace, and say, "Are you the guy with the dog?"

"Yeah, that's me."

So I finally come back to Seattle and run into Mike Hobi, and he says, "Listen, tell me that story about you and the dog again." And he's the guy that told it to me! There are some colorful things that you do, but that wasn't one of them! It just got completely out of hand. ↳

I'm sure some readers of the foregoing will still attribute the story to Red. It's the kind of thing that *should* have happened to him. In this way myths are born. As you read this book, bear in mind that these stories are more akin to legends than to affidavits. I've gone to the source wherever possible, but even eye-witness accounts are often colored by the palette of the imagination.

Contents

Jazz Anecdotes

chapter 1

Wild Scenes

When the individuality of jazz musicians combines with the capricious world in which they try to make a living, events are often produced which the musicians describe as "wild scenes." Pops Foster gives an early example:

Around 1923 the delegate of Local 44 got a one-night job over at Beartown, Illinois, for a little pickup band. It was a little coal-mining town where the miners come in and bring a jug to drink on all night. This one big tough guy with a long mustache came carrying a crock jug over his shoulder. He was unshaven, dirty, and chewed tobacco and sat in a chair he'd pulled up right in front of the bandstand. He laid a big pistol in his lap and told us to play nothin' but *Yes! We Have No Bananas.* We started playing it and the guy who put on the dance came up and told us to do what they guy wanted or he'd break the dance up. All night long we played *Yes! We Have No Bananas* and the people there danced to it. Sometimes during the evening he'd want us to drink with him and would pass the jug up. None of us wanted to drink behind him, but we did. He'd sit there and sing to the music, twirl the pistol on his finger, and point it at us. Once in a while he'd get up to go to the bathroom. He'd stand up and tell us to stop playing and not to hit a lick until he got back. We didn't care how long he stayed, we waited until he got back. When he came back he'd say, "All right fellas, let's go," and we'd start playing. After all the people left he asked us if we had a good time. We all said, "yes." I never will forget that guy and fifty years later I still can't play *Yes We Got No Bananas* without nearly getting sick. ↱

Wingy Manone found a job where the music was hot, but the band uniforms were a bit unorthodox:

Chief Blue Cloud, a real Sioux Indian who played good trombone, was the leader of the band. I was introduced to his wife, Ida Blue Cloud, in a musicians' hangout one night, and she told me she and her husband were organizing a band for vaudeville and needed some hot musicians.

I told her I was from New Orleans, and I might be interested if I could play the kind of music I wanted to play—the real New Orleans stuff.

The Chief and his wife were the only real Indians in the band, and the rest of us had to wear wigs with long, black, plaited hair.

We wore feathers in our hair, had on beaded costumes, with tomahawks in the belt, and moccasins for shoes. When the curtain went up we'd be sitting in front of a tepee, with one guy playing a tomtom. Everybody would give an Indian call: "Woo-woo-woo-woo," and then we would jump up with a big war whoop and bust into some hot jazz. ↱

When Glenn Miller put together a band for Ray Noble, the English bandleader, for an engagement at the New York Rainbow Room, he included several jazz musicians: Charlie Spivak and Pee Wee Erwin on trumpets, Bud Freeman and Johnny Mince on saxophones, George Van Eps on guitar, Will Bradley and himself on trombones, and Claude Thornhill on piano. Violinist Fritz Prospero said:

All the VIPs came into the Rainbow Room, and one night after finishing the job we were called back to the stand because a Rockefeller had come in. When we started to play, Claude was missing, having already gotten changed. A minute later, he casually assumed his seat at the piano, minus his trousers! ↱

Noble often neglected to tell the band which ending he wanted played on tunes for which there were alternate endings written. George Van Eps explained:

By the time Ray would get around to telling us it was the first ending, half the guys would be through the second ending. It was always
chaos. One night we were almost through a tune and were wondering what to do. Claude's piano was stationary, but Ray's was revolv-
ing and he would disappear among the dancers and would turn up
again every twelve bars or so. Claude had grabbed a tablecloth from
one of the waiters. He stood up with it over his head and announced, "Madame Zucka says to take the second ending." The
place broke up. ♪

Pee Wee Erwin remembered a wild New Year's Eve at the Rainbow
Room with that band:

It's a safe bet that since it was New Year's Eve the band was pretty
well stoned. I know for certain the customers were. It all started in-
nocently enough while the band was playing and Al Bowlly was out
front singing. I think a dancer passed by too close and accidentally
kicked a microphone which was in front of Noble's piano and pro-
jected well onto the dance floor. Anyway the mike the customer
kicked hit Al Bowlly, who took a pretty dim view of the idea, and he
threw something at the customer—a tom-tom, or something else at
hand. The customer went back to this table, picked up a couple of
rolls, and fired them at the band, and the band fielded them and
fired them right back.

   The next thing we knew all kinds of things were flying through
the air of the very sedate Rainbow Room. Some people were even
throwing ice cream balls and the band was returning them. It got to
be bedlam, like a pie-throwing scene in a Mack Sennett comedy.
One of the trombone players used a plunger mute that had a hole
cut out in the middle of it, and Ray Noble retreated to the brass section, picked up a horn, inverted the plunger over the mouthpiece,
and then held it in front of his face for protection. You couldn't see
him, only the plunger. After a while things settled down, but the
next day we received a lot of adverse criticism in the press.   ♪

Another wild scene happened on a different New Year's Eve, in 1968 at
Sunnie's Rendezvous Club in Aspen, Colorado. The club was owned by
pianist Ralph Sutton and his wife Sunnie. In Ralph's trio were Jack Lesberg and Jake Hanna. Sunnie cornered Lesberg and asked him to con
Ralph into playing "Auld Lang Syne." Lesberg agreed to try:

I told Ralph we really should play it for the crowd, but he said, "Fuck 'em. I hate to play for all those rituals." I reminded him that it was the big night for the people—that they had paid their money to come in, and maybe we should do it anyway. He finally said, "OK, we'll see about it."

A few seconds before midnight I said, "This'd be a good time to do it, Ralph." Well, wouldn't you know. He broke into "The Star-Spangled Banner," and Jake jumped up behind the drums and started saluting and shouting at the tope of his voice, "Fuck Communism! Fuck Communism!" The whole place broke up. Those people just roared with laughter, and I think they enjoyed it more than "Auld Lang Syne." They must have because they drank their champagne and wished each other Happy New Year anyway. 🎵

Benny Carter once had a band at the Club Harlem, on the location of the old Connie's Inn. The club was in financial trouble and was about to go out of business. George Rich, a sporting gentleman, told Benny, "They can't do this to you. You've got to have a place for your band. Come over to the house tonight after the gig."

Benny did, and after they talked it over, Rich said, "Well, I'm going to buy the place." From behind his sofa cushions he began to dig stacks of money that he had stashed there, and then he got in touch with the club owners. Carter said:

He made a deal for something like $9000, and became the new owner. He'd come in once in a while and have a drink, and sit around, and I'd say, "George, what's gonna happen about so-and-so?" And he'd say, "I don't know. It's your club." His only purpose for buying the club was to keep my band together, and I shall never forget him for it. 🎵

Milt Hinton once worked with Eddie South at Ben Marden's Riviera on the Palisades cliffs in New Jersey:

Paul Whiteman's Orchestra was the featured group and we were the relief band. At that time Whiteman had some excellent musicians. Frankie Trumbauer, the great saxophone player, was an officer in the Army Air Corps and used to fly a seaplane to work every night. I remember he'd land on the Hudson and then walk up a steep set of steps cut into the Palisades to the club. 🎵

Trumbauer told some flying stories to his friend Buddy Tate:

He used to tell me some of his experiences with Paul Whiteman. He had his own plane and used to fly to his gig. One night they were opening at some big hotel in San Francisco. On the way his plane developed engine trouble and it ended up falling on the hotel they were to play. He *swore* this was the truth, that the plane just sat right on top of the hotel. "See this?" he said, pointing to a scar on his nose. "This came from that." 🔖

At a musicale held in 1935 at the Hammond mansion on East 91st Street in New York, John Hammond and his mother presented Benny Goodman playing classical music in public for the first time. Goodman and a string group played the Mozart Clarinet Quintet. Hammond describes the event:

The recital took place in the second-floor ballroom, which could seat about 250 people. It had an eighteen-foot ceiling with two ornate chandeliers, and there was an adjoining library whose paneled doors could be opened to seat about a hundred additional guests.

My own guest list included Fletcher Henderson and his wife Leora, Walter and Gladys White, Charlie Buchanan, the manager of the Savoy Ballroom in Harlem, and his wife Bessie, Mildred Bailey and Red Norvo, and Charlie Barnet. Mother's guests included Mrs. Andrew Carnegie, Miss Alice Van Rensselaer, Aunt Edith Robbins, Cousin Gertrude Whitney, and other members of her circle. Father invited his present and former partners. Benny invited most of the music publishers he knew.

Some of the audience sat on spindly gilt Hammond chairs, the rest on rented folding chairs. At the conclusion of the first movement, Charlie Barnet, a tall man who was feeling a bit cramped, stretched, pushing his feet against the chair in front of him. There was a resounding crash as it collapsed, and Mrs. Murray Crane, the head of the newly opened museum of Modern Art and a woman of generous proportions, went sprawling to the floor. Mildred Bailey, sitting in the front row next to Leora Henderson, observed the downfall of Mrs. Crane, considered the fragile support under her own couple of hundred pounds, and asked aloud, "How'm I doin'?"

Several years later, when I was profiled in *The New Yorker* by E.J. Kahn, Jr., the 91st Street concert evidently came up in our talks, but like all subjects of Profiles I was not shown Jack's piece until it was published. The story of Mrs. Murray Crane's collapse was included and to my embarrassment she called and was furious. Her dignity, at least, had been bruised. ↷

During World War II Wingy Manone was playing at Café Society Downtown. One night some sailors got belligerent because Wingy had ignored their request for a tune. A fight started. A sailor grabbed one of Wingy's hands, but it was the wrong one; Wingy's prosthetic arm came loose. The sailor stood there holding the arm, looking bewildered, until Wingy grabbed it with his good hand and started hitting the sailor on the head with it.

In the 1940s three New York jazz musicians who were trying their luck in California shared a small house in Hollywood. Because they ignored the community's strict garbage rules requiring paper, bottles, and metal to be separated from kitchen waste, the collectors refused to haul away their garbage. It piled up until there were complaints from the neighbors.

A warning from the health department finally stirred them to action. They rented a trailer, and after their Saturday night gig they hitched it to their car, threw in all the garbage and hauled it up into the hills. Finding a lonely stretch of woods, they backed the trailer in, dumped the contents down a slope, and went home to get some sleep.

A couple of hours later the police were at their door. The car and trailer parked in front of the house had made them easy to find. The garbage had poured down the slope where they had dumped it, out of the woods on the other side, and into George Raft's swimming pool. They spend that Sunday morning cleaning up the mess under the watchful eye of a policeman.

Bobby Sherwood's band toured some state fairs with a package show. One of the acts on the show was a trumpeter who played two trumpets at once. As Bobby wandered along the midway at one fairground, he discovered a band drumming up business in front of a tent show. It featured a trumpet player who, on the finale of his number, played three trumpets. Bobby went back and told the two-trumpet trumpeter, who said, "Playing three trumpets at once is a cheap theatrical stunt!"

Al Rose hired Irving Fazola to play a jazz concert in Philadelphia. He extracted a promise from him to lay off the booze until after the concert:

About 7:00 p.m. I got a call from Horn & Hardart's Automat Restaurant—the one an earlier generation of Philadelphians had nicknamed "The Heel" for reasons not known to me. The manager was on the line and wanted to know if I knew a Mr. Fazola. He went on to explain that Mr. Fazola had eaten more than he had intended and as a result had found himself wedged in one of those captain's chairs. He apparently could not be pried loose, even with the efforts of the manager and a strong pair of busboys. I immediately sent an ambulance to "The Heel" and hurried over there myself. It was only a few blocks away.

The manager hadn't exaggerated. There was Fazola, clearly jammed into the chair. "What the hell happened?" I demanded, concerned for his condition and for my concert.

"Well, I gave you my promise," he reminded me, prepared to put as much of the blame as possible on me for the inconvenient circumstance. "I told you I wouldn't drink nothin' today and I didn't." But he went on to tell how he'd gotten into town on the train a bit early and had eaten a hamburger or two.

"How many did you eat?" I asked him.

"Thirty-six," he admitted. "I still feel okay. I just can't get out of the chair."

So the two ambulance attendants, the two busboys, the manager, and I carefully loaded him, *with* the chair, into the ambulance, drove to the Academy of Music, and unloaded him carefully right at center stage of the auditorium. I paid everybody off and sent them on their ways.

Patrons of "Journeys into Jazz" who remember that night may recall thinking it odd to come to their seats promptly at 8:30 and see one of the great stars of jazz sitting contentedly on the stage putting his clarinet together. Those who were present may be pleased to know, at last, how that came about.

During the first half of the concert, Faz kept his seat—playing magnificently, but not standing for his solos as was customary. At intermission time, pianist Joe Sullivan, a trombone player named Munn Ware, and I pulled him loose. The second half of the concert went off without a hitch, though I did substitute a chair without confining arms. Faz then got up to do his solos, and nobody could tell we had started the evening with an emergency.

After the concert, Faz sheepishly suggested he'd like to go somewhere to eat. I took him to Billy Yancey's and Faz ordered—you
guessed it—hamburgers. ↯

Joe Darensbourg played clarinet with Mutt Carey's band in Los Angeles:

Our drummer Ram Hall was bald and he was always looking for a
way to grow hair. He would do anything if he thought he could grow
a couple of strands of hair on that bald head of his. A guy told Ram
to try putting chicken crap on his head, make a poultice out of it.
Ram promptly went out to Les Hite's chicken farm and got some
fresh chicken droppings to make the poultice. This guy told him to
keep it on for 24 hours at a stretch, so he marches up to the Liberty
Dance Hall with the thing on his head. It was the summertime and
all that stuff was pretty ripe. Pretty soon Mutt gets suspicious and
says, "You guys must have stepped in some crap, got it on your
shoes."

   Well, we all looked and finally Mutt spotted Ram with this thing
on his head. Everybody started laughing and Mutt got mad. He
made Ram go to the bathroom and wash his head. Ram says, all
hurt, "If that's the way you feel about it. You don't want me to grow
any hair." Mutt says, "You'll get us all fired off the job. Clean it up."
Ram would have lit a stick of dynamite on his head if he thought it
would grow hair. ↯

Henry Jerome had a bebop band for a short while in 1944. Lenny Garment had talked him into changing from a dance band to a modern jazz
band, playing the sort of music the small 52nd Street bop groups were
playing, in a big-band format. They were a few years too early. The New
York musicians loved the band, but the public never accepted it. Boyd
Raeburn and Woody Herman inherited Jerome's musicians when he
broke up the band for financial reasons.
   While booked into Childs' Paramount in New York, Henry made a surprising discovery:

Childs' was a very proper restaurant, under the Paramount Theater. The guys went in through a tunnel that went under Walgreen's
drug store. I always had one person go get the band to make sure
they came back on time. This time the guy couldn't find them, and
I didn't know where they were. In Walgreen's there was a whole row

of phone booths. I looked up there, and they were all filled guys in my band uniforms, making "phone calls." It was where ... went to get high. In Dorothy Kilgallen's column it said, "What name band leader in a local restaurant has his whole band smoking marijuana in phone booths?" I got nervous, because it was very illegal then. ↱

When Pete Candoli was on Woody Herman's band the muscular trumpet player worked up a Superman number. His wife made him a caped costume, and when the band played theaters Pete would leap onto the stage as Superman with his trumpet, just in time to come in on the bridge of "Apple Honey." Comedian Buddy Lester, who was traveling with the band, found use for Pete's old costume when it was discarded for a new one Pete's wife made for him. After Pete's Superman number, Buddy, much smaller than Candoli, would come shambling out from the wings wearing the baggy old Superman costume and playing sourly on a beat-up cornet.

Igor Stravinsky heard records of the Herman band and sent Woody a cable from France saying he'd been very moved by the music. He also informed Woody that he was writing something for him. When Stravinsky came to New York he brought his Ebony Concerto and presented it to Woody. He said it was a challenge to write for Woody's instrumentation, though he added a French horn and a harp. The band was playing an extended engagement at the Paramount Theater at the time, so they scheduled rehearsals between shows in a room on the top floor of the Paramount building. Woody said:

The whole band hurried after the first show to this rehearsal hall on the top floor, but everyone stopped in the dressing rooms to change clothes and put on a dark blue suit and shirt and tie, things that are not normal with musicians, because it was such a great honor that this man had come.

So Stravinsky arrived, wearing a sweatshirt and a pair of slacks and a towel around his neck, ready to go to work. We rehearsed for about an hour and a half, and then the buzzer buzzed. And then someone would escort him downstairs to Sardi's where he would have a little champagne. Then they would say, "Okay, now we go back to rehearsal." We'd have just come out of the pit, having done another show.

This went on all day and all night. Finally someone got across to him the fact that we could only stay so long because we were doing shows. He said, "Oh, you're doing shows? That's lovely." So he came down and watched our stage show on the third day. We were slowly going under from lack of energy. ↓

Even with such a schedule, Woody's musicians managed to learn the Stravinsky opus and presented it at their first appearance at Carnegie Hall in 1946.

Charlie Barnet tells a story that reads like a script for a Steve Martin comedy. The scene is the Howard Theater in Washington, D.C.:

Trummy Young had a former wife living in the city, and he was far behind with his alimony payments. We were doing *Mood Indigo* in the show with a trio of trumpet, clarinet, and trombone opening the arrangement center stage at the microphone. The lighting was very subdued to fit the bluesy mood, and I sneaked offstage to get a drink after the number started. A U.S. marshal with a warrant for Trummy's arrest accosted me. He informed me that there were marshals on the other of the stage as well as out front. Trummy was in the trio at the microphone, but when they finished, a pin spotlight picked up Peanuts Holland back in the trumpet section, and the rest of the stage blacked out. I got hold of Trummy in the dark and told him about the marshals. Then we got a stagehand to hoist him up in the flies and, when the trio returned to finish the number, there was Eddie Bert playing trombone in the trio. Trummy had disappeared. [Eddie says it was his first night with the band, and he'd been hiding his non-uniform saddle shoes in the back row. When he had to go out front and play Trummy's part, the saddle shoes were revealed, and Eddie got the fish-eye from Charlie when the lights came up. Ed.]

When it was time to go, we put Trummy in Chubby Jackson's bass case and he was carried out of the theater and loaded on the truck for the railroad station. What we had forgotten, however, was that U.S. marshals can go anywhere. When we arrived at the Boston the-ater they were waiting for us. It took some string pulling to keep all concerned from durance vile. ↓

Shelly Manne remembered a tour with Stan Kenton:

We played an old theater in New England. The trumpet riser was very high. Ray Wetzel weighed almost 300 pounds. He'd jump off the riser to run down front to sing a vocal. He jumped off the riser this day and went right through the stage up to his waist, with his trumpet, and there he was stuck in the stage. The band couldn't play for about fifteen minutes. We were in tears, rolling around. Another time Stan kicked off the band and ran to the piano to play, and the bench collapsed under him.

Once we were playing a one-nighter in Kansas City in a ballroom. The dressing room was behind the bandstand, and the sprinkler system broke with all our music, our instruments, our uniforms, everything. Stan was standing there holding his hands around the sprinkler yelling, "Go get a plumber!" ♪

Willie "The Lion" Smith describes a wild scene on an airplane:

One fantastic junket I took with [Jack] Crystal was to Pittsburgh in 1950 or 1951. I didn't like the idea of flying around those mountains near Pittsburgh. I wasn't alone. Freddie Moore, drums and washboard, didn't go for it either. Before we started off I had a presentiment about trouble.

I was sitting next to Big Chief Moore, the 300-pound Indian trombonist, and he was sitting next to the window. We had left LaGuardia at 8:00 a.m. and all hell broke loose forty-five minutes later. The pilot announced, "We are now cruising at twelve thousand feet and will be in Pittsburgh in forty minutes." Then they hit the air pocket. Big Chief almost broke out of his seat belt, and the coffee which Wild Bill Davison was drinking flew out of the cup all over me from across the aisle.

We hit a storm and it stayed bumpy and shook us all up. Freddie Moore was praying his head off, offering prayers for the protection of his wife, kids, aunts, uncles, grandparents, sons-in-law. The plane was being bombarded by hailstones as big as baseballs. As the bumping continued, Big Chief almost pushed me out of my seat belt.

When it was all over, Crystal asked Freddie Moore: "What's the matter with you, you're a bachelor. Why were you praying for all those people?"

"I know," Moore answered, "but while I was about it, I wanted to cover all the possibilities." ♪

Jam sessions often developed at Mary Lou Williams's New York apartment. Some of the city's best jazz musicians gathered there, sometimes quite unexpectedly. Mary Lou said:

We'd come uptown around four or four thirty in the morning and stay up all day, playing. There was Tadd Dameron, Bud Powell, Erroll Garner, Mel Tormé, and Miles Davis. Let's see, another trumpet player, Fats Navarro. A tenor man that was with Benny Goodman when he came out East, Wardell Gray. And sometimes Leonard Feather. I had a white rug on the floor and we'd sit on the floor and each one would take a turn playing.

I remember once one morning I got sleepy so I said, "I'm going to bed." When the guys left, they left the door unlocked. Thelonious Monk rang the doorbell and came inside. He discovered that I was asleep. It was around eight o'clock in the morning. I had a big twin bed.

When I woke up I saw someone on the other bed, and I screamed. He yelled too, and ran out the door and into the closet, and the clothes fell on him. I said, "What are you doing here?" He said, "I wanted to play you something and you were sleeping and I didn't want to disturb you." He was lying on his back on the other bed with his tam on. That was the funniest thing. 🎵

Al McKibbon told about touring with Monk during the last years of his life:

We went out with the Giants of Jazz with George Wein. In about three months Monk said maybe two words. I mean, literally, maybe two words. He didn't say "Good morning," "Goodnight," "What time?" Nothing. Why, I don't know. He sent word back after the tour was over that the reason he couldn't communicate or play was that Art Blakey and I were so ugly. (Laughs)

In Tokyo we were having suits made, because they do it so fast and all that. Monk had his measured lying in bed. He wouldn't get up for them. 🎵

Al Cohn flew to the West Coast with Buddy Rich's band:

We had Jerry Thurlkild on alto; he was very good, but crazy. He started a fire on a plane! We flew to California, and he was complaining it was cold; everybody was complaining. It took us about 24 hours to make the trip. We stopped every half hour or something, to refuel. And Jerry tried to start a fire in the middle of the plane, in the aisle. 🎵

In New York in the 1950s, the sidewalk in front of Charlie's Tavern would be crowded with musicians on Wednesdays and Fridays after the union floor closed. One afternoon the metal doors in the sidewalk in front of Charlie's parted and the freight elevator slowly rose to sidewalk level. On the elevator stood Marty Napoleon's brother Andy, busily conducting an imaginary orchestra while he loudly hummed "Rhapsody In Blue." When he reached sidewalk level, he took a formal bow as the assembled musicians applauded.

Vinnie Bell had a record that was getting a little action on the charts one year and he wanted to know the latest figures, so between record dates in Manhattan he rushed into the newsstand at the Americana Hotel and said, "Where's your *Cash Box?*" The counterman, staring at the guitar case Vinnie was carrying, threw up his hands and cried, "Take it easy! Don't shoot!" It took Vinnie several minutes to calm him down enough to be able to buy the magazine he wanted.

Morris Levy's road tour called "The Birdland Stars of 1955" included Count Basie's band, Sarah Vaughan, the Erroll Garner trio, the George Shearing trio, the Stan Getz quintet, and Lester Young. Basie tells how they entertained themselves on the road:

> The band was divided into two groups that were always challenging each other in the games we used to play on the road and in various places, games mainly like softball, which may have been how it got started.
>
> Anyway, on one side there were the little guys like Joe Newman, Sonny Payne, Frank Wess, Frank Foster, Benny Powell, and so on; and they called themselves the Midgets. And the others, the big guys like Poopsie [Charlie Fowlkes], [Henry] Coker, Eddie Jones, and Bill Hughes, were known as the Bombers. Naturally since I was the chief, I didn't take sides, but when we were touring on a package show, I would line up on one side or the other. Usually the big guys would have to go with the Bombers, but naturally Lester insisted on being one of the Midgets. He was really too big to be a Midget, but he had to be with the underdogs, which was a joke, because the Midgets were the ones who were always coming out on top, beginning with softball and going right on through most of the other horsing around.

Well, Morris Levy was classified as a Bomber, and he was having a ball with all of the games and pranks, and when the tour went out to Kansas City, Morris went around to the novelty stores and bought up a supply of water pistols for the Bombers to attack the Midgets with, So they had the Midgets on the run, and then, according to Joe Newman, Sonny Payne found out where Morris had his supplies stashed, and the two of them stole them for the Midgets.

That's what led to what happened to Morris in Kansas City. We were at the Municipal Auditorium, and several of us were standing near the bus talking with some local people—reporters, officials, and businessmen, if I remember correctly. And they were asking about who was in charge of the tour, and somebody said Morris Levy.

"You mean Morris Levy, the manager of Birdland, is traveling with the show?"

"That's right."

"And he's in Kansas City right now?"

"Right now."

And right at that exact split second, we saw three or four of the Midgets heading in one direction, chasing a Bomber, shooting at him with water pistols. He was splitting, but they were gaining on him, and just as he got to a few feet from where we were, he tried to make a fast cut to go around the bus and he slipped, ending up under it.

The people standing there talking to us just sort of glanced at what happened, and then turned right back and continued the conversation.

"I'd like to meet him."

"Well, that's no problem. There he is."

"Where?"

"Right there under the bus."

"Under the bus? What's he doing under there?"

"The Midgets," I said. "The Midgets ran him under there. They were after him."

"The Midgets?" Who are they? Is this some kind of gag?"

So I told them about the Midgets and the Bombers. But when Morris came out from under the bus, it turned out that he had just had a serious accident. That fall had actually broken his arm. The minute the Birdland people back in New York were told about that, they started burning up the telephone wires to Kansas City, and Morris had to explain that it was all part of a game. Because as soon as he said that the Midgets were chasing him, they thought he was talking about a mob trying to cut in on the business. His business associates were ready to put somebody on the next plane to Kansas City to help him take care of the situation. ⸙

Jimmy Rowles played piano in every sort of jazz venue, and once had a brief encounter with the classical world:

I met Placido Domingo at Bradley's of all places. The girl that married Bounce [bassist George Mraz], Judy, she used to work up there at the opera. He had eyes for her, so she says, "I'll go out with you if you'll go to Bradley's." He says, "Where's Bradley's?" She says, "I'll show you." So she took him down to Bradley's [in Greenwich Village] and invited me over to the table, and I'm sitting down next to Placido Domingo. I didn't know who the hell he was. Never heard of him before.

When Judy told me he was a famous opera singer. I said, "Sing me something! Right now! Let 'em know you're here! Let out a roar! If you don't I will." So he goes, "RrroooOOORRR!" he let out a big thing, you know. Everybody said. "What was that?"

Bradley [Cunningham, the owner] got right up and came over to the table and said, "Don't ever do that again!" I introduced them. "This is Placido Domingo. You're not foolin' around with a bum— this is sincere! I mean, this is *ace!* And he and I are gonna do an opera together! Right, Plas?" By then he'd had a couple. He said, "That's right, Jim!"

Bradley went back and said down, and we started talking about doing Carmen. Carmen Lombardo! "I saw Carmen comin' home from school. He was broke, cause he'd been playin' pool . . ." that kind of stuff. (Laughs) We were workin' on this thing, you know, and *laughin'!*

So he gave me some complimentary tickets, and I went up there and heard him sing. Oh boy, he could sing! In his dressing room afterwards he came out in his bathrobe. He said, "You see, Jimmy, that's where *jazz* comes from!" ⸙

Lew Gluckin was playing a wedding party with a society piano player who found himself stumped when the groom asked them to play some Charlie Parker tunes.

"How about 'Scrapple from the Apple'?" asked Lew.

"Fine," said the groom.

The leader whispered to Lew, "I don't know that!"

"Don't worry, I've got it. Just play the chords to 'Honeysuckle Rose,' and I'll play 'Scrapple.' It's the same tune."

As Lew began Parker's classic melody line, the leader yelled,

"No, no, play the melody first!"

During the late 1960s Paul Quinichette disappeared from the jazz scene. He resurfaced some time later with a group called "Two Tenor Boogie," with Buddy Tate and pianist Sammy Price. They often played at the West End on upper Broadway, where Phil Schaap, the music director of the club, took an interest in them.

In 1975 Phil accompanied the group to Boston for a matinee. They were being driven to the job in a Cadillac limousine. Since Paul had been working and drinking late the night before at the West End, he wasn't in very good condition when the limousine picked him up. He slid into the back seat and immediately fell asleep.

Phil and Ditto Edwards, the drummer, discovered the limo had a television set, but they were unable to get it working. Ditto bemoaned their luck, since a pennant baseball game was being broadcast during the drive.

Somehow Ditto's complaint made it way into Paul's subconscious. He woke up and got the driver to stop and get him the tool kit from the trunk. With a terrific hangover, and little more than a screwdriver and pliers, Paul opened the TV set. As the limousine rolled on up the highway, he found the trouble and fixed it. He explained that he'd been working on the Lower East Side for the past several years as a TV repairman. Phil and Ditto happily watched the ball game as Paul closed his eyes and went back to sleep.

When Bobby Day was Fred Waring's featured banjo player, he often played golf at Waring's country club in the Delaware Water Gap. It was a favorite hangout of many famous cartoonists and comedians, and Bobby enjoyed their company. Waring constantly redesigned his golf course, making it tougher by adding traps and hazards. During one day's play, the golfers noticed that a section near the fairway had been marked out with stakes, indicating where Waring intended to add a small lake. Jackie Gleason, Bobby's partner in the foursome that day, drove his ball right into that staked-off area. He walked over, removed his shoes and socks, rolled up his pants, and, carrying a seven-iron, "waded" out in the imaginary lake and looked at his ball. He called out, "Bobby, this ball is playable!" and proceeded to knock it forcefully toward the green. He then "waded" back to shore, put his shoes and socks back on, and continued with the game.

Sonny Rollins often wanders into the audience while playing at jazz concerts. He says he likes to feel the people's reaction up close, and exchange vibrations with them. At an outdoor concert in Saugerties, New York, the stage and amphitheater were constructed of stone. During one number Sonny decided to jump down from the edge of the stage and play in the audience. The front of the stage was quite high, but there was only a five- or six-foot drop at the sides. Sonny walked to the side of the stage and, still playing, jumped down. He didn't reappear immediately, and the people in the seats closest to the stage could see that he was lying flat on his back. The rhythm section was about to stop playing and find out what had happened to Sonny when they heard his saxophone again, playing as lustily as ever. He was playing while still lying on his back beside the stage! Everyone thought Sonny was just being theatrical, but in fact he had fractured a heel. He was able to finish the concert without anyone knowing he'd hurt himself.

Beaver Harris described an appearance he made on television in Tokyo while on a jazz tour:

> Archie Shepp walked up to the microphone. Someone was going to interpret his conversation. The interpreter said, "Mr. Shepp, they would like to know how do you like Japan?" We're all standing in line, Lee Konitz and his band had played a tune. Archie looks into the camera, front and center, and says, "We come here in peace; not like the Americans who dropped the bomb on Hiroshima."
> And Grachan Moncour says, "Don't remind these motherfuckers!"
> This was all on television. I stepped in and said, "No, we came here to combine the rhythmical blah, blah—" If I hadn't talked, we'd be in jail.

When Motown Records staged a parade through the streets of Harlem one spring, they inexplicably included a marching dixieland band. While the parade was assembling, an elderly local resident came out his front door and found Herb Gardner with a group of musicians in red and white striped vests carrying tubas and banjos, surrounded by a sea of rock bands on trucks carrying giant sound systems. He broke into a huge grin and asked, "Are you boys lost?"

chapter 2

The Word "Jazz"

In a book titled *Jazz Anecdotes,* it seems appropriate to let one chapter deal with the word "jazz" itself. Many attempts have been made to pin down the origin of the word, none completely successful. Some scholars have detected roots in Africa and Arabia, and others hold, with perhaps a little more evidence, that it stems from the French verb *jaser,* meaning "to chatter." There are speculations that the word arose from corruptions of the abbreviations of the first names of early musicians: "Charles" (Chas.) or "James" (Jas.). Another source claims that a Chicago musician called Jasbo Brown was the genesis of the term.

Some historians find origins in slang terms for semen (gism, jasm). It is true that "jazzing" was widely used as a word meaning fornication, but no one has been able to determine for sure that this usage preceded the musical reference. Some early jazz musicians have remembered hearing "jazz" used erotically in both New Orleans and San Francisco around the turn of the century.

One story offers perfume as a possible source of the word. When he was a young man working in a circus band in Louisiana, Garvin Bushell discussed the subject with some older musicians:

> They said that the French had brought the perfume industry with them to New Orleans, and that oil of jasmine was a popular ingredient locally. To add it to a perfume was called "jassing it up." The strong scent was popular in the red-light district, where a working girl might approach a prospective customer and say, "Is jass on your mind tonight, young fellow?" The term had become synonymous with erotic activity and came to be applied to the music as well. 🏹

In 1916 Johnny Stein's band from New Orleans was playing a style of music that was new in Chicago. H. O. Brunn describes how "jazz" became the name of the music they played:

It was during their run at Schiller's that the word "jass" was first applied to music. A retired vaudeville entertainer, somewhat titillated by straight blended whiskey and inspired by the throbbing tempos of this lively band, stood at his table and shouted, "Jass it up, boys!"

"Jass," in the licentious slang vocabulary of the Chicago underworld, was an obscene word, but like many four-letter words of its genre it had been applied to anything and everything and had become so broad in its usage that the exact meaning had become obscure.

Harry James, the manager of Schiller's, never missed a bet. When the inebriate bellowed forth "Jass it up, boys!" the thinking machinery of the Chicago café expert was set in motion. The tipsy vaudevillian was hired to sit at his table and shout "Jass it up" every time he felt like it—all drinks on the house. The next day the band was billed, in blazing red letters across the front of Schiller's:

STEIN'S DIXIE JASS BAND

Chicagoans then had a word for the heretofore unnamed music. ↳

After some personnel changes, the band was booked into Reisenweber's restaurant in New York.

Ragtime's lusty successor had finally completed its evolution from "jass" to "jasz" and, in the *New York Times* of February 2, 1917, we find the first appearance of the word spelled "jazz." Reisenweber's ad on the amusement page of that issue vaunted "The First Eastern Appearance of the Famous Original Dixieland Jazz Band." Nick LaRocca avers that the word "jass" was changed because children, as well as a few impish adults, could not resist the temptation to obliterate the letter "j" from their posters. ↳

Ralph Berton has another candidate for first use of the word. He gives the following account:

In 1915 a vaudeville hoofer-&-comic named Joe Frisco, playing a date in New Orleans, heard a white *spasm band,* as it was called locally (homemade instruments & komic kapers), playing a kind of cheerful burlesque of the music they'd learned in black red-light districts, et cetera. Frisco got them a gig at Lamb's Café, in Chicago,

billed as "Tom Brown's Band from Dixieland." Business was good;
they were held over.

Respectable union musicians resented the invaders, and placed as
ad denouncing them as players of "nothing but cheap, shameless
JASS music." The shocking four-letter word had a predictable effect.
The next week Lamb had to put in forty extra tables, and thought-
fully changed their billing to "Brown's JASS BAND from Dixieland."
It was the first known public use of the phrase. ⇃

There may never be a clear determination of who used the word first.
At any rate, it quickly became the universal term for music improvised to
hot rhythm. Nathan W. Pearson, Jr., describes the dim view taken by certain moralists against the new music:

> Protests against jazz were plentiful. The town of Zion, Illinois, for
> example, banned jazz in January 1921, ranking it with tobacco and
> alcohol as a sin their citizens could do without. The term "jazz" itself
> was felt by many to have a sexual connotation. Worse, its rhythms
> and the "wild" dancing it elicited were feared to be leading young
> people to sexual abandon and degeneracy. Given the times, such
> fearful expressions probably heightened interest in the music and
> its social setting. ⇃

Whatever the origin of the word "jazz," it has resisted many attempts to
change it. Duke Ellington never approved of the word, preferring more
dignified terminology. He said:

> By and large, jazz always has been like the kind of man you
> wouldn't want your daughter to associate with. The *word* "jazz" has
> been part of the problem. The word never lost its association with
> those New Orleans bordellos. In the 1920s I used to try to convince
> Fletcher Henderson that we ought to call what we were doing
> "Negro music." But it's too late for that now. This music has become
> so integrated you can't tell one part from the other so far as color is
> concerned. ⇃

Others expressed the hope that the music could rid itself of the
"stigma" of the sexual connotation. Efforts during the 1930s and '40s by
music magazines to invent a new word resulted in lame substitutes like
"ragtonia," "syncopep," "crewcut," "Amerimusic," and "Jarb."

Now, in the twenty-first century, the sexual connotation of the word has almost completely faded away. "Jazz" is now used to identify a variety of musical forms, as well as a style of Broadway theater dancing, a patented exercise regimen, a toilet water, a basketball team, and at one time a brand of computer software.

chapter 3

Beginnings

Employment for jazz musicians developed wherever there was a demand for festive music. In the early 1900s the black and creole neighborhoods in New Orleans were especially fertile places since music was an important part of community activity there. Sidney Bechet contradicts the myth of Storyville as the cradle of jazz.

> People have got an idea that the music started in whorehouses. Well, there was a district there, you know, and the houses in it, they'd all have someone playing a guitar or a mandolin, or a piano . . . someone singing, maybe; but they didn't have orchestras, and the musicianers never played regular there. The musicianers would go to those houses just whenever they didn't have a regular engagement, when there was no party or picnic or ball to play at. But in those days there was always some party going, some fish fry, and there was always some picnic around the lakes. ↱

Sidney describes one kind of house party that he used to play:

> Sometimes in the section called "Back o' Town" they'd have contests like, they'd put a jug of wine in the center of the floor and cut figures around it. They'd dance around this jug of wine, a whole lot of kind of steps, dance as close to it as they could and still not touch it or knock it over. The man who touched it, he'd have to go out and buy another gallon. There wouldn't be any women where these men

got together. It was music and this cutting figures. Maybe somebody's wife would show up, but it wasn't any sporting place like Lulu
White's. Those bands, those days, there wasn't any piano to them. It
was guitar, bass, violin, drum, trombone, cornet. That was the original orchestra. ↳

"Montudie" Garland said that, when things got slow at the club where
he had a band, Freddie Keppard fired his bass player, guitarist, and violinist and replaced them with a piano player. "As far as I know, that was
the first time a piano was used in a jazz band."

When Sidney Bechet was just a little boy he figured out how to play a
clarinet his brother had given him. He describes the house party where
he got his first chance to play with the grownups:

It was my brother's birthday and there was to be a big party, all a
surprise. Freddie Keppard's Band had been hired for it. The band
came in and set themselves inside the house and waited, and when
my brother came home they let go all at once, and the people came
jumping out shouting "Surprise!" Well, it really did surprise him—
all that going on, people running around, the music. And after all
that had gotten under way, the party sort of settled down to the
music.

There was dancing, people getting together, things being real
lively. The band was playing back in the kitchen. It had been understood that the clarinetist, George Baquet, wouldn't show up till
later; he had another engagement on a parade. So the band went
along playing without him for a time, but it got going real good.

I stood around there hearing them play. I was standing back by
myself in the entry to the kitchen, and I couldn't help myself. I knew
I was too young for them, but I sure wanted to play along with them
all the same. So I sneaked away and got the clarinet and went into
the front room where nobody was at. It was dark in there. I began to
follow right along with the band with that clarinet of my brother's
what he had given me.

At first no one heard me. But then, the way I was told it, people
began to take notice. And then the men in Keppard's band, *they* noticed it and began to look at each other. Who the hell was playing?
They prowled all around and at last they found me. They opened
the door and they couldn't believe their eyes. One of them laughed

and said, "Well you're awful little, but we heard you, and you were sure playing like hell."

So they brought me back there, back into the kitchen with them and they put me in a chair by the window, and they gave me a drink. And then after a while Baquet showed up. There was an alley right in back of the house and the kitchen opened on to it, and being summer the window was open. Baquet came along this alley and *he* heard the clarinet and he wondered who the hell was taking his place. He stuck his head in the window and he looked around. He *heard* it, but he couldn't *see* it. But then he looked down: he saw me there in the chair. He just saw my head. About all he could see was the clarinet. He came on in, and he took out his clarinet and he ran his hand over my head and he just laughed. And he kept me there all evening, playing right along beside of him. 🎵

Herman Autrey was another early beginner. His father was a tuba player and kept his instrument in their living room standing upside down on its bell. Herman said he was about five years old when his father told him to leave the tuba alone when he was out of the house.

I figured out how I could play the doggoned thing and still be a good boy. I used to crawl on my belly over to the thing and I lay there and blow into it and make a "who-oo-oo," until I got so I could blow. So I'd have myself some fun and I'd play the doggoned thing until I got tired. When he came home, it was sitting right there where he left it. He had no way of knowing that I had bothered it. 🎵

When Herman grew up a little more he got a trumpet and went on to make quite a name for himself with Fletcher Henderson and Fats Waller.

Pops Foster started playing the bass before his family could afford to buy a real one:

Some of those critics and dicty teachers should see the first bass I had. My brother Willie did most of the work to make it. He put a two-by-four through the hollow of a flour barrel and nailed it on. We used some kinda wood for a bridge and carved some tuning pegs to stick in the two-by-four. Down on the two-by-four we pounded some nails in it to tie the strings to. We couldn't afford regular strings, so we used twine. It had three strings: we'd twist three pieces of twine together for the lowest, then two, then one for the highest. For two or three days we'd rub the twine with wax and rosin before we'd put them on the bass. The first bow was a bent stick with sewing machine thread tied on it. After awhile we got a regular bow without any hair in it. For hair we caught a neighbor's horse and cut the hair off his tail, but it didn't work, and we went back to sewing machine thread. My daddy made us use the bow on it, no plucking.

When he was a young boy Eddie Barefield asked his mother for a C-melody saxophone for Christmas. She got him an alto sax instead. She told him,

"Santa Claus didn't have any more C-melodies but he said the alto is going to be very popular so this is the one you should learn."

Eddie promptly unscrewed all the screws he could find on his saxophone, removing all the keys to see how it was put together. His mother had to put everything in a bag and take it back to the music store to have it reassembled.

She found him a teacher who charged fifty cents a lesson. At the first lesson Eddie learned the fingering for the chromatic scale. Eddie said:

Well, that's all I needed. We had records all of these years and I started fooling around playing what little things I had in my ear. I was copying Coleman Hawkins, the first saxophone player that I remember hearing.

When my mother gave me the fifty cents every week to take the lesson, I would go deposit my horn in the drug store and go to the movies and then come home and practice with the records. She would say, "Is that your lesson?" And I would say, "Yes, that's my lesson." This is actually the way I learned how to play.

Eddie "Lockjaw" Davis took a pragmatic approach to becoming a jazz player:

I didn't buy an instrument for the sake of the music. It's different if someone says he likes music and wants to get an instrument to try to be a musician. In my case I wanted the instrument for what it represented.

By watching musicians I saw that they drank, they smoked, they got all the broads and they didn't get up early in the morning. That attracted me. My next move was to see who got the most attention, so it was between the tenor saxophonist and the drummer. The drums looked like too much work, so I said I'll get one of those tenor saxophones. That's the truth. ⤵

Lester Young learned music from his father in the Young Family Band. His father and mother and sister were all musicians. Lester heard the bands in New Orleans going around on trucks to advertise for the dances they were playing and found the drummers exciting. He played drums with the family band before changing to saxophone. He told François Postif:

> Drums now? No eyes. I don't want to see them. Every time I'd be in a nice little place, and I'd meet a nice little chick, dig, her mother'd say, "Mary, come on let's go." Damn, I'd be trying to pack these drums, because I wanted this little chick, dig? She'd call her once and twice, and I'm trying to get straight, so I just said, I'm through with drums. All those other boys got clarinet cases, trumpet cases, trombone cases, and I'm wigging around with all that stuff. And, Lady Francis, I could really play those drums. I'd been playing them a whole year. ⤵

Nat Cole was the favorite pianist of many jazz musicians before he became a superstar as a singer. In the early days of the Nat Cole trio, his singing was considered a novelty that helped sell a good jazz group. Cole tells how it started:

> When I organized the King Cole Trio back in 1937, we were strictly what you would call an instrumental group. To break the monotony, I would sing a few songs here and there between the playing. I sang things I had known over the years. I wasn't trying to give it any special treatment, just singing. I noticed thereafter people started requesting more singing, and it was just one of those things. ⤵

Nat's wife Maria discussed the legend that Nat's singing career had begun when a drunk had insisted he sing "Sweet Lorraine" until he finally gave in and sang it:

> The incident of the insistent barroom customer, a guy who often spent as much as "three bucks a night" in the Swanee Inn, did happen. As Nat explained it, "This particular customer kept insisting on a certain song, and I told him I didn't know that one but I would sing something different, and that was 'Sweet Lorraine.'"

The trio was tipped fifteen cents—a nickel apiece—for that performance, and the customer requested a second tune. Again, Nat didn't know it but asked, "Is there something else you would like?"

"Yeah," the customer said, "I'd like my fifteen cents back." ↳

Frank Morgan was introduced to jazz earlier than most musicians:

My first influence was my father, Stanley Morgan, a bebop guitarist who played in Howard McGhee's band. He used to put the guitar against my mother's stomach and play while she was carrying me. After I was born, my father would practice next to my crib six or seven hours a day. I played guitar from three until I was seven.

I went to Detroit to visit my father and while there, he took me to the Paradise Theater to hear the Jay McShann band which featured Charlie Parker. After the show, we went backstage and I met Charlie Parker. Charlie played some more in the dressing room and I asked my father if I could play "one of those." That is how I decided that I wanted to play alto. ↳

Not every jazz musician started young. Some were reluctant to begin at all. Phil Woods said:

My uncle died and left me my alto and I went for my lesson. I didn't want to, but they said, "The man died. The least you can do is take a lesson." ↳

Art Blakey started to be a pianist in Pittsburgh, but became a drummer by default:

I was workin' steel mills and coal mines, I was a kid and they had child labor. I couldn't make that, I'd work my brains out. I was playin' piano in two or three keys—shit, I went out there and got me a gig. All I wanted to do was survive. I made so much money in the tip box, I was the biggest money maker in the house.

I used to make up dirty songs in E-flat. We'd have a little spinet piano and I'd move to different tables. Just filth, and they loved it and I'd get ten, twenty, forty dollars tips a night. I met a guy named Hitchcock, a trombone player who could really play, and we had a gig in a bar, trombone and piano, all in B-flat, E-flat, A-flat. I couldn't get out of them. And then I had this 14-piece band. We made $15 a week. Cats dressed in tails and played in the club.

They brought in Tondelayo and Lopez, an act from New York Raymond Scott had. I didn't know nothin' about music and I pretended. I'll never forget that ego, a lesson for my life. I'd tell the brass with authority, "All right, brass, run it down!" And the brass would run it down and pow!, we'd get to the piano part and I'd sit there, couldn't read. I say to the band, "That didn't sound too good, why don't you do it again." Tondelayo sitting there waiting and waiting and she played the record again. I went over to the piano and the band comes, pow! I looked at them and said, "All you son of a bitches know god damned well I can't read!"

So this guy sitting in the corner said, "Let me try it." And so he ran down through it like a dose of Epsom salts, and that was Erroll Garner. And that was the end of my piano career. [Garner couldn't read either, but he could play anything he heard. Ed.]

I was always running up showing the drummer, Skippy, how to play the drums. I didn't have them, but I always liked them. But Erroll played so well. The cat who owned the place was sitting over in the corner. He called me over, says, "Hey, Art, I think the kid should play the piano and you should play the drums." I said, "Listen, man, this is my band, you can't tell me how to run it." He said, "Now, how long you been here? You want to stay on, don't you?" He had a 350 magnum on his side. I said, "Hell, yes, I want to stay." He said, "Well, you dumb bastard, get up there and play the drums." I've been playing drums ever since. Just a matter of survival. ♪

Al Haig's first job in New York was with Tiny Grimes's quartet at the Spotlight Club. He played an audition there that was a complete surprise to him:

One night Dizzy [Gillespie] and Charlie [Parker] came in. It was kind of creepy, to tell you the truth. They both suddenly sprang up on the bandstand and were auditioning me. Nobody said anything. It was kind of weird, you know, somebody just coming up and sitting in and auditioning you without telling you that you're being auditioned.

But I got through it. They weren't the best circumstances, but they could have been worse. I could have had an off night. We played *I Got Rhythm*, a blues, a few things like that. I was only about twenty-two. One of the tunes I do remember was *Shaw 'Nuff*. To me it was like being in a maelstrom of sound. They just said, "I Got

Rhythm" and then started to play. I played, but honestly I didn't know what else to do because this was the first time I'd been on a bandstand with Charlie Parker.

When they stopped, Dizzy asked me if I would be interested in joining a group with him and Charlie. I said yes, oh yes, absolutely! ↳

Wynton Marsalis had a trumpet long before he developed an interest in being a trumpet player. He said:

I was about five or six, and Miles [Davis], Clark Terry, Al Hirt, and my father were all sitting around a table in Al's club in New Orleans—this was when my father was still working in Al's band. My father, just joking around because there were so many trumpet players sitting there, said,
"I better buy Wynton a trumpet."
And Al said, "Ellis, let me give your boy one of mine."
It's ironic looking back on it, because Miles said,
"Don't give it to him. Trumpet's too difficult an instrument for him to learn."
Ha! ↳

chapter 4

Inventions

While developing their music, jazz musicians invented ways of playing that were different from traditional techniques. Some of the special sounds of jazz were produced by blowing into the instruments in unorthodox ways, by using odd fingering combinations or holding valves or keys halfway down, by humming into the horn while playing, by sliding from one note to another, etc. To get the sound they wanted, the musicians sometimes redesigned their equipment. Drummers developed a wide variety of drums and cymbals. Reed players tried new reed and mouthpiece designs. Brass players found that holding a hand or some other object in front of the bell of a horn could create new sounds. Herman Autrey said:

You know where the bucket mutes came from? Bean cans. Sauerkraut cans. Any kind of can that we saw that was usable, we'd take them and fix them. The gallon pails, those buckets that they sold lard and syrup in, we used 'em. When you'd walk in an average club that had a band, you'd think you were looking in the garbage dump, because they were using all kinds of cans for mutes. Some smart guy walked in and watched them use these cans, and he took a pencil and paper and drew them and made them and sold them back to us, five, six, eight, ten dollars. We used derbies people had thrown away. And then instead of the derby hat, they made tin hats. When I recorded with Fats Waller I had a tin hat, but I took one of my old felt hats and cut the crown out, and stuck it in there to make it mellow. It was too brassy with just the tin. We used water glasses, cuspidors, everything, because everyone was looking for a different sound. ♪

Baby Dodds told of an unusual mute used by King Oliver in Chicago:

Joe Oliver had all kinds of things he put on his horn. He used to shove a kazoo in the bell to give it a different effect. A guy named Tony who played with us in Cairo, Illinois, got a guy to make a thing you put in your horn with two kazoos in it. He had another thing that had about four kazoos welded together that really gave the horn a funny sound. Those babies sold like a house on fire all over the country and Joe didn't get nothin' for it. ♪

Doc Cheatham remembered Freddie Keppard's reputation with mutes:

Freddie Keppard reminded me of a military trumpeter playing jazz. He was very loud, and he didn't have any of Oliver's polish. One night, he blew a mute right out of his horn and across the dance floor, and it became the talk of Chicago. After that, everybody piled in night after night to see him do it again, but he never did.

It was true about his fear of other musicians stealing his stuff. I saw him put a handkerchief over his valves when he was playing, so that nobody could follow his fingering. ♪

Wingy Manone preferred the sound of the open horn. He was looking for work for his band in New York:

I heard they wanted an orchestra at the Arcadia Ballroom on Forty-third and Broadway, to play opposite Teddy Cook on Saturday and Sunday nights. So I took my boys down there to try and sell a band to the man who ran it.

We got to talk to Mr. Harmon, the manager, and he told us we could audition. So we set up and started to play. I thought we were doing okay, until Harmon stopped me. He said he didn't like me playing open horn.

"Why don't you use a wa-wa mute?" he asked me. "You can't play jazz good without using a wa-wa."

"Listen," I hollered, "Wingy don't use none of those lousy wa-wa mutes in his band. That wa-wa stuff stinks, and so do those mutes."

As I kept on hollering, I noticed my boys all laughing their heads off and backing away from me. We started packing after I told Harmon off, and when they got me outside they broke the news to me.

Then I found out that the Mr. Harmon who owned the Arcadia was the same fellow who had the patent on the Harmon mutes. Ouch.

Just the same, I went back there a week later and sold him a band.

Garvin Bushell said that Mamie Smith's trumpet player Johnny Dunn was the first to use a plumber's rubber plunger as a mute. Plungers are made in two sizes, for sinks and toilets. They happened to have just the right diameters for trumpet and trombone bells. After Bubber Miley and Joe Nanton used plungers on recording with Duke Ellington, arrangers began to write for plungers and they became a standard mute.

While on staff at ABC, trombonist Charlie Small was given something to play that required a plunger, and he didn't have one with him. He ran out to a midtown hardware store and asked for a large regulation toilet plunger. When the man laid one on the counter, Charlie told him, "I don't need the stick." Charlie said that the puzzled expression on the man's face was rapidly replaced by one of sheer disgust.

"And to this day, when I go into that store, that man walks away and has a different clerk wait on me."

Herman Autrey worked with a tuba player named Clay Robinson, who had wired his tuba with colored lights that he could turn on and off with a foot switch:

One mash of his foot would make it red, green, blue, whichever you want. This particular time, we started to hit the overture, and he says *Whack! Prsst!* The thing lit him up! There was a short in the wire somewhere. I still believe Sandy Williams did that, the trombone player. Bass was trying to get this tuba from around his neck, and the sparks were flying—*Pffst!* I said,

"I told you to put that thing down! Now, let that be a lesson to you!" 🎵

Duke Ellington recalled the early experiments of his band with mutes, growls, and unusual instrumental sounds that eventually came to be known as "the Jungle Sound":

Before Tricky joined us, Charlie Irvis, who was known as "Charlie Plug," was our original player down in the Kentucky Club. He was called plug because of the device he used on his horn. In those days they manufactured a kind of mute designed to make the trombone sound like a saxophone. The sax was still regarded as new then. Charlie had dropped this device and broken it, so he used what was left of it, rolling it around the bell of his trombone. He couldn't use it the way it was intended, because of the part broken off, but he'd get this entirely different, lecherous, low tone, and no one has ever done it since. 🎵

The companies that made drum equipment flourished with the popularity of jazz. The New Orleans marching bands used parade drums: a large bass drum harnessed to the player's chest and a deep snare drum that hung slightly to the side to enable the player to walk. Drummers playing indoor jobs combined the bass drum and the shallower orchestra snare drum by adding a foot pedal attachment to the bass drum beater. Baby Dodds didn't think much of some of the further improvements:

I helped cause the sock cymbals to be made. I was in St. Louis working on the steamboat and William Ludwig, the drum manufacturer, came on the boat for a ride. He was very interested in my drumming. I used to stomp my left foot, long before other drummers did, and Ludwig asked me if I could stomp my toe instead of my heel. I told him "I think so." For a fact I thought nothing of it. So he measured my foot on a piece of paper and the space where I would have it and where it would sit and he made a sock cymbal. Two cymbals were set up and a foot pedal with them. One day he brought one along for me to try. It wasn't any good, so he brought another raised up about nine inches higher. Well, I had just taken the cymbal off the bass drum because I didn't want to hear that tinny sound any more and I didn't like the sock cymbal either. I didn't like any part of them and I still don't. ♩

It seems likely that some modifications and improvements on musical instruments were developed simultaneously by different people in different places. Cliff Jackson said:

The first foot cymbal was made by a fella called Happy Rhone, he was an ex-drummer and banjo player. He had a place called Happy Rhone's Club years ago in New York, had a band playin' there. He made this foot cymbal and I got one and started playin' the piano along with it for a novelty. I did a couple of recordings using the foot cymbal. ♩

Vic Berton had a flair for mechanical design and applied it to his drum equipment. His brother Ralph recalls:

If you look at old pictures of dance orchestras, say before about 1920, you will see that the drummer has only two cymbals. One hangs from a contraption atop the bass drum; the other smaller one is screwed to the rim of the bass drum. [It was called a zinger, and was played with a little metal striker that rode in tandem with the bass drum beater on the foot pedal. Ed.] Vic decided the little zinger must go. He removed it from its old spot and put it on top of the bass drum alongside the big crash cymbal where it could be played as an independent instrument. The little striker on the bass drum pedal was at first simply folded back out of the way; then it disappeared altogether.
    Next Vic became dissatisfied with the way the cymbals were suspended—by a rawhide thong hanging from a hook atop the bass drum. Clean fast licks couldn't be played on a cymbal bouncing wildly around at the end of a thong. Vic made a rude sketch of an improvement: a vertical rod on which the cymbal would fit, snug

enough for control yet loose enough to ring freely. Soon every drummer in the world had cymbals sitting on those vertical rods. I assume somebody somewhere took out a patent and made a bundle, but it wasn't Vickie. ♪

Berton also found himself a pair of afterbeat cymbals operated by a homemade board-and-spring pedal system, and a pair of wire brushes:

Wire brushes are now taken for granted as an indispensable ingredient of the sound of jazz drums. And yet again Vic Berton never made a nickel out of it. ♪

When Berton realized that his afterbeat cymbal was a patentable idea he sought the assistance of a lawyer:

In his ignorance, Vic handed over his precious brainchild to the first young schmuck fresh out of law school that he met at a party. Someone who had the brains to hire a real patent lawyer instantly got round Vickie's pathetic two-bit patent by "inventing" a patentable improvement; it's known as the hi-hat cymbal. The only money Vic ever made out of it was the wages he earned while using it. ♪

Quentin Jackson remembered Kaiser Marshall as the first New York drummer to have a hi-hat cymbal:

The rest of them had their cymbal like Cuba [Austin] had. They had a cymbal, you take two cymbals and you take a great big rat trap and you put a board on each end of the rat trap spring and then you put the cymbal on that board, a cymbal on each one, and you use the spring of the rat trap and put a strap across it to hold your foot in there, and that was your foot cymbal. ♪

Just before Duke Ellington moved his band to the Cotton Club, Sonny Greer came into a instrumental windfall that had a lasting effect on the setups of jazz drummers:

One of the executives of the Leedy Drum Company come to New York and seen me playing at the Kentucky Club. He said,
    "Sonny, how would you like to work for us?"
    I said, "What doing?"

"Designing and using all our advance products."

"All right. Send me a set."

Well, they sent me five trunks of drums. Chimes, vibraphones, everything. The picture's up there on the wall. [Pictures of the period show that Sonny's set also contained Chinese gongs and a pair of white enamel tympani. Ed.]

So I come in the Cotton Club. Ain't no drummer had that stuff! Nothing! They still ain't got it! Man, when them gangsters saw that, they say, "My God!" And when a guy want to get a job in a cabaret, the man say, "You got drums like Sonny?" And the guy say, "You must be crazy, that drum set cost $3000!" Didn't cost me nothing, but they didn't know that. I didn't have to play them. All I had to do was look pretty. ♪

Beaver Harris made an expedient change in his drum set that started a fashion:

I didn't have any money to buy a drum head for my bass drum, so I put a mesh on the back. I tucked the mesh and put it on the back. The next thing I knew, cats had mesh heads on the back of their drums. It was nylon mesh, a laundry bag. I cut it open and hooked it on the rim.

We did a benefit for Stokely Carmichael at the Village Theater and all the press was there. They all came in with their cameras and their pads. A cat said, "Why do you have that screen on the back of your drum?" I said, "It filters the air as you hit the bass drum; it purifies the sound." And he was puttin' all this shit down!

I went on a tour with Albert Ayler to Europe, and you know they throw your drums and things around. Somebody put a tom-tom on top of the mesh. Next day I looked at it and it was all sagged in, so I pulled it off. The next thing I saw, all the European drummers took the heads off the back. ♪

Frank Trumbauer made an improvement on Red Norvo's equipment when they worked for Paul Whiteman:

Frankie used to make my slap hammers when I was with Whiteman. I used to break them, and he used to sew them between shows. He'd have a needle and thread and those buckskin things, and fix them. Finally one day he said, "I'm going to make you a pair you won't break." So he got two steel golf shafts and he had them cut off and had washers welded on them. He must have spent a week wrapping this with yarn and put felt on it, and finally put the buckskin outside. We were in Cleveland or someplace, doing four or five shows.

I played the first show and they were wonderful. Third show, I thought, "Oh, this is going to be the greatest. I'm so happy." The fourth show, things started to happen. The washers had cut through the whole thing, and I'm gouging wood out. I had to keep hitting. I was doing the act, and Whiteman's standing there, so I had to keep going. I must have ruined a dozen bars. I had to send away and order new bars. And Frankie's sitting there laughing about it. Next day he had a couple of new pair for me. 🎺

Dizzy Gillespie designed himself a trumpet with an unusual shape that has become a Gillespie trademark:

The truth is that the shape of my horn was an accident. I could pretend that I went into the basement and thought it up, but it wasn't that way. I was playing at Snookie's on Forty-fifth Street, on a Monday night, January 6, 1953. I had Monday nights off, but it was my wife's birthday so we had a party and invited all the guys—Illinois Jacquet, Sarah Vaughan, Stump 'n' Stumpy, and several other artists—all the people who were in show business who knew Lorraine from dancing. This guy Henry Morgan, who had his own show in New York, invited me to come on his show and be interviewed; he was doing the show from a hotel around the corner. My horn was still straight when I left it on one of those little trumpet stands that stick straight up.

'When I got back to the club after making this interview, Stump 'n' Stumpy had been fooling around on the bandstand, and one had pushed the other, and he'd fallen back onto my horn. Instead of the horn just falling, the bell bent. When I got back, the bell was sticking up in the air. Illinois Jacquet had left. He said, "I'm not going to be here when that man comes back and sees his horn sticking up at that angle."

When I came back, it was my wife's birthday and I didn't want to be a drag. I put the horn to my mouth and started playing it. Well, when the bell bent back, it made a smaller hole because of the dent. I couldn't get the right sound, but it was a strange sound that I got from that instrument that night. I played it, and I liked the sound. The sound had been changed and it could be played softly, very softly, not blarey. I played it like that the rest of the night, and the next day I had it straightened out again. Then I started thinking about it and said, "Wait a minute, man, that was something else." I remembered the way the sound had come from it, quicker to the ear—to my ear, the player. I contacted the Martin Company, and I had Lorraine, who's also an artist, draw me a trumpet at a forty-five-degree angle and set it to the Martin Company. I told them, "I want a horn like this."

"You're crazy!" they said.

"O.K.," I said, "I'm crazy, but I want a horn like this." They made me a trumpet and I've been playing one like that ever since. ↱

John Kirkpatrick ran into Clark Terry at a concert and told him he had an Olds flugelhorn just like the one Clark was endorsing in the music magazine ads. Clark asked, "How do you like it?" John said, "Well, to tell you the truth, I'm a little disappointed with it." "What's wrong?" asked Clark. John said, "It doesn't sound anything like you!"

When Harvey Kaiser visited the Smithsonian Institution he wanted to see the jazz section, but had trouble locating it. He asked a couple of museum attendants to help him find it, but no one seemed to know where it was. Being a tenor player, Harvey was especially interested in seeing Ben Webster's horn, which he had heard was in the Smithsonian's collection. (Actually, it resides with the Institute of Jazz Studies at Rutgers.) Wandering through the galleries, Harvey finally noticed an alcove with large photographs of Duke Ellington and Katharine Dunham, and as he moved closer to the jazz display, he saw a tenor saxophone in a showcase. He hurried over to it and read the inscription. It said the saxophone had belonged to President William Clinton.

chapter 5

Pianos

The piano is an important element in most jazz groups, but jazz pianists are lucky if they find a good one to play when they arrive at work. It is necessary to spend money to own and properly maintain a good piano. Regular maintenance is needed to offset wear and tear on strings and playing mechanisms. At the very least a piano should be frequently tuned.

Many proprietors of jazz clubs and restaurants seem to find it difficult to resist the temptation to skimp when buying and maintaining a piano. A cheap piano is not constructed to take the punishment of constant use. In the classic story, a club owner receives a complaint from his pianist about the condition of his piano, and says, "Don't worry, I'm having it painted tomorrow." The joke does not exaggerate reality. Many owners would begrudge the paint.

Piano soloists with the leverage of stardom are able to specify the brand and dimensions of the piano that must be provided for them when they appear. Less fortunate pianists have often opted for electronic keyboards, usually not because they prefer them, but because they find them more bearable than untuned acoustic pianos with keys that refuse to respond to normal touch. As more pianists show up with their own equipment, some proprietors have become even more lax about keeping their pianos in shape. Those who own and scrupulously care for fine instruments in order to present properly the artists they hire are treasured by all musicians.

Jay McShann talked about the sort of pianos he regularly encountered when he was on the road with his band:

> We used to run into pianos. I'd be playing in one key and the band was playing in another key. Some of 'em were so bad I would just go get me a bottle and go on back to the hotel. ♩

Earl Hines's arranger Cliff Smalls knew the gypsy signs used by some pianists to warn each other of bad instruments:

We had a lot of trouble with pianos when we were on the road doing one-nighters, and piano players used to leave a little sign on them to tip you off. There was a girl called Jackie, who played with the Sweethearts of Rhythm, and a couple of other friends of mine, whose sign I'd always recognize. I'd walk up to the bandstand, see the sign, and tell the man:

"The piano's no good."

"How do you know? You haven't even touched it."

Then I would play a little, and maybe he could hear how bad it was himself. Sometimes we'd really wreck a piano after a dance, so they'd get another before the next group came in. They'd hire somebody like Earl, and a band like this, and pay out the money, but why would they think we were going to sound good with a really bad piano? ⸙

Billy Eckstine described the surgery that was sometimes performed on those unplayable pianos:

Here we come to some dance with Earl, the number one piano player in the country, and half the keys on the goddam piano won't work. So when we're getting ready to leave, I'd get some of the guys to stand around the piano as though we were talking, and I'd reach in and pull all the strings and all the mallets out. "The next time we come here," I'd say, "I'll bet that son-of-a-bitch will have a piano for him to play on." ⸙

Ernie Wilkins worked a string of one-nighters through the South with Count Basie. When the band arrived at one high school gymnasium they found no piano on the stage. The band manager made inquiries, but no one seemed to know anything about a piano. For a while it looked like Basie might have to sit the night out. Then a commotion at the rear of the gym revealed four students pushing an old upright through the doors. On its front was taped a sign printed in huge black letters that had unmistakably identified the instrument for them. PIANO.

Jimmy McPartland was in Europe during the Second World War with the 462nd Automatic Weapons group, stationed in the Ardennes Forest. He met his future wife in 1944 when he was transferred to Special Services and was assigned to play with Chicago bandleader Willie Shaw and his ENSA (British USO) Bandwagon. Margaret Marian Turner, using the stage name Marian Page, was Shaw's pianist and accordion player. They entertained the troops wherever they were, sometimes close enough to the front to hear small-arms fire while playing.

In Eupen, a rest area town, the theater where they gave jazz concerts had an unplayable piano. Seeing Marian's distress, Jimmy got a requisition order from the Special Services officer and went to the home of a family he was told had been collaborators with the Nazis during the occupation:

I took eight men, a truck and a tommy gun and went into this house and got a beautiful grand piano. Marian didn't know about it. We dismantled the thing and carried it out. These people were screaming bloody murder. I said, "See the mayor. You'll get it back later. We're taking it to the Capitol Theater." ↲

Marian was delighted with the piano, though shocked by the way it was requisitioned. Later she told Jimmy, "That was when I decided to really pay attention to you."

Acoustic pianists don't have to carry any heavy equipment, but they suffer with the poor quality of the instruments they are often faced with. On a job in Florida, Tony Sotos asked Derek to check out the piano when they arrived. "No," said Derek, "it's all right." Tony asked, "Don't you think you ought to check it out?" "Why," asked Derek, "have you got another one?"

Dick Katz found a strange piano on a job in Harlem with Oscar Pettiford:

One night during a colossal heat wave, we were working at Small's Paradise—what a misnomer!—during the summer of 1958. All power had failed in the city. I came to work five to ten minutes late, annoyed with myself for being late and thoroughly uncomfortable from the heat. All the lights were out, and the air conditioning was off. The band was already playing the first number, in the dark. I slid onto the piano bench and could feel Oscar's wrath. The piano keys felt unbelievably strange. To my horror I discovered many of the black keys were missing. Oscar was obviously unaware of this sad fact and blew his top when he heard me play something that would make Cecil Taylor sound like Art Hodes.

"I can't play—the black keys are missing," I told him.

"So what," he said, "I heard guys play with no keys!"

Then the lights came on, and we all broke up. The black keys were on the floor. We got some shoe glue from across the street and glued the keys back on. ♪

At a panel discussion on Birdland at Manhattan School of Music, Billy Taylor told how, when he was the house pianist at Birdland, he talked club owner Morris Levy into buying a Steinway. He had complained about the poor quality of the club's old piano, and Levy had told him that a Steinway was too expensive. Billy said, "You drive a Cadillac, don't you? You not only have a car that you know is the best, when you get ready to sell it, it's worth some money because it's a Cadillac. Same thing with a Steinway . . . even after years of being pounded to death down here in Birdland, it will still be worth some money because it's a Steinway. And it will sound so much better." Levy said he had a tin ear, and couldn't tell the difference. "Sure you can," said Billy. "I'll prove it to you. Come over to Steinway hall with me tomorrow." Levy agreed to do so. Then Billy called the Steinway company and told them, "I'm going to sell a piano for you, but you have to help me out. I want you to get the shiniest, newest, worst sounding grand piano you can find . . . really make it sound rotten . . . and put it next to a Steinway grand." They did as he asked, and when Billy played the two pianos for Morris Levy the next day, Levy said, "Yes, I *can* hear the difference!" And he bought the Steinway.

Dick Hyman often carries a portable practice keyboard with him when he travels. Dominick Cortese and Dick were sharing a plane seat on a flight to Toronto. Dick was in the aisle seat with his keyboard in front of him, giving his fingers a workout. Dom looked out the window and noticed that oil was spattering from one of the engines. He tapped Dick and said, "Take a look out the window." Dick looked, and saw the oil. Dom asked him, "What do you think we should do?" Dick simply reached across and pulled down the window shade, and resumed his practicing.

Rashied Ali had an instrumental adventure with piano virtuoso Cecil Taylor:

I bought this piano. It was secondhand, but a good one. Cecil was in the building at the time the piano came and as I wanted somebody to play it to find out what it was like, he came up. I was practicing at the time so he walked around the room for a few minutes, and then he sat at the piano and we played from about twelve at night close to about five in the morning, straight through without any letup. Every now and then I would look over at the piano and Cecil would make like a run down the piano, man, and the keys would be shooting out of the piano like bullets! They were just flying past me! I would look and I'd drop my head because my piano was being really messed around. Cecil is a very strong pianist. It's not that he's the kind of pianist that just wrecks pianos, it's just that the piano was old and it couldn't stand the way he'd strike those keys. I had to get a whole new set of keys, but he really broke that piano in for me, man! ♭

chapter 6

Teachers and Students

Very few musicians are completely self-taught. Even if they had no formal education, there is someone in nearly every musician's background who helped show the way. Often there were many who did so. Many jazz musicians refer to their "musical fathers," the musicians who taught or inspired them either personally or via performances and phonograph records.

Sometimes it took a fatherly remark to set a young musician on a better path than the one he had taken by himself. Al Hall remembered the day he stopped showboating with his string bass and started concentrating on playing it well. He was working with Bobby Booker in Philadelphia, opposite Charlie Gaines's band:

Gaines's bass player was Mr. Hayes. He was about thirty-seven, and I'm seventeen, and smart, you know. I'd get out on the floor, and I'd spin the bass and straddle it and slap it while wearing a red hat.

Mr. Hayes said, "Son, when you're spinning it, you're not playing it."

From that point on I stopped. ↳

Chick Webb was unimpressed with Art Blakey's early attempts to play the drums in a showy manner, with stick twirling and arm waving. Chick told him, "Son, the music is on the drum, not in the air."

Blakey picked up drumming on his own, and Idrees Sulieman claims he was not a good drummer until Dizzy Gillespie explained things to him:

A̲ny time he would come it, cats would turn their heads a different way. One day we were standing on the corner of Massachusetts and Columbus avenues in Boston and Art came up and said, "Hey, man, I got a chance to go with the Billy Eckstine band." We said, "What! How's he going to take that job?"

They say that the first time was so terrible that Dizzy Gillespie said, "Look, man. Drummer downstairs gonna show you how to play drums." And Dizzy took him down and showed him how to drop a bomb, and what to do, and they say from that night on he's been like he is now. Dizzy Gillespie taught him how to play drums.

I couldn't believe it. The band came through and I never have been so shocked in my life! I couldn't believe it was the same drummer. Dizzy knew how to explain things so you can learn it in one time. ↳

When asked about this story, Blakey said, "Idrees is crazy. Those cats just didn't hear what I was doing yet."

Fats Waller was the organist at the Lincoln Theater in Harlem when Count Basie first heard him. Basie spent a lot of time sitting in the front row near Waller's organ bench:

O̲ne day he asked me whether I played the organ. "No," I said, "but I'd give my right arm to learn." The next day he invited me to sit in the pit and start working the pedals. I sat on the floor watching his feet, and using my hands to imitate them. Then I sat behind him and he taught me. One afternoon he pretended to have some urgent business downstairs and asked me to wait for him. I started playing while he stood downstairs listening. After that I would come to early shows and he let me play accompaniment to the picture. Later I used to follow him around wherever he played, listening and learning all the time. 🎵

Art Blakey got a lesson from Sid Catlett one night:

When I was playing with Fletcher Henderson, one night I had a bottle of whiskey in my coat pocket and I was drinking through a straw from the bottle during the show. I thought I was hip. The chorus girls were out on the stage, and I did the show pretty well. When I came off the stage, Sid Catlett grabbed me, hugged me and picked me up. But when he felt the bottle, he put me down, hit me and knocked me to the floor. He told me, "Learn how to master your instrument before you learn how to drink. Next time I catch you, I'll break your neck." So this stopped me from drinking. It helped me, and I never got angry with him. If you did that now you would have a lawsuit on your hands. 🎵

Erskine Hawkins got some advice from Louis Armstrong about playing in the upper register of the trumpet:

It didn't come to me too hard, 'cause I was used to it. I was even doing it through my younger days. My first teacher was called "High-C Foster." It came to me a little easy. I didn't like to puff and act like it was hard for me. That's what Louis explained for me. He said,

"Now, you made your point. Now, let them think it's a little hard for you to do it." He said, "You're making it look too easy." 🎵

Johnny Guarnieri's father, the last in the line of the Guarneri violin makers of Cremona, Italy, hoped his son would become a concert violinist:

Unfortunately for my father's hopes, when I was fifteen a friend played me some Fats Waller records. Once I heard Fats, you couldn't hold me down. I had to play like that. I could think of nothing else and I could hear nothing else. I got those Waller records and began copying his style, including his singing. I wasn't the only one who was mesmerized by him. By the time I was known locally as the Fats Waller of Tremont Avenue [in the Bronx], a cousin of mine, Frank Barker, was the Fats Waller of Burnside Avenue, and Harry Raab, later known as Harry "The Hipster" Gibson, was the Fats Waller of Fordham Road. ♩

Art Tatum was a great inspiration to piano players, both for his technique and his harmonic conception. Other instrumentalists also learned from him. Eddie Barefield said:

Don Byas bought everything that Tatum recorded. He actually used to sit down and copy Tatum's solos and play them on saxophone. He said that that's where he got his greatest harmonic education, by listening to Tatum. ♩

Young Allen Eager asked for and got some lessons from his idol, Ben Webster:

Ben was playing on Broadway, with Duke. I walked over to him and said, "Man, I love the way you play, you're my favorite saxophone player. Could you give me lessons? I'm learning how to play." He said, "Oh well, I don't know about that. Coleman Hawkins is pretty heavy." I said, "Well, will you give me a lesson?" He said, "Well, all right," and he told me where he lived.

I went up there about one o'clock. It was the first time I went up to Harlem. I knocked on the door, they had a little hotel over Minton's, and then a big hand opens up the door. The room was so small the bed took up most of the room. He just leaned over from the bed and opened the door.

I set up and I played his chorus on "Cottontail" and he flipped. He ran out and woke up Russell Procope, Ray Nance, whoever else was there. Said, "You ought to listen to this white kid, listen to this white kid!" (Laughter) I was barely fifteen, something like that. He thought it was marvelous that a young white boy should be aware of him in that manner, even to copy his solos. I had three or four lessons. He gave me a lot of tips.

He didn't charge for the lessons. Of course, there's a tragic reverse side to it also. There I was, a full Ben Webster man, and then I went to the Coast just about the time Charlie Parker came to the Coast and played. I smoked some really good grass and went into a guy's room and started listening to some Lester Young, and did a complete about face. I just did a complete one-eighty. The next day I was at the club I filed my mouthpiece and was trying to play like Lester.

When I came back to New York about a year and a half later I was working at the Three Deuces and Ben came down to hear me, expecting to sound full and lush and everything, and I was a Lester Young fan. It was terrible. It was kind of a great disappointment to Ben and it made me feel weird.   🎵

When he left Benny Goodman's band and started playing trumpet for NBC in New York, Jimmy Maxwell went to hear a bagpipe band at Madison Square Garden and was moved to tears by the sound. His wife bought him some pipes, and he found a teacher, Mr. Gallagher.

"God, he was a great player," Jimmy said. "In the beginning he gave me free lessons. He wouldn't take any money. Then around January one year he said, 'Well, it's about time to be measured up for the kilt.' "

Jimmy said he didn't want a kilt. Mr. Gallagher told him,

"You don't have to march in the parade, but you can't do it without a kilt."

Jim said he didn't plan to march in the parade.

"Just because I gave you free lessons doesn't mean you're obliged to do it," said Mr. Gallagher.

By insisting on the absence of obligation, Mr. Gallagher eventually got Jim into kilts and into the parade.

Jimmy said, "As I marched down 5th Avenue past NBC, I thought, 'Oh God, I hope nobody comes out and sees me.' " He marched every St. Patrick's Day for six years.

After Mr. Gallagher retired, he spent some time traveling with the multi-instrumental Kim Sisters, who wanted to learn bagpipes. He wasn't able to get them to march in the parade.

Jim Hall was playing a week somewhere in the Midwest. During a break he was approached by a young man who wanted to talk about guitar playing. He spoke so knowledgeably about instruments, set-ups, and famous guitar players that Jim assumed he was the local virtuoso. After a pleasant conversation on a professional level, Jim excused himself to play another set. As the young guitarist headed back to his table, he said, almost as an afterthought, "You know, I have trouble with A-Flat minor seventh."

As colleges began including jazz studies in their musical curricula, they began to hire jazz musicians to give students professional advice at jazz clinics. Some were more articulate than others. At one clinic, Thelonious Monk listened to a student band play and gave careful consideration to what he wanted to tell them. After much musing and beard-stroking, he stood before them and said, "Keep on tryin'!"

The University of Cincinnati brought in Jaime Abersold and Red Rodney as co-clinicians. Abersold spoke first. He articulately parsed what the students had played, analyzing the music in exhaustive detail. When he turned the lecture over to his partner, Red said, "I agree with everything he said!"

After getting his laugh, Red added, "The only thing I would say is, God gave you these," and he pointed to his ears. "That's what guys like me use when we don't understand the intellectual terms. And learn the melody, because the melody is never wrong!"

Shortly before Woody Herman's death Red Kelly and his wife spent a day with him in Portland, Oregon. At dinner, Red reminded him of a clinic with a college band that Woody and some of his musicians had done while Red was the bassist with the Herman herd. Woody hadn't made many comments about the music that day. When he heard a problem in the student trumpet section, he would send his lead trumpet player up to sit with them and show them what to do.

He told Red, "Go sit in the rhythm section and tell the drummer what he's doing wrong."

Woody had one piece of advice for the saxophone section. He stopped the band and told them, "Don't pat your feet. When you pat your feet, you can't hear the rhythm section."

Red reminded Woody of this, and Woody said, "Nobody ever hires anybody to pound foot."

When Pee Wee Erwin and Chris Griffin were operating a music school in New Jersey, Buddy Christian taught some of the drum students. The mother of one of his pupils complained to him one day, "All I hear is banging! He doesn't know any music! Not even the Alley Cat, like they play at weddings!" To reassure her, Buddy had her son play a steady beat on the hi-hat while he took the lady by the hand and led her through the steps of the Alley Cat: "Right side, right side, left side, left . . ." The mother was delighted. "He *does* know the Alley Cat!"

John La Porta reportedly had a little talk with one of his pupils: "I have good news and bad news about your playing. The good news is: you've got a lot of technique. The bad news is: you've got a lot of technique."

A concert in New Jersey included several trumpet players including Joe Shepley, John Glasel, Bobby Hackett, and young Glenn Zottola, who was then a teen-ager. Everyone was impressed with young Glenn's talent, and when they all got together afterwards in a restaurant, Hackett complimented Glenn's parents. "Who has he been listening to?" asked Hackett. "Louis Armstrong?" "No," said Glenn's father, "he doesn't like Louis Armstrong." Hackett looked at them gravely and said, "Your kid's in a lot of trouble!"

At a jazz demonstration concert at a Greenwich, Connecticut, school, Glenn Drewes showed his trumpet to the kids, talked a little about how it worked, and then demonstrated its sound and range. Then John Fumasoli did the same with his trombone. John said, "This instrument is in the same family as the trumpet, but it goes much lower," and he demonstrated the low register. "And it can also go up into the trumpet's range," and he played some very high notes to illustrate. A young boy raised his hand and asked John, "Then, isn't it a waste of money to buy a trumpet?"

At a Rahway, New Jersey, public school, a mature group of jazz musicians were demonstrating their skills to the assembled students in the music department. The teacher wanted to impress on his pupils the fact that the music was all improvised, and no one was reading music. He said to them, "Now, what is it that we have in our orchestra that none of these musicians has?" One of the kids offered, "Hair?"

Joe Puma was working with a talented young drummer who tended to overdecorate Joe's solos. Joe had a talk with him afterward. "Look," he said, "You don't have to *make* me swing. I can do that by myself. Just keep time. You have to learn to let things glide along. Every time you stick your paddle in the water, you slow the boat down!"

Dwike Mitchell's piano teacher Agi Jambor gave him an unorthodox sendoff at the Philadelphia Musical Academy, when he had to play a classical piece in performance:

It was Khachaturian's Piano Concerto, and it was the first piece I
had ever played well, because Agi had worked and worked with me.
But I was a nervous wreck when it was time to go out on the stage. I
was standing there in the wings, and I was so frightened, and I said,
"I'm not going out there." Agi said, "You're going—don't worry
about." Just as I was starting out on the stage, shaking in my boots,
she kicked me in the ass just as hard as she could possibly kick. I've
never had such a shock. It just blipped out all that nervousness. That
was the sendoff she gave me. The next day the critic for the Philadelphia newspaper gave me the write-up of write-ups. I still have it
somewhere; it's all yellow and torn. ↰

chapter 7

Stage Fright

Stage fright is considered a normal hazard among actors, but musicians are often unprepared for it. Finding themselves before an audience in an unusual situation, they may suddenly be surprised to
discover that their mouths are dry, their palms sweaty, their minds
blank.

Garvin Bushell saw it happen to Bubber Miley. After recording with
blues singer Mamie Smith in 1921, Bushell went on to tour with her
show. Somewhere along the way, Bubber Miley was hired to replace
trumpeter Johnny Dunn. Bubber had never done a show before and was
nervous about being on stage.

On opening day at the Pershing Theater in Pittsburgh, Mamie got the
hooks and eyes on her costume caught in a drawer in her dressing room
and was late coming on stage. The band kept vamping, but Mamie didn't
appear.

Mamie's husband said, "Play the introduction again." The band complied, but still no Mamie. They had already played the "Royal Garden

Blues," but they played it again. They repeated Mamie's introduction. Still no Mamie. "Play it again," shouted Mamie's husband. By this time Miley's lip was beginning to give out. Bushell said:

> I looked over there at Bubber and he was so nervous he had his trumpet down on his chin trying to blow it. And he's backing off of the stage at the same time he's trying to find his mouth, scared to death. Mamie's husband, out in the wings, took his foot and booted Bubber back on the stage, and the audience yelled! They had to bring the curtain down. ♩

Barney Bigard tells of a time when stage fright struck the Ellington band:

> We were booked into the Palace Theater in New York. If you played there, and went over big, then you had made it. It was like a testing ground for acts of all kinds. We were all set to open and we had on our new white ties and tails, but most of the guys were real nervous because this was such a biggie. There was just two shows a day and if the public liked what you did, and you got those good first-edition notices, then you would work fifty-two weeks of a year automatically. This all being at stake, we were shivering with apprehension in the dressing room. We knew all the critics and Broadway "big wigs" were out there. We took the stand behind the curtain. Then they pulled the curtain and we like to froze. Out came Duke and took his bow. He turned to us and waved the baton to get us to hit that great big chord that would start out our show. Down came that baton . . . nothing! Nobody moved or blew a note. Duke's eyes were blazing at us all but he turned and smiled sweetly to his audience just as if he were conducting for a "tea dance." He turned back to us, still smiling, and said in a loud voice, "Play, you bastards!"
>
> We got through that first week somehow and I'll never know how, but we got good press and we were on our way. ♩

On another occasion, Bigard said:

> At that time *Black and Tan* was one of the big numbers. While we rehearsed I was foolin' with the horn and I made a glissando, you know, and Duke says at once, "Keep that in, that's what I want."
>
> That's how things happened in that band. The funny part of it was

when we opened at the Palace Theater in New York, and that was the big number. And tricky Sam and I, we had solos in this.

So when I get up there—this is my first stage appearance and I'm all trembling—I get to make the slur and all I can do is say "peep, peep, peep," and the people started laughing. Then I went into the blues and it was all right.

Well, I turned green, you know, thinking I really did a good bit of messin' it up. Then Tricky Sam started his solo with the plunger, and he had it in so tight, the inner mute, that he blew the back of the horn out. [The tuning slide]. The people started laughing again. They thought that was in the act. ↳

Lucky Thompson was overwhelmed when he first arrived in New York in 1943 with Lionel Hampton's band. He was hired to replace Ben Webster at the Three Deuces, and on the first night looked down from the bandstand to see Coleman Hawkins, Don Byas, Lester Young, and Ben Webster sitting there listening.

"I never played so horrible in my life," said Lucky. "I don't know how I survived, believe me. For the first time I found my fingers in *between* the keys."

Roy Eldridge was such an ebullient, competitive player that nervousness seemed out of the question, but he said he always felt nervous before playing. He thought the reason dated back to his childhood:

I joined the drum and bugle corps. That, I really enjoyed. I couldn't wait til the parade on Decoration Day. I'd get up about six o'clock in the morning and go out and get my snare drum and tune it up. When you get home at night, those drums are still beating in your ears. It was such a good feeling, marching in front of all those people.

They got short of buglers, and they just handed me a bugle. That was before I started playing trumpet. I could play it, except for one thing. Something that hasn't left me in all these years—being nervous when I had to play. See, what they did, they stationed each bugler a certain distance in the graveyard. ↳

Roy described how one bugler would begin "Taps" and each bugler in turn would play the next phrase.

It had nothing' to do with it bein' in a graveyard. It was just that all my buddies were there from my side of town. We lived on the north side. If I'd been the second one, I don't think I'd have been nervous. But, like, they went *there,* and they went *there,* and they went *there,* and it looked like I was the last one. When it got to me, I was in a cold sweat, and I went: (sings, with shaky tone) Talk about soundin' like a nanny goat! And that's something that stuck with me ever since, you know?   ↱

Like many young musicians, Roy felt intimidated when he first came to New York:

New York musicians, cats that had been here, had a certain attitude, you know. I got in this band. First of all, I'd never played in a band with a good string bass and a good drummer with that kind of time, with a sock cymbal, you know. And it was different. Plus, these cats are playing so great, and I was scared to death. Every time I'd have a chorus coming up, the first trumpet player, Leonard Davis, he would take my part. When I did get something, I was so beaten down I just couldn't play nothing.

When intermission came, my brother and Chu Berry got me and took me up to the bar across the street from the Renaissance and bought me about three shorties of gin, or corn, or whatever it was. And said,

"If you don't play, we gonna kick the shit out of you! Forget this cat! Stomp on him!"

In those days, if you would take a chorus, near the end of your chorus I would stomp; that means "I'm comin' in! So open the door!" Right? So by the time we got back on, man, I was feelin' no pain. So Davis got up and took my chorus from me, and I stomped on him, and played, and I haven't looked back since!   ↱

chapter 8

Reading Music

Though a musician needs a good ear to play jazz well, it is possible to be musically illiterate and still excel in jazz. Erroll Garner was the most shining example. Erroll had such a quick ear as a child that he never bothered to learn to read. One hearing was usually enough for him to learn any new piece of music. When someone mentioned his not being able to read music, Garner said, "Hell, man, nobody can hear you read."

In the early days, a jazz musician who could read music was usually called "Professor." Written notes were viewed with suspicion by the unschooled and were considered to be devoid of soul. But men like Eubie Blake could read and write music very well. He said:

> In those days Negro musicians weren't even supposed to read music. We had to pretend we couldn't read; then they'd marvel at the way we could play shows, thinking we'd learned the parts by ear.

As bands became larger and arrangements more complex, the ability to read *and* play good jazz became an asset. The musically literate often helped their section mates improve their reading. As a fair ability to read became the norm, the few holdouts became figures of fun.

Brad Gowans told a leader who asked if he could read: "Not enough to hurt my playing."

Phil Urso felt the same way when he took over one of the tenor chairs on Woody Herman's band. Woody inquired,

"How well do you read?"

"Just enough so it doesn't screw up my jazz."

Jack Teagarden heard Wingy Manone's trumpet playing on the *Kraft Music Hall* radio shows with Bing Crosby. Jack wired Wingy, "If you can read, come on."

Wingy wired back, "Can read. Am coming."

At the first rehearsal they tried "Waitin' at the Gate" four times. Wingy couldn't cut it.

Jack called him over. "Why did you wire me you could read? You can't read."

Wingy replied, "Man, I can read." He pointed to a piece of music.

"Now here goes Wingy," he said. "That's an F, that's a G, that's a C-sharp, that's a D. I can read 'em; I just can't divide 'em."

Wingy went back to New York, and about two months later Jack got a letter from him saying he'd been taking lessons and now could read anything.

Jack sent him a ticket to come out to Chicago.

When Wingy got there Jack called a rehearsal, and discovered that Wingy still couldn't read. Jack said, "You got a lot of nerve, man, making me send you money to come here and take up all my time."

Wingy answered, "I don't see what you getting so excited about. You don't realize how rusty a guy can get on them long train rides!"

Earl Hines recalled playing with Louis Armstrong at the Sunset, on the south side of Chicago:

Punch Miller was a friend of Louis's from New Orleans, and he came into the Sunset one night. He walked up to Louis during intermission, when we were changing music and talking to some song-pluggers who wanted us to play their tunes.

"Let me play some of these things," he said to Louis as we passed out the sheets of the arrangements.

"Man, you can't play this music," Louis said. "Everybody is reading in this band."

"I can read now."

"Are you sure?"

"Yes, I can read."

"All right," Louis said, "you go ahead and play if you think so."

I got off the stand, because Fats Waller was up there on the second piano. I wanted to hear Punch Miller, because I'd heard so much about him. Louis came off, too, and we stood at the back of the room.

"All right," said Fats, "let's stomp it off!" And he stomped it off.

Punch evidently couldn't get it together, but there was a little strain he thought he was familiar enough with to take a solo on. Well, he got into the strain, but he couldn't get out of it, and that's when Fats came up with an expression that would make musicians crack up for years afterwards: "What key are you struggling in?" he hollered. "Turn the page!" ♩

Herschel Evans, one of Basie's tenor stars, was not a good reader. Dickie Wells recalled:

Herschel was a slow kind of reader and didn't care about reading at all. So after we had spent about three hours rehearsing, Basie would call out that night: "Get out that number Kirkpatrick made!"

"I can't find my part," Herschel would say.

We'd all be down looking under the stands, and Basie would be looking through the piano music. Herschel would be real busy helping Basie look for it, but after the gig he'd tell me: "Man, I tore that damn thing up and sent it down the drain—all them sharps and things. I didn't feel like fooling with that."

That happened three or four times, until Basie got wise. He said, "I believe that rascal's tearing up our music." But I don't think he ever actually *knew*. Herschel would wait until after rehearsal and tear it up, six or seven sheets for saxophone. Well, he read slow, but that was one of the reasons why he swung so much. ♩

When Herman Autrey first arrived in New York he met a friend from Washington, D.C., who told him Fletcher Henderson was looking for a trumpet player. Autrey took the address and went to Fletcher's house.

"I heard that you wanted a trumpet."

"Okay, sit down."

Henderson passed out some music, picked up his baton, and started. Autrey played his part perfectly. Henderson pulled out some more music, and Autrey did the same thing.

Henderson said, "What's your name?"

"Herman Autrey."

"Where you from?"

"Alabama."

Henderson called his wife. "Babe, come here! I want you to meet someone!"

He told Autrey, "Nobody's ever played my music like that! You couldn't have played it before. I wrote it last night."

Henderson's wife came in and listened, and said, "You'll be a nice trumpet player some day."

Autrey later found out she was a trumpet player herself, Leora Henderson.

Autrey moved right into Fletcher's first trumpet chair. One of the numbers was a new arrangement Fletcher had done for Benny Goodman. He said as he passed out the parts, "Run this down for me. I just want to see if the notes are right."

Fletcher liked the way it sounded and put it in the book to use on a job that night. Autrey forgot to take his part with him and didn't discover it was missing until Fletcher called the number on the job:

All the band pulled it out but me. I couldn't tell him, "I haven't got it." So when he brought his hand down, I closed my eyes and played the whole arrangement from memory. Thank God I'm capable of doing that. I have what they call a photographic memory. If I see a letter or an arrangement or anything, I don't know, I seem to make a picture of it if I can remember where I saw it. I was only worried about one spot that was in the second ending. Went through and it was beautiful.

I told Fletcher, and he said, "What!" Oh, he almost had a heart attack. He said, "Why didn't you tell me?"

"I did, but you couldn't hear me." 🎵

When John Bunch was conducting for Tony Bennett, he got a surprise when they rehearsed for one concert:

In the middle of our first rehearsal with Duke Ellington's band, Johnny Hodges got up, put his horn down and walked right out in the middle of a tune. Clear out of the room! It didn't really upset me because I'd heard so much about the fellows in the band and what they were like. Shortly afterwards we took a five-minute break and Russell Procope came over to me and said, "Come here, John, I want to talk to you. Come on over in the corner. I just want you to know that when Johnny got up and left right in the middle of a tune like that, it's not because he was mad at you. He's mad at himself. He couldn't read the parts."

I'd already heard that Johnny wasn't a good sight reader. It's amazing because he was such a great player! I later found out that he learned a lot of his parts by hearing Procope play them. He learned as he heard the music being played every night. He played his parts by ear, a lot better than most do by reading! 🎵

Teddy McRae remembered a time with Jimmy Lunceford's band when memory was more important than reading:

We're going to Washington, we played Trenton, that's when they left the books on the train and we had to play the whole two shows without music. Mr. Lunceford said, "Don't worry about it, because y'all been playing the music all your life."

We played that show without any music, man. Played the whole show. 🎵

Nowadays most jazz players can read, but they still may run into situations they aren't prepared for. Saxophonist Jack Nimitz, a Stan Kenton alumnus, had no problem with reading or improvising, but when he took a job with a club date band that faked harmony to standard tunes, he had trouble. Club date fake bands play long medleys, one chorus of each song. The trumpet or the lead alto will play the melody, and the rest of the horns find harmony parts by ear.

Jack was doing all right with the harmony lines until the band began to play a tune he didn't know. He tried to catch it by ear, but in the process he played a few wrong notes. The leader shouted over the music, "If you don't know the tune, just play the melody!"

A local bass player once filled in with Thelonious Monk's group at a Seattle jazz club. When he was called for the job, he asked, "Will there be a rehearsal?" He was told to be at the club at two p.m. The bassist arrived fifteen minutes early, tuned up, rosined his bow, warmed up a bit, and waited. Around three-fifteen, when no one else had turned up to rehearse, he stopped practicing and went home. When he returned that evening and was introduced to Monk, he gingerly asked if there wasn't supposed to be a rehearsal that afternoon. Monk said, "Yeah. The rehearsal was for you. Did you show up?"

When Kenny Berger joined the band that Thad Jones and Mel Lewis co-led for several years, he found a change that Pepper Adams had made on one of his saxophone parts. Pepper had penciled in a comma, turning Thad's title, "Quiet Lady," into "Quiet, Lady."

Derek Smith reads well and is able to handle a wide variety of musical styles. But when he came home after a gig one night and found a message that he was booked for the *Good Morning America* show on ABC to accompany Luciano Pavarotti, he was a little worried. He had never played for the tenor and had no idea how difficult his piano music might be. Derek showed up at the studio promptly for the 5:00 a.m. call and found that no one knew anything about the music. Pavarotti arrived an hour later, but he immediately became the center of a social clamor that made it impossible for Derek to get near enough to ask any questions. When air time arrived and everyone was concentrating on the morning news segment, Derek finally got Pavarotti's attention.

"Could I have a look at the music?" he asked.

Pavarotti referred Derek to his manager, who fumbled through his briefcase and produced a sheet music copy of "We Wish You a Merry Christmas."

chapter 9

Hiring and Firing

Jazz musicians who stay with the same band for years are in the minority. They will usually tire of traveling or of the music they are playing, or will have a falling out with someone. There may be an offer of more money or more solos somewhere else, or a band will have a layoff or break up, and changes will be made. During the height of the swing era, musicians moved from band to band so frequently that *Down Beat* magazine ran a column called "Sideman Switches" that helped the musicians and fans keep track of who was with whom.

Some good stories arose in the course of all this hiring and firing and quitting. Jo Jones told how he was hired by Count Basie:

> In 1933 I joined Tommy Douglas in Joplin, Missouri. I replaced Jesse Price on the drums, and I was a singer. Walter Page came up and sat in the band and he says, "How would you like to join Count Basie's band?" I says, "Sure." I played one night and quit. I played Topeka, Kansas, and they played "After You've Gone," and when Hot Lips Page got through playing, Lester Young stood up and took the second chorus, and I went downstairs and refused to accept my money. I said, "I'm going back to Omaha to go back to school." Basie begged me to stay. I said, "I'm not staying. I can't play with your band, Mr. Basie." My heart went in my mouth when Lester Young got up and took the second chorus on "After You've Gone." I died.
>
> I came back to pick up my drums and they told me, "You can't leave." I said, "I'm picking up my drums because I'm going back to school. I won't be playing in no band." And Ben Webster wanted to slap me. "Why, are you crazy!" And Herschel Evans says, "You're crazy, you can play in the band." So I said, "All right, Mr. Basie, I will play with you for two weeks until you find a drummer." That lasted fourteen years. ↷

Lester Young was one of Count Basie's principal soloists when the band came out of Kansas City, and admirers of the band couldn't imagine the band being without him. But Basie fired him in 1940. After waiting two hours for him to show up on a record date, Basie called his hotel. Buck Clayton said:

> He got him on the phone and told him that we were all waiting for him to show up, and for him to hurry and get his butt down there.
>
> Prez said to Basie, "Man, I don't make no records on the thirteenth of no month." So Basie had to let him go. ↷

Jo Jones described Lester Young's rehiring by Basie in 1940, just before he was drafted into the army:

> Lester had left the band. He stayed out of the band for about two and a half years. When we went to the Lincoln Hotel something happened with Don Byas, and Basie told me to go find Lester. Lester by that time had left the USO show and was playing on 52nd Street.

I went around to the White Rose and got Lester. I told him, "You're due at work tomorrow night at seven o'clock. You come to the Lincoln Hotel."

And there he was! Nobody said nothing! He just sat down and started playing, and nobody said nothing. They didn't say, "Hello, Lester, how have you been?" or nothing. He came back in the band like he'd just left fifteen minutes ago. ↶

When Don Byas left Basie he gave his notice this way: "Basie, in four weeks I will have been gone two!"

And when Sonny Stitt asked Miles Davis for a raise and was told there was no more money, Sonny said, "No money, no Sonny!" and left the band.

Milt Hinton met Oscar Pettiford when the Cab Calloway band traveled to Minneapolis. Oscar was playing bass with a band at the local Elks' club, and Milt couldn't get over how well he played. He wanted the rest of Cab's band to hear him, so he invited him to visit them the next day at the theater where they were working.

When Oscar dropped by, Milt took him up to the rehearsal hall and organized a jam session. Milt says, "He played, and Cab came up and heard him and fired me! I said, 'That's the last time I ever do that!'" He wanted to hire Oscar right then and there, and kick me out. Oscar wouldn't go. Later on, he went with Duke."

Milt has often told the story of Dizzy Gillespie's altercation with Calloway that resulted in his being fired. On stage at the State Theater in Hartford, Connecticut, Milt was out front with Cab's small group, the Cab Jivers. When he finished his bass solo he looked back to the trumpet section for Dizzy's reaction. Just at the moment that Dizzy held his nose with one hand and waved deprecatingly with the other, a spitball rose from the trumpet section and landed in the spotlight next to Chu Berry. Cab, watching from the wings, saw Dizzy wave and saw the spitball land, and was sure he'd seen Dizzy throw it. When he called Dizzy aside after the show to reprimand him, Dizzy denied that he was the culprit. Cab said, "I saw you do it," and Dizzy called him a liar. After more heated words Cab threatened to slap Dizzy around, and Dizzy dared him to do it. Milt says:

Cab slapped Diz across the side of his face. A split second later Diz had his case knife out and was going for Cab. I was just a couple of feet away. So when Diz took a swing at Cab's stomach with his knife, I hit his hand and made him miss. Then Cab grabbed Diz around the wrist and tried to wrestle the knife away. Within seconds the big guys, Chu and Benny [Payne], had made it to where we were and quickly pulled them apart. ♪

Calloway discovered he'd been nicked on the leg and wrist during the scuffle. He told Dizzy, "Pack your horn and get out of here." Dizzy left, and apologized when he met Cab again in New York. Later, Cab found out it was Jonah Jones who had thrown the spitball. He and Dizzy eventually made up and became friends.

The grapevine quickly carried the story of Dizzy's fight with Calloway around the music world, with appropriate embroidery, and Dizzy gained the reputation of being a very bad cat. Dizzy said:

Les Hite appreciated our music and liked my playing, but he was afraid of me because of the incident with Cab. He had heard about that scuffle, and Les Hite thought I had to be some kind of nut, so we didn't have too much to talk about. ♪

One night Dizzy sat down in the middle of his solo because he didn't like what the drummer was playing behind him.

Les Hite looked at me, but he was scared to say anything because of my reputation, so he fired the whole band. Les fired the whole band, and then hired back the men he wanted. Bandleaders use to do it like that, and it's a good idea. You say, "I'm breaking up my band, everybody's fired," and then say, "I want you, you, and you in my new band." That's better than pointing at one person and saying, "It's you I want to get rid of." Can you believe Les Hite fired a whole band to get rid of me? ♪

Clark Terry worked on a riverboat with Fate Marable, the bandleader who first took Louis Armstrong out of New Orleans. When Fate fired a man, he literally gave him the axe:

Fate was quite a character. He had changed his name from Marble to Marable. Whenever Fate was going to fire a person, he'd take one of the fire axes from the wall of the boat and put it in the cat's seat. When the guy came on board, we would start playing. Naturally the cat would figure he was late, and as he ran up to the band, we would start playing, "There'll Be Some Changes Made." ♩

Charlie Barnet recounts the complicated events that enabled him to hire Jack Purvis:

Jack Purvis was one of the wildest men I have ever met in my life. He was also one of the greatest trumpet players, certainly head and shoulders above most guys around then. He had a great high-note ability and he could play just like Louis Armstrong; but he could also turn around and hold down a chair in a symphony. Jack had been hired to play with Waring's Pennsylvanians when they opened at the Roxy Theater in New York. The Roxy was then the newest and largest theater in the country, a truly magnificent place that rivaled the future Radio City Music Hall for sumptuousness. Fred Waring had augmented the band for the occasion and it was to play the 1812 Overture in the huge rising pit.

Now Jack Purvis's pride and joy was a little moustache that he spent hours shaping and waxing to a fine point. It upset Waring, because he tried to project the image of a collegiate-type organization with all the musicians clean-shaven and dressed in sweaters and slacks. So he went to Jack and told him to remove the moustache before the next show.

The 1812 Overture opened with a solo trumpet. Waring had it staged so that the band came up from the pit in the dark. Then a pin spot picked him up and followed him to center stage. He gave the downbeat and the spot went to Jack Purvis, the only guy who could handle the assignment. At the next show, Waring made his trek across the pit and gave the downbeat. When the spot hit Jack, he had shaved off not only the moustache but every hair on his head, and very uncollegiate he looked. Jack suddenly became available for my band. ♩

Lionel Hampton hired young Betty Carter to sing with his band:

He'd look at me and ask dumb questions like, "Whose band do you like best, mine or Dizzy's?" I'd say Dizzy's, and he would fire me, and Gladys Hampton would rehire me. We went through that for two and a half years. 🖎

Lester Young had hired a drummer who wasn't playing what he wanted to hear. During a break, the drummer tried making conversation:

"Say, Prez, when was the last time we worked together?"

"Tonight," sighed Lester.

Red Norvo visited a dark little club in New Jersey where he heard a bassist who sounded good to him, and found out his name was Red Mitchell. When he needed a new bass player for his trio he asked around and found that Red was living at a small musicians' hotel in New York. He called the number.

"Red?"

"Yes."

"This is Red Norvo. Would you like to make a gig with my trio in Chicago?"

"Sure."

Norvo laid out the details and arranged to pick him up and drive him to Chicago, where they would meet Mundell Lowe, the third member of the group.

The new bassist fell asleep in the car not long after they left New York. After driving for several hours, Norvo stopped to eat. He shook his companion and said, "Hey, Mitchell."

"Mitchell? My name's Red Kelly."

The two redheaded bassists were roommates in New York.

Many years later, when Mitchell was living in Los Angeles, he got a call from a local club to play a week with Marian McPartland, who was coming in from New York. Red had known Marian for many years, but had never played with her before. He asked the booker how he had happened to call him. The answer:

"She asked me to find her a bass player who sounds like Red Mitchell."

In the 1950s Dave Lambert was scuffling to survive a rough spot in his career. (This was before he met Jon Hendricks and formed Lambert, Hendricks & Ross.) He had heard that the King of Thailand was an amateur clarinetist and jazz fan, and decided to offer his services, hoping the King might fly him to Thailand and put him on an annual retainer. Dave got his secretarial ex-wife to write the King a letter, suggesting that he might like to have a resident arranger and bebop singer. He got a courteous reply, on royal stationery, to the effect that, "If you're ever in town, look me up."

Jimmy Giuffre brought his trio to New York in 1957. His group included guitarist Jim Hall and Chicago bassist Jim Atlas, a replacement for Ralph Pena, who had stayed in California. In New York, Giuffre discovered that Bob Brookmeyer was available. He wanted to add him to the group, but he had bookings for a trio and couldn't afford a fourth musician. He decided to eliminate the string bass and let Jim Hall cover the bass notes on the guitar. He told Jim Atlas of his decision and sent him home.

Atlas hadn't been paying much attention to national and world news, so he was unaware of the latest missile developments at Cape Canaveral. His dismay was understandable when he got off the train in Chicago and saw the morning paper's banner headline: "ATLAS FIRED."

Mel Tormé tells about a musician that Stan Getz offered to hire at the Copa Club in Pittsburgh:

> The engagement went well, and one night, in walked José Ferrer, the Broadway Wunderkind. He was a jazz buff, and after my last performance of the evening he suggested that we slip across the street to the Carousel, where Stan Getz was fronting a quartet. Getz was his usual miraculous self on tenor, and late in his set he invited me to play drums with the group. As I rose, José Ferrer whispered to me, almost pleadingly, "Ask him if I could sit in on piano. Please!"
>
> As I settled behind the drums, I asked Stan if my friend could join us. Getz nodded, and José practically leapt onto the small bandstand. We decided on "Indiana," and when José's solo turn came, he knocked us all out with his playing. I was only minimally surprised. José Ferrer could—and can—do anything. At the end of the final chorus, there was a roar from the crowd, and José had earned his share of it. We went back to our table, and when Ferrer excused himself to go to the men's room, Getz came over.
>
> "Hey, man," he asked, "who's the old cat?"

"Old cat?" I laughed. "Stanley, that's José Ferrer. He pulls down about a grand a week on Broadway."

Getz shrugged, looked around, and said offhandedly, "Makes no difference to me. If he wants to play with my group, he'll have to work for scale!" Getz was dead serious. Ferrer told me his publicity people about the remark. It was hilariously reported in all the trade papers as well as the *Pittsburgh Press* next morning.   ↱

chapter 10

Managers, Agents, and Bosses

The business people of the music world are necessary to jazz musicians who want to make a living. Unless a musician is good at marketing his own skills, he needs the assistance of bandleaders, agents, managers, promoters, publicists, club owners, and record producers. He may not deal with them all directly, but they all affect his life and his music. He tries to find those who value his work and want to see him prosper.

Some bands managed themselves on the commonwealth system. When money came in, expenses were taken off the top and the remainder was divided evenly into as many shares as there were musicians. There were many commonwealth bands in the Midwest. Buster Smith played with one in Kansas City, the Blue Devils:

> A commonwealth band was what the trouble was. That's where I found out that anything commonwealth could never amount to nothing. The thing is, there's thirteen of us, whenever we wanted to do something, accept a job, we have to sit down and have a discussion, and we'd always have voting on it and seven would vote for it and six would vote against it. Or vice versa. It looked like everywhere we'd get a chance to get a good job somewhere, that seven would vote against; they'd want a little more money.
>
> Like when we got to Cincinnati, Fats Waller was playing at

WLW, and he had a little four- or five-piece band. He liked us and wanted us to sit in with him out there and work regularly. He offered us, I think it was $800 a week. We wasn't doing anything there. So we got to talking on it, and seven of 'em said we ought to get $1000.

"That's Fats Waller, he's making plenty of money."

We couldn't never get together on it so we ended up going back down to Virginia. Went all the way to Newport News, and that's where we got stranded. ⇃

In bands owned by bandleaders, the leader makes the decisions, sets or negotiates wages, pays expenses, and takes whatever profits or losses that ensue. Some bandleaders have done very well under this system, as have some high-priced soloists, but the average sidemusician has usually been paid a minimum scale.

Fletcher Henderson had a great band that never had the success it deserved despite its first-class musicians and an excellent library written by Henderson himself. His mild disposition may have been part of the problem. He was not skilled at promotion and salesmanship, nor at instilling discipline. His musicians were so lax about getting to work on time that the boss at the Steel Pier in Atlantic City, New Jersey, said,

"Mr. Henderson, you've got a good band, but that's the worst conduct I've ever seen. I'm going to have to let you go."

Henderson replied, "You're right, I can't argue with you. But you know, when I'm lucky enough to get them all on the bandstand, I've got the baddest-ass band in the world, so I'm just going to have to stick with them."

Henderson eventually broke up his band and made his living as an arranger. His excellent scores became the solid footing under the phenomenal success of the Benny Goodman band.

The records that the Count Basie band made for Decca in 1937 had a wonderfully fresh approach to swing and introduced Lester Young, Buck Clayton, and Jimmy Rushing to the listening public. Those records caused great excitement in the jazz world and launched the Basie band into the major league of music. John Hammond tells about Basie's introduction to the record business by one of the sharks at Decca:

I spread the news of Basie's band to everyone interested in jazz, and I went to Dick Altshuler at the American Record Company to urge him to sign Basie for the Brunswick label. Dick agreed, so back I went to Kansas City to sign the band to its first recording contract. Basie said, "A friend of yours was here to see me, John."

"Who?" I asked. "I didn't send anyone to see you."

"Dave Kapp."

Dave, the brother of Jack Kapp, the head of Decca Records, was no emissary of mine, but I knew why he had come to see Basie. "Let me see what you signed," I said, fearing the worst.

Basie showed me the contract. It called for twenty-four sides a year for three years for $750 each year. To Basie it seemed like a lot of money. To me it was devastating—for both of us. There was no provision for royalties, so that for the period when Basie recorded "One O'Clock Jump," "Jumping at the Woodside," and the rest of those classic hits, he earned nothing from record sales. It was also below the legal minimum scale demanded by the American Federation of musicians for recording.

Back in New York I called Local 802 to protest these outrageous terms, and did manage to raise the per-side payment scale, but there was nothing the union could do to break the contract. The loss of Basie to Decca was partially my own fault. I had praised the band in *Down Beat* for months. I had talked about Basie to everybody I knew, and in the music business there are no secrets. Every record executive knew about Basie by the time I went out to sign him. Even Joe Glaser, the head of Associated Booking Corporation, had hurried to Kansas City before me, except that he thought Lips Page was the star and that Basie was no leader; so he signed Page and not Basie.

Glaser's mistake turned out well for Basie. We replaced Lips with Buck Clayton, one of the best—as well as one of the handsomest—trumpet players in jazz. Buck had been playing for Lionel Hampton in Los Angeles, and by accident had burst into a wrong room to the embarrassment of Hampton's wife, Gladys, the real boss of that band. She fired him. Buck joined Basie, and you'll just have to believe me when I say Lips was never missed. ❧

When Roy Eldridge left Fletcher Henderson in the late 1930s he was a rising star, beginning to place high on music polls. He signed a contract with Sam Beers and took a group into his Three Deuces club in Chicago. The radio wire from the club brought in a lot of business:

We were on the air late. During those years, most of the big bands that traveled, they'd have a radio on the bus and they'd hear us. When the guys would get in town, that's the first place they'd come, to the Three Deuces. That was the *only* place to hang out. Meantime, I got an offer to go to California, with Bing Crosby's brother. Everything was going along great, except the guy didn't want me to leave the Deuces, 'cause we were doing business for him. So he stopped it. How he stopped it I'm not too sure, but he did. That was Sam Beers. He also sold my contract to Joe Glaser. Unbeknownst to me! The union said his contract was null and void, so to get out of that, he sold it to Joe Glaser. He had it here in New York, waiting for the moment to swoop down on me, which he did!

Joe Glaser came in to the Savoy one night to listen to me. I didn't want to be with no one after this cat in Chicago kept me from going to California. Glaser told me to be at his office at ten o'clock one morning, and I told him "I won't be there. I don't want nobody to book me." He said, "You be there or you won't work around New York."

I went up on a tour of New England with my little band, left them up there with Max Kaminsky playing for me, and came back to New York with Mal Hallett's band, the first white band I worked with, at the Palace Theater. I got this wire from the union, said if I don't go sign up with Glaser, I can't work. They'll tear up my card. Well, that's politics, you know. ⟁

Eldridge hired Panama Francis for his band after hearing him at a jam session. A management problem arose at the rehearsal the next day. Panama said:

While we're at rehearsal, Joe Glaser, who was Roy's manager, came in and saw me sitting up there and he said, "Where's Sid Catlett?" So Roy said, "Well, this is my drummer here." And that's one reason why I have a lot of respect and a warm spot in my heart for Roy, because he stood up for me with Joe Glaser, when Joe Glaser said, "Well, look, I want Big Sid in this band." So Roy takes his horn and puts it on the stand, and says to Joe Glaser, "Well, I tell you what you do. You play this god damned trumpet, then, if you want to run my band." And he left and went upstairs. And that's how I stayed with Roy. ⟁

Roy finally accepted an offer from Gene Krupa to join his band, and Gene's manager worked out a deal with Glaser to let Roy buy back his contract with weekly deductions from his salary with Krupa.

Wingy Manone had second thoughts about having signed a long-term contract with Irving Mills:

I went to all kinds of people—lawyers, musicians, and friends of Mills—trying to get my release from Irving. But nobody could help me. Then I was tipped off that Mills was afraid of gangsters. I went to Joe Marsala and asked him to assist me.

Joe agreed and I got him one of those black hats and a black over-coat like the mobsters wore. He pulled the hat over his eyes and we went up to see Irving.

Before we got to the office I said to Joe, "You don't have to say nothin'. I'll do all the talking. Just sit there with your hand in your pocket and look tough. I figure Mills will understand the situation."

Irving let us in his office and I laid it on him.

"Pops, I just dropped in to tell you I don't need no manager no more," I told him. "My brother here is gonna handle me. He just blew in from Chicago where he's working with the Capone mob. I guess you better let me have that contract, 'cause he's got some-thing in his pocket, and it's going to make a noise if I don't get it."

Joe's act must have been good, 'cause Irving got nervous and dug out the contract. Man, I guarantee you I snatched that father-grabbin' contract out of his hand and ran out of there like a bastard.

A few nights later Mills came parading around Fifty-second Street, saw Joe sitting in the band, and found out who he really was.

"Hey, I thought that guy was your brother," he yelled at me. He promised to get even with me, but he never did. I saw him at Palm Springs not long ago, and he wanted me to make some records for him, so I guess he ain't sore. ⑂

Stuff Smith visited the musicians' union in Chicago to seek a favor from the president. Jimmy Jones told the story:

When James Petrillo was president of Local 10 in Chicago there were a lot of people that wanted to get in to see him at that time.

Stuff wasn't a bad guy, he was just loose and would get into trouble. He knew he had to go see Petrillo. He went to his office. There were a lot of people outside that also wanted to see him. Stuff went down with his violin and just started walking the halls out in front of Petrillo's office playing Italian songs. He was about tenth on the list, you know, and Petrillo says, "Come in here, Stuff." He took him inside, you know, and there was Stuff, sitting on Petrillo's desk, still playing these songs. He got his bargain. ⤷

Honest managers and promoters were jewels to be prized. Too many of them, attracted to the money that good entertainment can generate, found ways to overpay themselves at the expense of the talent they represented. In some corners of the music business, the word "talent" is still used by the wheelers and dealers, when talking among themselves, as a synonym for "pigeon."

Joe Darensbourg remembers a promoter who went to unusual extremes to avoid coming up with the money he owed Joe and trombonist Gus DeLuce:

We worked jobs for various promoters, and one that you was always running into was Ragtime Billy Tucker. Some of these guys didn't pay you your money and one of the most notorious was this Billy Tucker. He probably owed money to every musician in Los Angeles. We worked a job for Billy and he disappeared without paying us. We didn't see him for about six months, so finally we ran into another musician and he says, "Hey, you seen Billy Tucker? Maybe you can get your money. Billy's round here at the Circus Museum on 5th and Main playing a wild man. They got him in a cage there, with a wig on and everything."

So Gus and I went down and sure enough, old Billy was in this great big cage. I guess he thought people wouldn't know him. He was real ferocious looking, with chains and a big long beard and a kind of leopard-skin outfit. They opened the cage door and threw a ham bone in there and Billy started chomping on it, pretending he was eating, and growling. Gus goes up to the cage and says, "Billy, you ain't fooling us in there, we know who you are. How about hat money you owe us?" He looked at us and growled. In the bottom of the cage they had a lot of dry hay, so Gus says, "OK, Billy, you won't talk to us, we gonna fix you." And he pulls out a box of matches.

Billy sees Gus about to set light to this hay with the cage locked, so he says, "You dirty bastards, you gonna set a man on fire for 25 dollars apiece?" Gus says, "Hell, yes, we gonna burn up your rear end." Billy started hollering for help and the promoter ran over there, so Billy says, "You give these people their money before they set light to this damn hay. I owe them 25 dollars each." That's how we got our money from Billy Tucker. ♪

Gus Johnson said the band he worked with around Kansas City often were cheated by promoters who ran off with the cash before the band finished playing:

Sometimes you'd see them coming around at intermission with a bushel basket full of half-pints of whiskey. They'd try to get everybody loaded so they would forget to keep an eye on the cash. And sure enough, when the end of the night came, the money'd be long gone! ♪

Some musicians became good negotiators and managed to pocket a larger share of the money than their talent generated. Miles Davis's agent Jack Whittemore told of a negotiation he conducted between Miles and some concert promoters:

Back in the days when he was only getting a thousand dollars for a concert, Miles was booked into Town Hall. The tickets were selling very well, so the promoter suggested doing two shows instead of one. As was customary in such cases, Miles was to get half fee, $500, for the second concert, but when I approached him with this, he looked puzzled.

"You mean I go on stage," he said, "pick up my horn, play a concert, and get a thousand dollars. Then they empty the hall, fill it again, I pick up my horn, play the same thing and get only five hundred? I don't understand it."

I told him that this was how it was normally done, but he was not satisfied. Finally he said he'd do it for $500 if they would rope off half the hall and only sell half the tickets. When the promoters heard this, they decided to give him another thousand for the second concert. ♪

Mary Lou Williams remembered how one good manager got his start at Café Society Downtown:

I never smiled when I was playing and Barney Josephson, the owner of the club, did everything he could to try to get me to smile. Eddie Heywood said, "Leave her alone. She'll get into it." One night I was playing and Johnny Garrett used to walk in back of me to make me smile. He'd do the Bronx cheer and I'd laugh. Barney happened to be there and he said, "What do you mean doing that to my star act?" Johnny said, "You wanted her to smile, didn't you? Look at her now." And so he gave Johnny a raise. Johnny came to the Café as a valet for us; he pushed the piano on and off. He just watched and learned and became a great manager. He went out with Sarah Vaughan and helped make her great.

Phil Schaap, well known in New York for his in-depth coverage of jazz history on radio station WKCR, was the musical director of the West End club for a while. Jo Jones appeared there regularly on Wednesday nights. When the club changed hands, the new owner was warned to handle Jo with kid gloves: "He's crazy, but he draws a good crowd." Phil treated Jo with great deference and courtesy and usually got along well with him. During Jo's frequent angry outbursts, Phil became even more formal and polite.

One Wednesday Jo started the night by screaming repeatedly into the microphone, "Where's the manager? Whe-e-ere's the MAA-NAA-GER!?" Phil shut off the mike, but Jo simply increased his volume, screaming for the manager with his face contorted in a maniacal grimace.

Phil convinced the manager to come out of hiding. "Mr. Jones, I'd like you to meet Mr. X, the manager." Jo glared at him, and changed his scream to "Where's the BASS PLAYER?" Brian Torff, the bassist, had arrived early, set up his instrument, and was having dinner in the next room. After summoning Torff and indicating to Jo that he was present, they asked what the problem was.

"The bass player has put his case in front of the *fire exit!*" yelled Jo. "*You're* the manager. What are you going to *do* about it?" The new club owner had come in and observed the end of this scene.

"Mr. Jones," he said, "The previous owner warned me that you were difficult to deal with, but I'd like to say that you are the first entertainer I've met who ever made a constructive suggestion concerning the welfare of the club owner."

Jo turned on him and screamed,
"I DON'T GIVE A FUCK ABOUT NO CLUBOWNERS!"

At the same club, the bartender, who everyone called "Jack the Ganif,"
had regularly been helping himself to money in the cash register. The
boss accepted this as part of the cost of doing business. But one night
when closing up the boss opened the register and found nothing there
but a roll of pennies. He said to the bartender, "What's the matter, Jack,
aren't we partners anymore?"

When Gerry Mulligan put together the first edition of his Concert Jazz
Band in the late 1950s he realized he needed help to get organized. He
delegated a lot of the internal responsibility to section leaders Mel Lewis,
Bob Brookmeyer, and Nick Travis, got Joe Glaser to handle the booking,
and hired a bandboy who said he had worked for Gene Krupa and the
Sauter-Finegan band. Gerry mentioned his name to Bill Finegan and his
wife Kay and they said he was good. He was.

The bandboy was so efficient that Gerry gave him more responsibility.
He was getting Gerry's scores microfilmed for safekeeping and was deliv-
ering the checks from concert promoters to Glaser's office. Glaser was so
impressed with the way he took care of business that he let him use his
box at Yankee Stadium when he was in town.

During a week when there were no bookings, Gerry called a couple of
days of rehearsals at a midtown studio. On the second day the bandboy
didn't show up. Phone calls to his hotel room weren't answered. No one
could discover what had become of him. Talking to Glaser, Gerry mentioned some money the bandboy was supposed to have delivered and
found that Glaser hadn't received it.

When they checked the guy's hotel room they found no sign of the
scores he was supposed to be having microfilmed—about half of Gerry's
library. And Gerry's favorite horn was missing. About $800, the scores,
and the horn just vanished into thin air. Gerry was stunned by the loss of
the horn, since it was an especially responsive old Conn that the factory
had modified and adjusted until he was really happy with it.

The next time he saw the Finegans, Gerry told them what had happened with their ex-bandboy. Kay looked crestfallen. She had known the
guy had a problem, but hadn't mentioned it because she thought he'd
straightened up.

"Son of a bitch!" she said, "he did it again!"

chapter 11

On the Road

Most jazz musicians have found it necessary to keep moving in order to make a living. A band might get lucky and stay in the same club for a month or two, but most jazz establishments prefer a more frequent change of attractions.

When bands were in demand during the swing era, the most profitable schedule for bandleaders was a constant string of one-nighters. Sometimes the string got so long that the musicians fell into a road trance, never seeing any more of the places they stopped than the hotel room, the diner, and the bandstand.

Phil Woods proposed a curriculum for teaching young students of jazz about the realities of the road:

> If I taught at a school, I would charter a bus and after I picked out my A-lab band, I would get this bus and I'd get all the kids and I'd have them get their libraries together and their music stands. I'd get uniforms for them. Have them get all their crap together, pack, get on the bus, close all the blinds, and just drive around the campus for about eight hours—don't go anywhere, no visual delights to intrigue them. Get off the bus, set up, pick out a set, tune up, put their uniforms on. That's it. They're not going to play any music. Pack up, back on the bus another eight hours, circle some more, and then have a talk with them:
>
> "All right, now. Who wants to do this? Because this is what it is."
>
> It's an exaggeration. I admit it doesn't have to be that way, but it's just an exaggerated reality. They're not getting any reality from the people that are teaching them in school. Most of the teachers have never been on the road.

Before networks of reliable promoters existed, traveling bands took a chance when they went on tour. If a band on the road ran into bad business or the promoters ran off with the money, they might have to break up, and the penniless musicians would get back home however they could. Jesse Stone told how his band solved the problem on one occasion when they ran out of money on the road:

> Eddie Durham was one of the trombone players, and this woman who ran this hotel, oh, she was ugly. But she liked Eddie Durham and she told us that we could stay there. Eddie didn't want to be bothered with that woman, you know, but we dressed him all up, a necktie from one guy, a shirt from somebody else, carried him downstairs to her room and knocked on the door, pushed him in. Eddie did more to save the band than anybody in the group. 🎵

When he was a young man, Jimmy Maxwell found a band stranded in his home town, Tracy, California:

> I remember bands being down on their luck. After I'd been down to Los Angeles about 1936 or '37, I saw four or five familiar faces standing around the street in Tracy one day and said to one of them, "Aren't you Buck Clayton?" And he said, "Yeah."
>
> "What are you doing here?"
>
> "I'm here with my band and the promoters ran out."
>
> No money and everything. Buck Clayton and Lee Young and about six of the others. They said they hadn't eaten for a couple of days, so I took them home to my house and my mother gave them all dinner. 🎵

Eddie Barefield was stranded several times with Benny Moten. A cooperative band, they shared equally in whatever profits were made, but they were often taken advantage of by promoters who ran out on them with the proceeds from the ticket sales:

> We were stranded in Zanesville, we were stranded in Columbus, Ohio, we were stranded in Cincinnati, and we were stranded in Philadelphia. 🎵

In Philadelphia, after working a week at the Pearl Theater and putting rooms, food, and whisky on the tab until payday, they found that the man who had lent them money to buy new uniforms the last time they were in town had attached the box office receipts and taken all the money and the band bus. Benny contacted a local promoter, who helped them out. Barefield said:

They got a big old bus and took us over to Camden, New Jersey, to a pool hall, and this guy took a tub and one rabbit and made a big stew. We got a lot of bread, and stood around and sopped up this stew and ate this gravy. I always called it cat stew because I didn't figure out where this guy got a rabbit. I always kid Basie and say that we ate cat stew that day. ⤵

Then they went to a Camden church which was used for a recording studio:

We recorded an album which has been re-released and re-released and we never did get paid for that, either. In fact, I have a tune on there, *Toby*, that I wrote and arranged. Never did get anything out of it. ⤵

There often were crap games on Count Basie's band bus. Billie Holiday was singing with the band, and she hoped the crap game would augment the fourteen dollars a day she was earning:

Fourteen dollars a day sounded real great. Nobody bothered to tell me I'd have to travel five hundred to six hundred miles on a hot or cold raggedy-ass Blue Goose bus; that it would cost me two or three bucks a night for a room; that by the time I was through having my hair fixed and gowns pressed—to say nothing of paying for pretty clothes to wear—I'd end up with about a dollar and a half a day. Out of that I had to eat and drink and send home some loot to Mom.

Whenever I had a couple of bucks it was always so little I was ashamed to send it home, so I would give it to Lester Young to invest. I hoped he could shoot enough dice to parlay it into a bill big enough I didn't have to feel ashamed to send home.

The first time out we had been riding for three months, and neither Lester nor I had a dime. Both of us were actually hungry. Jimmy Rushing, the blues singing "Mr. Five by Five," was always the only one who had any loot. We went to him once and asked him real nice for a buck to buy a couple of hamburgers. He wouldn't give us nothing but a lecture on how he saved his money and how we petered ours away.

When we were on the bus coming back to New York from West Virginia, I couldn't stand the thought of coming home to Mom broke. I had four bucks when that crap game started on the bus floor.

"You're not shooting these four," I told Lester. "I'm shooting these myself."

I got on my knees, and the first time up it was a seven. Everybody hollered at me that the bus had swerved and made me shoot it over.

Up came eleven. I picked up the four bucks right there and won the next three pots before someone said something about comfort.

I thought they said, "What do you come for?" I said, "I come for any damn thing you come for." I didn't know the lingo, but I knew Lester did. So I told him I'd do the shooting and he could be the lookout man.

I was on my knees in the bottom of that bus from West Virginia to New York, a few hundred miles and about twelve hours. When we pulled up in front of the Woodside Hotel everybody was broke and crying. I was filthy dirty and had holes in the knees of my stockings, but I had sixteen hundred bucks and some change.

I gave some of the cats in the band enough loot to eat with and for car fare. But not Rushing. I didn't give him back a dime. I took what was left and split on uptown to Mom's. When I walked in she looked at me and like to died, I was so dirty and beat up. I just waited for her to say something, and she did.

"I'll bet you ain't got a dime, either," Mom said.

I took that money, over a thousand dollars, and threw it on the floor. She salted a lot of it away and later it became the nest egg she used to start her own little restaurant, "Mom Holiday's," something she always wanted. ↶

Mezz Mezzrow took a road trip through New England with the Red Nichols band:

That was a bunch of wild men Red Nichols got together; besides a couple of foreigners from California on trumpet and trombone, there was a sax section of Pee Wee Russell, Bud Freeman and me; Dave Tough on drums, Eddie Condon on banjo, Joe Sullivan on piano, and little Max Kaminsky on the cornet.

Our bass player, a little sixteen-year-old named Sammy, practically had to stand on tiptoe to reach the bridge of his instrument, but he was supposed to be a genius, and Red saw a commercial angle in his age and size, so along he came. Well, we set up headquarters in Boston and took off to rock New England, traveling around in two seven-passenger touring cars, and little Sammy just came along for the ride because he sure never got to play that bass much. We tried tying the big fiddle to the roof of a car but it kept sliding around so much, poking its nose down into the window every few minutes, that we decided to ship it by Railway Express. Now Railway Express, in its own quiet way, is a real friend to hot jazz. Regular as clockwork, that bass showed up in each town on our itinerary the morning after we left, dogging us round just one day late. Little Sammy fiddled with his tie and plucked his suspenders.

Finally the remaining dates were cancelled. Back in New York we rolled, unemployed once more and no meal-ticket in sight. Sammy's bass fiddle showed up in town about three weeks later, after it made the rounds slow and steady, just one day behind schedule, playing all the cancelled engagements by itself. ⇂

When a busload of musicians appeared in town, some restaurant owners would gather up the menus and quote prices that were considerably higher than what they usually charged. If certain hotel managers realized they were dealing with a traveling band, their room rates would immediately go up. Teddy McRae described the way the musicians would outwit such opportunists:

So what we did, we would get in town and we wouldn't park the bus in front of the hotel. We would park two blocks down, around the corner where nobody in that neighborhood would know we were in town. We'd go in the hotel one or two at a time. The girl on the desk wouldn't know what was going on. Before she find out, we done rented the whole hotel for a dollar and a half a day.

The guy'd come back, the fella that owns the hotel, he'd say, "Did the band get in yet?"

"What band? I didn't see no band. A lot of fellas been here renting rooms, but I ain't seen no band."

The road manager would take the things to the ballroom, set up the bandstand and everything. Take the uniforms to the tailor and have them cleaned and pressed and brought back to the ballroom where we were playing.

At nighttime when we got through work, here we come walking in with instruments in our hands in uniform. We would be just laughing and carrying on, because we beat them to the gun. ⇂

The Eddie Condon All Stars, with Buck Clayton, Vic Dickenson, Pee Wee Russell and Bud Freeman, were flying from Australia to Tokyo. Condon fortified himself for the flight with repeated extractions from the private stock of liquor that he carried with him. Everyone settled down in the dimly lit cabin to sleep during the long flight. A few hours later, Clayton woke up and noticed a small figure at the door of the plane. It was Condon, struggling to lift the bar that opened the door. Buck dived across the plane and tackled Eddie, preventing him from depressurizing the cabin and causing a catastrophe. Condon said he was looking for the men's room.

When Terry Gibbs joined Buddy Rich's band, he found himself in the mercurial drummer's good graces:

Buddy told me, "You're going to be a star. You ride in my Cadillac with me." In the car, every time he'd get mellow, I'd suggest he let the guys play. "They're good soloists, and you should give them more of a chance to play." He'd say, "Really?" and that night he'd say, "Let's play." Next night in Buddy's car, he's driving 100 miles an hour, I'd say, "Why not let Johnny Mandel play." "Okay." This went on for about a week.

Finally, one night, going through the desert, in the middle of the night, he gets mad. "Wait a minute. I've had enough of this shit. You've been telling me how to run my band for a week. Get out of my car and take the bus."

He stopped the car and put me out! The bus was a couple of hours behind him. I was panicked, standing out there in the desert all that time, until the bus came. ♪

Terry, Jackie Carman, and Frank La Pinto left Rich's band in California and headed for New York in La Pinto's car. As they were short of money they stopped at a casino in Elko, Nevada, to see if they could win enough money to travel home in style. Instead, they lost what money they had. La Pinto had $100 wired to him from home, and they made the trip on that, surviving on salami and cheese. After many days of driving, their car broke down in the Lincoln Tunnel. Terry says:

Everybody's ringing horns and we're pushing the car through there. By the time I got home I swore I would never ever in my life go on the road again, ever, after making a trip of like eight days, whatever it was—no sleep, no food, filthy. I get home and it wasn't an hour later that I got a call from the Woody Herman band. Would I join them in Chicago? I got dressed, showered, shaved, was on the next plane and joined the band that night. ⇃

Many road musicians from the 1950s remember a brash young alto man from Texas named Jimmy Ford. He was an aggressive player, never in doubt, which gave a certain zing to his playing and a unique quality to his relationship with the rest of the band. On a one-nighter he leaned across the sax section and snapped at the baritone player, "Gimme a reed!" The puzzled baritone player handed him a brand new Rico, wondering how Jimmy was going to use it on an alto sax. Jimmy snatched the reed from him, whipped out a Dixie cup, and proceeded to eat his ice cream using the reed as a spoon.

Carol Easton describes the peregrinations of the Stan Kenton band as it grew larger and larger to accommodate Stan's grandiose orchestral vision:

> The size of the band necessitated two buses, which were quickly designated "The Quiet Bus" and "The Balling Bus." Bob Gioga was in charge of the Quiet Bus, which contained the string players—headed by concertmaster George Kast, they considered the jazz players barbarians—and an occasional exile from the Balling Bus, the scene of a perpetual poker game and party. Stan once sent a scout from the Balling Bus to "see what those intellectuals are doin' in there!" The scout came back shaking his head, mystified.
> "They're *reading*!" he reported. "And *sleeping*." ⇃

Kenton was pacing the aisle of the band bus after a concert, expressing his dissatisfaction with the band's musical direction.

"We're in a rut," he announced. "We're just repeating the same old stale thing. We've got to find something new, something we've never done before!"

Trumpeter Al Porcino, who took a dim view of Stan's "Innovations in Modern Music," had a suggestion. His slow, nasal drawl came from the rear of the bus:

"How . . . about . . . swing . . . Stan?"

On the road, big bands had one advantage over small combos: they had enough members for a baseball team. An eighteen-piece band could have two teams, though this rarely happened. News of bands with ball teams passed along the musicians' grapevine, and challenges went back and forth when the paths of traveling bands crossed. Milt Hinton was on Cab Calloway's team:

Cab organized a baseball team and bought uniforms, gloves, bats, and had a big truck for us to put all the equipment in. When we got into a town a little early, we'd get out the stuff and have a little infield practice or batting and whatnot, and if we got into a town like Los Angeles, we'd play some band out there. We'd play Woody's band sometimes. Oscar Pettiford broke his arm in about three or four places playing baseball with Woody Herman's band.

Cab made Tyree Glenn the manager. Cab was in a batting slump, and Tyree benched Cab. He was furious. It's his team, and his bats and his balls, and Tyree benched him. He got so mad he sold Tyree the whole team for a penny, one cent! ↴

Rex Stewart tells of a baseball game with the Fletcher Henderson band:

The Hendersons had been challenged by some other band when we were playing at the Southland Club in Boston. The game was to be played with regulation equipment, hard ball, etc. Smack was the starting pitcher and did pretty well for an inning or so. Then Jimmy Harrison left first base to take over the pitching chores.

Just then, a weird sight ambled across Boston Common. I looked, blinking my eyes from left field, at the spectacle of a fellow wearing a Panama hat, tuxedo, and patent-leather shoes, Coleman Hawkins's uniform for participating in the national pastime. The ensemble was set off by an even funnier note—the tender way he carried a new first baseman's mitt.

When he announced that we were in the presence of the world's greatest shortstop, Jimmy laughed until tears came to his eyes and said, "Hawk, that's a first baseman's mitt you've got there." This made Coleman quite indignant, and he replied, "Any damn fool knows that, Stringbeans, but I've got to protect these valuable fingers or you won't eat." So, to keep pace, Fletcher put Bean in at shortstop. Batter up. And the first ball was hit right to Hawk. He fielded the ball, threw the man out, stuck his mitt into his hip pocket, and walked off the field. That was the end of Coleman's baseball career, as far as I know. ↳

When recording producer George Avakian was a New York City high school student, a fledgling pianist, and a jazz fan, he met Teddy Wilson, who introduced him to guitarist Freddie Greene (Freddie used that spelling then). Greene was playing behind Amanda Brown at the Black Cat in Greenwich Village, but he soon replaced guitarist Claude Williams with Count Basie, and George was happy to have the resulting "backstage in" with the Basie band. He said:

The following summer (1938), after my freshman year in college, Freddie took me along to a softball game in Central Park between the Count Basie and Jimmie Lunceford orchestras. Buck Clayton was Basie's right fielder, but didn't care much about playing, so after an inning or so he tossed me his glove.

The Lunceford band was pretty good. As I recall, the score ended up something like 19 to 3, with Lunceford pitching against Lester Young. Lester wouldn't play unless he could pitch, and Basie was hard put to field nine players. I became a semi-regular, and I don't believe we won a game all summer.

Jimmy Crawford [Lunceford's drummer], the biggest man on the field, was the star first baseman of the Lunceford team. He belted a single, and the next batter lined a hit to right field so hard that I saw a chance to throw Jimmy out at third. I nailed him, but his slide knocked our third baseman, Harry Edison, ten feet past the bag.

At the end of the inning, Sweets came up to me and said, "George, next time that happens and it's Willie Smith on first, you can throw to me. But if it's Crawford again, please throw home to Ed Lewis!" ↳

George added that Lunceford had a wicked underhand pitch.

I struck out against him, but later poked a single over the shortstop. At first base, Crawford hooked a hand around my belt and said, "If Jack [Washington, Basie's baritone sax man and leadoff batter] gets a hit, *you* are getting thrown out, right here at first base." ↳

George went to Central Park one day to watch the Harry James band play baseball. He suggested to James that they arrange a game with the

Basie band when they got back to New York. James's bus always carried a full supply of bats, balls, and gloves. George said, "Harry used to joke about checking on a musician's ball playing ability before he hired him. When I proposed a game with the Basie band, he laughed, because he knew Basie's guys were no match for his crew." James told George, "Forget it. We don't play bands that use ringers." But there was a rumor around the musicians' bars that James carried a pitcher with the band who didn't play a musical instrument.

George wasn't the only one from outside the Basie band who played in those games. The late Bob Bach, radio producer and husband of documentary movie producer Jean Bach, was also a frequent fill-in.

Al Thomson, a tenor player who clocked many road miles with various big bands, was an enthusiastic baseball fan. Talking baseball at Jim and Andy's bar, he discovered there were enough ball players among the musicians gathered there to make a team or two. They met occasionally for an afternoon of baseball in Central Park.

Whenever Thomson heard that a band that played baseball was in New York, he'd call their hotel and challenge them. Then he'd assemble the team, known at Jim and Andy's as "Al Thomson's Drunks." Dave McKenna sometimes pitched, and Zoot Sims played whenever he was in town.

Al was proud of the day the Drunks beat Harry James's team. He told the drinkers at the bar that night.

"We were so far ahead I decided it was safe to put myself in at third. But I struck out once and bobbled a ground ball, so I sent myself to the showers!"

In a game Al organized in Central Park one day, Zoot Sims was playing center field with a very old, ragged fielder's glove. The opposition batter hit a powerful fly to center. "I've got it!" yelled Zoot. He got his glove under it, but the ball broke through the rotten webbing and hit Zoot right in the face before it fell to the ground. As the batter pounded around the bases, Zoot bent over in agony, blood streaming from his nose. Thomson, in the coaching box at third, began to leap frantically up and down. "For chrissake," he screamed to Zoot in center field, "Pick it up! Pick it up!" ⮱

Al Cohn remembered a great catch made by Zoot Sims on Woody Herman's ball team:

He was running to his left after a long fly to the outfield. He caught the ball in his left hand, and as he caught it, his hat flew off, and he caught his hat in his right hand! ↲

Sometimes a musician who had saved a little money on the road might buy a car. In the early days, a buyer of one of these luxury items didn't require any special training. He learned by having the salesman show him the controls, and then getting in and driving the thing. Al Hall told of a car Stuff Smith bought in 1936:

When Stuff's record of *I'se A-Muggin'* started making him some money, Stuff walked into a LaSalle auto showroom in Chicago and bought a shiny new car. He wrecked it driving onto the street from the showroom. Undaunted, he walked back in and bought a second LaSalle.

The next time he played Chicago his fans were bringing requests to the bandstand written on pieces of paper. Stuff took one and looked at it; it was a summons for that last LaSalle. They garnished the whole band's salary to pay for it. ↲

Milt Hinton tells of traveling in style with Cab Calloway's band:

I was in the band for six months before we hit New York. We traveled the road, playing one-nighters mainly, all through the South and Midwest and Southwest. I couldn't get over the band traveling in its own Pullman—strictly first class, all the way. There's never been any band, black or white, that traveled any finer than Cab's band did. Behind the Pullman was the band's baggage car with all the H & M trunks in it. Everybody in the band had the same kind of H & M brand of trunk. When I looked into the baggage car my eyes nearly popped out.

In the middle of all these trunks and instruments was Cab's big green Lincoln. Right in the baggage car. Everywhere Cab went he took that beautiful car with him, and when he got into a town the rest of us would get taxis, but Cab would roll that old Linc down off the train, with his coonskin coat on and a fine Homburg or derby, and drive off into town looking for the action. ↲

George Paulsen traveled from Connecticut to California with the Claude Thornhill orchestra:

> We stopped at the Grand Canyon in Arizona. Claude asked us to get out our instruments and we all lined up facing the canyon. He called off the chords and we played them and then listened to the echoes. Some very interesting sound effects resulted and we drew quite a crowd of tourist spectators. ↯

Charlie Shavers and Louis Bellson were roommates on Tommy Dorsey's band in 1949. Shavers liked to take a hot bath before going to bed at night. One night Bellson awoke in the middle of the night to find the light still on and Charlie's bed empty. He found his roommate asleep in the bathtub, up to his chin in cold water. When Louis called to him, Charlie reached to pull up the covers and pulled a wave of water over his face. After that, Bellson made sure Shavers was out of the tub before he went to sleep.

Everyone got a good laugh when Serge Chaloff's mother, Margaret, a teacher at the Boston University School of Music, suggested that her son stop hanging around with Red Rodney and Brew Moore. She thought they were a bad influence. Serge was a great player, but when it came to drugs, he was a bad influence on everybody. Terry Gibbs remembered Serge on the road with Woody Herman's band:

> He would fall asleep and his cigarettes would burn holes three feet long in hotel mattresses. But when the hotel manager confronted him with the burnt mattresses he would say, "How dare you talk to me like that? I happen to be the *Down Beat* and *Metronome* poll winner. How dare you even suggest that I—." Finally the manager would wind up on his hands and knees apologizing.
>
> Once Serge put a telephone book up against his hotel room door and decided to get in some target pistol practice. He shot through the book, or around the book, and into the door. So the manager accused him of this. Serge tried to lie his way out. He couldn't. The manager told him, "You'll pay $24 for that door or you'll go to jail." When we left, Serge insisted that, having paid for it, it was his door. I helped him to drag it down to the band bus! ↯

Zoot Sims was Serge's roommate on the Herman band. He remembered Serge shooting his air pistol out a hotel window:

Serge was hitting this guy who was waiting for a bus, I told him, "You could put that cat's eye out!" Serge said, "I don't shoot that well." And he was serious! 🎵

Al Cohn was also with Herman's band when Chaloff was there:

I was in Serge's car. I don't know how we kept from being killed. Serge would always be drunk. One time after work, we're driving at four o'clock in the morning, we wondered why the road was so bumpy. Serge had made a left onto the railroad tracks, and we were going over the ties. 🎵

Steve Voce wrote of Woody's adventures with Chaloff, who was his baritone saxophonist on the "Four Brothers" band:

Serge was instrumental in introducing some of the other men to his habit. Eventually, despite the brilliance of his jazz playing, Woody decided that Serge had to go. Since he came from Boston, Woody decided that he should leave when the band next visited the area. He told Serge in advance, and Serge was distraught since he depended on his income to finance his habit. The break was to be made at a famous dance hall near Boston, Nutting-on-the-Charles, a picturesque building backing onto the River Charles.

At the intermission on the fateful night Serge called Woody over to a window overlooking the river.

"Look out there, Woody. What do you see?" Herman peered through the window.

"A lot of water," he said.

"Look more closely," said Serge.

"Well," said Woody, "there's some litter floating about."

"That litter," said Serge, "is the band's baritone book. Now you can't fire me, because I'm the only person in the world that knows the book by heart."

It took Woody another six months before he was able to unload Chaloff from his band. 🎵

Woody Herman told Gene Lees how he got his revenge before Serge left the band:

Woody began to be aware of what was wrong with his collection of sleeping beauties. And he found that Serge Chaloff was the band's druggist, as well as its number one junkie. Serge would hang a blanket in front of the back seats of the bus and behind it would dispense the stuff to colleagues. This led to an incident in Washington, D.C.

The band not only looked bad, it sounded bad. And Woody, furious at what had happened to it, had a row right on the bandstand with "Mr. Chaloff," as he called him, emphasis on the first syllable.

"He was getting farther and farther out there," Woody said. "And the farther out he got the more he was sounding like a faygallah. He kept saying, 'Hey, Woody, baby, I'm straight, man. I'm clean.' And I shouted, 'Just play your goddamn part and shut up!'

"I was so depressed after that gig. There was this after-hours joint in Washington called the Turf and Grid. It was owned by a couple of guys with connections, book-makers. Numbers guys. Everybody used to go there. That night President Truman had a party at the White House, and afterwards all his guests went over to the Turf and Grid. They were seven deep at the bar, and I had to fight my way through to get a drink, man. All I wanted was to have a drink and forget it. And finally I get a couple of drinks, and it's hot in there, and I'm sweating, and somebody's got their hands on me, and I hear, 'Hey, Woody, baby, whadya wanna talk to me like that for? I'm straight, baby. I'm straight.' And it's Mr. Chaloff. And then I remembered an old Joe Venuti bit. We were jammed in there, packed in, and . . . I peed down Serge's leg.

"You know, man, when you do that to someone, it takes a while before it sinks in what's happened to him. And when Serge realized, he let out a howl like a banshee. He pushed out through the crowd and went into a telephone booth. And I'm banging on the door and trying to get at him, and one of the owners comes up and says, 'Hey, Woody, you know, we love you, and we love the band, but we can't have you doing things like that in here.' And he asked me to please cool it.

"Well, not long after that, I was back here on the coast, working at some club at the beach. Joe Venuti was playing just down the street, and I was walking on the beach with him after the gig one night, and I told him I had a confession to make, I'd stolen one of his bits. [See Chapter 35.] Well, Joe just about went into shock. He was horrified. He said, 'Woody, you can't do things like that! I can do things like that, but you can't! You're a gentleman. It's all right for me, but not you!'" ↳

Gus Johnson illustrated the sort of foolery that often lightens long road trips:

George Duvivier and I were going to California. I was driving his car and we had to stop for a light in downtown Denver. He was arguing about my driving, so I told him to get the hell out of my car—his Cadillac. He got out, slammed the door, and I drove off around the block. When I came back by where he was standing. I called, "Hey, what do you know? You want to ride?" People looked on were amazed when he said, "I don't mind if I do," and then got back in the car. ⅄

The road for musicians got longer as promoters began to book overseas jazz tours. When he went to Europe with the Basie band, Buddy Tate got the wrong band member to interpret for him:

We went to Lyon, and Jimmy Rushing says, "Now, don't worry about the language problem. I'll order for you, I'm over here all the time." So we go into this restaurant and I decide I wanted some veal chops, so Jimmy talked to the waitress. She went away and we waited and waited. Then here she comes with six hard boiled eggs. I can't tell you what name I called him.

So he gets to talking again and she goes back and she come out with more eggs—fried! I called him some more names I can't repeat, and Rush says, "Well, she can't speak English. She's just not getting it right." The waitress was listening to us arguing back and forth, and then she says, "Excuse me, what would you like to have?" Speaking better English than either of us! ⅄

During a tour with the Dave Brubeck Quartet, Steve Voce was helping Paul Desmond with his travel arrangements:

During the Quartet's first tour he decided to catch the midnight train back to London (the rest of the group were staying overnight)—a decision which gave us 90 minutes to kick our heels in a station waiting-room full of tramps and drunks.

It was February and very cold outside. The waiting-room was smothered in that stifling British Railways heat which knows no moderation. Sweat and beer fumes contributed to produce a sticky jungle humidity. Occasionally the drunks convulsed into two or three bars of song. Every so often one would fall off a chair and lie, still asleep, sprawling on the floor. The whole impression was that of a prison camp during the height of the Indian mutiny.

Paul and I squeezed into a corner and after about ten minutes had become a part of the scenery, rendered partially unconscious by the atmosphere and the fact that we were both wearing overcoats— there was hardly room to take them off.

From outside came sounds of approaching turbulence and dis- cordant voices yelled the lyrics of one of Mr. Presley's current million-sellers.

Finally the door burst open and three teenage girls rioted into the room, causing instant chaos and enforced re-shuffling amongst the drunks and layabouts.

For some reason we attracted their attention, and one of them came across and tried to pick up Paul's alto case. He snatched it back with a quick movement and smiled at her nervously. He held the case on his knee, apparently to protect it and himself from fur- ther onslaught.

"Hey mister," the hoyden shrieked accusingly, "you're a caveman, aren't you?"

"Huh? Who, Me? No, I guess not. I guess not." Desmond's voice cracked as he shrank back in his chair.

"He is. Isn't he?" she turned accusingly to me. It was all rather like a denunciation in the French Revolution.

"Isn't he a caveman?" She turned to her two colleagues who were eagerly closing in. "Doris! You come and look at this feller. Isn't he a caveman?"

Without hanging around for further enlightenment we picked up our things and, pursued by the accusing cries, fumbled our way out into the cold. The harridans showed every sign of joining in pursuit so we ran.

Paul's train had by now arrived at its platform, so I saw him onto it. He huddled into a corner seat, swathed in coats and scarves look- ing miserable enough to convince me that he wouldn't sleep so well during the journey.

It wasn't until I was on the bus going home that I found the solu- tion. Looking through the window I saw a poster lit momentarily by the lights from the bus. It advertised the show at the local music- hall, and in big letters at the top it said: "TOMMY STEELE AND THE CAVEMEN." I often wondered how Desmond figured it out. ❧

Bud Freeman became an Anglophile when he was a young man in Chi- cago. His clothes, hair, speech, and courtly manner rang with overtones of the British upper crust. On his first trip to England he was met at the airport by a Rolls-Royce and driver belonging to the Hon. Gerald Lascelles, a jazz anthologist, pianist, and ardent fan. The limousine whisked him off to a party at the Lascelles stately home, Fort Belvedere. They rolled silently through beautifully tended gardens to the mansion's great entranceway, where Bud stepped out onto a red carpet. Liveried footmen held the door open for him and carried his luggage away to his room. Bud sighed happily as he was greeted by his host, "England is exactly as I always knew it would be."

During a grueling tour, on the way from one gig to the next, Stan Kenton made an announcement from the front of the bus. He was disturbed that, while packing up the night before, someone had shouted out the "F" word, and an older couple a few feet away had nearly dropped in their tracks. He asked the band to watch their language in public. After Stan's lecture, a pall settled over the twenty-one band members. The next day, after Stan had flown ahead to New York to take care of some radio publicity, the bus was filled with discussion of how to deal with Stan's "pep talk." Dalton Smith suggested they make a list of every vulgar word they could think of. He and Bob Fitzpatrick made a list and assigned a number to each word. They made copies at an office supply place they found during a stop, and the rest of the trip was spent memorizing the numbers associated with the words. Milt Bernhart said:

> That night Dalton Smith passed Kenton on his way to the bus and said, to no one in particular, "Boy, this was a seventeen night! What a thirty-one audience! Five, I need a taste!" To add to Kenton's bewilderment, Fitzpatrick strolled by with, "Seventeen you, Stanley. Another thirty-one town! How about telling those seventy-threes in New York who book this six band to give the forty-seven a rest?" Kenton assumed this had something to do with his announcement the day before, but he held out for a couple of days before finally asking what the numbers meant. He laughed when the musicians explained the joke, and said, "I had a feeling you guys were a bit pissed at me the other night." One of the trumpet players yelled out, "Hey, Stan, on this band we say 'two-ed!'" Kenton got a copy of the list and committed it to memory, and was later heard to tell a promoter he was having trouble with, "And a good seventeen to you, too, you eighty!" ⟱

Milt Bernhart never played on the same band with Porky Cohen, but the two trombonists often met on the road when Stan Kenton's band, with Bernhart, would be checking into a hotel as Charlie Barnet's band, with Cohen, would be checking out. One night in Washington, D.C., when both bands were in town, Milt was awakened shortly after dawn by the sound of a trombone coming from another hotel just down the street. Porky practiced when the spirit moved him, whatever the hour. Recognizing Porky's sound, Milt listened for a while, and then got out his trombone and joined in. Then he called Porky and they traded choruses on the telephone. There were no complaints from the neighbors.

When Louis Prima's band was working in Boston in the 1940s, the New York contingent in the band would often drive down to Coney Island on their day off, just to get some hot dogs at Nathan's. That was nothing compared to the trip Prima and four of his hometown sidemen would make whenever the band had a three-day break. They would jump in their car and drive day and night (over the relatively primitive roads that existed then) to New Orleans for a Creole feast. Then they would drive back, arriving just in time for the next Boston downbeat, after a 3,250-mile round trip.

Dan Levine, who traveled with the Ray Charles band for a while, noticed that one of the musicians began wearing an Indian headband on the bandstand to keep his long hair in place. Ray's manager reported this unusual departure from the regulation band uniforms:

"Ray, one of the musicians is playing with an Indian band!"

Ray ordered curtly, "You tell him he don't play with no band but mine!"

Woody Herman's band was booked for a one-nighter at the Regency-Hyatt in Atlanta. When they got there, Woody discovered they were playing a wedding in the center atrium. He called his agent to ask why his jazz band had been booked instead of a regular club-date band. The agent told him, "I've already got the money . . . just get through the night however you can."

Woody started the band off with some dance music, and before long he felt a tug at the leg of his trousers. He found a matron looking up at him, who said, "Play the Alley Cat." "We don't know it," Woody told her. A couple of minutes later, the same lady tugged again at Woody's cuff and yelled, "I said, play the Alley Cat!" Woody got a little hot under the collar. "Look," he said, "I lied when I said we don't know it. We know it, but I won't play it!" The lady bridled. "Do you know who I am?" "No," Woody replied, "but I know who I am!"

On a 2003 gig in Boston with Bobby Short's band, a young fan approached Eddie Bert after his name had been announced and asked, "Was that your father on Woody Herman's band?" No, it was Eddie himself, back in the 1940s and 50s.

All through a European tour with Thad Jones and Mel Lewis, Eddie had no trouble carrying his trombone in its soft case onto airplanes as hand luggage until the last flight, from Frankfurt back to New York City. A uniformed attendant at the Frankfurt airport stopped Eddie, pointed to the trombone case, and said, "You can't carry that onto the plane with you." Eddie said, "It's my trombone. I always take it with me." The attendant said, "What if everyone took a trombone on board?" Eddie said, "You'd have a big band!" The attendant laughed and let him pass.

When Gerry Mulligan's Concert Jazz Band made its first European tour, saxophonists Gene Quill and Zoot Sims were roommates. They spent much of their free time sampling the indigenous alcoholic beverages. Impresario Norman Granz had booked such a tight schedule that the band was never in one place long enough to have their laundry done. Toward the end of the tour he finally found a place in one German city that would give fast service. Granz told the musicians where to find the laundry, and they hurried over in taxis to deposit their soiled linen. Zoot and Gene were among the last to make the trip. Bob Brookmeyer was standing at the front desk of their hotel when Zoot and Gene returned, each carrying a small bundle of dirty laundry.

"What happened?" asked Bob. "Were they closed when you got there?" Gene scowled and snapped, "They refused our shorts!"

chapter 12

Arrangers and Arrangements

Early jazz musicians found their own notes and harmony lines by listening and remembering, and this tradition continues to the present day. But when bands began to get bigger, the ones that could afford it hired arrangers to help organize the music. Imaginative arrangers accounted for the success of many bands, and were highly prized, though not always well paid.

Duke Ellington added Lawrence Brown to his band before he had written anything for him to play:

> There were no third trombone parts, so I had to sort of compose my own parts. Then as the new numbers came out they started arranging for the third trombone. All bands at that time were mostly ear bands. Whatever you heard you'd pick up a place to fit in, a part to fit in. What ever you heard was missing, that's where you were. 🎵

When Bill Berry joined Duke he wasn't sure what to play:

> I had a library of music, it must have been six inches thick, but none of it was titled or numbered, and we didn't play any of it anyway! I know that sounds fantastic, but it's the truth. You can ask anyone who was ever in there and they'll tell you. There wasn't any music. 🎵

Since he had nothing to play, Bill just sat there. Duke told him, "Put your horn in your mouth. Dress up the bandstand, whether you've got anything to play or not."

Bill asked Cat Anderson what he should play on the end of one number. Cat told him, "Pick a note that sounds wrong and play it."

With the help of his section mates, Berry eventually figured out his parts and stayed with the band for three years.

Paul Quinichette was with the Johnny Otis band when they picked up some new arrangements:

> It was a Basie-structure sound; he loved Basie. At that time Preston Love, who I worked with before with Lloyd Hunter, he was with Basie's band. Preston would write out some of the Basie arrangements and give them to us. Sometimes the band would be off and Preston would go get all of the arrangements out of the book and have them copied and give them to Johnny Otis. One time he gave one to Georgie Auld, a tune called "Taps Miller," and Basie heard it and said, "Hey, wait a minute, this guy got my own arrangement before I recorded it." Georgie had it note for note; Basie was so flabbergasted. ♩

Herman Autrey told of a similar situation on the Fletcher Henderson band:

> The Fletcher Henderson and Chick Webb bands were frequently booked opposite each other in a "battle of bands." Fletcher's problem was that his brother Horace would copy his arrangements and sell them to Chick. Fletcher, preparing to amaze Chick with something he hadn't heard, would find that Chick had gone on ahead of him and was playing it first. ♩

While drumming with Jimmy Lunceford's band, Jimmy Crawford had a difference of opinion with arranger Sy Oliver. Sy liked a two-beat feeling and wrote directions on the drum part for Jimmy to stay in two on the "out" chorus of his arrangements. Jimmy preferred a four-four beat when the band began to ride out, and ignored Oliver's instructions. Sy collared Jimmy and said, "Why don't you play in two there? What's wrong with two-beat?"

Jimmy answered, "What's wrong with two-beat is, there are two beats missing!"

Ray Conniff joined Bunny Berigan's band in 1938:

> There were some great stars in the band. Georgie Auld on tenor saxophone, Joe Bushkin on piano, and then Buddy Rich came with the band; it was a great thrill when he joined, he was playing great. ♩

The Berigan outfit was Conniff's first big name band. He hoped to write some arrangements for it.

When I joined the band I was practically in my teens, and Bunny said my salary would be $60 a week. I thought he was talking about a month when he said that. I'd just come from a small town. It was my first break. So I mentioned that I also arranged and he asked me to bring something around for him to hear. I took a couple of things along and Bunny thought they were fine and put them in the book, and we played them every night. Bunny seemed to like them, so after a few weeks I asked him if he was going to pay me for them. You know, what's the deal? Finally we settled on thirty-five bucks an arrangement, and I thought that was great.

Three, four, five six weeks go by and I still hadn't been paid, and by this time I had done a couple more. So I reminded Bunny about the talk we had, and that I had still not been paid. He seemed surprised and asked what we had agreed. I told him it was thirty-five bucks an arrangement and he said, "Let's make it fifty." We shook hands. You know, he raised my price five times while I was with the band, and I never got a cent for arrangements! ♪

After Chris Griffin left the Benny Goodman trumpet section and began doing studio work around New York, he found himself under Mark Warnow's baton playing the *Lucky Strike Hit Parade*. The other trumpets were Nat Natoli, Snapper Lloyd, and Andy Ferretti. Because of his stint with Goodman, Chris was elected to be the "hot" man in the section.

One Saturday morning while running down a new chart at rehearsal Chris saw a falloff marked in what he thought was an inappropriate spot. "Since I thought I knew everything there was to know about falloffs— Louis Armstrong's influence—I told the brass to just play the note without the gimmick," said Chris. The arranger called Warnow's attention to the missing falloff, and Warnow asked Chris about it. Chris said it was in a bad spot.

"Did you get up on the wrong side of the bed?" snapped Warnow. "Now, start four bars before letter C, and play it like it's written!"

Chris was known for his low boiling point in those days. On the note in question, part of a B-flat chord, Chris ripped out a loud run from high C down through a C chord. Warnow stopped the band again. Chris, expecting to be fired, reached for his horn case.

"That's exactly what we want," said Warnow. "Now the rest of the trumpets must play up to Chris."

Andy looked at Chris and then told Warnow, "I can't play that loud. I'm not as mad as he is."

Benny Payne, Cab Calloway's pianist for many years, remembered an arrangement Andy Gibson wrote for the band:

Andy could write a complicated arrangement in a minute, but he was unreliable as all get out. One time Cab got angry because Andy was supposed to do a new arrangement of "St. Louis Blues." As the days went on Andy kept getting drunker and Cab kept getting angrier. Finally Cab said, "Andy, if you don't have an arrangement of 'St. Louis Blues' by tomorrow morning you can pack ass."

Andy didn't know what to do. At that moment he was already loaded. Couldn't write a line. Three of us at sat up all night and got him sober. He wrote and we played and in the morning he had it. I can't say that it was the greatest arrangement of "St. Louis Blues" but I ain't ever heard no better. Andy was in such a hurry he wrote the thing without a score sheet. It had three singing choruses in addition to the orchestra instrumentation and three solo choruses for Chu Berry on sax. It was some piece of writing. ♪

Shelly Manne met Neil Hefti when Neil was still a trumpet player:

When he first came from Omaha, he came to play with Sonny Dunham's band. Something happened between him and Sonny, and he joined Bob Astor's band instead. We roomed together. One night we didn't have anything to do, up at Budd Lake, and I said, "Why don't you write a chart for tomorrow?" Neil was so great, he just took out the music paper, no score, and wrote, be-de-de-de-dup, trumpet part, be-de-de-de-dup, another trumpet part, be-de-de-de-dup, trombone part. And when we played it the next day, it was the end! A cookin' chart! ♪

Shelly remembered a record date where they forgot to hire an arranger:

We did a session on Manor. There was a big band, with Clyde Hart, Dizzy, Serge Chaloff, Al Casey, Oscar Pettiford. It was for Bob Shad.

We all came in and sat down to play, and nobody had written anything! So we ran out into the hall, and Dizzy and Clyde Hart started
writing charts. To make it easier, we got Rubberlegs Williams, and
the band backed him singing the blues, on some of the sides, because it was easy to do. But that was a funny scene, nobody had any
arrangements for a big band. Weird! ↯

Marion Evans was a busy and much admired New York arranger in the
1950s. Then he developed a successful career in investment banking that
kept him out of the music business for years. He once did the arrangements for a record date for Dick Haymes.

Haymes had a reputation for not paying his arrangers," said Marion, "but I wasn't worried, because I was getting paid by the record
company. At the end of the date, I saw him going around gathering
up the charts off the music stands. I knew he planned to use them on
his night club dates. I told him an additional payment was required
for using that music for anything else besides recording. I also told
him that he ought to know that the copyist that did the parts had developed a kind of ink that would disappear off the pages in twenty-
four hours unless they were sprayed with a special fixative that would
make them permanent. I said that the copyist wouldn't accept a
check, so we agreed that Haymes would get the cash together while I
took the music over to be sprayed. I went over to the copyist's place
and we watched television for a couple of hours, and then Haymes
came by with the cash, and we gave him the arrangements." ↯

The Smithsonian Institution wanted Lee Konitz to do a concert using
the Nonet arrangements by Gil Evans, Gerry Mulligan, John Lewis, and
John Carisi that had been used on the Miles Davis "Birth of the Cool"
band in the late 1940s. Lee said:

I didn't know where the arrangements were, so I called Miles. I
hadn't had any communication with him in years, and he wasn't interested. He didn't want to hear about it. ↯

After getting the four arrangers to laboriously re-create their arrangements, Konitz phoned Davis:

I said, "Miles, remember my asking you for the arrangements of the
'Cool' sessions? Well, we've transcribed them and rewritten them

and put them together again." He said, "Man, you should have asked me. Those mothers are all in my basement." ↷

Later, Konitz reported the conversation to Gil Evans, who said,

Miles wouldn't have told you he had everything in the basement if you hadn't first told him you'd gone to the trouble to transcribe the records. ↷

chapter 13

Cutting Contests

Musical rivalry has existed ever since there first were two musicians who played the same instrument. In the early days of jazz, where ensemble playing was the game, rivalry existed mainly between bands. Baby Dodds describes an early form of competition in New Orleans:

Sometimes the groups would have several bands in a parade. Then the main band had to start first and finish last and all the other bands had to go through this leading band at the end of the parade. Of course the head band would always be the best. And it was one of the most exciting things I ever did to play music and go through another band that was playing. The main band was lined up on both sides and we had to go between them and keep playing. I remember the first time it happened. My snare drum was a four-inch drum, and this fellow had a six-inch snare drum. When we got going through I couldn't hear my drumming anymore so I didn't know what I was doing. And I picked up with the other drummer who was playing six-eight in contrast to the two-four time we had been playing. I should have displaced the other fellow's drumming with concentrating on what I was doing, but that time I heard the other guy's part and not my own, and of course we were playing altogether different numbers. But it's those experiences which make you know what music is, and it's the hard way of learning. ⤷

Sidney Bechet tells about competitions between bands during the same era:

Sometimes we'd have what they called in those days "bucking contests"; that was long before they talked about "cutting contests." One band, it would come right up in front of the other and play at it and the first band it would play right back, until finally one band just had to give in. And the one that didn't give in, all the people, they'd rush up to it and give it drinks and food and holler for more, wanting more, not having enough.

It was always the public who decided. You was always being judged. It would make you tremble when one of those bands, it came into sight. One of them would come up in front of the other and face it, and you'd hear both of them. There'd be the two. And then you'd start noticing onliest the one. Somehow you'd just hear it better. Maybe it was clearer, maybe it was just giving you a lot more feeling. And so you'd want to hear it closer and you'd get up nearer. And then, it seemed it was *all* you was hearing. It was the only one that came through. And the other band, it would get away farther and farther until finally you just didn't hear it at all. ⤷

Baby Dodds describes a confrontation between two bands advertising dances:

The only advertising they had would be to get the band on a wagon and put a couple of posters on the side. We would sit there and go from block to block or corner to corner, and play.

When some other outfit was also advertising and we met each other along the street in those wagons it used to make it very interesting. The guys would put the wheels together and tie them so the band that got outplayed could not run away. That made us stay right there and fight it out.

We ran across Ory's band. Quite natural the Ory band had the best of it all. Besides Ory, my brother [clarinetist Johnny Dodds] was in that band, and Joe Oliver. Of course we didn't have a chance, but we had to stay there. When we played a number there wouldn't be much applause, but when Ory played we would hear a lot of people whistling and applauding. When we heard that, quite naturally our courage went down and we wanted to get away. But the wheels were tied together. It lasted about hour and a half or two hours and it was very discouraging. ↘

Jazz musicians usually respond with enthusiasm to news of a jam session, especially with musicians they admire. Some musicians go to sessions to hear and participate in good music, some want to test their own progress against better players, and some want to do battle. During the big band era, when the band business moved a steady stream of musicians around the country, jam sessions with local players were important. Word of a good musician would swiftly be spread all over the country by traveling musicians who had heard him play. Reputations could be made quickly by challenging the famous, and reputations were upheld by mowing down upstarts. A lot of this rivalry took place in public, since "sitting in" was a common practice.

Rex Stewart tells of a challenge Louis Armstrong met:

Jabbo Smith tried on several occasions to prove he was better on trumpet than King Louis. He was never able to convince any of the other musicians, but he certainly tried hard.

One such occasion comes to mind. It was an Easter Monday morning breakfast dance at Rockland Palace, Harlem's biggest dance hall. Jabbo was starring in Charlie Johnson's band from Small's Paradise, but Don Redman's band, featuring Satch, from Connie's Inn was the top attraction. For weeks before the dance arguments raged, bets were made, and finally the great moment came.

When I entered the hall I found that more than a hundred musicians had beaten me to any choice spot, so I pulled out my horn and got on the stand with Charlie's band. Nobody said anything, which figured, because I always sat in with anybody around town in those days.

Jabbo was standing out in front, and I'll say this, he was *blowing*— really coming on like the Angel Gabriel himself. Every time he'd fan that brass derby on a high F or G, Altis, his buddy from Small's would yell, "Play it, Jabbo! Go ahead, Rice!" (Everybody from Charleston called each other Rice. It was the hometown nickname.) "Who needs Louis?" he yelled, "You can blow him down anytime." When Johnson's set ended with Jabbo soaring above the rhythm and the crowd noise, everybody gave them a big hand. I could tell from the broad grin on Jabbo's face that he felt that once and for all he'd shown Satch who was king.

Then all of a sudden, the shouts and applause died down as Louis bounced onto the opposite stage, immaculate in a white suit. Somehow, the way the lights reflected off his trumpet made the instrument look like anything but a horn. It looked as if he were holding a wand of rainbows or a cluster of sunlight, something from out of this world. I found out later that I was not the only one who had the strong impression of something verging on the mystical in Louis's entrance. I can still see the scene in my mind's eye. I've forgotten the tune, but I'll never forget his first note. He blew a searing, soaring, altissimo, fantastic high note and held it long enough for every one of us musicians to gasp. Benny Carter, who has perfect pitch, said, "Damn! That's high F!" Just about that time, Louis went into a series of cadenzas and continued into his first number.

Since everyone is not a trumpet player and cannot know how the range of the instrument has grown over the years, I should explain how significant a high F was. Back in the twenties, the acceptable high-note range for the trumpet was high C, and to hit or play over C made the player exceptional. That is until Louis came along with his strong chops, ending choruses on F. Lots of guys ruined their lips and their career trying to play like Satchmo.

Louis never let up that night, and it seemed that each climax topped its predecessor. Every time he'd take a break, the applause was thunderous, and swarms of women kept rushing the stand for his autograph. They handed him everything from programs to whiskey bottles to put his signature on. One woman even took off her pants and pleaded with him to sign them! ❧

Kansas City was a great jam session town. The local musicians seized every opportunity to play with the good jazzmen that passed through with traveling bands. Buck Clayton had a memorable introduction to the K.C. jam session scene:

Lips Page was a "carver" who used to invite or, rather, I should say dare visiting musicians to come down to the Sunset Club on 12th Street and join in a jam session. For example, if Duke Ellington would play Kansas City, Lips would find out at what hotel they would be staying and slip notes under the doors of the trumpet players, such as Cootie Williams or Rex Stewart, and dare them to come down to the Sunset Club after they had finished their engagement. Lips would sometimes get drunk and play all night in the Sunset Club until it closed.

One day, shortly after Maceo Birch and I arrived in Kansas City from L.A., Maceo said to me, "Buck, why don't you take your horn out and go jam in some of the clubs so that people will know that you're in town? It is good if all of the guys know you and you can get acquainted with all of the best musicians in Kansas City."

I thought it was a good idea so I decided to go down to the Sunset Club and jam with Pete Johnson, who was playing piano there. I went down to 12th Street with my horn and started playing with Pete and pretty soon one lone trumpet player came in with his horn. I though, "Good, I'll have somebody to jam with." Then after a few minutes about two more trumpet players came in and started jamming. That was OK with me too as I figured we'd all have a ball. Then about a half an hour later in came about three more trumpet players. I thought to myself, "Damn, there's no shortage of trumpet players in Kansas City, that's for sure." Then, as the evening went on, more and more trumpet players came in to blow. To me, it seemed as if they were coming from all directions. Soon the room was just full of trumpet players. They were coming from under the rug, out of the woodwork, behind doors, everywhere. I never saw so many trumpet players in my life. Some had even come from as far as Kansas City, Kansas, because they had heard that the new trumpet player from Los Angeles was going to be there that night, and they all had their weapons (trumpets) with them. They really had blood in their eyes.

We all stayed there and jammed until about five in the morning. Then some of them started clearing out and about seven they were all gone. I really had been shown how they jammed in Kansas City. I think, though, that Maceo Birch had put out the word that I was going to be at the Sunset Club that night and from there on things just happened like they always did in Kansas City. Lips Page would have died if he knew he missed all that. He had left for New York, thank God. 🎺

Budd Johnson was living in Kansas City during those glorious days and participated in jam sessions with Lester Young:

Prez used to come and get me, wake me out of a deep sleep, pour whiskey down my throat, and say, "get up! So-and-so just came into town, and he's over there blowing. Let's go get him!"

One guy in particular I remember—Georgie Auld. Prez said, "Let's put him in the middle. You get on one side, and I'm going to be on the other, and we're going to blow him out of the joint!" That was Kansas City for you. ♪

Benny Moten's band had played a dance in Indianapolis, and was due the next night in Terre Haute. They were loading the bus in front of the Indianapolis ballroom when a beat-up Ford pulled in front of the bus and stopped. Tenorman George Johnson jumped out and shouted. "Where's Eddie Barefield? I've come to cut him!" Barefield said:

Everybody got right out of the bus, went into the ballroom, opened up the piano, and Basie started playing. The first thing you know the whole band was in there jamming and we didn't get to the dance that night. Bennie sent out and got some booze and things, and we just had a jam session right there. ♪

Buster Smith tells about the competition between two Kansas City bands, Walter Page's "Blue Devils" and Andy Kirk's "Clouds of Joy":

Our reeds had them going, but we couldn't get our brass to hit like Andy Kirk's boys. It was me and Lester Young and Theodore Ross. Ross and I would put tenor reeds in our horns [alto saxophones] and Lester would put a baritone reed on his tenor and then that brass wouldn't drown us out. We played as loud as the brass did. People thought it was great, the reeds being as loud as the brass section. Of course they didn't know the real story. ♪

Bassist Gene Ramey was in Kansas City with Jay McShann's band when a chance came for the band to go to New York:

Before we went to New York to play at the Savoy Ballroom, we got a postcard from Lucky Millinder which said, "We're going to send you hicks back to the sticks." McShann had one of those big old long Buicks, and I was driving, with about five or six guys in it. We finally got to New York, raggedy and tired. When we got up on the bandstand the people were looking at us like we were nothing. Lucky Millinder was on the main bandstand.

Everything we had was shabby-looking, including our cardboard stands, and we only had one uniform—a blue coat and brown pants. But from the time we hit that first note until the time we got off the bandstand, we didn't let up. We heated it so hot for Lucky Millinder that during his set he got up on top of the piano and directed his band from there. Then he jumped off and almost broke his leg.

Well, that opening was on Friday, the thirteenth of February, 1942. That Sunday we had to do a matinee at four o'clock. In fifteen minutes we played only two tunes, *Moten Swing*, I think, and *Cherokee*. Bird started blowing on *Cherokee* at that extremely fast tempo. It was way up there.

The program was going out on the radio and somebody in the studio called the man with the earset and said, "Let them go ahead. Don't stop them!" We played about forty-five minutes more, just the rhythm section and Bird, with the horns setting riffs from time to time. That night you couldn't get near the bandstand for musicians who had heard the broadcast. "Who was that saxophone player?" they all wanted to know. ♪

Benny Payne spoke of the difficulty other bands had trying to cut Chick Webb's band at the Savoy:

Benny Goodman used to bring his band up to the Savoy from time to time, and the story was that Chick Webb, who had the regular Savoy band, would give Benny and his band a little face-washing and send them back downtown. There was no way that Benny Goodman's band could stand up to Chick Webb's band. It was reputed that Chicklet had three different books, or types of musical program. The third was mild stuff, number two was hot stuff, and number one would blow you away. Chick used his number three book on Benny Goodman; he and his band didn't even work up a sweat. But if Earl Hines was in town playing with Chick, then Chick would have to dig into that number one book and bring out the hot numbers. Earl was the only one who could put any pressure on Chick for sheer showmanship, musicianship, excitement, and energy. ♪

New York became one of the hottest spots for jamming. All the clubs in Harlem and on 52nd Street were places where a musician could sit in if he was good enough. Guitarist John Collins attended many Harlem jam sessions:

We used to go to a club called the Victoria Bar and Grill. All the tenor saxophone players would congregate there every night. There would be Hawk, Dick Wilson with Andy Kirk, Joe Thomas with Jimmy Lunceford, Prez. This was just about every night. Right next

to the Woodside Hotel, on 141st and Seventh Avenue. We would go
there to cash our recording checks and never got out with a quarter.
We would spend the money right there in the bar. They played there
all night, just jammed all the time, all night long. ↷

Most musicians who couldn't play well enough to keep from embarrassing themselves would pack up their instruments when better players
appeared at a session. There were one or two who would hang on despite
being outclassed. A tenor sax player that everyone called "Demon"
would dominate the jam sessions at Minton's by glaring murderously at
everyone else until they left the stand. Dizzy Gillespie referred to him as
"the first 'freedom' player—free of harmony, free of rhythm, free of
everything!" Joe Wilder remembered:

> Demon would play chorus after chorus. Bad? It was awful! Lock-
> jaw Davis was the house tenor man. He would go get Teddy Hill,
> the manager. Teddy would stand in front of the bandstand with
> his arms folded and growl loudly, "Demon! Get off my band-
> stand!" ↷

Some of the guys at Minton's developed difficult chord substitutions
on standard tunes as a way to make the music more interesting for themselves. At the same time, the new chord structures kept the less skilled
players from sitting in. As the new music developed into what was later
called "bebop," a chasm began to open between the modernists and
members of the old guard who preferred traditional harmony. A few of
the masters of the earlier style like Coleman Hawkins and Don Byas
moved comfortably along with the new wave. Red Allen, a fierce competitor at the cutting session, had his own way of dealing with bebop.
Kenny Davern saw him in action at Minton's one night:

> I was with some friends, a bebop band on the stand. The classic
> one, with the pianist's nose about four inches from the keyboard,
> just about to nod out. Everybody was into whatever they were play-
> ing. It went on for half an hour and the place was packed. In walks
> Red Allen, like the Red Sea opened up, and he's all spiffed up with
> his shirt, tie and jacket.
> "Hey, Red! Hey, my man!"
> And he's putting his hand out like he's mayor of Harlem. He
> walked right up to the bandstand while these guys were playing,

thumped his case onto the stand from the floor, took his horn out and, while these guys are still playing he's warming up: paa paa paa-paa paapaa. And then he stopped them in the middle of the tune and said, "Rosetta." Womp, womp. And he started playing "Rosetta," walking through the crowd playing to all the people. These cats were in a tempo half of "Rosetta" and all of a sudden they're in "Rosetta." Whether they knew it or not, didn't matter.

When he got finished playing he just took his mouthpiece off, put the horn in the case, slammed it shut, and says, "Goodnight, y'all. What a ball, what a ball."

He was shaking hands and went out the door. These cats went back on and one of them says, "What are we doing? Who was that?" ↳

Roy Eldridge had been given some preconceptions about the New York jazz scene before he arrived in town:

Horace Henderson used to tell me all these wonderful stories about New York. How you'd walk in a night club, and a guy would be sitting over in the corner in overalls, and you think you're playing real great. And this cat'll get up and stretch and have him a drink of wine, and reach in this brown paper sack and pull out his trumpet and start on low G, and when he stopped playing he's up to high G above C! (That was a high note in those days.)

That story stuck with me all those years, 'cause when I first came to New York, I would always look around before I played to see if I see anybody acting like he was sleeping, you know. In fact, to tell the truth, I played that trick on some trumpet players myself, in the thirties. [chuckles] Act like I was too drunk to play, you know, and they'd jump all over me, and then I'd wake up and [claps hands like a trap snapping shut]. I'd wake up like I was in a stupor, get up, and blow everybody out of the building! Making the fantasies come true, you know. ↳

Roy didn't always come out on top. He lost a cutting contest one night in Harlem:

There was a place, where I got wiped out by Rex Stewart, called Greasy's. I was working at Small's with Charlie Johnson. Rex had stayed at the house, showed me some of my first riffs, and I had so much respect for him. I even wanted to *be* like the cat, you know? He came down, and he didn't have his horn, and I told him, like you do in New York,

"I'm gonna get you after the show. Go home and get your horn."

We started to go to the Rhythm Club, but he said,

"No, no, let's go down to Greasy's."

So we went down there, and I don't know how the word got around, but before you know it, that joint was packed. There was Gus Aikens and Red Allen, and some other trumpet player, and we started to play. All of Fletcher's cats were in there. They could really load up a cat.

"Roy? Shit, he ain't playin' nothin'! Go get him!" And then when I'd play,

"Yeah, Little Jazz, yeah!"

So he got bigger and bigger, and I made a mistake by coming in on his chorus. I screamed a G and the whole house fell out. He didn't let them other cats in; he jumped in and caught my ass. Hit a B-flat, and I ain't *never* heard a B-flat that high and that loud and big, in my life! I start feelin' around on my horn to see what it is. I said, "oh-oh." I took my horn and put it in the case. I told the cats, "You can't play as high as him. Might as well give it up!" I had tears in my eyes.

I went home and sat on the side of the bed and said, "Now, what did he do that really tore my ass up?' And I dug what it was. He only screamed that note, but he didn't play up to it or back down. Now, if I could get so I could play up to B-flat and back down, make that part of my natural range, then I'd have him.

So that's what I did, and the next time we met, we played "China Boy," and every time we went to that bridge in A-flat, I was up on that B-flat! And I *played* up there. I didn't just scream it, you know. So that was my round.

The next time we got together, I figured he was going to do the same thing I did, so I'm waitin' on him to see what he's gonna come out with, and he's waitin' on me, and neither of us played shit! The night was over, and neither one of us did nothin'! That's funny, man. 🎵

Dizzy Gillespie spoke of Roy's competitive spirit:

Roy Eldridge is the most competitive musician I've ever seen. Every time he picks up his horn and another trumpet player's there, he wants to blow him out. Roy used to come into places, and we're on the bandstand, the younger players, playing gentlemanly. He'd take out his horn at the door and start on a high B-flat, the next chorus, and come walking in, and everybody'd look around. That's Roy, coming up on the bandstand walking with it. Roy used to always get the best of us by playing real high. 🎵

On a radio interview, Dizzy added:

Roy would hurt himself before he'd let you blow him out. One night we were standing outside a club and Roy said, "Come on, let's go inside and blow!"

And I told him, "Roy, would you mind if *I* went in by myself and played a while first? 'Cause when *you* get up to play, you don't know how to act!" 🎵

In Dizzy's autobiography, trumpeter Duke Garrett talks about challenges:

Nowadays they don't go in for battling, but when I came up, it used to be a battle. If Dizzy walked in where Roy was, well, Roy would be waiting for Dizzy. And if he didn't beat him, Roy would get off the stand and get drunk, just stay at the bar and start to cussing and calling everybody different names.

What Charlie Parker and Dizzy would do, they would put their horns under their coats and run in on Coleman Hawkins, and run in on Illinois Jacquet and all of them, and start to playing down on Fifty-second Street. And they would just wipe out the session. But if the cats saw them coming with their horns, they'd get off the stand before it started. In the middle of a tune, they'd slip up on the stand and eat them up. 🎵

Dizzy's footnote says, "This was known as an ambush."

Teddy Charles once did a Voice of America broadcast opposite Milt Jackson. To save set-up time as the groups alternated during the broadcast, Milt agreed to use Teddy's vibraphone. Milt played first, and when Teddy took over he discovered, too late, that Milt had disconnected his damper bar from its pedal. Teddy had to play a whole number without being able to sustain a note by releasing the damper. Teddy countered by moving the front row of bars one notch to the left, so all the sharps and flats were in the wrong position when Milt played again.

"It didn't do any good," said Teddy. "He still played better than me!"

When Joe Wilder joined the Count Basie band in the 1950s, Joe Newman had been playing all the trumpet solos. On the first job, Newman leafed through his book and pulled out half a dozen parts that had solos in them. "Here," he said to Wilder, "give me your parts on these." Wilder accepted the solos gratefully, and later said to Marshall Royal,

"Joe Newman sure has changed. He used to want all the solos for himself, but he just gave me a whole bunch of them." Marshall asked,

"Which ones did he give you?"

Joe showed him.

"Hell," said Marshall, "we haven't played any of those charts for a year!"

chapter 14

52nd Street

In the 1930s and '40s New York's 52nd Street was the jazz mecca. There were nightclubs and restaurants in most of the brownstones that lined the two-block strip, and most of them featured jazz groups. Willie "The Lion" Smith tells how the first jazz club on the Street got started:

In those days the two long blocks on Fifty-second Street from Fifth Avenue to Seventh Avenue were packed with those old-fashioned brownstone houses. Damn near every one had a blind pig or speakeasy hidden away somewhere. Some of them were fancy while others were just a onetime bedroom without beds. You got the same bad whisky in them all.

Several of the musicians were working in the big radio studios. They couldn't wait to get loose from the job and run over to a speak for a taste. They made one place their second home, stashed their instruments there, took telephone calls from chicks that they didn't dare receive at home, and even used the place for a mailing address.

This place was only a short block north from the studios. Off of the hall were parlors, called "drinking rooms." In the back was a room where they had a beat-up bar, a push-ball game, an old up-right piano, and a few shabby wicker chairs and small tables. You couldn't get more than twenty-five people seated in the place at one time.

The guy behind the bar was named Joe Helbock and he was the owner. He called the setup "the joint," a club for musicians. He liked music.

The Lion got in the habit of stopping by and giving the piano a workout once in a while. One day Joe said, "Lion, why don't you stop by every day around five and I'll give you a little salary for your trouble?" That deal, the engagement of the Lion for the cocktail hour at Helbock's in 1930, was the beginning of Fifty-second Street as "The Cradle of Swing." That was long before they had all those jazz traps on the street and called it Swing Lane.

When Prohibition went out in 1933, Helbock moved downstairs and across the street into larger quarters. He decided he needed a fancy name for the spot, so he called it the Onyx.

Besides the excellent talent like Stuff Smith, Art Tatum, John Kirby, Cozy Cole, and Maxine Sullivan that Helbock hired at the Onyx, there was a constant stream of visiting musicians who came to listen and sit in. Songwriters and publishers also liked to gather there, and occasionally good spenders who appreciated the music, like Mr. and Mrs. W. B. Armstrong of Orange, New Jersey, who called one night while they were on a trip to Hollywood. They were homesick for the Onyx, and wanted to hear some music over the telephone. "I put the receiver down," said Helbock, "and asked the boys to play a bit. About an hour later I realized that the phone was still off the hook. But there were the Armstrongs still listening. It cost them more than drinking in my place all night, but I could have kept the phone off the hook for the rest of the evening so long as the music was going."

When the Onyx got too popular with the general public, the musicians began to congregate at other clubs on the Street. Jazz attracted enough business to keep several establishments alive, especially since the musicians were available at low cost. It was easy for clubowners to underpay them because they knew how much they loved to play. Some places only hired a pianist or a trio, knowing that there would be plenty of other musicians who would sit in. The musicians' union tried to control the situation by forbidding sitting in, but found enforcement impossible. The musicians wanted to play together, and they did so whenever the union delegate was not around.

The Onyx was joined by Jimmy Ryan's, the Famous Door, the Hickory House, the Three Deuces, Kelly's Stables, the Yacht Club, the Downbeat, and several rooms that vacillated between jazz and cabaret entertainment. Clubs sometimes moved to other locations on the block or closed and opened under new names, but for thirty years, until the brownstones were razed to make room for large office buildings, there was jazz being played somewhere on 52nd Street. During the Street's busiest years a festive social climate evolved. Musicians and music lovers wandered in and out of clubs and around the corner to the White Rose Bar on Sixth Avenue, which became the common watering hole because of its reasonable prices.

The clubs on the Street featured all kinds of jazz. Jimmy Ryan's usually hired the more traditional groups. One of the highlights of an evening at Ryan's was the parade. The band would play "When the Saints Go Marching In," and the horn players would leave the bandstand and march all around the club. When Brad Gowans and Tony Parenti worked there, they would sometimes extend the march out the front door, across the street to the Famous Door or the Three Deuces, and return like pied pipers, bringing some of the patrons of those clubs back with them.

George Brunis continued the tradition when he worked at Ryan's. On his way back into the club after an outdoor parade, Brunis would march into the ladies' room and out again, holding up fingers to indicate how many ladies he'd surprised. Back on the bandstand, he might lie down and play his trombone slide with his foot. While on his back, he would offer to let anyone stand on his stomach while he played, excepting anyone who weighed over 150 lbs., and women with high heels.

Willard Alexander, Count Basie's manager, was looking for a New York venue for the band in 1938. He talked it over with Al Felshin and Jerry Brooks, the managers of the Famous Door. The club could only seat about ninety people, but it had a radio wire that would help promote the band. The Famous Door did little business in the summer because it lacked air-conditioning, so Alexander got the Music Corporation of American (MCA), of which he was then a vice-president, to lend them enough money to have air-conditioning installed. A dressing-room area was removed and the wall moved back to make room for the band, and Basie's piano was put on the floor in front of the bandstand. Alexander said:

> Although the Door did tremendous business all through Basie's stay, collecting the loan from Felshin and Brooks was another matter. Just about this time, Sonny Werblin and I gave a start to a new agent. Today, he's one of Hollywood's top literary agents. He's short and bald. But they don't call him Swifty for nothing. He's one of the sharpest agents on the film scene. I mean Irving P. Lazar. One of his first assignments at MCA was to get our money back from Felshin and Brooks.
>
> And it was a tough one, let me tell you. Even Brooks was bigger than Lazar. As for Felshin, he could put Irving into one of his pockets. And they were tough babies. You had to be to run a club in those days. But Swifty was tough, too. He used to show up on Saturday nights— after they had Friday and Saturday receipts in the till—and he used to grab, but I mean *grab*, as much money as he could. Finally, MCA had its money back—I don't think we ever got all of it—and Count Basie was launched as one of the big, new name bands of 1938. ⟩

John Hammond, also interested in the success of the Basie band, claimed to have been the one who put up the money for the air-conditioning unit at the Famous Door. It is quite possible that Felshin and Brooks borrowed the money from both Hammond and MCA.

Max Kaminsky described working at the Famous Door with Jack Teagarden's sextet, opposite Sid Catlett's group. The moment he finished his set, Teagarden would head for the door carrying his horn. He would go next door to the Three Deuces or across the street to Jimmy Ryan's and sit in with whoever was working there. Felshin told Teagarden that he was supposed to be playing exclusively at his club, and asked him to stop playing for his competition. Jack didn't see what all the fuss was about.

"Jes' bein' neighborly," he said.

Being neighborly was the name of the game on the Street. Shelly Manne, a teenager at the time, was made welcome by neighbors like Ben Webster and Roy Eldridge:

> You'd go into the club and listen and play, and then a set would be starting in another club, so you'd go over there. And you didn't have to ask to sit in. They'd see you and say, "Hey, man, come on and play!" Everybody knew everybody in those days. 🎵

Shelly got his first break hanging around the Street. Dave Tough, working at the Hickory House with Joe Marsala, got sick one night and asked Shelly, who had been playing drums for about a year at that time, to play for him. Benny Goodman came in that night to get Tough for a date in Washington the next day, and was disappointed to hear he was ill. Goodman sat at the bar for a set and listened to the band, and then left. Shelly said:

> About an hour later the phone rang. A call for the drummer.
> "What's your name, kid?"
> I told him.
> "This is Benny Goodman."
> "Yes, Mr. Goodman!"
> "You want to go on the road with my band?"
> "Sure!"
> "Just be down at Grand Central Station at eleven tomorrow morning with your cymbals. I've got the drums."
> I must have been down there about eight, with my cymbals and my little suitcase. And about two hours after I'd gotten there, here they come: Cootie! Georgie Auld! Charlie Christian! Helen Forrest! Man! I was really going berserk; I was scared.
> I got on the train and sat all by myself. We were going to the March of Dimes President's Ball in Washington. Benny came up and said,
> "What are you worried about, kid?"
> "Well, I haven't seen the book or anything."
> "You've been listening to my music for years."

And he walked away! I played with the band for two or three days, and then Davey joined. ↳

When bebop hit the Street during the 1940s, all the musicians felt the excitement of the change, though many had a negative reaction to it. The younger musicians adapted more easily to the new ideas. Since everything about jazz was fairly new to them, this new way of playing was just one more thing to assimilate. Al Cohn said:

I played at the only square club on the Street, the 51 Club, opposite the Three Deuces, same side of the Street as the Onyx Club. They just had a trio; Bob Barron was the leader. Piano, drums, and tenor. Just a corny club with singers. I don't know what it was doing there. One of the piano players was Al Haig, before he played with Dizzy and Bird. He was still in the Coast Guard, I believe. Apple cheeks, clean cut young fellow, playing a little like Teddy Wilson. We didn't get a chance to play a lot there, but it was great, because we were right on the scene. Between sets we could go hear all the other guys. ↳

On the way to work one night, Red Rodney was stopped by a stranger with a British accent who wanted to find 52nd Street. Red said, "I'm working there with Charlie Parker, follow me." The stranger introduced himself as Bill Le Sage, and they struck up an acquaintance as they walked along.

Twenty-five years later, Red was in London. He stopped a passerby and asked if he knew where Ronnie Scott's club was. The man looked at Red and burst out laughing. It was Bill Le Sage.

Cliff Leeman often worked at the Three Deuces, which had a kitchen in back but didn't serve food. Cliff and Harold West took turns on Sundays cooking for the musicians who worked the clubs on the Street. On one Sunday, Cliff would make a slumgullion stew and salad, and the following week Harold would cook soul food. Cliff describes how he started the operation:

I went shopping one Sunday morning down in the Italian section, which was open on Sundays. The first week I left a dish and a sign on the kitchen table reading: "Wash your own pots and dishes and don't forget to feed the kitty." All day long the kitchen got busy, and as word passed around the street, Charlie Parker ducked in, Dizzy

Gillespie, Ben Webster, countless musicians. I think Charlie Parker came back for threesies.

The guys playing on the Street were only a few of my patrons, because there were a gang of musicians at the White Rose Bar on 6th Avenue. The word spread, and the food was all gone before closing. I just about broke even with the kitty. I think there was $25 in there. Food was much cheaper then.

The following Sunday, Harold West wiped my reputation off the slate. He made pigs' feet and lima beans and ham hocks—things that I had never tasted before. He added insult to injury by baking, from scratch, biscuits and cornbread.

Leeman worked in several clubs on the Street. He was in the band at the Famous Door when it finally closed. The manager told the band to take any souvenirs they might want since the club was going into receivership the next day. Being an amateur chef, Cliff wanted the cleaver he'd seen in the kitchen.

During the last set at the club, Kenny Kersey began having a little fun with Ben Webster, the leader. Kenny wedged his knees under the keyboard of the piano until he raised front legs of the instrument an inch or so off the floor, and then dropped it quickly, making a loud thump. Every time he did this, Ben Webster glared at Cliff, thinking he was making the noise on the drums. Cliff got mad at Kenny for getting him into trouble, and yelled at him when the set was over. Then he remembered the cleaver he wanted and ran to the kitchen to get it before someone else did.

Ben Webster and Eddie Barefield misinterpreted his action. When he came running back out of the kitchen with cleaver, intending to put it in his drum case, they grabbed him and "disarmed" him. They were sure he was after Kenny.

Jimmy Ryan lost his lease on the 52nd Street club when CBS bought the building to raze it and build a new office tower. With the nine thousand dollars Ryan and his partner Matty Walsh were given to relocate, they moved to 154 West 54th Street. When they reopened, Tommy Nola, the recording engineer, came in carrying a picnic refrigerator. He opened it and took out an ice cube, which he presented to Jimmy. He had saved it since the farewell party that closed the 52nd Street club, five months earlier.

chapter 15

Jazz Records

The recording industry developed at the same time that jazz was developing. The profits that could be made from exploiting the novelty of recorded sound caused the birth of many record companies, all eager to find marketable talent. Some early jazz artists turned down offers to record because they were afraid that recordings would make it easier for their competitors to copy their work, and some rightly suspected that musicians would eventually be competing for work with their own recordings. The value of records as a means to build a musical reputation was overlooked until the Original Dixieland Jazz Band's recordings popularized that group almost overnight.

H. O. Brunn describes some of the problems at the first date at Victor with the ODJB:

> The stamping of a foot would be heard very clearly, and at this time they had not yet discovered a method of "erasing" an unwanted sound from a record. For this reason LaRocca was not allowed to "stomp off" his band in the usual fashion. Instead, the musicians were instructed to watch the red signal light, count two after it came on, and then begin playing. It is indeed miraculous that they were able to start out together, and even more of a wonder that they immediately fell into the same tempo. [Musicians are not awed by these "miracles." Ed.] ↷

Musicians have always had to adjust their playing to the limitations of the recording equipment of the day. The earliest recording machinery couldn't tolerate any sudden loud sounds such as bass drum beats or rim shots on the snare. Each technical development that freed musicians from one restriction came at the price of other restrictions peculiar to the new equipment.

Even today most engineers set up the musicians in their studios in physical relationships they would never choose for themselves, citing the requirements of the recording equipment. Those same engineers manage to produce perfectly acceptable recordings at concerts and in nightclubs where they can't rearrange and isolate the musicians, but in their studios the requirements of the recording equipment come first. Musicians have been remarkably adaptable to these limitations, managing to produce wonderful recorded music in spite of them.

Rudi Blesh writes of the technical problems on King Oliver's record date for Gennett in 1923 with Louis Armstrong and Lil Hardin:

> The music had to be played into a long tin horn which was connected at its narrow end to a steel needle that cut grooves in a revolving disc made of beeswax. The vibrating sounds were transformed onto the disc in the shape of wavy lines.
>
> The King Oliver Creole Jazz Band, apprehensive but well prepared, was about to make musical history. But when they grouped around the bell of the big horn, there were problems. The two trumpets drowned out the rest of the band. King Oliver and Louis had to move back away from the horn, while Dodds's clarinet was pointed directly into it.
>
> Baby Dodds's bass drum couldn't be used. He had to get along with snares and a set of woodblocks. Then when Oliver and Louis began playing side by side as usual, it became evident that Oliver couldn't be heard. To achieve a balance, Louis was moved back even farther, away from the band. Lil later said that "he was at least twelve or fifteen feet from us on the whole session."

When American bands first began to tour Europe, they discovered that some of the local musicians, especially in France, had learned to play jazz from the records that were made with these limitations. The result was horn players who achieved the same hollow sound heard on the records, and drummers who felt they were playing "authentically" because they only used a snare drum and woodblocks.

Chris Albertson describes some of Bessie Smith's adventures in the recording studio:

> Four of her acoustical recordings with Louis Armstrong had been released, and sales looked very promising. Frank Walker was anxious to record her again, particularly since Columbia was converting

to the electrical method, which allowed greater flexibility and produced an infinitely superior sound. A larger backup band could now be used without drowning out the singer's voice. Walker arranged Bessie's next recording session for May 5, 1925.

The new technique was still in the experimental stage. The old system of waxlike discs, which had to be metal-plated and processed at the factory before a playback could be heard, was still being employed.

The band was a choice group consisting of musicians from the Fletcher Henderson band, including Henderson himself, Buster Bailey, Coleman Hawkins, and Joe Smith.

Bessie had never recorded with so many musicians and engineers. She had previously been accompanied by a trio at most, along with one engineer. Since the new system was being tested, Columbia's own engineers were assisted by their colleagues from Western Electric.

One of Western's engineers felt that the Columbia Studio was too large for the carbon microphone, and that a proper sound could only be achieved if its acoustics were altered. He had a theory to meet the problem, and it was put to the test that afternoon: a conical tent made of monk's cloth, large enough to cover Bessie, her six musicians, Frank Walker, the engineers, and the recording equipment, was suspended by a wire from the ceiling.

The session would probably have yielded additional sides had it not come to an unexpected end: two minutes after the group finished the second take of "Yellow Dog Blues," the tent collapsed. "I'm telling you," said Walker, "it was the wildest scramble you ever saw."

As the musicians, the engineers, Frank Walker, and Bessie tried to get out from under the huge blanket, the Empress contributed her favorite expression: "I ain't never *heard* of such shit!"

Neither had her tentmates. The session ended, and, with it, the tent theory. ⤵

Baby Dodds and his brother Johnny made some trio records with Jelly Roll Morton. Baby recalled:

When Jelly made those trio recordings he patted his foot to keep his tempo. He was so determined about his time that he stamped his foot. Once the technician said that Jelly stamped his foot so loud it sounded like two bass drums. In order to keep it from the recording they had a little mattress made, about eight inches square, which they put under his foot so he could stamp all he wanted to and yet not be heard. ↳

Kid Ory told about a record session Morton had in Chicago in 1923 on the old OKeh label:

Zue Robertson was on trombone, and he refused to play the melody of one of the tunes the way Morton wanted it played. Jelly took a big pistol out of his pocket and put it on the piano, and Robertson played the melody note for note. ↳

Cuba Austin described some technical problems on a date at Victor with McKinney's Cotton Pickers in 1928:

We had a lot of trouble with the engineers. In those days everybody took off their shoes and had a pillow under his feet so the thud from beating the rhythm didn't ruin things. Well, on *Milenburg Joys* the band was beating a fast rhythm and then, bit by bit, the pillows kept sliding away. We ruined several takes that way.

Now the worst of all was Prince Robinson. Don Redman hit on the idea of lashing Prince's ankles and knees together with rope to hold him steady. We started another time and things went smoothly 'til Prince started a solo; then he began to bob up and down with his feet tied together, and finally gave up in the middle of it—looked at Don and said, "Aw, Don, I can't play tied up like this." But finally we got by with a good one. ↳

Jess Stacy thought that part of the problems in recording studios stemmed from the attitude of the record producers:

In those days jazzmen were looked down on. A record company acted like they were doing you a favor to let you in the front door. ↳

Jimmy McPartland made an OKeh date with Red McKenzie and Eddie Condon where a little progress was made with the engineers:

This was the first time I ever played with Krupa. And it was the first recording session on which any of our guys had seen a bass drum used.

We came into the studio there, and Gene set up his bass drum, tom-toms—the whole set. Then we made a take to see how it sounded, and immediately the recording manager, Mr. Ring, ran out saying, "You can't use all those drums; throw those drums out; just use sticks, cymbals, wood blocks, and so forth."

After some protests, they finally worked the thing out by laying down rugs that took up the vibration. The vibration was the thing they worried about mostly. So they let Gene play the drums, and he beat the heck out of them all the way through the set, which was fine for us, because it gave us a good, solid background. ⇂

When Sam Woodyard joined Duke Ellington he decided it was time to make the engineers adjust to the musicians. Woodyard said:

The first time I went into Columbia with this band, a guy came out of control with a blanket before we ever started playing. I broke him out of that.

"Put it over your bass drum." He said.

"For what?"

"We do it for all the drummers who come in here. If you don't cover the bass drum the needle starts jumping."

"That's your business. Don't tell me how to play my drums. You just move the microphone back, because I'm going to play the way I usually play for the band." ⇂

All the problems in the studios weren't caused by the equipment. Some musicians found it difficult to transfer their music from late-night gin-mills to the business world of nine-to-five. Sidney Bechet described the fiasco that occurred when Hugues Panassié came to New York to record some of the jazz greats that he admired. The band included Tommy Ladnier, Mezz Mezzrow, James P. Johnson, and Sidney DeParis:

The men were supposed to be there pretty early in the morning. But something had got going the night before and when they showed up at the studio they were really out; they'd been drinking all night. That was a session I wasn't scheduled to be at, but I heard about it quick enough. Tommy, he showed up dead drunk. James P. Johnson, he just stretched himself on the piano and passed out. Some of the musicianers didn't know how many fingers they'd got on each hand. But they went ahead and recorded somehow. And after it had all been cut, Tommy knew the records weren't what they could have been and he wanted to say something to appease Panassié, who was sitting in the corner holding his head—something he thinks will fit the occasion. So he pulled himself up and called out *"Vive la France"* and then fell almost flat on his face. ↳

Early in his career Earl Hines made a recording date that he wasn't eager to be identified with:

W̲e began to record for Victor early in 1929. I was on the Victor staff as a pianist for three years in Chicago and recorded with all kinds of groups and singers. I'll never forget a session one snowy morning with a hillbilly group from Louisville led by a violinist named Clifford Hayes. The producer assured me the records wouldn't be issued, but they were. I was sitting in a restaurant with Louis [Armstrong] and Zutty [Singleton] about 5 o'clock one morning when one of these records was played on the radio.

"Man, that cat sounds so much like you," Louis said, "he could be your twin brother."

We all stopped to listen, and then he said, "That *is* you!"

"Oh, you're kidding," I said. "You know I wouldn't be playing with a group like that!"

"Well, he sure had got your style. That's the closest I've heard anybody play like you."

During the course of the record I realized it was me, but I never told Louis. If he had seen that band, I never would have heard the end of it. ↳

Eddie Condon was once hired by Ralph Peer of Southern Music Company to deliver Fats Waller, who he had advanced some money, to the recording studio. He wanted him on time with a well-rehearsed band. Condon found Fats at Connie's Inn and introduced himself:

E̲arl Hines told me to look you up," I explained.

"Ol' Earl?" Fats said. "Well, that's fine. How's ol' Earl? I'm so glad to hear about him. Sid down and let me get a little gin for you. We'll have a talk about Earl."

He was so amiable, so agreeable, so good-natured, that I felt almost ashamed of my mission; but I performed it; I asked Fats about making a record. A recording date? He'd be delighted, he'd be proud; just any time. In four days. Fine. At Liederkranz Hall? Wonderful. At noon? Perfect. ↳

For three days Condon tried to get Waller to talk about the music for the session. On the night before the date he asked:

After we get the band together, what shall we play?"

"Why, we'll play music," Fats said. "Now, let's have a little drink and talk about it."

Things grew faint and finally dark. When I awoke I was lying on the wall cushions at Connie's Inn, fully dressed. It was half past ten in the morning. On another cushion Fats was curled up, also fully dressed, asleep.

"It's half past ten!" I croaked. "We're due at the studio at noon!" Fats sat up, stretched, and yawned.

"That's fine! That's wonderful! That's perfect!" he said. "Now let's see about a band. Look around for some nickels so I can make the telephone go." ☙

They gathered a cabful of musicians and headed for Liederkranz Hall. In the taxi Waller said,

Now here is what we are going to play."

He hummed a simple, basic pattern of rhythm and melody, a blues in a minor key. When we had it memorized he explained what each of us was to do. At ten minutes before twelve we walked into the hall. ☙

After recording two successful sides with the band, Fats went on to make some piano solos.

We must have some more of these dates," the recording executive said. "This is an excellent example of the wisdom of planning and preparation."

After that the Southern Music Company, with careful planning and preparation, brought out the record on the Victor Label with the titles reversed: *Harlem Fuss* was called *The Minor Drag* and *The Minor Drag* was called *Harlem Fuss*. ☙

Herman Autrey was there when Waller began recording with his own band:

Phil Ponce was handling Fats then. He talked Victor into letting Fats have a small band, six pieces, and they screamed murder! Never! They'd never had a small band like that before, and they didn't think it would be advisable. They didn't think it would pay, and would be nice, and so and so and so and so. They finally agreed, for some reason I do not know, but I'm glad they did, because when we started recording, well, it was fair. (Laughs) They paid us thirteen dollars for the first day. The next time we recorded we got a raise, three dollars, I think it was. We worked it up until we got into money.

Squirrel Ashcraft, a Chicago lawyer who doubled on jazz piano, invested in some good recording equipment, hoping to capture the jam sessions that took place at his house. One night Joe Rushton, an avid motorcyclist, came out with his bass sax strapped on his back, eager to record with visiting firemen Eddie Condon, Georg Brunis, and Jimmy McPartland. The visitors were more interested in Squirrel's well-stocked bar than in recording, and Joe couldn't get them started on the music. Finally he wheeled his motorcycle onto Squirrel's porch, ran a microphone wire outside, started up the bike and recorded it.

Maxine Sullivan's singing career got a boost when Claude Thornhill suggested she record some old traditional ballads and "*Loch Lomond*" became a hit:

> Claude selected these things. I don't know whether you noticed *Lover and His Lass*. We used Dave Barbour as a guitarist, but there was no part for guitar. So Claude handed him the bird whistle. If you listen to the record you'll hear that bird whistle. I don't know how many people played the record out to the last groove, but at the end there is a door slammed. In the studio there was a prop door for sound effects. For Dave to earn his money, he had to go shut the door. I'd say "Goodnight," for no good reason at all, except to keep it in the song.

When Osie Johnson came to New York with the Earl Hines band, Milt Hinton invited him to a recording session that he was doing with the Billy Williams Quartet. Osie hadn't seen a recording studio before. He sat beside Jo Jones during a take, and go so excited that he yelled "Oh, yeah!" at the end, before they had stopped the tape. Milt said reprovingly, "You don't do that, you know. You don't say anything until the guy says, 'That's it.'" Osie started to apologize, but Bill Williams said, "Leave that in. That sounded good." He had them give Osie a payroll form and paid him for the date, and "Oh, yeah!" became a tag line with Williams's group.

Trummy Young was on a record date for Continental with Rubberlegs Williams, Clyde Hart, Dizzy Gillespie, Charlie Parker, Mike Bryan, Al Hall, and Specs Powell:

Rubberlegs was a big sissy, you know. Great big guy, about six-four. He weighed about 240. This particular day we were making those records, we were doing some of Bessie Smith's songs. *What's the Matter Now, You Been a Good Old Wagon, But You Done Broke Down,* and some of those things. It was late at night or early in the morning, and we all had about ten cups of black coffee. In those days these benzedrine inhalers were very popular. Charlie Parker, he didn't have any stuff this time, so he broke open a Benzedrine inhaler. This thing was equivalent to 75 benzedrine tablets, and he put it in his coffee to let it soak.

Rubberlegs was already half drunk. He wanted some coffee, so Teddy Reig—he was running this date—he grabbed the coffee up, and Rubberlegs drank it. Later on Bird went and got his coffee and drank it, and he told us, "Man, my constitution is getting terrible. This stuff ain't even fazing me." We didn't know what had actually happened, but Rubberlegs had got hold of it.

He kept saying, "This is bitter coffee, man." We're recording along and he's breaking out in a sweat and cussing. He called everybody Miss So-and-so. He told Dizzy, "Miss Gillespie, you keep playing those wrong notes behind me, I'm going to beat your brains." He had fists big as hams, so we all was getting kind of frightened because the guy was getting so wild around there.

He got after Teddy:

"Put out these lights; it's too hot in here."

So Teddy put out the lights. The only light was back in the control room. He told Charlie Parker,

"What are you playing? They're some wrong notes!"

You know how Charlie played flatted fifths? He's getting after Charlie and Dizzy. He sang one of those tunes, I think it's *What's the Matter Now?* He's going all out of tune and all, and we die, we almost roll on the floor laughing, man, and this is when we found out that he had got Charlie Parker's cup by mistake. This was the wildest record date you ever saw in your life. We never did get through with it. And they put those things out! It was the funniest thing I ever heard.

When the Ellington band recorded Lawrence Brown's tune "On a Turquoise Cloud" in 1947, they had a problem with the penetrating sound of Kay Davis's voice, which was to be used wordlessly as one of the instruments in a trio. Lawrence said:

We had to find some way to shade her voice down without destroying her delivery. So I finally rigged up a metal derby, which we use in orchestra work, and put a cloth towel inside the derby, and let her sing with this right directly in front of her mouth. When you hear this record it sounds like she is open like the rest of the horns, but actually she is singing into a metal derby with a towel inside it. ♪

Stanley Dance described a scene at another Ellington recording date:

There were no parts for the percussionists in the *Afro-Bossa* album, complicated though their roles often were, and a certain amount of mock disaffection with this state of affairs was sounded on one occasion.

"Where's my part?" Billy Strayhorn (on "second cowbell") demanded of Tom Whaley.

"And where's mine?" asked Sam Woodyard, who never gets one.

A few seconds later, Whaley handed Sam a sheet of manuscript paper with a big letter B on it.

"What's that mean?"

"Be natural!"

"Be ready, I thought."

"Be there!" Johnny Hodges called. ♪

Before recording studios began providing house amplifiers for guitar players, these musicians had to carry their own from date to date. In the 1950s a group of New York guitar players started the Guitar Club, which placed locked guitar amps in most of the midtown recording studios, with a key for each member.

One day Don Arnone was finishing a date at Fine Sound and discovered that Andres Segovia was recording in the next studio. He asked the studio manager if he could slip into the control booth and listen.

"Oh, no, said the manager. "Nobody gets in there. Orders from Segovia."

"Okay," said Don, "then tell him he can't use our amps!"

A recording contractor called Jim and Andy's bar one afternoon looking for a trombone player at the last minute. Jim Koulouvaris handed the phone to Jack Raines, the only trombonist in the place at the time.

"I need you to play bass trombone on a date starting in half an hour," said the contractor.

"I'm sorry," said Jack, "I don't play bass trombone."

"I'll rent one for you. Okay?"

"Sure, said Jack, "and while you're at it, rent me an alto saxophone. I don't play that, either."

When Gary McFarland turned up in New York fresh from the Berklee School of Music, Gerry Mulligan recorded a few of his arrangements with his Concert Jazz Band. As a result the word got around town pretty quickly that a new talent was in town. Before long Gary found himself writing his own record date. He was slightly awed at the prospect of conducting some of New York's best recording musicians. On the first take Gary did fine all the way to the last chord, which the brass section was holding. A look of doubt crossed Gary's face as he stood there with his arms out and then he made a swooping upward gesture, hoping that was the correct signal for a cutoff. Instead, the entire brass section, still playing, stood up. The ensuing laughter ruined the take, but it was worth it.

Teddy Reig supervised a record date with Erroll Garner for Savoy Records.

I was an A & R man for Savoy when Erroll had his famous version of "Laura." When we got to the WOR studios at 1440 Broadway, we had to walk up to the eighteenth floor. The elevators were on strike. As hungry as we were for money, up the stairs we went. Before we started up the stairs somebody suggested getting a jug, so we got some brandy. We would go up a few stairs and sit down and sip, and by the time we got upstairs in the building, we were crocked out of our nut. John Levy, Jr., and a kid by the name of George DeHart, the drummer, were with us. But what makes it interesting is that a masterpiece like "Laura" came out of all that! 🎶

Record producer Ralph Bass claims Erroll never forgave Herman Lubinsky, head of Savoy Records, for making him climb all those stairs.

Nat Pierce attended one of Garner's record dates in 1969:

The red light went on and he started to play. The red light went off and he kept on playing. Everybody waved to him from the booth, and when he eventually finished they said,

"Erroll, we turned off the light. You were supposed to stop."

He looked at them and said,

"I couldn't stop. I wanted to find out how it would come out." ↲

Milt Hinton made a number of recording dates with Dinah Washington:

Dinah would have laid out her arrangement with the arranger, and if the date was seven o'clock, we'd go in the studio and get a balance, set up at seven, get all the mistakes out of whatever the arrangement was, get the proper balance, how it's to be played, and by eight o'clock we had that done. And eight o'clock, Dinah was nowhere to be found. Nine o'clock, Dinah wasn't around. She'd come in about quarter to ten and she's say, "Well, you guys got it?"

We'd say, "Yeah." She would say, "Let's make it." One take. She never wanted to do over one take. She'd walk in and do four tunes, one right after the other. Sometimes the producer would say, "Dinah, would you give me another one?" And she'd say, "Why? What's wrong with that one?" They would really have to talk her into doing that second one. She just wouldn't do it. ↲

At a record date at Manhattan Center for a Jackie Gleason album, a large brass section sat at the rear of an even larger string section. Gleason looked back at Charlie Shavers who sat among the trumpets. He knew Charlie would have a flask with him. "Hey, Shavers," he called, "gimme a taste!"

Shavers was already feeling his liquor. He could play, but was in no condition to walk up to the podium. So Gleason trundled his large frame back to Charlie's chair and got his taste. As he headed back to the podium, Shavers said to the brass section,

Mohammed couldn't go to the mountain, so the mountain had to come to Mohammed.

Henry Mancini once hired trombonist Frank Rosolino for a 10 a.m. recording date in Los Angeles. Frank told Henry, "I have a gig the night before in San Francisco, but don't worry, I'll catch the early plane back and be here in plenty of time." Henry did worry, but Frank reassured him that he had a booking on the early flight. On the date, Frank arrived fifteen minutes late, apologizing to Henry with, "Sorry, I was fogged in at San Francisco." Henry fumed, "I knew you'd come in here with that B.S., so I called the airport at San Francisco, and they said it was clear there!" Frank said coolly, "I didn't say the airport was fogged in . . . I said *I* was fogged in!"

Paul Desmond was working on an album with Jim Hall at RCA. It was during the days that George Avakian was leaving the company to become an independent producer, so his office was whatever studio he happened to be in at the moment. Consequently, during the dates, George was constantly on the phone.

The musicians were scuffling with one tune, doing take after take until they finally got one they thought might work. Paul looked into the control room for some indication from George that he approved of the take and saw George on the phone. He ran to the hall, found a pay phone and called RCA.

Can I have studio B?"

"Certainly sir . . . That line is busy. Can you hold?"

"Yes, ma'am. (A slight pause.)

"I can ring now." (Rrring.)

"Hello, is this George Avakian?"

"Yes, who is this?"

"It's Paul Desmond. How was that last take?"

Kenny Davern discovered that one engineer had equipment that went too far:

> This recording engineer was considered one of the greatest geniuses since Rudy Van Gelder. I forget his name right now. I've wiped it from my mind. He put Al McManus, the drummer, in a little house, looked like a dog house. And if I growled, he had this very funny little machine that, when it got to playback, the growl would be gone. If I wanted some spittle coming through, or air— phee, phee—it was gone, vanished. I said,
>
> "How would you record Ben Webster? You'd have two sides of silence! You're taking out unique aspects of my playing. So put them back in again!"

Al Haig must have run into an engineer of the same school on a record date in 1949. When the A & R man asked for the name of one of Al's original tunes, Al told him it was "Earless Engineering," and that title was printed on the record label.

When Lynn Seaton's wife was pregnant, she made an appointment with her doctor for an ultrasound scan to check on the baby's progress. Lynn marked it in his date book, but when the week arrived and he saw the entry for Tuesday: "3 p.m. Ultrasound," he drew a blank. "My God," he thought, "I didn't write down who I'm working for, and I don't even know where that studio is!"

When Alan Rubin was in California making the first Blues Brothers movie, he bought a gull-wing Mercedes 300SL sports car. Back in a New York recording studio, he was showing photographs of the car to his section mate, Joe Shepley. The record producer looked over their shoulders at the pictures and said, "You own that car? But you're only a trumpet player!" Alan replied, "Yeah, but I play the flugelhorn, too."

Andy Fitzgerald was on a record date at the old Capitol studios on West 46th Street. The young A & R man in the control room was trying to impress his guests, but was unaware that the microphone into the studio was open. The musicians heard him say, "I wish someone would go out there and show that drummer how to lay down a Lunceford two!" The band broke up, because their drummer was Jimmy Crawford, who had been the mainstay of the Lunceford band during its years of success. Andy said, "Jimmy just smiled that beautiful smile of his."

Eddie Fisher had a pleasant voice, but was famous for a seriously deficient sense of meter. A stagehand at a telethon was seen wearing a tee-shirt that bore the inscription: EDDIE FISHER OWES ME 8 BARS.

Carmen Mastren once contracted a 15 minute Coca-Cola show on NBC for Axel Stordahl. One night on one arrangement, Fisher, the star, got hopelessly lost on the air, and wound up two measures ahead of the band. Stordahl frantically waved the horns out and signaled the rhythm section to catch up with Fisher. Andy Ferretti, the lead trumpet player, whispered to Yank Lawson, his section mate, "I don't know where the hell he is, but at seven fifteen, I'm going home!"

Jazz tenorman J. R. Monterose traveled to New York City from Albany to play a gig and recording date at Birdland with Eddie Bert. The band got together at Ben Aronov's house for a rehearsal beforehand. Eddie pulled out some Shorty Rogers originals, and J. R. made suffering noises after they read through the first one. He wasn't sure he wanted to take any choruses on it. "It's just 'I Got Rhythm' changes," said Eddie. J. R. shook his head and said with disdain, "I have nothing further to say on 'I Got Rhythm.'"

Much of the recording work that musicians used to do has been taken over by producers of electronically synthesized music. Entire film scores have been made with an electronic drum machine and a rack of keyboard synthesizers. At a film date in Los Angeles one day the recording studio was filled with a huge orchestra. One of the musicians looked around the room and said, "This is putting two synthesizer players out of work!"

chapter 16

Jazz on the Air

Radio broadcasting came along in the 1920s, just in time to help spread the sound of jazz. Many people in small American towns found out about jazz by hearing a radio broadcast from a big city ballroom or nightclub. When such broadcasts were aired via clear-channel stations late at night, they carried great distances, helping to build a new audience for jazz that bought records and flocked to see traveling bands.

Paul Whiteman didn't really have a jazz band, even though he was known as "The King of Jazz" (to his press agent, not to musicians). But he hired good jazz soloists and presented them well, and he was one of the first bandleaders to realize the benefit of radio exposure. Smith and Guttridge tell of a couple of early Whiteman radio shows:

Once just before going on the air, Paul Whiteman lifted his baton to lead the band into *Chinatown, My Chinatown*. A last-minute impulse seized him and he switched the command to *China Boy*. A rustle of paper sounded coast-to-coast as the musicians changed their music while the red light flashed on. The baton fell and a chaotic burst of discords went out over the air-waves. Without panic, White-man realized that the men in the rear hadn't heard him.

Softly he directed the band back to *Chinatown*. But by now the *China Boy* order had filtered from the front line to the more remote members. When Whiteman again gave the downbeat, the stunning clash of chords was repeated. Whiteman's self-control ebbed. And just then the restraining screw on his podium came loose, the heavy top crashed to the studio floor. Whiteman roared. But by now he was safely off the air.

On another occasion Whiteman was to accompany a concert diva singing 3000 miles away. For its day, this was a bold experiment in radio broadcasting. The engineers, leaving nothing to chance, in-sisted that each musician wear a set of headphones to enable him to hear the singer. Whiteman objected. His were trained musicians. They would instantly obey his every signal. There was need, there-fore, for only one set of headphones. His own.

Alas, as he swung his baton downward, it caught the wire lead con-necting the headphones to the control booth. The phones were given a sharp twist. Whiteman tried to straighten them while contin-uing to conduct his band. It was no use. The sight of their leader, one headphone in the middle of his forehead and the other on the back of his head was too much for the band and its performance slid unmusically to a halt. The diva sang on magnificently, unaware of the chaos on the East Coast, and quite unaccompanied. ↱

Charlie Barnet's band played an engagement at the Paramount Hotel on West Forty-sixth Street in New York, where a similar foul-up occurred:

We had a coast-to-coast CBS wire several times a week. Disaster al-most struck on opening night during the first of these broadcasts. Paul Douglas, later to become famous as an actor, was the an-nouncer. We were supposed to play *I Got the World on a String*, and he announced *Avalon*. When I kicked the band off, half of it began playing *String* and the other half *Avalon*. The brass section finally prevailed, *Avalon* won out, and my heart started beating again. It was very humorous on the Street afterward when a lot of musicians praised our "wild" introduction to *Avalon*. ↱

David Walter was a teen-ager just out of college when he began to work around New York playing bass with musicians that are now remembered as stars of the Swing Era: Teddy Wilson, Bunny Berigan, Bud Freeman, Jack Teagarden, Miff Mole, Benny Goodman, Artie Shaw, etc. Excepting Louis

Armstrong, the band of that era that impressed him the most was the Casa Loma Orchestra, a cooperative band led by Glen Gray. And so, when their bassist suddenly became indisposed, it was with great excitement that he responded to a call to sub with them at the Essex House. When the contractor asked him to wear tails, he told him that didn't own any. "Okay, we'll lend you a white tie. But Glen wants to see plenty of shirt-front."

The band did a remote broadcast over NBC every night at 6:30. David arrived a few minutes early, quickly looked over the book, and the band began to play "Smoke Rings" as they went on the air. The hot, dry air in the Essex House, coupled with David's nervousness and excitement, resulted in a tickle in his nose. He gave a mighty sneeze, which caused his nose to begin bleeding all over his stiff shirt-front, his white tie and his bass. He stood there for the rest of the program, sniffing back blood and looking like a war casualty, while he continued to play. "You okay, kid?" whispered sympathetic band members. "Yeah, great, great!"

David said, "For half an hour I stood in the midst of the most elegantly dressed band in the world with my bloody shirt and tie, wanting to die. And afterwards, I suffered the mortification of finishing the job in a shirtfront the headwaiter cut out of a table cloth. I never was called again. But I'll bet they never forgot me."

"Remote" radio wires were run into many jazz clubs to provide listeners with entertainment. This helped many musicians and nightclubs to become better known. Pee Wee Erwin did regular broadcasts from Nick's in Greenwich Village, where Kenny John was his drummer:

It was customary for the announcer to acquaint the radio audience with the members of the band by mentioning their names and instruments. One night it came out this way:

"... Pee Wee Erwin on trumpet, Andy Russo on trombone, and Kenny Drums on the John."

The most traumatic broadcast of all occurred on a show called "Bandstand," a weekend program with a roving format where odds and ends of entertainment were picked up from almost any place on the NBC network. Naturally, it was tough to be precise about the time a particular segment would be aired, but they tried to give some forewarning or an approximate time.

One night we were taking a break and I was sitting alongside the bandstand, when without any warning the announcer gave me the cue that we were on the air. It was a shock—because not only was the bandstand empty, I knew that most of the band members were in

Julius's bar around the corner. I sent someone to alert them and then climbed on the bandstand just as the announcer was saying, "And now from Nick's in Greenwich Village, Pee Wee Erwin and his band."

Under such duress, I'm not very quick on the draw, so I looked at him and asked (on the air),

"What do you suggest?"

He looked right back at me and said, "It's your show. What can you do?"

"How about a few bugle calls?"

He shook his head. "That's hardly Dixieland. What else do you offer?"

Just then I saw Billy Maxted scrambling through the door and knew the situation was in hand, so I told him with more confidence than I felt, "Well, I'll start the theme song and we'll see if we can build a band over the air waves."

I went into "Tin Roof Blues," the house theme, and by the end of the verse and the first chorus we had the full band, winded and flushed but complete, back on the stand. ♪

Erwin also worked in the radio studios for many years:

Richard Himber was a great prankster. He enjoyed pulling practical jokes on members of his orchestra on the *Studebaker Hour*. This included a number of the really great studio men, like Arnold Brilhart, Manny Klein, and Charlie Margulis. After putting up with Himber's gags for some time, the musicians cooked up one of their own to get even, and it was a beauty. With the cooperation of the studio engineers and personnel, every clock in the broadcasting studio was set ten minutes ahead. Then they all sat back to wait for Himber.

He showed up a few minutes before air time and, when the hands of the clock reached the hour and the red light signified they were on the air, he gave the band the down beat—and nothing happened. Nobody blew a note, they all just stared back at him. A little flustered and unbelieving, Himber gave the down beat a second time, with the same result. Then, red in the face and furious, he tried one more time and almost collapsed when the orchestra still refused to start. At that point, he was greeted by a gale of laughter and he realized that, for a change, he was the victim of a gag. ♪

Himber was an amateur magician. He worked a little sleight-of-hand on Joe Bennett once while paying him. Himber counted out $175 into Joe's hand, but when Joe recounted it there was only $150. He called

Himber's attention to the shortage, Himber again counted out $175 for Joe, and Joe's recount still only came to $150. Joe handed him the bills and said, "Look, just write me a check." Himber willingly complied, but when Joe got the check home, he discovered it was blank. Himber had written it with disappearing ink.

Billy Butterfield and Bobby Hackett were in Paul Whiteman's trumpet section on the Goodyear Tire show on ABC. Hackett specialized in playing great jazz with a beautiful mid-range tone. He never played loud or high.

The ABC musicians all knew that Hackett had recently recorded a Pathé News film with the legendary classical trumpeters William Vacchiano and Harry Glantz. At a rehearsal for the Goodyear program, when the music for the overture was handed out, Butterfield noticed a fortissimo fanfare in the lead trumpet part that ended on a high E-flat. He mischievously handed Hackett the part and said, "Here you are, Bobby. You play lead on the overture." Bobby glanced at the music and handed it back. "No thank you," he said politely. "I don't play first trumpet unless I have Vacchiano on one side of me and Glantz on the other."

In the days of studio orchestras at ABC-TV, Leon Merian found himself sitting in the trumpet section next to Hackett. Knowing Leon's ability in the high register, Bobby whispered, "Leon, at the end of this tune, I'll give you twenty bucks to hit a double A!"

To make sure that Leon believed him, Bobby took out a twenty and slipped it into the breast pocket of his jacket with the edge peeping out like a handkerchief. Leon had an F written as his last note, but he couldn't resist. He played the F, then popped up to a double A and held it, loudly. He was still holding it for a moment after the rest of the band cut off. Conductor Abe Osser looked at him in disbelief, and Frank Vagnoni, the contractor, ran out of the booth. He told Leon, "If you ever do that again, you're through here!" Leon nodded, whisked the twenty from Hackett's pocket and put it in his own.

Henry Jerome's new progressive jazz band was scheduled for weekly broadcasts from the bandstand of Childs' Paramount:

> With my four-beat band we had a theme called "Night Is Gone." So Lennie Garment and Al Cohn, the spokesmen, say, "Henry, we can't have this corny theme song."
>
> I said, "What do you mean it's so corny? It's my theme song!"

"Well, no, we can't have that. We've gotta say what we are when we come on."

"All right, if you guys feel that way, we'll use 'Night Is Gone' for the closing theme, and you figure out something modern for the opening." So, I think it was Al who wrote the thing up.

So they say, "And here he is, Henry Jerome and his Orchestra!" and the band went "POW! Bup-baaa-bedeedlyup!" Well, the first time we went on the air, we put the transmitter *off* the air. We blew the limiter at the transmitter! ⇂

On a record date that Lennie Hambro did with Ray McKinley years ago, the engineers had installed a cue light on the podium to indicate that recording was taking place. At the end of the first take, Ray waited until the cue light went out, and then addressed some comments to the engineers in the booth, at which point Lennie started laughing. "What's so funny?" asked McKinley. "You might try using the mike," said Lennie. The whole band cracked up when they saw that McKinley was talking into the light bulb.

On the Arthur Godfrey radio show, Andy Fitzgerald and a couple of other musicians discovered they shared an interest in horse racing with Godfrey. They used to meet now and then at Aqueduct to enjoy the races and bet on the ponies. At the taping of the show one day, a promo for Aqueduct was aired which said, "The fastest animal in the world runs at Aqueduct." Godfrey started a discussion with the band about that statement. "Not true," he said. "A cheetah can run faster than a horse. Right, Andy?" Andy quipped, "Not with Willie Shoemaker on his back!" Lou McGarity, who knew as well as everyone else how Godfrey hated being topped, whispered, "Goodbye, Andy." Arthur took it with a laugh, but he did cut Andy's remark out of the tape before it was broadcast.

Alfredo Antonini was the conductor of the CBS Symphony of the Air. CBS also wanted Antonini to occasionally conduct the staff orchestras on other shows, but he refused to do it under his own name. He used the pseudonym Eddie Collins whenever he was required to lead a non-symphonic group. At a rehearsal for one such program, the lead alto player, Johnny Pepper, took the maestro aside and told him, " 'When you try to conduct everything in a big band arrangement, you throw us off. You can start us and stop us, and the rest of the time, just follow along." Later, during a rehearsal of an aria from *Tosca* with the Symphony of the

Air, Antonini stopped the orchestra during a clarinet solo that Pepper was playing. "Mr. Pepper," he said, "When I am Eddie Collins, I will follow you. But when I am Antonini, you will follow me!"

Television offered an even more compelling form of exposure for jazz musicians, when they could get access to it. Early TV variety shows included jazz groups in the roster of boookable acts. Jackie Gleason liked mellow jazz. He included jazz players in his studio orchestra and recorded several albums featuring Bobby Hackett. He sometimes invited jazz groups to appear on his show. When Erroll Garner's trio appeared, Garner's well-known inability to read music presented a problem. Erroll's bassist, Eddie Calhoun, said:

Jackie Gleason had a little song that he used as an opening for his show. It was a funny little ditty. Anybody could play it, but Erroll couldn't remember the damn thing. He wanted Erroll to play this thing on the show. Every time Gleason would hum it, Erroll would play it different. What they finally had to do was to put up a screen in back of him, and then Hank Jones stood behind this screen and hummed it to him while we were on. The funniest damn thing was that Hank was out there, and he still didn't play it right. Boy, I tell you, I could have went through the floor, I was so embarrassed. But Erroll played close to it. With Erroll's talents you just could not buckle him down like that. ↰

On a club date, Al Gallodoro and Sid Jekowsky were reminiscing about their years on staff at ABC. When television came in, the station image-makers prescribed hairpieces for the baldest members of the orchestra, and they suggested to conductor-pianist Buddy Weed that he visit a cosmetic surgeon to improve his visual appeal. Buddy underwent a reshaping of his nose, chin and ears, and when the healing process was complete, he finished off his new look with a visit to a hair stylist. As the newly handsome pianist was having a taste with some friends at the musicians' bar near the studio, Jack Teagarden walked in.

"Buddy Weed!" he said, "I haven't seen you for fifteen years! Man, you haven't changed a bit!"

A German film of The Modern Jazz Quartet in one of their concerts has often been shown on Public Television. In it, John Lewis, Milt Jackson, Percy Heath and Connie Kay play "Django," "Summertime," and "A Day in Dubrovnik," with introductions by John and Milt. "Bags' Groove," the one number that no one on camera announced, seems to have thrown the producers a bit of a curve. The staff evidently didn't know that "Bags" was Milt's nickname. As the quartet begins to play the tune, a subtitle appears on the screen that reads: "BACKGROOVE." Another slip occurs when Percy takes a few choruses. Throughout the entire bass solo, the camera remains on John Lewis.

When Merv Griffin's talk show used to be aired from the stage of the Little Theater next to Sardi's in New York, Mort Linsay's band included jazzmen like Danny Stiles, Bob Brookmeyer, Jake Hanna, and Bill Berry. One day Merv began asking his audience if they remembered their school songs, and got several people to sing theirs. When he ran out of volunteers from the audience, he turned to the band. "Do any of you guys remember your school songs?" There was no response from the musicians. Merv persisted. Pointing to Bill Berry, he said, "Bill do you remember yours?" Bill nodded. "Can you play it?" Bill nodded again. After a moment, Merv said, "Well, will you, please?" Bill put his trumpet to his lips and played, all on the same mid-register note: (rest) ta-da dut, dut, (rest) ta-da dut, dut, (rest) ta-da dut, dut. The band broke up, but no one else seemed to understand what was so funny. Bill was playing the third trumpet part he had played in high school.

A guest singer on the Griffin show agreed to an impromptu performance, and said to Jake Hanna, "Give me four bars." Jake called out: "Charlie's, Juniors, Joe Harbor's, and Jim and Andy's," the musicians' four favorite New York watering holes.

chapter 17

The Well-dressed Jazz Musician

Most early jazzmen were very conscious of the way they dressed. Sharp clothes represented maturity and success. A good portion of a jazzman's income might go into improving his wardrobe. Some musicians dressed so distinctively that they influenced men's fashions. Jelly Roll Morton, a flashy dresser whose teeth were encrusted with diamonds during his peak earning years, often boasted of his extensive wardrobe. He would tell other musicians scornfully, "I've got more suits than you got handkerchiefs!"

Morton told Alan Lomax about the sartorial styles prevalent in early New Orleans among the "tough babies" he associated with:

They frequented the corners at Jackson and Locust and nobody fooled with them. They all strived to have at least one Sunday suit, because, without that Sunday suit, you didn't have anything.

It wasn't the kind of Sunday suit you'd wear today. You was considered way out of line if your coat and pants matched. Many a time they would kid me, "Boy, you must be from the country. Here you got trousers on the same as your suit."

These guys wouldn't wear anything but a blue coat and some kind of stripe in their trousers and those trousers had to be very, very tight. They'd fit 'em like a sausage. I'm telling you it was very seldom you could button the top button of a person's trousers those days in New Orleans. They'd leave the top button open and they wore very loud suspenders—of course they really didn't need suspenders, because the trousers was so tight—and one suspender was always hanging down.

You should have seen one of those sports move down the street, his shirt busted open so that you could discern his red flannel undershirt, walking along with a very mosey walk they had adopted from the river, called shooting the agate. When you shoot the agate, your hands is at your sides with your index fingers stuck out and you kind of struts with it. That was considered a big thing with some of the illiterate women—if you could shoot a good agate and had a nice high class red undershirt with the collar turned up, I'm telling you, you were liable to get next to that broad. She liked that very much.

Those days, myself, I thought I would die unless I had a hat with the emblem Stetson in it and some Edwin Clapp shoes. But many of them wouldn't wear ready-made shoes. They wore what they called the St. Louis Flats and the Chicago Flats, made with cork soles and without heels and with gambler designs on the toes. Later on, some of them made arrangements to have some kind of electric light bulbs in the toes of their shoes with a battery in their pockets, so when they would get around some jane that was kind of simple, why they would press a button in their pocket and light up the little-bitty bulb in the toe of their shoes and that jane was claimed! It's really the fact. ⤵

Al Rose patronized a tailor who in later years made clothes for Morton:

There was a tailor in Philadelphia who sometimes used photographs of me in his window in the fond belief, or so he said, that my irresistible appearance would attract customers into this shop. The legend above identified me as "Impresario Al Rose. Suit by Mike the Tailor." By agreement, I got 40 percent off the price of any suit I ordered.

One day Mike said to me, "Al, I've got a real impressive piece of imported English goods. It's a remnant, but I might have enough for a three-piece suit. You wanna see?"

In those days that was a lure I couldn't resist. The "goods" turned out to be a polychromatic, green-striped worsted, truly beautiful.

Mike had no trouble selling it to me. The suit was finished two weeks later on the day of my appointment with Reese Dupree [composer of the "Dupree Blues" and "Shortnin' Bread," who had an Ellington concert in mind that he wanted Rose to help him promote].

"Look," Mike had suggested (a good tailor knows how to flatter his clients), "I don't have to tell *you* what looks good, but I'd like you to consider a pink shirt with this, with a white detached collar and a dubonnet tie, handkerchief, and buttonhole. Can you *see* it?" I could see it. Cordovan shoes, too.

So when I joined Reese in the [Showboat Room of the] Douglass [Hotel], that's what I was wearing. I couldn't help being aware of the contrast I made with Dupree, whose suits always looked like mattress covers. I was ever so conscious of such matters in 1938.

We had just begun to talk when I noticed a flurry of activity in the entrance. Two noisy, light brown ladies, both grossly overpainted, came in; they were followed by none other than Jelly Roll Morton. He and Reese saw each other and exchanged waves as Jelly escorted his two friends to a table, then returned to have a word with Dupree. I was impressed with the elegance of Jelly's attire—very much impressed indeed. Polychromatic, green-striped suit, pink shirt with detached white collar, dubonnet tie, buttonhole, and handkerchief—and even a pair of cordovan shoes. Obviously there had been more than a single suit in Mike's remnant. Jelly Roll appeared equally impressed with my attire.

He shook hands with Reese, who then introduced us. Jelly and I had both begun to laugh, and Dupree became uncomfortable, fearing that our joke might have been on him. Reese was not one to notice how people dressed. In a moment, Jelly got up to join his party; as he said goodbye he leaned over and said quietly in my ear,

"Next time you see Mike the Tailor, you tell him I'm gonna kick his ass." ⸙

Lips Page told a group of jazz buffs at the bar at Jimmy Ryan's on 52nd Street about an experience he had dressing his hair with Conkolene, a heavy pomade used to keep the hair slicked down:

We were traveling on the road, doing one-nighters, and some of us were sleeping at this rooming house. I came in drunk, and didn't put my head-rag on before I got in bed. I was using lots of Conk on my hair in those days. My bed was by the window, and in the morning the sun came in on my head while I was asleep and melted that Conk right into the pillow. Then, when the sun moved off me, the Conk hardened up again, and when I woke up, the pillow was stuck to my head! Everybody else was ready to get in the bus, and I'm still trying to get that damn pillow off my head. We had to get the landlady's teakettle and heat that stuff up until it melted a little, and then I could go on and get dressed. ⸙

When they were both living in Kansas City, Lips shared his wardrobe with Count Basie:

Lips Page had a couple or three fine special suits, and at that time he and I were the same size. So one night we were supposed to go out somewhere, and I said I couldn't go because I didn't have anything to match up, and he said,

"That's all right. Why don't you borrow one of my suits?" And I said okay. I figured that would be great. Because he had three real sharp, truly great outfits. But I didn't know what I was getting myself into. I couldn't get rid of him. Everywhere I went he was right there with me, saying, "Don't lean on that."

Or he'd say, "Hey man, that chair is kinda dirty."

"Hey, Basie, watch it sitting down."

He couldn't think of anything else all night but that suit of his I was wearing. That was one of the most uncomfortable evenings I've ever had in my life. I never was so glad to get back home and take off a suit. ⸙

Rex Stewart told about Duke Ellington's appreciation of elegant footwear:

Duke was making *Check and Double Check*, his first movie. En route to California, he met the people who ran a theatrical shoe firm in Chicago. He had them make a dozen pairs of a shoe he designed; feather-weight, thin-soled, square-toed. This evolved, over some twenty or so years, into what is now known as the Italian shoe. But at the time, this way-out footwear was a real conversation piece. Duke continued to order these shoes by the dozen, in every imaginable color and leather, and had soon accumulated so many pairs that he had to have special trunks made to accommodate them.

It was always his custom to change shoes between sets, choosing between the blacks in calf and patent leather, the browns in crocodile, alligator, and suede, and all the other colors in the spectrum. When I attended a few concerts by the band recently, I was amazed that he didn't change shoes. Later I found out the reason. These were the pumps he had worn when he was presented to the Queen of England, and despite their shabby appearance, they now were his favorites.

Stewart also told of a coat that broke up a friendship between Coleman Hawkins and trombonist Jimmy Harrison:

Coleman is essentially a loner, and with the exception of Harrison, I don't know anyone with whom he was ever really close. There was always a lot of good-natured teasing between them, but when Jimmy bought a Pontiac, Hawk accorded him a lot more respect than he had previously, and stopped kidding Jim so roughly. They ate together, hung out as a team, and got along fine, until Coleman made the mistake of buying a raccoon coat, which became the talk of Harlem. I've heard how a woman can break up a friendship between two men, but this is the first time I ever came across a situation in which a fur coat was the cause.

It started at one of those breakfast dances that Harlem was noted for at the time. At the peak of the evening, Hawk made his entrance looking like an Oriental potentate, with a beauty on each arm. When he was seated, all the pretty little showgirls converged upon his table, where, of course, Jimmy also was seated with his date. The showgirls went into ecstasies, raving about Hawk's coat. And Jimmy's date, not to be outdone, draped the garment around herself, remarking in a loud, clear voice, "This fur piece is the living end, and to get its twin, I for one, would take anything that goes along with it, including you, Coleman."

I'm sure she was only joking, but by a strange coincidence, two weeks later she was sporting a coat that looked exactly like Hawk's. Jimmy looked rather glum for a spell. I don't know if it was poetic justice or not, but only a few months later Coleman's raccoon went up in smoke. It caught on fire from the exhaust pipe that heated the bus we were using to make a series of one-nighters. ↯

Billy Eckstine accentuated his good looks with an extremely sharp wardrobe. The wide shirt collars he favored came to be known as "Mr. B. collars." Duke Ellington remembered a competition that developed between Eckstine and himself:

He worked with us at the New York Paramount once, and it was a ball hearing him five shows a day. There was also a little thing going on between B. and me. For four weeks, neither of us wore the same suit twice. He flattered me by ordering his valet to call Los Angeles and have two more trunks shipped out immediately. By the third week, people were buying tickets just to see the sartorial changes. ↯

Joe Darensbourg found a way to dress properly for jobs when he was scuffling in Los Angeles:

Al Pierre was originally from Tacoma, Washington, and he owned his own tuxedo. We got hooked up with the Spikes Brothers agency, and they often used to book us on different jobs, like in the movies, where you'd have to have a tuxedo. We never had the money to rent a tuxedo, so we used to hustle over to Al Pierre's house and borrow his. We used it so much the knees was stretched out of shape; look like they had a couple of footballs in there. It was all frayed to hell. Anybody would see us they'd say, "I see you got Al's tuxedo!" ↯

Jesse Stone found a backer willing to outfit his band with uniforms:

There was a guy named Frank J. Rock, an undertaker; he took over the management of the band. He bought us all new instruments and he sent us down to have these costumes. We decided to get tuxedos, but nobody thought of getting shoes. So we went to this photographer with these hobnail shoes on, and wing collars with bow ties. As a novelty thing everybody kept a shot of that because it was funny. ↳

Many bandleaders invested in flashy costumes, realizing the need to keep their bands looking sharp. Louis Jordan bought everything new for his men, suits, shirts, ties, shoes, instruments. An ex-sideman commented, "When you left Louis, you left in your underwear!" Jordan was an exception; the cost of band uniforms was usually passed along to the musicians via paycheck deductions.

Eddie Condon told how he and George Wettling cut their uniform expenses on a job in New York.

Artie Shaw had a string sextet. His playing impressed George Gershwin, and Artie found himself booked for a run at the Paramount Theater. He organized a full band for the date, with Wettling on drums. Just before the opening his guitar player went to a hospital with appendicitis and I replaced him. The band wore uniforms and ugly brown suede shoes. At one point in the performance I had to stand up, put my right foot on a chair, and play a sixteen-bar solo. Otherwise both my feet were hidden by a music stand. Wettling's right foot was hidden by his bass drum; his left was visible to the audience. We wore the same size shoe, and since each musician had to buy his own uniform and accessories, we shared a pair of the brown suede atrocities. George wore the left one, I wore the right one. ↳

When Roy Eldridge came to New York, he felt the necessity to build up his wardrobe:

I made thirty-two dollars a week at the Savoy, and every two weeks I bought me a suit! Wasn't a hundred dollar suit. Wohlmuth was the thing then, like Bond's. I bought all them suits, and all of them went out of style! Suits with all them buttons on the vests, you know, and all of a sudden the *louds* came in, and there I am stuck with all these things! (Laughs) Money went a little farther then. You could take ten dollars and go out and have a good time. You can't take ten dollars and do nothin' now! You go in Ryan's and have two drinks, you're dead! ↳

As time went on, especially during the postwar era, clothes of a deliberately scruffy nature became standard among the younger musicians. Since the older generation was still dressing sharply, for a while it was almost possible to tell the style a man played by the clothes he wore. Of course, there were always jazz musicians who were completely indifferent to clothes. Bix Beiderbecke may have been the pioneer of this school. Wingy Manone wrote:

> Bix didn't give a damn for anything but music, except maybe his gin. He ran around in raggedy old clothes and was always jiving me for dressing up in my fancy garb.
>
> "How come you put so much money in clothes?" he asked me one time. "You don't have to wear fancy bow ties and shined shoes and stuff to play good. If you didn't spend so much money on clothes you could buy more gin." ↳

When the armed services began to deplete the big bands and young replacements arrived with modern musical ideas, Woody Herman welcomed them with open arms. He let his musicians recommend arrangers who wrote a modern book for him. Tommy Dorsey was more conservative. He wanted no bebop in his arrangements, and said so for the record on several occasions. In response, Woody went to a San Francisco men's store and bought the squarest jacket he could find, a loud plaid with a belt in the back. He sent it to Dorsey with a card that read, "If you want to play that way, why not dress that way?"

When Count Basie broke up his big band and started working with a septet during the 1940s, he dressed his musicians in uniforms that had seen considerable wear with his old band. When the septet members complained about their seedy appearance and asked for new clothes, Basie told then, "Never mind about the uniforms. Just get out there and play good." In Toronto, Clark Terry decided it was time for drastic action. He took his uniform and those of Wardell Gray and Marshall Royal, slashed them to ribbons and hung them on the doorknob of Basie's hotel room. Then he set them on fire, knocked on the door and hid. When Basie opened the door, he was definitely not pleased with the conflagration he found.

That night the musicians, dressed sharply in their own clothes, were expecting Basie's wrath as he climbed onto the bandstand to kick off their first set. He looked them over and said drily, "You mothers weren't kidding, were you?" They got the new uniforms they wanted.

Working with Earl Hines, Art Blakey learned about maintaining a band's public image:

> I love him; he is something else. I learned so much from him about band leading. He's a dealer. He bought us all bathrobes and pajamas and he'd send in flowers every morning to put in your bathrobe lapel—"You never know when the press is coming." (Laughter) "The curtain never comes down, Gate." 🎵

The beginning of the bebop era caused the news magazines to focus on the externals of the musicians involved in the music, and Dizzy Gillespie's beret, goatee, and horn-rim glasses became symbolic of the new generation of jazz musicians. Dizzy told the story behind the stereotype:

> Lie number one was that beboppers wore wild clothes and dark glasses at night. Watch the fashions of the forties on the late show. Long coats, almost down to your knees and full trousers. I wore drape suits like everyone else and dressed no differently from the average leading man of the day. It was beautiful. I became pretty dandified, I guess, later during the bebop era when my pants were pegged slightly at the bottom.
>
> We had costumes for the stage—uniforms with wide lapels and belts—given to us by a tailor in Chicago who designed them, but we didn't wear them offstage. Later, we removed the wide lapels and sported little tan cashmere jackets with no lapels. *Esquire* magazine, 1943, America's leading influence on men's fashions, considered us elegant, though bold, and printed our photographs.
>
> Perhaps I remembered France and started wearing a beret. But I used it as headgear I could stuff into my pocket and keep moving. I used to lose my hat a lot. I liked to wear a hat like most of the guys then, and the hats I kept losing cost five dollars apiece. At a few recording sessions when I couldn't lay my hands on a mute, I covered the bell of the trumpet with the beret. Since I'd been designated their "leader," cats just picked up the style.
>
> My first pair of eyeglasses, some rimless glasses, came from Maurice Guilden, and optometrist at the Theresa Hotel, but they'd get

broken all the time, so I picked up a pair of horn rims. I never wore dark glasses at night. I had to be careful about my eyes because I needed them to read music.   ⟡

Miles Davis always dressed with flair. He selected his own clothes carefully, but he didn't interfere with the way his musicians chose to dress. He didn't permit others to interfere, either. Eric Nisenson describes his reaction when a club owner tried:

Miles refused to be told by anybody what he should wear. Once when he was appearing at Birdland with his sextet, Oscar Goodstein requested that Miles have his band dress in uniforms, as many groups were doing at the time. According to Nat Adderley, Cannonball's brother, the next night Miles kept the group in the dressing room until it was time to go on. When the group went on stage, they were wearing the same disparate clothes they had worn the night before. Miles pulled a rack of uniforms that he had obtained from a nearby clothing store onstage and told the audience,

"Oscar Goodstein wanted to see uniforms onstage so here they are. If that's what you came for, to look at uniforms instead of music, that's what you got. Now we're going to leave so you can enjoy these uniforms."

Needless to say, Goodstein quickly backed down on his demand, and the group played in their usual clothes.   ⟡

When Frank Vicari was Woody Herman's road manager, the musicians wore white turtlenecks with their band jackets on informal jobs, and white dress shirts with neckties on the fancier ones. Sal Nistico discovered that if he put a dress shirt on backwards, it could pass for a turtleneck, saving him the expense of buying a second set of shirts. So every night before the job, Sal would call Frank and ask, "Fronts or backs tonight?"

One night in Los Angeles, Woody told Frank, "Those band jackets are looking ragged. Get some new ones." The next day Frank took everyone's size to a men's store and found an acceptable model, but discovered that, because there were some very large musicians on the band at the time, the store wouldn't be able to fill his order right away. Frank noticed some dashikis, which came in sizes large enough for everyone, so he bought enough for the whole band and they wore them on the bandstand that night. Woody came in dressed in a tuxedo and looked a little put out when he saw the dashikis, but he got so many positive comments from the customers that he kept them for casual gigs. "But," he told Frank, "make sure everyone is wearing the same kind of shirt sleeves!"

chapter 18

Prejudice

Jazz helped to start the erosion of racial prejudice in America. The music was a strong magnet to those who had ears for it, and it drew whites and blacks together into a common experience. It was difficult to admire the music without admiring the musicians, and for many whites, educated in prejudice, it was their first chance to discover that blacks could be admirable. The process continued in other popular venues like professional sports and pop music.

In the 1920s and '30s, black and white musicians enjoyed the social freedom they constructed for themselves within the jazz world, so different from the state of affairs in the rest of the United States at that time. Jazz musicians formed many warm and enduring interracial friendships. But it took a while longer for a few white bandleaders to risk presenting black musicians with their bands. The black pioneers in those bands told many stories of the bitter resistance in the music business to this change. Meanwhile all traveling black musicians faced the hard realities of going into hostile territory to work. John Best described a situation in Parkersburg, West Virginia, when Billie Holiday was singing with Artie Shaw's band:

> On this tour, Billie usually rode in my car, together with Lester Burness and Zutty Singleton (a famous black drummer who Shaw had temporarily hired to "coach" the band). When we reached Parkersburg, Zutty asked to be let out at a black hotel and suggested to Billie that she get out there too, as they were "down South" and

couldn't stay at the "white only" hotel downtown. However, Billie was determined to find this out for herself. She found out, the hard way, and was told that there were no rooms available. I had to take her back to the place where Zutty had checked in, and in the meantime he had the only room with a private bath. For a few minutes it seemed as though Billie was as mad at Zutty as she was at the whole South. 🕩

The problems weren't confined to the South. Billie did a show at the Fox Theater in Detroit, with the Basie band:

After three performances the first day, the theater management went crazy. They claimed they had so many complaints about all those Negro men up there on the stage with those bare-legged white girls, all hell cut loose backstage.

The next thing we know, they revamped the whole show. They cut out the girls' middle number. And when the chorus line opened the show, they'd fitted them out with special black masks and mammy dresses. They did both their numbers in blackface and those damn mammy getups.

When he saw what was happening, Basie flipped. But there was nothing he could do. We had signed the contracts to appear, and we had no control over what the panicky theater managers did.

But that wasn't the worst of it. Next they told Basie I was too yellow to sing with all the black men in his band. Somebody might think I was white if the light didn't hit me just right. So they got special dark grease paint and told me to put it on.

It was my turn to flip. I said I wouldn't do it. But they had our name on the contracts, and if I refused it might have played hell with bookings, not just for me, but for the future of all the cats in the band.

So I had to be darkened down so the show could go on in dynamic-assed Detroit. It's like they say, there's no damn business like show business. You had to smile to keep from throwing up. 🕩

Bessie Smith was a star of the black entertainment world while relatively unknown to the rest of the country. White audiences discovered Bessie through her records. Some of those who came to see her traveling show weren't all that happy about her success, but Bessie was a match for them. Chris Albertson writes:

Bessie must have known that many of the Southern followers who flocked to her tent, laughed at her jokes and applauded her singing were Klansmen who had left their sheets at home. But like many Southern blacks, she ignored the Klan and assumed she'd receive no more malice than she gave.

Still, Bessie often found trouble whether she looked for it or not. In July, 1297, in Concord, North Carolina, she was forced out of her complacency toward the Klan. It was a hot July night, and Bessie's electric generator was creating additional heat, making the packed tent almost unbearable, especially for the lively performers. Halfway through the show, one of the musicians was close to passing out. He left his seat and stepped outside.

As he walked around the huge tent, he heard soft voices and a grunting sound nearby. Following the sound, he came upon a half dozen hooded figures, the moonlight showing up their white robes. They were obviously getting ready to collapse Bessie's tent; they had already pulled up several stakes.

Unseen by the preoccupied Klansmen, the musician hurried back to the rear entrance of the tent. Bessie had just come off stage, and the audience was hollering for her to return. Before she could raise hell with the musician for not being inside with the rest of the band, he managed to blurt out what he'd seen.

"Some shit!" she said, and ordered the prop boys to follow her around the tent. When they were within a few feet of the Klansmen, the boys withdrew to a safe distance. Bessie had not told them why she wanted them, and one look at the white hoods was all the discouragement they needed.

Not Bessie. She ran toward the intruders, stopped within ten feet of them, placed one hand on her hip, and shook a clenched fist at the Klansmen. "What the fuck you think you're doing'?" she shouted above the sound of the band. "I'll get the whole damn tent out here if I have to. You just pick up them sheets and run!"

The Klansmen, apparently too surprised to move, just stood there and gawked. Bessie hurled obscenities at them until they finally turned and disappeared quietly into the darkness.

"I ain't never *heard* of such shit," said Bessie, and walked back to where her prop boys stood. "And as for you, you ain't nothin' but a bunch of sissies."

Then she went back into the tent as if she had just settled a routine matter.

When Cab Calloway and Duke Ellington toured through the South, they dealt with the problem of being barred from good hotels and restaurants by hiring private railroad cars. Duke gave his reasons:

> In our music we have been talking for a long time about what it is to be a Negro in this country. And we've never let ourselves be put into a position of being treated with disrespect. From 1934 to 1936 we went touring deep into the South, without the benefit of Federal judges, and we commanded respect. We didn't travel by bus. Instead, we had two Pullman cars and a 70-foot baggage car. We parked them in each station, and lived in them. We had our own water, food, electricity, and sanitary facilities. The natives would come by and say, "What's that?"
>
> "Well," we'd say, "that's the way the President travels."

Snub Mosley made a trip into the South with Lil Armstrong's band in 1937:

> Teddy McRae was with the band, Dick Vance, Stumpy Brady, it was a nice band, but it didn't draw no people. Didn't draw flies. We got down in Knoxville, Tennessee, and didn't have no place to eat. None of us had very much money. We finally got enough money from someplace to get us back, in the cars. We were coming back from Tennessee, and there was a little stand on the edge of the highway, and the man was so happy we stopped there, 'cause he didn't have no business. We bought hot dogs and soda and things like that.
>
> All of a sudden I heard somebody cursing like hell. This guy opened the door to his bathroom and there was McRae on the stool! (Laughs) I never heard so much—this guy was hurt to his heart. He says, "Oh, my God!" (Can I tell it like it is?) "Oh, my *God!* This nigger's got his *ass* on my *stool!* Ohhh, Lord have *mercy!* What am I gonna *do?*" As if somebody had hit him in his head or something!
>
> "Nigger, get up!"
>
> Went and got his big pistol—this pistol was this *big,* and it looked to be like it was *that* big! So we all rushed back to see what it was about, and McRae said, "Man, I can't get up! I can't stop!"
>
> The man said, "If you don't get up I swear to God I'll blow your head off!"
>
> "I can't stop now, man!"

I went and grabbed McRae by the hand and pulled him up! He'll never forget about that. ↷

Stan Shaw had a close call when he went to Virginia with Lips Page's band:

I was one of the first white musicians that ever went below the Mason-Dixon line with an all-black group. Lips Page took me, when I was fifteen, on a tour of the South. Before I went in the service. I remember Billy Taylor, Sr., the bass player from Washington, D.C., and I can't remember who the other guys were. Piano, trumpet, saxophone and myself playing. We played at the Star Theatre in Norfolk, Virginia. It was a segregated theater, they had the whites in the orchestra and the blacks in the balcony. I don't know why Lips accepted the engagement. I guess they were all segregated. There was a tremendous uproar when the curtains parted and there we were. Apparently white people thought I was lowering myself to play with a black group, and the black people thought I was intruding on their music. The whole audience started towards the stage; they came to get us.

Lips ran out the back door of the theater yelling "Cops, Police!" And the cops came swinging their clubs at *us!* We ran like hell for the train station. I left four hundred dollars worth of drums in the Star Theatre in Norfolk, Virginia. We got out of there with our lives, and we were lucky. ↷

Jimmy Maxwell, Benny Goodman's lead trumpeter for many years, spoke of Goodman's hiring of Teddy Wilson, the first black to work as a member of a major white band:

Benny is a very mercenary man. He's very interested in money. But he cut off almost half the country for Teddy Wilson. He didn't want to travel in the South with the band, so he cut off a large part of his income. I've heard him stand up, even in the New Yorker, the first time we went in there. We had Sid Catlett, John Simmons, Charlie Christian, Cootie Williams, five or six black guys, and I remember the manager saying, "I don't want these black guys coming in through the lobby and through the restaurant. In fact, I don't even want them here." And Benny said, "Well, I'm sorry. This is my band. If you don't want them in the band then screw yourself. We're walking out." So then he said, "Well, they'll have to go through the kitchen." Benny said, "They do not go through the kitchen." Then he said, "All of the musicians go through the kitchen." And Benny said, "None of the musicians go through the kitchen." "Well, then, they can't wear their uniforms when they come." "All right, they won't wear their uniforms."

But he stuck up for them. It wasn't just he put black guys in the band and then said, "Good luck," you know. He didn't give any particular race or guy a bad time. If he was giving anybody a bad time it was just he felt that way. It wasn't because of their ethnic background. ↷

Trummy Young also worked with Goodman, and had a different perception of him:

I remember once with Benny Goodman, it was Teddy, Slam and myself, we had a problem in Providence in a hotel. They didn't want us. So Teddy approached Benny. Said, "We can't get a room in the hotel. We thought you made a reservation. They don't want to let us have a room." Benny didn't go to the front for this, you know. He said, "You know, I have problems, too. I can't belong to this club or that one because I'm Jewish." So we told him we was going back to New York. We told him thanks very much, but we were going; we didn't have to go through that. Then he got somebody to do something about it. He wouldn't battle those things out.

I liked Benny, you know, I don't think Benny would go too far for nobody. Not only us but nobody else, you know. He didn't think like that. He just thought clarinet, and that was it, you know. He didn't let anything else bother him. Clarinet was it. ↷

Maxwell was with Goodman when Cootie Williams joined the band:

I generally liked to room alone, but we would get into a place like Ohio or someplace and they wouldn't have any place for Cootie to stay. So I would check in in both names and then Cootie would come in the room. And it broke my heart the first time he said,

"You check in and I'll carry the bags in and act like I'm the bandboy." I said,

"Bullshit. I'll check in and you walk in and I'll carry my own bags. That much I'll do.

Then he didn't want to go down to the dining room and he said,

"We'll have room service."

I didn't want to go out and eat and leave him alone, so it cost me a lot of money. But when I said,

"Look, we'll go down to the dining room. You don't have to do anything. If they say anything at all, I'll pop them." And he said,

"No, I don't want to embarrass the band. Leave it alone. It's all right." ⤵

Trummy Young spoke of the Harry James band when Willie Smith was the lead alto player:

Advance word would get to these southern cities that Harry James had a mixed band; there was one negro on the band. The sheriff would come up and say, "You can't go on with a mixed band." And Harry would say, "All right, point out the one that mixes it." They couldn't tell. ⤵

Gary Giddins tells the story of Red Rodney's southern tour with Charlie Parker.

The weirdest road incident came about in 1950, when agent Billy Shaw arranged a southern tour for big money.

"You gotta get rid of that redheaded trumpet player; we can't have a white guy in a black band down south," Shaw insisted. Bird said,

"No, I ain't gonna get rid of him, he's my man. Ain't you ever heard of an albino? Red's an albino."

Shaw knew Red was Jewish—he'd heard him speak Yiddish to Parker, much to the delight of the saxophonist, who called Rodney "Chood." [Red was born Robert Chudnick.] Shaw raised hell. Bird said,

"Leave it to me."

Red knew nothing of the conversation. When the band arrived at the first gig, Spiro's Beach in Maryland, he was surprised to see a sign reading, "The King of Bebop Charlie Parker and His Orchestra featuring Albino Red, Blues Singer."

Bird said, "You gotta sing the blues, Chood baby."

"But I don't know any blues."

"Sing 'em anyhow."

He did. The other guys chanted behind him like a choir, and the audiences loved it. In three weeks, nobody ever questioned the masquerade.

"They were very polite," Red says. ♪

In a later interview, Red explained that he knew no blues lyrics, so he sang "School Days," a doggerel rhythm tune that Joe Carroll recorded with Dizzy Gillespie.

Benny Carter had a band at the Plantation Club in St. Louis, in 1944. The club featured black bands and had black employees, but the customers were all white. The band's pianist, Joe Albany, attracted the attention of some of the dancers on the floor. Carter recalled.

W̲e were on an elevated stage. I noticed one couple that kept looking up at us while they were dancing. They danced up to the bandstand and the lady leaned forward and said to me, "Pardon me, Mr. Carter, but is your pianist white or black?" I looked over to Joe, turned to her and said, "I don't know. I never asked him." They seemed very surprised. ♪

When Nat Cole bought a house in a white suburb of Los Angeles, some of the other homeowners in the area drew up a petition against undesirable people moving into the neighborhood, and began passing it around for signatures. When Nat found out about it he went to a neighbor's house and asked if he could sign the petition. He said he didn't want any undesirables moving in, either.

Barney Kessel appeared in the classic movie short *Jammin' the Blues*, filmed by Gjon Mili in 1944 for Warner Brothers under the supervision of Norman Granz. Kessel was asked if it was true that, in deference to the southern market, he had been put in shadows in the background because all the other participants were black:

W̲ell, that's absolutely true. They wouldn't be able to sell it below the Mason-Dixon line. Jack Warner didn't really want to go through with the project when he saw that everyone was black but me. He spoke to Norman Granz about it and asked why he didn't just get a black guitarist. He felt it would be much simpler to do it that way. Norman said no, because the people that were here are not here because they are black or white, they're here because they are the people he (Norman) wanted. They kicked it around for a while, trying to find a solution and finally the solution was that I was in the shadows. It kind of inferred, pictorially, that I might be black.

When they did a closeup of me they did stain my hands with berry juice. Now that might seem farfetched, but this was in 1944 before the civil rights movement and at that time it didn't seem too far out. It was a time, whether you liked it or not, it seemed like that was the thing to do. That was the way it was.

I saw one of the stills and it showed Lester Young and myself sitting there on the soundstage. Now, Lester was a very light complexioned black and he is sitting there with the lights on him and I'm sitting next to him, kind of in the shadows. When I saw this still I turned around to these other black musicians, showed them this picture and I said to them laughingly, "What's he doing sitting here with us?" He looked much lighter than I did. ❧

Miles Davis visited Ronnie Scott's London jazz club, where he was to play the next night. The comedian at Scott's was Professor Irwin Corey, "The World's Foremost Authority." Scott said:

Miles came in with a whole entourage—girl friends, barber, lawyer, shoe shine boy, you know. And they all sat down front. And he had these huge wrap-around sunglasses on. And Corey suddenly bent down and whipped the glasses off Miles and put them on. And said, "No wonder you're smiling—everyone looks black." ❧

Dizzy Gillespie wrote about a solution to prejudice in America that was chosen by some black jazzmen:

For social and religious reasons, a large number of modern jazz musicians did begin to turn toward Islam during the forties, a movement completely in line with the idea of freedom of religion. Rudy Powell, from Edgar Hayes's band, became one of the first jazz musicians I knew to accept Islam; he became an Ahmidyah Muslim. Other musicians followed, it seemed to me, for social rather than religious reasons, if you can separate the two.

"Man, if you join the Muslim faith, you ain't colored no more, you'll be white," they'd say. "You get a new name and you don't have to be a nigger no more." So everybody started joining because they considered it a big advantage not to be black during the time of segregation. When these cats found out that Idrees Sulieman, who joined the Muslim faith about that time, could go into these white restaurants and bring out sandwiches to the other guys because he wasn't colored—and he looked like the inside of the chimney—they started enrolling in droves.

Musicians started having it printed on their police cards where it said "race," "W" for white. Kenny Clarke had one and he showed it to me. He said, "See, nigger, I ain't no spook; I'm white, 'W.'" He changed his name to Arabic, Liaqat Ali Salaam. Another cat who had been my roommate at Laurinburg, Oliver Mesheux, got involved in an altercation about race down in Delaware. He went into this restaurant, and they said they didn't serve colored in there. So he said, "I don't blame you. But I don't have to go under the rules of colored because my name is Mustafa Dalil." Didn't ask him no more questions. "How do you do?" the guy said.

Milt Hinton worked with Powell on a Chicago group called the Enjoyment Band. They made a trip to Omaha, Nebraska, for a theater date:

We had a guy in the band named Rudy Powell. He changed his name to Musa Kalim. He wore a fez and grew a little beard. They got into town after midnight and found everything closed. Having no way to locate the rooming houses that accepted black musicians, they decided to park the bus in front of the theater and sit there until morning.

Rudy had a better idea. He walks into this white hotel, and the minute he hit the door, the man said, "I'm very sorry, we're filled up." Rudy says, "Where's the manager?" The manager comes out and says, "Well, it isn't the policy of this hotel to rent rooms to colored."

Rudy says, "I'm not colored." He whips this card out, which says, "My name is Musa Kalim, and I am a descendant of Father Abraham, and the mother, Hagar, and I'm entitled to all the rights and privileges of the Mystic Knights." He's wearing this fez.

He says, "Call the State Department in Washington. I want to speak to someone in the State Department right now." The man got scared to death. "I'm very sorry, sir," he says. "We'll get you a room."

Rudy says, "I've got nine of my brothers out in the bus there, and they don't speak English. I've got to have room for the nine." So the guy claps his hands, says to the bellhop, "Get this gentleman nine rooms." And it's Jonah Jones, Shad Collins, Kansas Fields, nine of the guys in the band. Rudy got up the next morning and collected the money from all the guys and paid the bill and walked out. Since then, change, integration started. He's back to Rudy Powell again now. ↳

Quite a few black American jazz musicians found the social attitude in Europe so agreeable toward them when they toured there that they moved there to live. Of course, prejudice can crop up anywhere. Johnny Simmen wrote of an incident in Switzerland while Duke Ellington's orchestra was touring there:

On one of the band's yearly appearances in Zurich (probably 1967) Harry Carney and Ray Nance paid a visit to a watch and jewel shop near their hotel. They asked to see a certain number of Swiss watches, inspected them, could not make a decision right on the spot, promised to come back and left the shop.

A few minutes later it was discovered that three precious jewels were missing, and the shopowner and his staff immediately "combined" that only the two "black people" could have stolen them. They hurried out of the shop and had no difficulty locating Harry and Ray, who were quietly window-shopping one or two blocks further down the street. ↳

They were taken back to the shop, searched by the police, and were taken to the police station where they were interrogated and held until the shopowner called to report that the jewels had been found, having been misplaced by a salesgirl. No apologies were offered to the accused musicians, either by the police or by the shopowner. Carney later said:

I thought of the poor shopowner who had so unjustly suspected us. I could imagine how bad he must have felt about it all. Well, I went back to that shop. I bought the most expensive watch that I could find. The man in the shop looked happy, and so was I. ↳

Along with the changes in American society brought about by the civil rights struggle came a feeling on the part of some black musicians that jazz should be an exclusively black expression. But it was too late for that. The music had already integrated itself. Once a good idea gets out, it's out; the genie can't be forced back into the bottle. However, there were hard feelings among some musicians. When Joe Gordon joined Shelly Manne's group, he was asked by black friends, "What are you doing, working in Whitey's band?" Sonny Rollins was criticized for hiring Jim Hall, and Miles Davis for hiring Bill Evans. Miles was contemptuous of this attitude:

> When I first hired Lee Konitz years ago, some guys said, "Why do you want an ofay in your band?" I asked them if they knew anybody who could play with a tone like Lee's. If I had to worry about nonsense like that, I wouldn't have a band. I wouldn't care if a cat was green and had red breath, if he could play. ♪

In 1958, George Wein arranged to stage a jazz festival at the old resort hotel at French Lick in southern Indiana. He demanded and received assurances that there would be no discourtesies shown the black musicians and fans who would be visiting that formerly lily-white resort. The hotel manager told George that French Lick had changed with the times. When the Gerry Mulligan Quartet arrived there, however, Art Farmer and Dave Bailey expressed doubts about using the swimming pool. They wanted to avoid any ugly scenes.

From the lobby the blue water of the pool looked inviting, and Art and Dave had just about decided to go get into their swim suits when Dizzy Gillespie stepped out of the elevator. He was wearing bathing trunks from the French Riviera, an embroidered skull-cap from Greece and embroidered slippers with curled-up toes that he'd picked up in Turkey. A Sheraton bath towel draped over his shoulders like a cape was fastened at the neck with a jade scarab pin from Egypt. With a Chinese ivory cigarette holder in his left hand and a powerful German multiband portable radio in his right, he beamed cheerfully through a pair of Italian sunglasses.

"I've come to integrate the pool!" he announced. He led the way to the beach chairs at poolside, enthroning himself in one with plenipotentiary panache. After he had the attention of everyone at the poolside, he grabbed Jimmy McPartland, who had also come down for a swim. Arm in arm, the two trumpet players marched to the diving board and jumped in together, and the last barrier to integration at French Lick was down.

chapter 19

Songs

The American popular song form and the twelve-bar blues have been used by most jazz musicians as the basis for their improvising, though modernists have moved on to the exploration of other forms. The standard repertoire made it possible for disparate musicians to play together. A jazz musician from Dallas who knew the standard tunes could sit in with a band in Boston or Paris or Stockholm without difficulty even if he played with a regional style.

Since composer royalties are a source of income, jazz musicians eventually realized that a new melody based on a standard set of chords could be copyrighted. Original jazz tunes proliferated on records, and publishers and managers found that it was profitable to talk jazz composers into adding their names to the credits. Many of Duke Ellington's early hits list Duke and his manager, Irving Mills, as the composers. Mills had little to do with composing, but he did fight to get Ellington's music into the recording companies' general catalogues, and he got Ellington and himself into ASCAP.

Pops Foster told why New Orleans pianist Clarence Williams's name was on so many jazz tunes:

Clarence wasn't down there too long when he and Armand Piron opened a little music store and music publishing house. I think that was around 1910 or 1912. We used to rehearse there sometimes. If you had written a number, you'd go to Clarence to write it down. He could write very fast; as fast as you could do the number, he could write it down. After he'd write it down, he'd arrange it and send it to have it copyrighted and published. Clarence always managed to cut himself in on a number. When a number was published, it would have four or five names on it. Clarence would get as much of it as he could. His name would be in two or three places and the guy who really wrote it was usually way down the line. After he got through, he had more of your number than you did. Louis Armstrong wrote *Sis-*

ter Kate and had Clarence put it down, copyrighted and published it, and Louis never did get nothin' for it. Clarence was a real horse thief. ↱

Jazz musicians will play any song that has an interesting melody or chord structure, but they try to avoid requests for the uninteresting tunes that often become popular. Joe Darensbourg discovered that one popular tune suddenly became quite unpopular in Louisiana:

It Ain't Gonna Rain No More was a heck of a popular tune. We used to have to play it about seven or eight times a night. By some kind of coincidence they had a big drought in Louisiana. This was in the summertime and it didn't rain for two or three months. We'd have to drive on dirt roads and the dust would be six inches deep. The crops was dying and the cotton was dying, so, being superstitious, the Louisiana people thought a song like *It Ain't Gonna Rain No More* was causing the drought. They got the idea of passing a law, and believe it or not, it was made illegal to play that tune. Several times musicians and bands got put in jail when they got caught playing that tune. ↱

Earl Hines described an encounter on the South Side of Chicago between some jazz musicians and a certain songwriter:

The Sunset also became quite a hangout for musicians. We played seven nights a week til 3:30 or 4 in the morning and we never had a night off. Most of the clubs and hotels where the white musicians played closed between 1 and 2 o'clock, and they'd come down either to King Oliver at the Plantation or where we were. Benny Goodman used to come with his clarinet in a sack. Tommy Dorsey was there with either his trumpet or trombone, because he hadn't decided then which one he wanted to specialize on. His brother, Jimmy, would come with his alto and clarinet. Muggsy Spanier, Joe Sullivan, Whitey Berquist, Jess Stacy, and I don't know how many different musicians came to sit in and jam with us.

Fats Waller used to take over on Hamby's piano and we'd play duets. [Willie Hamby was Hines's second pianist.] I also remember a fellow who often came in and wanted to sit down and jam with the guys, but all he wanted to play was a sweet old number he had written. Nobody at that time wanted to hear it.

"Look," the guys said, "get this cat off that piano so we can go to town!" But he was constantly playing his new composition and trying to make everybody listen to it. It was *Stardust*, and he was Hoagy Carmichael. ↳

Hines encountered another songwriter at the Apex Club on 35th Street:

One incident that I always remember at the Apex had to do with *Rhapsody in Blue*. I had been playing it in the Sunset because they had a show built on it, and because I had played it so long I really knew it backwards. We used to get some very prominent musicians and theatrical people in the Apex, and I used to sit up there on its very small bandstand and play this piece with quite a lot of success. One night, after I finished playing it, I went to the men's room.

"You play *Rhapsody in Blue* very well," a gentleman said.

"Thank you," I said.

When he went out, the attendant asked if I knew who he was.

"No."

"That was George Gershwin."

You know, that really upset me. You never know who's listening to you. ↳

Jack Teagarden had a successful collaboration with Glenn Miller on one song:

I was home in New York the evening before the *Basin Street Blues* record date when Glenn called me from his apartment in Jackson Heights.

"Jack," he said, "I've been running over *Basin Street* again and I think we could do a better job if we could put together some lyrics and you could sing it. Want to come over and see what we can do? My wife will fix us some supper."

After we had worked out a first draft of verse and chorus, Glenn sat on the piano bench and I leaned over his shoulder. We each had a pencil, and as he played, we'd each cross out words and phrases here and there, putting in new ones. We finally finished the job sometime early in the morning.

Next day, we cut the record. It's been the most popular I've ever done! The lyrics were later included with the sheet music, but it never carried our names. ↳

Maurice Waller and Anthony Calabrese add a songwriter story to the long list of Hollywood movie fantasies supposedly based on real events about musicians:

Fats Waller and Andy Razaf wrote "Honeysuckle Rose" in 1928 for a revue at Connie's Inn. It only gained popularity much later, when it was highlighted in a film short of the same name. When Razaf saw the film he was incensed by its depiction of the song's creation. The screen version showed two white men writing the song while they were in jail. Waller felt that the film treatment was inconsequential and refused to join Razaf in a lawsuit. Razaf then wrote a letter to Louis B. Mayer, president of MGM, expressing his resentment and remarking that the film was an affront to Waller and himself as well as to all their race.

Mayer did not reply directly to Razaf, but wrote in Variety that the songwriters were "poor sports," and should be "proud to have had their song featured so prominently in a big Hollywood musical." Razaf wondered "how they would've placated Irving Berlin if they had presented a scene showing *Alexander's Ragtime Band* as being written by a colored boy behind bars." ↳

Red Callender once applied for work to a famous songwriter, "The Father of the Blues":

Alexander Valentine was a friend of W. C. Handy and had written me a letter of introduction to him. I was proficient at copying music. So I presented myself in Handy's office at 1619 Broadway in the Brill Building. Handy himself received me. He was a bald, stocky man, ensconced behind a big oak desk. He still had his sight then, was very cordial, inquired after Alexander's health. After he read the note he sat silently for a moment. Clearly I was bubbling with enthusiasm and hope. Handy let me down easy. "Son," he said, "I've got to tell you that this office is just a front to get me out of the house. I've been living off the *St. Louis Blues* for the past twenty years." So much for my career as a copyist! ↳

Callender was there when the famous joke began about Billy Strayhorn's tune:

Sweet Pea came into the Capri one evening and brought us some music scratched out in pencil which we played on our nightly broadcast. It was "Take the A Train" before Duke had seen it. When Duke heard it, he adopted it for the band's theme song. Billy Berg, a very personable Jewish fellow, used to announce for the broadcasts. He said on the air, "Ladies and gentlemen, now the boys will play 'Take a Train.' " Lawrence Welk usually gets credit for that slip, but it was the club owner Billy Berg. ♭

Steve Voce revealed the origin of the title *Lady McGowan's Dream*, a tune Ralph Burns wrote for Woody Herman:

When the band was resident at the Panther Room of the Sherman Hotel in Chicago, a woman by the name of Lady McGowan checked into a suite and several other rooms. The hotel regarded her as some kind of visiting dignitary. Nobody knew her, but she was evidently a Woody Herman fan and came every night to listen. One night she threw a big party for the band in her suite and caviar and champagne were laid on. A day or so later the management decided to check up on who she was and when they did they discovered that there was no such person as Lady McGowan. She had run up a tab of $4000 and when it was investigated her luggage turned out to be empty trunks. She had played hostess to the band at a splendid party and was gone, to be immortalized in Burns's composition. ♭

Dave Lambert was hanging out with songwriter Henry Nemo one afternoon. They were short of cash, but Henry told Dave it was no problem; he'd get an advance on a song. He led Dave into the Brill Building. On the way up in the elevator, Nemo hummed a melody to himself. He burst into a publisher's office and sang him the song he'd just made up.

"How do you like it?" asked Henry.

"Love it," said the publisher, handing him a $50 advance. "Get me a lead sheet on it right away."

Henry pocketed the fifty and headed for the elevator. On the way down, he asked Dave, "Now, how did that go?"

Andy Farber asked Joe Gianono if he knew where the title of Miles Davis's "Nardis" came from. Joe was all ears . . . he was writing a chart on it, and had been searching for the source of the title for weeks. Andy told him, "Miles and Bill Evans were doing a gig together somewhere and somebody asked Bill if he would play some stupid tune. Bill said, 'I don't play that crap . . . I'm an artist.' " (He pronounced it "a nardis.")

A club date leader booked a wedding party and got a list of tunes from the bride. For the first dance she had typed, *Move*. The puzzled leader consulted his musicians and was told that *Move* was a jazz classic recorded by Miles Davis. Eager to satisfy his client, he found the Davis record and learned the tune. At the wedding, as they began to play the newlyweds' first dance, a cry of dismay came from the bride. Of course, what she had wanted was the pop tune, *More*. The happy couple had their first quarrel about the bride's spelling.

chapter 20

Goofs

Jazz musicians are adept at turning their musical mistakes into new ideas, but their nonmusical mistakes, usually called "goofs," are embarrassing for the perpetrators and a source of good stories for everyone else.

Count Basie told this one on himself:

Whenever it was that I moved down to 138th Street, I'm pretty sure I was already living there when the second Joe Louis–Max Schmeling fight took place, because I distinctly remember stopping by the Woodside to join the celebration on the way home from Yankee Stadium.

Here's my little story on that famous fight: John Hammond took me along as his guest, and he had ringside tickets. So what happens? We're getting settled in our seats just as the fight is about to begin, and I dropped my goddamn straw hat. It's rolling around down by my feet and I'm trying to pick it up. I'm bending down there looking for my hat so I can settle back in my seat and watch Joe take that cat apart, and everybody started jumping to their feet, hollering, and I looked up and the goddamn fight was all over. ♪

John Chilton tells of a golf game on Catalina Island during a Bob Crosby engagement there:

Matty Matlock was a keen golfer, but he was a much better musician. On one of his early visits to the Catalina course he managed to drive a ball straight onto another player's head, rendering him unconscious. When the cry went up for a doctor, it was discovered that Matty had knocked out the only M.D. on the island. ↲

Muggsy Spanier lost the little finger of his right hand in a youthful accident of some sort. Johnny Frigo saw a review of one of Spanier's performances in a Detroit newspaper that said: "Mr. Spanier can play more on the trumpet with four fingers than most trumpet players can play with five."

Frigo once played a fancy Jewish wedding at the Palmer House in Chicago, doubling on violin and amplified bass. His bass was plugged in and ready to go, lying on the floor next to Barrett Deems's drum set. Just before the ceremony of slicing the challah, one of the spurs on Barrett's bass drum slipped its moorings, allowing the whole drum set to roll over against the amplified bass strings. Johnny said it sounded like World War Three.

As he reset his drums, Barrett crouched beside his bass drum to adjust the spur. The host announced that the rabbi would now say the traditional prayer over the bread. Barrett didn't notice the microphone beside the bass drum as he muttered directly into it, "Fuck the bread, say a prayer for my drums."

When Bill Krinsky was twelve years old, he got his first job as a musician at a very small hotel in the Catskills. As he was about to go onstage for his first show, he noticed a sign over the door that read, "Positively No Blue Material To Be Used Onstage." So Bill went back to his room and changed into his brown suit.

At a White House party on Duke Ellington's birthday, President Nixon pumped Cab Calloway's hand with such special warmth that Cab assumed that the President was a fan of his. Then Nixon said, "Mr. Ellington, it's so good you're here. Happy, happy birthday. Pat and I just love your music."

Cab smiled and thanked him and stepped on down the receiving line.

Buck Clayton was on a record date with an all-star band that included some trumpet players for whom he wanted to sound his best: Charlie

Shavers, Rex Stewart, Billy Butterfield, and Yank Lawson. Buck couldn't
get his horn to play the way it usually did. He took out the valves and
cleaned them, cleaned out all the tuning slides, checked his mouthpiece, but nothing seemed to help. He played carefully and uncomfortably and got through the date somehow. Later he got a long bore-brush
and pushed it all the way through the horn, and out came a little mouthpiece brush that had been in his horn case. It had slipped into the bell of
the horn, worked its way around the bend and become lodged there, ob-
structing the flow of air just enough to cause the trouble.

Bud Freeman never made very many mistakes while playing his horn,
but Wingy Manone saw him make a different kind of mistake early in his
career:

> One time Bud Freeman came to my room at the Marie Antoinette
> Hotel. He was tired and wanted to rest a while. I was goin' out to
> walk my dog, so I told him to make himself at home.
>
> He asked me if I had anything to eat, in case he got hungry, but I
> didn't have nothin' in the icebox except some dog food for my dog.
> I told him I was sorry, but I didn't have anything to eat.
>
> When I got back I found a note from Bud saying he hoped I
> didn't mind that he ate the meat loaf that was in the icebox. Man,
> that wasn't no meat loaf. That was just plain dog food. I didn't care
> if he ate it, but my dog sure did.

Dinah Washington arrived at a party at a Manhattan hotel. She heard
music coming from an inner room and asked someone who was playing.

"Meyer Davis," she was informed. Dinah listened to a few bars of music
by Meyer's popular society band.

"Shit," she said, "that ain't Miles Davis!"

When Chet Baker first traveled to Italy, he was invited to a party in
Rome. One of the guests was Romano Mussolini, the jazz pianist son of
the Italian dictator whose life came to an ignominious end when Italy
was defeated in World War II. As Romano was introduced, Chet muttered uncomfortably, "Oh, yeah, man, it was a drag about your dad."

During his early days on the New York music scene, Chubby Jackson often brought scuffling musicians home to his mother's house on Long Island for a free meal. Mrs. Jackson was getting tired of feeding her son's hungry acquaintances. One night when Chubby appeared at her door with another stranger, she said, "That's it! No more bums!" and slammed the door in the faces of Chubby and José Ferrer.

Elvin Jones was hired to play at a festival with Harry Edison:

It was funny traveling with him. We had a contract to play a jazz festival in this resort at French Lick, Indiana, in I think it was October of 1959, and so all five of us—Jimmy Forrest, Tommy Potter, and Tommy Flanagan were also in the group—squeezed into this station wagon, and because there wasn't any room inside I tied my drums on top and we drove eight hundred miles non-stop through rain and hail—the drums out in it all—and when we get there we get the greeting, "Where have you been? You were supposed to play *yesterday.*" 🎵

Eddie Calhoun once played a concert with the Erroll Garner trio at St. Mary's College, across the street from Notre Dame:

I remember this very well, Erroll opened up with "Love For Sale," and I could have died, but nobody really caught on to the tune. Can you imagine him opening up St. Mary's College with "Love For Sale?" Man, we laughed about that later, I said,
"Man, how could you possibly have come up with "Love For Sale," and he said,
"I don't know! It just popped up into my head, and I played it." I expected them to stop the concert with all those nuns out there.   🎵

Always hoping to find a jam session or a place to sit in, Roy Eldridge carried his trumpet with him wherever he went. But if the drummer was tired, Roy was also able to take over on that instrument. Roy tells why he finally gave up on the drums:

I played drums a couple of times while I was with Count Basie in 1966, when Sonny Payne was late. Basie kept me up there, but, goddam, I could hardly play my trumpet when I got through with that. I don't play drums any more, and I'll tell you what stopped me.

There's a clarinet player on Long Island named Herb Myers, who used to be a policeman. Naturally, he liked Benny Goodman. I did a lot of club dates with him. He got a date playing for the policemen, with an organ player, a singer, and me. Gene Krupa had given me a drum set one Christmas, and after Herb got through playing forty minutes with the tom-toms going, I'd play a thirty-minute drum solo! I knew all Gene's solos, and everything went along nice.

We played about two hours overtime, and when we got through, I had forgotten how to tear those damn drums down! I'd been juicing and was pretty well out of it by then, but when I used to play drums as a kid, they didn't have stands like they have now. When I played with Gene Krupa, Gene had always set them up. So they were like a jigsaw puzzle to me. Man, I messed around there and couldn't get those drums broken down for nothin'!

"Come on, Roy," the man said, "we've got to close."

Eventually, he got a couple of waiters, picked up the drums just like they were, and put 'em in my station wagon. When I got up, and was sober, and remembered how to break 'em down, I put 'em away, and they ain't been out since.

Some drummers have arrived at a job, opened their trap cases, and discovered they failed to pack the snare drum or the cymbals. Even more pitiful is the traveling drummer who gets to the job and finds that the airline has sent his drums to some other city. One drummer piled his cases on the scale at an airline counter in New York and said to the clerk, "I'm flying to Los Angeles. I want the square case to go to Denver and the two round ones to go to Seattle."

"I'm sorry, sir, but we can't do that."

"Why not? You did it last time!"

Arranger Gene Roland was traveling with the Stan Kenton band. He brought his trumpet along and sometimes sat in with the brass section. Once he left his trumpet behind on the bandstand and only realized it after the bus was on its way.

"Why didn't somebody pick up my trumpet?" he shouted. "You know I'm not responsible!"

Gigi Gryce called Danny Bank to work a gig with him. Danny wasn't home, but his mother took the message. When Danny returned, she told him, "Jesus Christ wants you to work with him Friday night."

A similar mixup happened to Sonny Russo. His grandmother told him Mr. Mondello had called him for a job. Sonny called Toots Mondello, who said, "I didn't call you. I don't book any jobs, I just play them." Further detective work on Sonny's part uncovered the identity of the real caller, Mundell Lowe.

Sidewalk Stanley picked up a little work now and then helping drummers transport their equipment from place to place. He got his nickname from hanging around on the sidewalk outside jazz clubs and musicians' bars, waiting to say hello to the musicians. He knew how to set up a drum set and sometimes sat down and tried out the sticks. At rehearsals the drummers he worked for sometimes let him sit in for a tune.

When the old Half Note made its short-lived move to 54th Street in 1972, Ronnie Turso was playing drums there with his brother, Turk Mauro. On the way into the club one night they were greeted by Sidewalk Stanley. During the first set, the bartender sent Turk a message: "Stan wants to sit in." Turk shook his head. "Not now." Later, the same message was passed to the bandstand from the bar, and again Turk said no.

When the band finished their set, Turk went to the bar, where he was surprised to see a famous tenor saxophonist get up from his barstool, give him a dirty look, and walk out the door. It hadn't been Sidewalk Stanley asking to sit in. It was Stan Getz.

A few years later Hod O'Brien was playing piano on a cold January night at Gregory's in New York, with Joe Puma on guitar and Ronnie Markowitz on bass. The only customers in the place were three camera-laden jazz fans from Japan. A big limousine pulled up outside the window, and Stan Getz and a socialite friend emerged. They came in for a drink, and after listening for a bit, Stan got out his horn and sat in. While he was playing, the door of the tiny club opened and a guy looked in, casing the bar for single girls. Seeing none, he stood for a minute and listened to the saxophonist. Then he turned back toward the door. As he left, he said to the owner, "Well, he ain't no Stan Getz."

When Dick Johnson was chosen by Artie Shaw to front the new edition of his orchestra, Dick called a musical supplier on the West Coast to order individual music folders for the band. The young man who took

Dick's call was very helpful and took down the information about color, weight, and printing style. Dick told him to emboss "The Artie Shaw Orchestra" on the front of each folder.

Dick made two mistakes. He assumed everyone had heard of Artie Shaw, so he didn't spell the name. But the clerk was too young to be familiar with stars of the 1940s. Dick's second mistake was forgetting that he spoke with a Brockton, Massachusetts, accent. When the folders arrived, beautifully embossed on each one was the legend: "THE OTTIE SHORE ORCHESTRA." Dick insisted on keeping them.

Drummer Ed Metz, Jr., played some concerts in Germany with a traditional jazz band. Ed noticed that the printed program listed the title of each number and then gave a German translation. In one case, "Struttin' with Some Barbecue," the translation was so long that Ed asked someone to translate the translation back into English. It came out: "Walking Pompously Down the Avenue With an Animal Carcass Roasted Whole."

Pee Wee Erwin found a lot of work in the New York radio studios. He met a conductor there who was famous for his way with words:

One of the radio conductors I often worked with over a span of years was Al Goodman, who had been a Broadway theater conductor of some note. He was a very nice guy as well as an excellent conductor, but much of his reputation with musicians was based on his dry sense of humor and his way of twisting words. Billy Gussak, who played drums with him for an extended period, actually compiled a collection of Goodman's sayings.

I played the fabulous "Fred Allen Show" for some time with Goodman, then he went away to California for a year or so. When he came back he greeted the orchestra with the words, "Well, we've passed a lot of water under the bridge since the last session, haven't we?"

During rehearsal, if a musician said, "I think I have a wrong note in bar 12." Goodman would tell him, "Make an X around it." Then if questioned as to what the note should be he'd squint at the score a while and then answer, "Oh, I'd say that's about a C7th." ♪

Vido Musso was famous for his malapropisms. He was as illiterate in music as he was in English, but he had a quick ear and a powerful tone.

Pee Wee Erwin was with Benny Goodman when Vido was being considered as an addition to the band:

> Vido's sitting in with the band had created a lot of talk among the
> guys. He couldn't read music, but he was a tremendous musician
> with a fantastic ear. He could sit in a sax section and once over he'd
> have the arrangement memorized. All of this must have impressed
> Benny, so riding home with [his brother] Eugene one night he
> asked, "What do you think of Vido Musso? I'm thinking of adding
> him to the band." Eugene wasn't a musician, but he did his best to
> answer the question logically and honestly:
>
> "Well, Benny, he can't read music. And if he can't read, what good
> will he be to the band?"
>
> Whatever the answer Benny wanted to his question, this wasn't it.
> He got so sore he put Eugene out of the car and made him walk the
> rest of the way home. 🎵

Leonard Feather and Jack Tracy chronicled some of Musso's mangled
language while he was with Goodman:

> On long bus trips, some of the men would play word games to
> break the boredom. One of them called for a man to give the initials
> of a bandleader he was thinking of and the others would try to guess
> who it was.
>
> Then it came to Vido. "E. C.," he said.
>
> The men kept coming up with names like Eddie Condon and
> Emil Coleman, but Vido just kept shaking his head. Finally they gave
> up. "Who are you thinking of?" they asked.
>
> "Ex-avier Cugat," said Vido. 🎵

When Benny Goodman saw Vido puzzling over his part, he tried to
offer some help.

> What seems to be the trouble, Vido?" Benny asked.
>
> "It's not the notes I can't read Benny," came the answer, "it's the
> rest-es." 🎵

Carol Easton adds some more Vido-isms:

> The mysteries of the English language always eluded Vido, whose
> references to boats that drowned and Cadillac conversibles kept his

fellow band members entertained. Once when on the road with Harry James, he remarked, "If somebody don't open a window on this bus, we'll all get sophisticated!" And it was Vido who was once heard to observe, to nobody in particular, "Music is a very hard instrument." ♪

Art Rollini was on the road with Vido on the Goodman band:

He asked if he could dictate a letter for me to write to his wife Rose, because he couldn't write. I agreed and got out a pad and pen. He dictated, "Dear Rose, How are you? I am fine. Love, Vido." I addressed it and mailed it. ♪

Kenny Rupp was sitting next to Jack Gale in a New York trombone section one day, and Jack said, "I'm sorry to hear about your trouble." Kenny looked puzzled. "What trouble?" Jack said, "My brother Dave told me you might lose your house." Kenny looked even more puzzled. Jack said, "Dave saw you at Giardinelli's yesterday, and told me you said you were in danger of losing your house, and had to sell your trombones!" Kenny thought a minute, then grinned and said, "What I told him was: 'I've got to get rid of some of these trombones . . . they're taking over my house!'"

Clark Terry and his wife Gwen celebrated their wedding at a party that started at a country club near Dallas, Texas, and continued for a week at their new home nearby. They sent invitations to friends all over the country, expecting about seventy-five to attend. Three times that many celebrants showed up, and one of the reasons was the final line at the bottom of the invitation, which read, "BRING YOUR AXE AND JAM." Gwen told Clark, "You know, some people aren't going to know what that means." Clark assured her that all his friends understood the term. But he forgot about his new next-door neighbors, non-musicians, who also had received an invitation. When they arrived at the party, the husband was carrying a woodsman's axe and the wife had brought a jar of her own home-made preserves.

chapter 21

Pranks

In the jazz world there is a tradition of pranks, practical jokes, and general devilment. Most bands have had at least one prankster. Sometimes pranks become epidemic, especially on long road trips.

Jimmy Rushing never forgot one that Count Basie played on him while they were in Dallas with the Blue Devils. Basie said:

> Jimmy Rushing got in touch with a girlfriend of his who worked in a restaurant, and during a certain time of day he could go around there and get himself a free meal. I had been there and had seen him do it a few times. So one day while he was fooling around in the pool room or somewhere I got hungry and slipped around there and told his girl friend that Jimmy said he won't be around today and said for me to eat his meal. I ate my head off and cut out, and later on he went around there and sat at the table. She kept walking by without bringing him anything. At first he thought she was just busy and then he started wondering. She finally came and stood looking at him.
>
> "Hey, what you doing here?"
>
> "Aw now, baby. Don't I come here every day?"
>
> "Yes, she said, "but you sent Basie around here."
>
> "What?"
>
> I don't even have to imagine the look on his face. I know that bulb began to light up right there.
>
> "Basie was here and said you weren't coming so I gave him your meal."
>
> Old Jimmy came back and just sat and cut his eyes at me for hours, as if to say, "You dirty dog. You lowdown dirty dog." Then all he did was shake his head and walk away. But finally he had to laugh about it, and he was still telling about that until he died some forty-odd years later. ⤴

Buck Clayton describes a prank that took place on stage with Basie's band:

Earle Warren had been singing a song which was titled *I Struck a Match in the Dark*. So when Basie was preparing our show to be presented in the Paramount, Earle's introduction to his vocal on the song was doctored up in a something like Frank Sinatra style. Before singing the song Earle was to stand in front of the band in complete darkness and just before Basie was to bring the band in on the introduction Earle was supposed to strike a match which would illuminate only his face. We rehearsed the song until we had it down pat. The light technicians knew that they were not supposed to illuminate the whole stage until Earle had struck that match and the band was going into the introduction.

The first show that morning at the Paramount went down like clockwork. Earle had struck the match in the dark and it really was a nice intro to the song. But the next day Earle went out to do the song and as he was out there in the dark we were waiting to see the match ignite so that we'd be ready for the introduction. We waited and waited but nothing was happening. What really was happening with Earle was that he couldn't get those damn matches to light. He struck one and it didn't light. He struck another one and it fizzled out. Then he started getting panicky as the audience was wondering what was happening. Earle kept striking one match after another and not one would ignite. Somehow Basie dug what kind of trouble he was in and had the band go into the introduction without the lit match. Earle was saved from embarrassment.

Later I was told that Jo Jones had slipped onto the stage between shows and, when nobody was around, had taken the matches that Earle had placed on the stage as props and had dipped them in a glass of water. 🎶

Evidently the number was dropped soon after that. Harry Edison said:

Basie wanted a production number and Jimmy Mundy did an arrangement on *I Struck a Match in the Dark*, which Earle Warren was to sing. When the lights went out and Earle started, we were all supposed to strike a match and light up the stage. Well, when Earle made his introduction, Prez stuck a match, held his part up, and set fire to it! That was the end of that. 🎶

Edison revealed the real reason that Freddie Green didn't play an amplified guitar on Basie's band:

Freddie could have been a fine soloist, and was a good soloist at one time, when it became fashionable for guitarists to play solos. Of course Charlie Christian and he were very close friends, and Christian gave him an amplifier. But whenever Freddie would lay out of the band to take his solo, the whole rhythm section used to fall apart. It got to the point where we had to do something about it. So one night I would remove the plug from Freddie's amplifier and it wouldn't work. Next night Herschel Evans would break a wire in it so it wouldn't play, and Freddie would have it fixed. Next night Prez would take the plug out, you know. And that was how we did it. I mean, the band wasn't swinging.

At that time we had a group in the band called the Vigilantes. If there was something in the band we didn't like, we would get rid of it quick. [On Cab Calloway's band "The Bat" was blamed for such vigilante action. On Lionel Hampton's band it was "Barracuda." Ed.] So finally we took all the guts out of the amplifier. Freddie got ready to play one night and there was nothing there but a box. Naturally he got furious but nobody paid him any attention.

"Did you do this?" he asked. "No." So he reached the point where he said, "Well, to hell with it. I won't play any more solos." That rang a bell with us. "Great," you know. So that's the reason he's not a soloist today. He probably could have been one of the best at that time, but we had to sacrifice him for the good of the band.

Bobby Hackett also played guitar, but had no desire to be amplified. In 1941, Glenn Miller hired him as a rhythm guitarist and made him buy an electric guitar, which at the time was a relatively new instrument. Hackett carried the amplifier with the band wherever they traveled, but never plugged it in.

Xylophones and chimes were added to some early jazz percussion sections because they looked good on the stand and could add a little tonal color now and then. The drummers who had to play these instruments often didn't know much about them. Earl Hines told of Zutty Singleton's first xylophone, on Carroll Dickerson's band at the Savoy Ballroom in Chicago:

He didn't have but one note to play at the end of a number, but everybody was going up there to hear him play this xylophone. He had put a piece of paper on the note he wanted to hit, but during intermission somebody moved it, so when the band finished he hit a note completely out of tune. Everybody fell out on the floor, and he didn't know what to say. Zutty almost quit the band right then. 🎵

If a greenhorn on Lionel Hampton's band showed up carrying a raggedy looking suitcase tied shut with a rope, someone might remark, "Oh, I'm afraid Barracuda is going to get that suitcase!" If someone wore an old greasy baseball cap, heads would nod in agreement that "Barracuda will get that cap!" Sometimes little notes would be found attached to the offending article. "Barracuda is watching this raggedy coat." And, if the situation did not improve, before too long the offending article would either disappear or be discovered in such a state of total destruction that it would have to be thrown away. Any questions were answered in tones of wonder: "Barracuda must have been here! Oh, Barracuda got it!"

Joe Wilder remembered that Barracuda disposed of a couple of Lionel Hampton's loud hats. And one of the beat-up house slippers Dinah Washington was wearing on a Pullman car went flying out the window. Everyone told her, "Barracuda did it."

Freddy Martin had a few jazz players on his band in the 1930s. Pee Wee Erwin was one of them:

We had a drummer named Ernie Schaff, a real nice guy from Fort Lee, New Jersey. Once the band was booked to make a movie short for Warner Brothers at their studio in Brooklyn. Claude Thornhill used to double on vibraphone once in a while, hit last chords and such. But Ernie decided that it would be nice if it was made to look on the screen as though he were the one playing vibes. Well, in those days you made the soundtrack one day and the next you did the posing. Thornhill had played a beautiful passage at the end of one number and Schaff asked him to let him hit the vibraphone for the camera as though he had played it. Thornhill agreed readily enough, but then some jokester hid the mallets.

While the sound of the passage was being heard on the soundtrack, the movie showed Ernie looking for the mallets. 🎵

There were several pranksters on Duke Ellington's band. Barney Bigard recalled the tricks they played on each other:

Looking back, we did some terrible things in that band. Like one of the guys would be trying to sleep it off before the job in the band room and we would sneak up and tie his shoe laces together. We had a great big bell. We'd hit that bell and yell, "Fire! Fire!" and the poor guy, whoever it was, would jump up and fall all over his shoes, banging his head on the floor, with his hangover and all. Those guys would be so mad it would be way into the second set before they calmed down. We were like kids really with all that, but it seemed fun at the time. Of course, Duke, he would have been up all night writing music and so he'd sleep through the intermission in a corner somewhere. He never said anything about our crazy pranks.

Another time we put Limburger cheese and cayenne pepper on Freddie Jenkins's mouthpiece. He had a habit of leaving it on the stand before the show started, then putting it to his lips in the dressing room ten minutes before we hit. He jumped like mad. We took Artie Whetsol's valves all out of his trumpet and turned them around. Naturally his horn wouldn't work and he was there on the stand shaking it, and Duke just looking straight at him all the time.

The worst prankster of the whole bunch was Juan Tizol. You would never believe it if you met him casually. He always seemed so far above everything, but he was the ringleader of us pranksters. We used to play *Mood Indigo* and Tricky Sam, Artie Whetsol, and I had to come right to the front of the stage for the three-part harmony on the first chorus. It was a real small stage and the curtain made it even smaller, so the three of us were real close up, and Tizol burst a stink bomb right behind us. They had those Klieg lights up full and they hit us full in the face. We had no idea of something thrown in back of us. Pretty soon I started to get a whiff of this thing. So I looked at Whetsol, and Whetsol looked at me. I looked at Tricky and he began to giggle. This thing was getting stronger and stronger and the worse it got the more Tricky and I would be giggling.

Arthur Whetsol was always the "prissy" one. Oh, so sophisticated. He couldn't laugh if he saw a Charlie Chaplin movie. We had to give up for the laughing, Tricky and I, and went back to our chairs, but not Whetsol. He just kept playing a solo.

Afterwards we came to find out it was Tizol—and we ought to have known right then and there. We fixed him. There was a novelty shop in the next block so went out and bought some itching powder next day. We got to the dressing room early and put this stuff all in Tizol's tuxedo. All over his shirt. Everywhere. Hodges was in on it, in fact everyone in the band was in on it. I guess they'd had enough of those pranks and seeing how he was the instigator we were going to give Tizol holy hell.

We went up on the stage and the Klieg lights hit him. After half of the first number, and we were all watching him closely, the itching powder starts to work and Tizol starts moving around. When he started perspiring that made it even worse and after a few more choruses he was really going with that stuff. He couldn't make the end of the piece and had to run off the stage cussing everybody. He couldn't take it and it wasn't funny to him any more. That kind of broke him of that habit, and the pranksters in the band cooled off now the ringleader was off it. ⤵

Jimmy Crawford told a story about the Ellington band that Bigard left out:

When everyone on Duke Ellington's bus was sleeping, Junior Raglin would take a swig out of any bottles left where he could reach them. Barney Bigard didn't appreciate waking up to find half of his whiskey missing. He took an empty bottle to the lavatory and filled it with urine. He pretended to fall asleep, leaving the bottle in plain view on the seat beside him. Sure enough, Raglin filched the bottle and took a heavy swig. He looked up to see Bigard fixing him with a scowl. "Now, I hope you know what you just did," said Barney as Raglin, realizing what had happened, rushed to the lavatory to rinse out his mouth. ⤵

Cootie Williams remembered how Rex Stewart solved the same problem:

Rex had a bottle, a big bottle of whisky, in his locker. And some of the rest of the guys cottoned to it. They raided his locker when he was out of the room and when he returned he found his bottle was drained dry. Turned it over and not a drop left in it. Rex said nothing. He replaced the bottle next night with another. Only this time he mixed castor oil with the whisky. The guys found this bottle, too. Oh, what a time on the stand that night! ⤵

Limburger cheese seemed to be a favorite item in the arsenal of pranksters. Smith and Guttridge tell how it was used on Ben Pollack's band:

Dick Morgan [banjo] was also featured in "Boop-a-Doop" comedy vocals but perhaps his most memorable attempt was to discourage Ben Pollack's urge to sing. It happened shortly after Ray Bauduc had joined the band as a drummer. Pollack, released from the drums, was now able to conduct his men as he felt a bandleader should. Then Bernie Foyer took over as band manager. He conceived ideas which, if practiced, would have turned the band into a vaudeville act. Some were and did. But when Foyer persuaded Pollack that he might be a second Rudy Vallee, they suspected he was going too far. They were sure when they heard Pollack sing.

He sang through a megaphone in the then popular Vallee fashion. One night the band played the introductory chords, Pollack beamed, waved the megaphone, and pressed it to his lips. He broke into *I'm a Ding Dong Daddy from Dumas*. His smile vanished. He spluttered. Behind him the band romped through its well-rehearsed accompaniment with difficulty. Some of its members were convulsed. They included Dick Morgan, who might have been seen earlier smearing limburger cheese over the mouthpiece. ⤵

Eddie Condon was working in the pit at the Commercial Theater, on the far South Side of Chicago:

For convenience we took an apartment near the theater. When the wind was right we got perfume from the stockyards. One night Mezzrow dropped in and rubbed limburger cheese on Bud Freeman's pillow. All night Bud moaned and complained about the odor from the stockyards. ⤵

Eddie "Lockjaw" Davis discovered the devilish side of Don Byas:

Don Byas was helpful to everybody. Anyone that could play. He'd give you reeds, he'd answer your questions, direct. He didn't give you no tap dance, he'd just tell you. But he was full of tricks, too. He used to broadcast every Friday from the Downbeat. They had a bar on Sixth Avenue; between sets everybody would be around. He'd come in, see you with your horn.

"You wanna play the next set for me? I go on in about ten minutes. I don't feel so good."

I'd say, "Yeah, okay, sure."

"It'll be broadcast."

I'd say, "Fine, great."

And by the time you'd get there, start the first tune, you look up, he's on the stand next to you.

"Thought you didn't feel good."

"Oh, I feel better now."

He needed that inspiration. Somebody up there he could nail. ↷

Buck Clayton found himself on the receiving end of one of Byas's pranks when he visited Paris:

We had been invited to Pepe's home [André Persiany] for dinner. His mother was half Italian and naturally was an expert on cooking Italian cuisine. All the boys showed up and we were having one great time listening to records, telling jokes, and in general just enjoying ourselves. Don Byas was invited, since we were old friends. Madame Persiany cooked a beautiful dinner and we ate like pigs.

I went over to Bish [Wallace Bishop] and asked him what we could give Madame Persiany as a token of appreciation. Bish suggested that we give her a bouquet of flowers. So I went downstairs to the street where there was a flower vendor and bought a beautiful bunch of roses and brought them upstairs. Without Madame Persiany seeing me I went to Don and asked him to write out a speech for me to say, since I couldn't say that much French yet and Don could. He scribbled out something on a piece of paper and went in the bathroom with me to help me learn it. It began with something like, "Madame Persiany, we hope that you will accept these flowers for such a beautiful dinner, etc." After coaching me a bit Don left and went back in the room with all of the rest of the guys and I stayed in the bathroom and practiced.

Finally, when I thought I had it down pretty well, I came out of the bathroom. With everybody watching me, everybody smiling, I began. I said, in French,

"Madame Persiany, we have enjoyed this dinner so much that we want you to remember us." She was smiling and beamed as I went on. "We would like for you to accept these flowers."

She was still smiling at this point. Then I continued on with the speech until I got to his word that I didn't understand, but anyway I went on and said it. Then I looked at Madame Persiany. She was no longer smiling, her eyes bulged, she got red, and she had that awful embarrassing look on her face. Everybody else, especially the

French cats, looked at me like I was crazy or something. Madam Persiany left the room in a huff.

Nobody said a word and I got the feeling that I had said something very wrong, and when I looked over at Don and saw him laughing like hell I *knew* that I had said something wrong. Finally Pepe came over to me and said,

"Buck, we know that you didn't know what you said so we don't blame you for it."

Then, after a few minutes, I was told. I had said, "Madame Persiany, we enjoyed that wonderful dinner so much that we hope you will accept these flowers and stick 'em up your ass!" That one word that Don had added to the speech in French was "enculez" and enculez is a bad word. ↴

Shelly Manne and Al Epstein were the cut-ups on Bob Astor's band:

Al Epstein, used to be Al Young, played baritone, but he could play trumpet. He could only play high notes. He'd play baritone, and then at the end he'd grab his trumpet and play the high note. We used to do wild things. We were at Budd Lake in New Jersey with Bob Astor's Band at the Wigwam. Al says,

"I'll give you fifty cents if you eat that spider with some mustard!"

And you know, you do it! You'd do anything. One day he put iron glue in my hair while I was sleeping. My hair was long in those days. I woke up, and it was standing up like this! It was like that for weeks, I couldn't get it out. One night we got arrested in Budd Lake, we went out with the guys and had a few beers, we were just kids, and we opened a big truck that was full of ducks, let them all out. They put us in jail.

In Boston, I dressed up like the hunchback of Notre Dame, and I got the girl vocalist to make up my face. I was skinny and gaunt in those days. I stuck a pillow in my back. At the Copley Square Hotel they had fire escapes that ran all around the building. I found out what rooms the guys were in, they'd been playing cards or something, and I got out there. I think there was another band in there, too, with Al Cohn and those guys. Will Bradley's band, I think it was. I jumped in the window and everybody ran. I went in the bathroom and opened the shower curtain and there were three guys standing there, terrified. ↴

Lee Young, Lester Young's brother, worked a job in Aspen, Colorado, with Oscar Peterson and Ray Brown. He discovered that they were addicted to practical jokes:

W e're getting ready to play, and I can't find my snare drum. They had taken it out of my trap case and hidden it from me. Ray used to call me "Ripty," he said, "C'mon, Ripty, we got to hit it." I was really up a tree, because I couldn't imagine how you could leave your snare drum out of your trap case. They opened up with "Air Mail Special," just as fast as you could play it, and I had no snare drum. All of a sudden, here comes a waiter with a tray, my snare drum on it! ♪

One afternoon in California, after a golf game on their day off, Ray Brown and Herb Ellis were walking back to their hotel. They saw a sign in a drug store window advertising hair coloring that would wash out with shampoo, and decided to have some fun with their leader, Oscar Peterson. They took the dye to their hotel room and colored their hair, Ray's a flaming light red and Herb's jet black. Then they called Oscar and insisted he come over to discuss something important before going out to dinner with some friends.

When Herb answered Oscar's knock, Ray was sitting in a chair reading a newspaper. Oscar looked right at them and, without batting an eye, said, "What did you want?"

Ray said, "Don't you get it?"

"Get what? You guys detained me from my dinner. I'll see you tomorrow." And he left. Oscar maintained for a year that he never noticed anything unusual during his visit. "Now, that's control, isn't it?" said Herb.

Oscar wouldn't let his sidemen stay one up on him, however. After that, Oscar would secretly loosen one of Herb's guitar strings before a concert and then engage him in conversation right up to the moment they began playing. Or he'd pretend to be untuning the guitar without really changing anything, then would make Herb think he was out of tune by starting the next piece in a higher key than they usually played it.

On a Jazz at the Philharmonic tour of Japan in 1953, Oscar played the same trick on Brown, loosening the G string of his bass several turns and then distracting him with conversation while Norman Granz announced the trio and Ella Fitzgerald. When they took the stage and began to play, Ray's G string was so loose it didn't make any notes at all, just thwacks and buzzes. Ella gave him a dirty look as he cranked his string taut again, while Oscar and Norman laughed with delight.

Later, Ray went to a Japanese Pachinko parlor and pocketed a handful of the little steel balls that are used to play Japan's most popular game. During the next concert, as Oscar was on his way to the piano to accompany a Bill Harris solo, Ray reached into the grand piano and scattered the Pachinko balls across the strings. Harris announced *But Beautiful* and nodded for Oscar to begin the introduction. Every note Oscar played sizzled and twanged as the Pachinko balls danced among the strings.

Oscar picked the balls out of the piano with one hand while playing with the other. As he retrieved each ball he tossed it at Ray's bass. Bill Harris suffered through his solo, rather poorly accompanied. On his way offstage he whispered to Oscar, "One day. One day."

That day didn't come until the next year's tour, at the Rome opera house. Harris overheard Peterson agreeing to Granz's request for him to sing a number. When the trio went onstage, Bill gathered up a huge tray full of glasses and empty bottles and put it on top of a ladder behind the back curtain. Oscar started to sing *Tenderly*. Bill waited for the title word, then pushed over the ladder and ran. The crash was gratifyingly dreadful. Because the stage was steeply raked, the noise seemed to go on forever; the bottles and glasses that hadn't broken kept rolling to the footlights at the front of the stage.

Harris had run upstairs so fast that he was able to rush down again after the crash, protesting.

"Norman, what's going on? Don't you realize there's an artist performing out there?"

Granz was so furious that no one dared identify the culprit.

On another Jazz at the Philharmonic tour, the musicians were playing poker in the basement during the section where Ella Fitzgerald and her trio were onstage. There was a table in the theater wings where they would park their instruments as they filed downstairs. Oscar Peterson and one other musician who didn't gamble stayed in the wings to listen to Ella, and Oscar's eye wandered over to the table. He noticed that the mouthpiece on Dizzy Gillespie's trumpet had a shallow cup with a large bore, and that Roy Eldridge's had a deep cup with a small bore. He asked his colleague, "Shall we switch mouthpieces?" They did it. When Ella went into "Lady Be Good," it was a cue for the other musicians to return to the stage for the big finale. They all rushed up, picked up their horns and ran onstage. Ella finished her scat, turned to Gillespie and said, "Take it, Diz!" He put his horn to his lips and went, "Splatt!" Roy, quick to the rescue, said, "I got it, Diz!" He put up his horn and went, "Squeeeak!" Oscar Peterson didn't tell the trumpeters who had perpetrated the sabotage.

In 1938, long before special personalized license plates were available in New York, bassist Artie Shapiro managed to get a plate number that he and his fellow members of Musicians' Local 802 found entertaining: 4Q802. George Avakian took a picture of it with his box camera, but when he sent the film to be developed, instead of a print, he got a blank negative and a note from the photo lab informing him that it would not print obscene material.

Because of Bill Harris's conservative dress and dignified mien, only his friends knew what an irrepressible joker he was. Chubby Jackson said that Bill couldn't walk by a novelty store without buying something: a dribble glass, disappearing ink, a squirt rose, a rubber chicken.

By stretching a heavy rubber band across a crescent of coat-hanger wire and winding a large metal washer on it, Harris made a device that mimicked the sound of flatulence when sat on and carefully released. Al Cohn recalled:

> He'd wind the washer up real tight, and put it against a chair seat. After a while you could learn to control it—"high and dry," or any way you wanted it. He used to do it in an elevator. He's taller than anybody else, and he'd look around with disgust, as if to say, "Who did that?" ↴

There was a lot of good-natured horsing around on the bandstand when Chubby and Bill were working together in a small group, but Chubby got complaints from fans who loved Bill's ballads. Bill specialized in a passionate ballad style. People would ask, "Why can't you stop laughing and carrying on while Bill is playing so beautifully?"

Chubby didn't know how to explain that while Bill's perfectly serious right profile was toward the audience, his left profile was doing everything it could to crack Chubby up. Bill's left eye would roll insanely, and whenever he took a breath he'd stick his tongue out at Chubby and do a dance with it. Chubby tried, but he never could keep a straight face all the way through one of Bill's ballads.

When he was on Woody Herman's band, Harris had a little right-angle crook of tubing made to fit between his mouthpiece and his trombone. One night on his way to the front mike to take a solo, Bill surreptitiously slipped the crook onto his horn. This allowed him to play with his horn at right angles to its normal position. When Bill finished his solo he put the crook back into his pocket. Woody had been standing behind Bill where he couldn't see the gimmick, and he couldn't figure out how Bill managed to play with his slide pumping sideways.

Bill told section mate Eddie Bert that he wanted to have these crooks made for the whole trombone section. "Then we could spell out dirty words with the slides while we play."

Harris and Red Norvo got two life-size dummies from some dancers that had used them in their act. Bill dressed his in a Woody Herman band uniform and had it sitting next to him in the trombone section holding a horn. During rests Bill would argue with his dummy. "Man, come in when I tell you!" The dummy traveled as a passenger in Bill's car, riding three in the front seat, with the dummy in the middle. When they got tired of dummy jokes, Bill and Red faked a double suicide, pushing the dummies out of a hotel window.

One of Harris's schemes never worked out. He had seen vaudeville comics secretly slip special brackets mounted to the soles of their shoes over cleats that had been screwed to the stage floor. Hooked firmly to the stage that way, they would lock their knees and lean about at impossible angles.

Bill had Woody chasing all over Philadelphia looking for the guy who used to make the cleats. Unfortunately he had passed away. Bill wanted to use them to lean out over the audience while he played his solo on the romantic ballad, "Everywhere."

Mel Tormé was the object of a few of Buddy Rich's practical jokes:

In 1973 Buddy Rich had "fronted" a little club called "Buddy's Place" on Second Avenue and Sixty-second Street [in New York]. One night he cooked up a prank that was really funny. I had been playing the Maisonette. I called to tell him that I and a good friend, Rudy Behlmer, were going to come and hear his last show on Saturday night. Buddy seemed delighted.

When we arrived, the place was jammed. Rich, heading a sextet in those days, played a knockdown, drag-out set that left everyone breathless. When the cheering subsided, he made his way to the microphone, towel wrapped around his neck.

"Thank you," he puffed, holding up his hand for silence. A few people continued to stamp and whistle. He glared at them, then smiled. "I don't blame you. I know I was great."

More cheers. "I just want to take a minute to introduce one of my best friends. I'm really flattered that he came over tonight, after doing two shows of his own over at the St. Regis. What else can I say, except—Ladies and gentlemen, the absolute greatest—Mr. Mel Tormé!"

I smiled and stood up.

Not one person applauded.

Not a single soul.

Total dead silence.

My jaw dropped and my eyes popped. Ten seconds went by. I looked at the audience, dumbfounded. They looked at me. Then came a burst of laughter from every single person in the room and wild applause.

In that split second I "got it." Rich had pre-programmed the entire audience. ("Listen, everyone, Tormé's coming over. Now, when I introduce him and he stands up, I don't want to hear one single whistle, hand clap, or cheer. Dead silence, understand? He'll flip.") It was a great gag, and no one laughed harder than I.

Stanley Kaye, Buddy's manager, prevailed on me to play the club for a pair of weeks. It sounded like it would be fun.

Opening night, Rich was already knee deep in "shtick." I came to work to find all my clothes gone. Buddy, highly agitated, informed me there had been a robbery. The police had been notified; they were working on it. Meanwhile, I would have to go on, in front of a packed house, in my street clothes. Knowing Victor Venom's penchant for practical jokes, I shrugged and said, "Let's go." When his gag bombed, he immediately produced the missing garments and we got down to business.

I opened the 1975 fall season at Buddy's Place. Rich's juvenile sense of humor was working overtime. He had planned an elaborate practical joke that might have had serious repercussions.

Stanley Kaye and Marty Ross let me in on what Buddy had cooked up for me. He had arranged with a couple of his buddies, a pair of plainclothesmen from a precinct house, to come into the club just before the first show, pretend to be hoodlums, abduct me, drag me out of the place, up the stairs, throw me into the trunk of a car, and drive around town for an hour or so before returning to the club and letting me in on the merry "gag."

Only the angry, forceful intervention of Stanley, Marty, and Buddy's wife, Marie, prevented this stupid stunt from actually taking place. Had it come off, I would either have had a heart attack or I would have run amok.

Rich sulked about this aborted practical joke. He figured out another one for closing night. The place was jammed. Rita Moreno, then starring in *The Ritz*, had purposely rushed her show that night so she could come to my closing performance. Gary Berghof, of M*A*S*H fame and an amateur drummer, was in the audience. The band played its final set. Now it was my turn.

I stepped out in front of the orchestra and began to sing. Twelve minutes into my act, Buddy walked onto the stage and stopped the proceedings cold. Hands behind his back, he announced, "Ladies and gentlemen, I want to thank Mel for a marvelous engagement. [Applause] I'm particularly proud of him because he'd been dieting all the time he's been here. Tonight, closing night, I think he deserves a little dessert." Before anyone could stop him, he slammed me in the face with a lemon meringue pie. Not, mind you, one of those show-biz shaving-cream prop pies, but a genuine lemon meringue job that went way beyond my face. Women shrieked out in surprise and disgust as their dresses were splotched with whipped cream and meringue. Men were furious to find their pants and jackets suddenly fouled by flying goop. Buddy laughed.

I stood there covered in dripping lemon pie. My suit was ruined and so was the show. Twelve minutes into my performance, it was all over. (Why, in God's name, hadn't he waited, at least, until the end of the show?)

I went backstage, having to apologize to the audience for the shortened performance, and tried to clean up. The sink in that makeshift dressing room was one of those tiny affairs, and I simply could not wash away the gunk. My hair felt like I had doused it with a full tube of Brylcreem and, of course, my suit was a complete disaster. Buddy walked into the dressing room, patted me on the back, and said, offhandedly, "You're a good sport." That was it.

We held a post-mortem on Buddy's untimely act. Stanley Kaye, shaking his head in anger, said, "Jesus! Do you know how Buddy reacted when Marty and I raised hell with him about it? He pouted like a little kid and said, 'Okay, so we won't have fun anymore.' "

chapter 22

The Put-on

There is a form of teasing that is loosely referred to by musicians as "putting people on." "Squares," those who don't understand jazz and musicians, are natural targets for put-on artists. But insiders are not exempt. The first story is from Pops Foster:

> Papa Lorenzo Tio was a nice old guy. He was tall and drank a lot. One night he was playing for the Magnolia Band. He was drunk and sleeping through the numbers. He'd get the clarinet up to his mouth and finger the horn but nothin' was coming out. I got a broomstick, picked up his clarinet, and put the broomstick on his lap. He played the whole next number on the broomstick. When Joe Oliver got ready to knock off the next number he asked Tio, "Tea, you gonna play this next number with us?" Tio said, "I been playing all night man, don't you like my playing?" Joe said, "What are you playing with?" He said, "My clarinet," and took a look at it. Then he turned to me and said, "You did this." ♪

When bassist John Simmons was twelve years old and living in Tulsa, Oklahoma, he spent an afternoon at Barry's Park, where Oran "Hot Lips" Page was playing with Benny Morton's band:

> A lady came to the door and called me over.
> "Little boy, would you give this note to Lips Page?"
> I took the note up to the bandstand and announced, "Lady there at the door sent this letter to Mr. Warm Jaws."
> Everybody in the band fell out in hysterics, and Lips got mad. ♪

Years later John found himself on a New York bandstand with Lips. At the end of a number, John leaned across his bass and asked Page:

What note was that, Mr. Warm Jaws?" Lips whirled around and said, "I'll knock you down! I've only been called that once in my life!" "That was me!" 🎵

In Louisiana, Wingy Manone put together a band that left him wide open for a put-on:

I picked up Snoozer Quinn in Bogalusa. Me getting Snoozer for this band was the cause of a practical joke being played on me by Eddie Connors.

Snoozer only had one eye, but he could play a mess of guitar, and nobody ever paid any attention to his lamps. However, in the same band there was "Hooknose" Joe Loyocano on bass, with a cork leg, and me with one wing, and a few other cats with parts missing. Altogether I had nine men.

Connors laid for me, after looking those guys over. Things were rough, and we were in there at bottom scale. He was payin' me for just so many men.

So at the end of the week I went to get paid, and he handed me the dough. I counted the money, and there was a man short. I only got paid for eight instead of nine.

"Where do you get that jive at?" I asked Connors. "This ain't the right money. You paid me for eight men, and there's nine up there."

Then he told me: "Just look around among you. Among the nine of you, there's a whole man missin'. Here's your salary for eight men."

Of course, it was only a gag—but for once he had me stopped. 🎵

Quentin Jackson told of a spur-of-the-moment put-on with the Basie Band:

Dickie Wells noticed that Vic Dickenson, who had been up all night the night before, was asleep on the bandstand during a number. He shook him and said, "It's your time to play!" It wasn't, but Vic grabbed his horn and started playing before he woke up enough to realize it. 🎵

In 1945, a famous jazz critic interviewed Barney Bigard. To have a little fun, Barney invented some imaginary details about his early days in New Orleans. He talked about a jazz group called the Pelican Trio which supposedly played at Mahogany Hall and made some cylinder recordings. The writer published his new found "facts" in a jazz magazine, causing himself some embarrassment when the put-on was revealed. Many years later, Bigard recorded a trio album and called it *Barney Bigard and the Pelican Trio*.

John Chilton tells about a put-on that was devised by the Bob Crosby band:

> Gil Rodin [a better manager than he was a saxophone player] was never accorded any saxophone solos, and this in itself became something of an "in" joke. By 1940, *Down Beat* magazine had already started its policy of publishing transcribed solos by famous jazzmen. That year the band arranged that the magazine print a "special" solo by Gil Rodin, the first twelve bars of which consisted of a single long note. ♪

Chilton also tells a story about Matty Matlock. The Crosby band was playing at the Casino De Paree in New York:

> One night, while the band was accompanying a cabaret artiste called "Cardini," Matty began to feel distinctly ill at ease. He had totally misjudged his bladder capacity during the previous intermission's drinking time, and now urgently felt the call of nature. He whisperingly asked his colleague Eddie Miller for advice, but Eddie couldn't suggest any course of action. Suddenly, Matlock had a brain wave. During a piano solo he called quietly to Bill McVea in the trombone section. "Say, Billy, I was thinking of using that big mute of yours in an arrangement. Would you mind passing it to me?" The trombonist obliged, and passed a receptacle that was soon to bring relief to Matlock, who laid his alto saxophone across his lap to shield his action. At the next intermission, one of the big plants in the night club was irrigated, the mute was washed out and handed back to the trombonist, who remained blissfully unaware of his great humanitarian deed, but was always puzzled as to why an arranger should need to see a mute rather than hear it being played. ♪

Chilton describes another show at the Casino De Paree featuring the Ben Pollack band:

> An uncharming dancer insisted that he had to have a guitarist on stage with him for his act, one who could play seated at the top of a lad-

der, while wearing a sombrero. Nappy [Lamare] cheerfully obliged and raised no objection when asked to smoke a cheroot while strumming. The stage was dimmed and only Lamare's silhouette was seen by the audience, until he began puffing away at his cheroot with a ferocity that turned it into what Eddie Miller describes as "a fiery Roman candle." The band became convulsed with laughter, and so too did the audience. The only person not amused was the egotistical cabaret artiste. From then on he managed without a guitarist up aloft. Lamare was philosophical about the debacle: "Those damned cheroots were a lousy smoke. Give me my Picayune cigarettes any day." ♩

Bunny Berigan taught Al Rose a trick he used as a defense against jukeboxes:

Bunny's custom was to carry several packages of chewing gum in his pocket, not because he was addicted to the vigorous mastication of chicle. He had an even more practical use for the stuff. He'd put three or four sticks of gum in his mouth as we approached a boite with liquor in mind. Once inside, we'd sit at the bar and order our drinks. Then he'd excuse himself, promising to come back in a moment. He would walk purposefully off, to the men's room I assumed incorrectly. Early on I discovered that what he was doing was finding the jukebox, putting a wad of Wrigley's Doublemint through the coin slot, then pushing the slide in to assure the device's inoperability for at least as long as we'd be there enjoying our drinks. He'd return to the bar secure and relaxed in the knowledge that our ears wouldn't be assaulted by bad music. Later on I took to doing that myself. ♩

When Coleman Hawkins was with Fletcher Henderson's band, he practiced some subtle one-upmanship. Rex Stewart writes:

At that time, the only rival in the group that could come close to competing with Hawk for the crowd's favor was Big Charlie Green, an ex-carnival trombonist from Omaha, Nebraska. Green, a six-footer, was a beautiful instrumentalist with perfect command of his horn, and his playing ran from very sweet to a braying, raucous shouting style.
    Bean used to cool Charlie's horn off whenever he wanted to by saying to Buster Bailey or Don Redman, in Green's hearing, "Well, I guess I'd better call my old lady. It's not that I don't trust her, but I want her to know that I'm thinking about her." This remark never

failed to upset Green, who was a jealous husband, and when he got upset, he'd hit his gin bottle. As the evening drew on, Charlie's playing grew sadder and sadder. Yet, he never seemed to realize that Hawk planned it that way. ⤵

Artie Shapiro spent some time with Wingy Manone's band at the Hickory House on 52nd Street. Around 1937, Artie had bought a new car and wanted to try it on the road, so he invited his section-mate, Carmen Mastren, to take a trip upstate on their day off. On the way back, they got the idea of sending postcards to Wingy from every little town along the way, with a bogus name signed to each, praising him and the group for their remote radio broadcasts from the Hickory House. They filled the cards with all kinds of compliments, but when they got to Suffern, they wrote, "Dear Wingy, We're stuck every night having to listen to your stale imitations of Louis Armstrong. In fact, just like the name of this town, we're Suffer(i)n." On the job the next night, Wingy proudly showed them the cards he had received . . . but not the one from Suffern.

Some jazz musicians entertain themselves by putting on the writers that interview them. As a result, a number of articles in jazz magazines have carried phony historical items that were invented on the spur of the moment by the interviewees. The biographies of one or two of these fabulists remain permanently confused.

Writers who become "authorities" on jazz leave themselves open to put-ons. Charles Edward Smith had begun to develop a reputation in the literary world as a jazz authority, and Eddie Condon decided it was time to bring him back down to earth. Art Hodes tells the story.

We all hung out at Julius's Bar and Grill, which was around the corner from Nick's. That's where we got our mail, it was our country store, it was our library, this was it. Eddie Condon would wheel his baby up and leave her outside in the buggy. This is where we lived, part of the day.

Charles Edward hung out there, and was getting to be a pain in the ass to Eddie. Eddie's got a good mind, so he started thinking,

"What are you going to do about it?" So he set this up.

Smith came in one night, and Eddie introduced him to this guy who looked like a Russian. A little like Kenny Davern with a moustache. And a little hat.

"This is Vladimir Steenevitz, a great Russian jazz critic. And this is
Charles Edward Smith, a great American writer, jazz critic."

"Oh, glad to know you"

And the Russian says to him, "What do you play?"

And Smith says, "I don't play anything." And the Russian looks at
him and says,

"You wrote a book on jazz music and you don't play an instrument? In Russia, we shoot you!"

Smith got the point after a while because the whole bar broke up.
From then on, we got along very well with him. 🎷

A small inside joke mushroomed to a put-on of surprising proportions
when Gene Lees became the editor of *Down Beat* magazine in 1959 and
offered a job to Don DeMicheal:

I asked him to be Louisville correspondent for the magazine and
he began to send me tidbits of information about jazz activities
there. One time he included an item about the legendary blues
singer Blind Orange Adams.

Because I so respected and therefore trusted Don's knowledge of
the earlier forms of jazz and the blues, I didn't question the item.
When the next issue came out, Don phoned in panic. "That was a
joke," he said. "I thought you'd get a laugh and take it out of my
copy. It's a pun on Blind Lemon Jefferson! Jefferson, Adams—get
it?"

"Too late now," I said, and started to laugh.

Later I told Jack Tynan, the magazine's West Coast editor, about
it on the phone. And of course I told Chuck Suber [*Down Beat*'s
publisher], who found it as funny as Tynan did. We began dropping references to Blind Orange into the Chicago and Los Angeles copy, and among us we had the non-existent Mr. Adams
appearing at rent parties and other functions all over America.
🎷

DeMicheal eventually moved to Chicago as an assistant editor of *Down
Beat*, and the joke continued:

The career of Blind Orange Adams blossomed during those years.
Soon there was mail about him, and DeMicheal went so far as to
rent a postal box and to found the Blind Orange Adams Appreciation Society.

Blind Orange Adams was becoming the legend we said he was. One day I got a letter from a New York record label that specialized in folk music. They wanted to find and record Blind Orange Adams! I tried a desperate ploy. I wrote to the company saying that Blind Orange didn't trust people, and the only one he would deal with was DeMicheal. He would agree to do an album only if DeMicheal and I produced it.

One of my frequent companions of that period was the tenor saxophonist Eddie Harris, who used to sing incredibly funny satires on the blues. If I could seduce the label into going for it, I planned to record Eddie as Blind Orange and make the put-on complete.

But the company was immediately suspicious, and insisted on meeting Blind Orange face to face. I can no longer say with certainty what we did to resolve the situation, but I seem to recall that Don wrote a story killing Blind Orange off in a car crash.

Jack Miller had the orchestra on the Kate Smith show. Two of his musicians, Sal and Eddie, were close friends. Eddie had never married. His only companion at home was a dog. Eddie answered an ad in *Popular Mechanics* magazine for a device that would feed his pet while he was away from home. You put the food inside, connected it to your telephone, and when you called your own number, a tray of food would slide out for your dog. Eddie began feeding his dog this way while he was at rehearsals.

Sal decided to have some fun. He told the other musicians to watch Eddie the next day when he went to the phone, and the following morning he called in sick. He had a key to Eddie's house. Around the dog's feeding time, he went to Eddie's place and waited. When the phone rang, he picked it up and barked into the receiver. At the studio, Eddie's face went pale. He said to the waiting musicians, "The sonofabitch can answer the phone now!"

When Chubby Jackson put together his own band in the late 1940s he hired some of the coolest beboppers in New York and turned them into show-business extroverts. Teddy Charles, his vibraphonist, described the opening number:

The stage would darken, and an off-stage voice on the microphone would announce, "The Chubby Jackson Orchestra! Featuring . . ."

A spotlight would light the center of the stage, and a white football would be tossed out from the wings. The first musician to be introduced would run out wearing a football jersey and white pants, would catch the football and turn his back to the audience, showing his first name on the back of the jersey. The lettering on the front said, "THE HAPPY MONSTERS." Each guy would throw the ball to the next as he ran on, and the offstage voice would announce each name and instrument.

"And now, ladies and gentlemen, we are proud to present one of the handsomest men in the business, a most talented fellow, not to mention one of the *sweetest* guys in the music world, a really *swell* guy with a *great* personality . . ." and Chubby would walk onstage, still talking into a hand-held mike. 🎵

Sometimes the introductions that Chubby gave to his arrangements were longer than the arrangements themselves. His comments fractured the band so much that they often found it difficult to start a number when Chubby finally kicked it off. The audiences were sometimes mystified. To understand what the musicians were laughing at, one needed a working knowledge of New York City, Jewish food, old vaudeville routines, traveling bands, and bebop.

When Chubby took a band to Sweden in 1947, he was delighted with the enthusiastic response of the audiences there, but he couldn't resist teasing them a little. He would sometimes announce a number this way:

"And now, ladies and gentlemen, we'd like to yam out a little yazz tune written by Yay Yay Yohnson."

Harry Edison described the announcements he made when co-leading a band with Eddie "Lockjaw" Davis:

Something I usually announce when I'm at the end of every set. I introduce the musicians and then when I introduce my partner:

"He's one of the jazz greats, one of the giants in the jazz world and it's my partner, cohort, and colleague, Eddie Lockjaw Davis."

Then, when the applause dies down for him, I usually say,

"And of course, the gentleman I'm about to announce is one of the most lovable, adorable, sensuous, impeccable gentlemen you've ever had the pleasure of meeting. I daresay, without a doubt, he is the epitome, the echelon, the sine qua non of sartorial splendor. I have nothing but accolades for this man. As we say at the college where I teach, Yale University, he is the alpha and the omega, which is the beginning and the end, the first and the last. Ladies and gentlemen, the magnificent, the talented, the lovable, the effervescent, the magnificent, his eminence, Harry 'Sweets' Edison! (Laughter)

And I'm not fooling, either, because if you don't love yourself, nobody else is going to love you. (Laughter) 🎷

Stan Kenton once opened at Birdland on the heels of the departing Woody Herman band. Kenton's musicians decided to have a little fun. Pee Wee Marquette made the opening announcement, Kenton stepped into the spotlight and gave the downbeat, and the band went into Woody Herman's theme song, "Blue Flame." Kenton never batted an eye. He waited until they finished the chorus, and then announced,

"That was our tribute to Woody Herman and his wonderful band."

Pepper Adams was working at the Apollo Theater with Duke Pearson. Pepper would hang out with Julian Priester between shows:

We used to go out on the intermissions and sit at a bar just around the corner from the backstage door. People came in there selling whatever they happened to have that day: watches, billfolds, anything. Julian liked to talk to these folks, bargain with them. One fellow came in with a great big paint brush, about six inches across, that's obviously for house painting or some such thing, and he's trying to peddle that up and down the bar. Julian is bargaining with him; the fellow isn't getting anywhere with Julian. He turns to me and says, "How about you? Would you like to buy this?"

"Well, no, I do mostly miniatures, and little locket paintings, and things like that."

I got such a disgusted look from that cat! I did that primarily for Julian. I knew he would enjoy that. 🎷

French hornist Don Corrado met Merv Gold carrying his trombone case down the street one day. Merv said, "I just got a new axe. It's the best one I ever had."

Don asked to see it, and Merv proudly opened the case. Inside, instead of a trombone, was a brand new long-handled single-bladed woodsman's axe.

Merv stopped by the bar at the China Song one night with a small package in his hand. "Have you seen the Polish shell game?" he asked. No one had. He took out three small clear plastic domes and placed them on the table. He placed a peanut under one of them and carefully mixed them up. "Which one is it under?" he asked, owlishly. As the musicians laughed, the bartender inspected the plastic shells carefully, and then pointed to the one which clearly housed the peanut.

"There it is!" he cried triumphantly.

Merv and Pete Hyde were sitting at the bar of the old China Song one night when they heard a siren. An ambulance pulled up at the sea food restaurant down the block, and Merv went to the window to see what was happening. He sauntered back to his seat and explained, "Somebody hit a clam."

At the old Spotlite Bar on Broadway, Joe Harbor looked out the window and spotted Merv Gold coming up the street. Joe hurried over to the door, and as Merv walked in, Joe held out his hand and said, "Merv, you got something for me?" "Yeah, Joe," Merv replied, "here's the bread I owe you." With that, Merv opened his wallet, took out a slice of Wonder bread and placed it in Joe's outstretched hand.

A friend walked by as Merv was talking on a pay phone. Merv raised his voice and shouted into the receiver, "I can't talk now, I'm on the phone!"

Merv liked telephone jokes. While he was working on a Broadway show he had a stagehand rig his trombone case with a battery-operated bell that could be activated by a secret button near the handle. While standing at a bar with friends, Merv's case would ring. He would open it and take out a telephone and pretend to be accepting a jingle date from Radio Registry.

Merv hacksawed huge jagged sawteeth around the rim of an old trombone mouthpiece and had it silver plated. He had engraved on the outside of the cup: "SURE GRIP COMFO-RIM." Merv got a laugh from every trombone player that saw the mouthpiece except Urbie Green, who just slipped it on his horn, executed a few flawless runs and high notes and handed it back, saying, deadpan, "Not bad."

In order to pay the rent, Johnny Cresci found himself working regularly with a society band led by Lester Braun. The music was boring, so John looked for ways to liven things up. He noticed that, even though the band's first dance medley was always the same tunes in the same order, Lester, playing leader, always gave the standard finger signals to indicate to the musicians the key of the next song in the sequence. He always gave these signals exactly four bars before the end of the tune being played.

Knowing how many fingers Lester was about to hold up, Johnny devised questions that he would ask just loud enough for the musicians around him to hear, and Lester's hand signal would seem to be the answer. He might ask, "How many guys made it with your old lady last night, Lester?" just before Lester held up five fingers for the key of D-flat. Or, "How many balls you got, Lester?" just before Lester held up one finger for the key of F.

Lester never found out why his band always started the night in such good spirits.

At a taping of a TV show with Tony Martin and Cyd Charisse, bandleader Glenn Osser wanted to keep the audience happy between takes. He called "In the Mood." As the band began to play the Glenn Miller stock arrangement, Johnny Frosk whispered to Joe Wilder, "Joe, let me have the trumpet solo."

Joe nodded, and when the time came Frosk stood up and played the famous Bobby Hackett solo—from "String of Pearls." With Osser looking completely bewildered, John played the wrong solo in the wrong key all the way through and sat down with a straight face to finish playing the arrangement. Later he told Joe, "I've wanted to do that all my life!"

Eddie Tone was leading a club date band composed of Mel Davis, Carl Janelli, Ray Cohen, Buddy Morrow, and Bobby Shankin. There was a show to rehearse, and when the singer walked in, Eddie said, "I know this chick; she's going to be a pain. Let's put her on. Everybody switch instruments."

Each musician picked up an instrument he couldn't play, and they began to run down the first chart. Mel, at the drums, played a crippled roll on the snare and the band played the opening fanfare. All they got right was the rhythm of the figure. The notes were bleats, squawks, and crunches. The singer waved the band to a stop.

"No, no, it's too slow!"

Eddie said, "I know how to fix this. Buddy, you play the trombone, Mel, play the trumpet, Carl, you play sax, Bobby, play drums, Ray, you play piano, and I'll play the bass!"

Everybody switched back to their own instruments, and they took it again from the top. This time, of course, the music was perfect.

"No, no," said the singer, "It's still too slow!"

Gunnar Jacobsen attended the Flip Phillips 80th Birthday Party that was given by Arbors Records in Deerfield Beach, Florida, in 1995. Matt Domber, owner of Arbors, asked Gunnar to help Barney Kessel with his wheelchair after the concert. But Barney's wife said she preferred to handle the chair herself, and asked Gunnar to instead sit with Barney while she went to get it. While they sat together, a big guy came over and began fawning over Barney with statements about being extremely honored to be in the same room with him, and telling him he was the greatest guitarist ever, etc. The guy overdid his praise for so long that Barney was embarrassed. When he finally came to the end of his encomium, the guy said to Gunnar before leaving, "I have always admired Kenny Burrell's playing." Barney grabbed Gunnar's arm, shaking with convulsive laughter. The next morning, as Barney's wife wheeled him through the lobby on their way to the airport, she stopped to say goodbye to Gunnar. And she added, ". . . and Kenny says goodbye, too."

In a small town on the West Coast a young trombone player was working at an informal night spot with a small combo. He noticed that a couple of unshaven guys at the bar wearing old fishing clothes were laughing at his crude attempt to play Tommy Dorsey's theme song, I'm *Getting Sentimental Over You.*

"What's so funny?" he asked them. "If you think it's so easy, you come up here and try it!"

One of the guys said, "Okay," and took the trombone from the surprised young man. "Where do you blow, in here?" he said, and proceeded to play Dorsey's solo flawlessly. When the young trombonist expressed amazement, the fisherman said,

"Hell, anybody can do that!"

He called to his friend at the bar,

"Hey, Joe, come over and try this!"

The friend walked over, took the trombone, and repeated the performance. He handed the instrument back to the astonished youngster, and the two fishermen left the bar talking over the possibility of buying one of those things. The poor kid may never have found out that he had been put on by vacationing Los Angeles studio trombonists Joe Howard and Lloyd Ulyate.

(This story has been attributed to several other pairs of famous trombonists, but these seem to have been the original protagonists.)

Musicians often find work with bandleaders who are better businessmen than they are musicians. On such bands, the put-on becomes a form of occupational therapy. Ed Hubble used to work at a New Jersey club called The Ferryboat:

It was an actual ferryboat moored to the dock, owned by George Morrow. George was a trumpeter who could play for three hours at 150 decibels. He had iron chops. I've never heard anybody with chops like his. His highest note was a C concert, and he could play that continually for hours, louder than Conrad Gozzo, but always slightly flat. And then he'd walk away, smiling! *Winter Wonderland* was his specialty.

One of his strong points was lack of meter. He would go astray and the band would get back with him, then he would lose another beat and we would shift with him. It would get to the point that it wasn't funny anymore continually shifting, so all of a sudden we would modulate and be playing half a step higher. He would be playing in C and suddenly the band is in D-flat. It was hysterical—absolutely mind-blowing.

George Morrow had a phenomenal memory, he could remember parts of ten thousand songs, but he couldn't remember which bridge went with which song. He would go along playing one tune and then bridge from another, so it got to be a habit with us that when we got to the last eight bars, we would play a third tune.

It got so bad that we didn't tell anyone where we were working anymore. [Dick] Wellstood, with his sly humor, took a dollar bill and cut the letters "LOVE" out of it and pasted them on the piano right where it said "Steinway." Whenever anything went crazy, he would sit staring at those letters to remind him he just loved that money.

Kenny Davern was on that band, but only remembers how much he enjoyed having a steady job playing with Wellstood and Hubble. He said, "It was the best job I ever had."

British musicians have a fondness for the put-on. Ronnie Scott improvised a gag for the benefit of touring American brass players Clark Terry,
Bob Brookmeyer, Benny Morton, Doc Cheatham, and Maynard Ferguson. Heading across the border in a bus for some concerts in Scotland,
they pulled into a large parking lot and parked beside a shed-like building. Scott shouted, "Quick, everyone in a line!"

As the Americans lined up in the aisle of the bus, Ronnie made sure
they all had their passports in their hands. Then he led them in an or-
derly file into what turned out to be the bus stop café.

Eddie Thompson was trying to play a set in a very noisy night club. The
roar of conversation made the piano nearly inaudible. A few customers
down front were trying to hear the music, and one of them rose in righteous indignation. He loudly went "SHHHHH!"

From the piano, Eddie said, "I'm sorry. I'm playing as quietly as I
can."

Johnny Knapp once was called to sub for a pianist who had a steady gig
in a cocktail lounge. Johnny was reluctant, but his friend said it was a very
sophisticated crowd that loved good songs, and told him he could play
anything he wanted. John agreed to go, and when he got there, he found
a rather seedy looking room and an audience that didn't look all that sophisticated. He got up to the keyboard and played a set of all his favorite
obscure musical songs, with the verses included. The audience didn't
pay much attention, and when he finished the set to no applause, he
walked back near the kitchen door and asked the manager if he could
get a cup of coffee. She brought him one and sat down at a table with
him, starting the converstion with, "What do you do for a living?" John
decided to put her on a little. "I'm a toll collector on the Henry Hudson
Parkway," he said. She commiserated with him on the wear and tear such
a job must have on the hands, and John reassured her that he wore
gloves.

On his second set, John decided to try a different tack with the audience. He played tunes like "Four Leaf Clover," using double octaves for
the melody, and pounding his foot heavily on the floor. He was an im-
mediate hit. The audience crowded around the piano and begged for
more. At the end of that set, the manager came over with another cup of
coffee and said, "You were just kidding me, right? You really ARE a piano
player!"

Joe Wilder is such a perfect gentleman that it often comes as a surprise to anyone getting to know him that he has a devilish sense of humor. In its mildest form, it expresses itself in outrageous puns, but in his youth Joe was known as an expert in the administration of the hotfoot. Somewhere between these extremes lies his expertise at the put-on. He can tell you all sorts of whoppers with the straightest face imaginable.

On a record date for Lester Lanin, Joe started a put-on that nearly got out of hand. After a run-through of an arrangement of "Sweet Leilani," Lanin stepped into the studio and suggested to guitarist Everett Barksdale that he follow each phrase of the melody with a little rising arpeggio that he sang to him. Joe wasn't sitting near Everett, but he overheard their conversation, and so, when Lanin returned to the engineer's booth, Joe spoke into the microphone in front of him, suggesting to the engineer, "You know, it would make this sound better if you would have Everett play (and he sang Lanin's arpeggio) after each phrase of the melody."

Lanin was amazed. "You know, I just made the same suggestion!"

Joe couldn't resist. On the next number, Eddie Bert was playing the melody to "Lassus Trombone," and Lester came out and suggested that Eddie play more exaggerated smears. When he returned to the booth, Joe called in on his microphone and said, "Why don't you have Eddie exaggerate those trombone smears?" Lester still didn't catch on. "You won't believe this," he said, "I just suggested the same thing!"

Joe went through the entire session repeating Lanin's suggestions word for word. "I was putting him on so much," said Joe, "that I started to feel bad. But I just couldn't stop."

On the last tune, "Hello, Dolly," Lanin asked the whole band to sing a chorus, but wasn't happy with the result. Joe called in again: "Lester, what we need is for you to come out here and sing it with us, to get us in the right spirit." Lanin came right out and sang, and the effect on the band was wonderful. Marky Markowitz, sitting next to Joe in the trumpet section, was laughing so hard he could barely play.

After the date, the engineer told Joe that Lanin had said, "I wish I had someone as conscientious as Joe Wilder on every one of my dates."

Charles Earland's bass player got interested in playing extended solos with the bow. Charles let him go for a few nights to see where he would go with it, but one night he felt his bassist's explorations had gone on much too long. Charles went to the microphone, cupped his hands around it to imitate the hollow sound of a SWAT team bullhorn, and called out with deliberate authority, "Put the bow down! Slowly! Put your hands in the air, and step away from the bass!"

After years on the road with Woody Herman, Stan Kenton, and Harry James, bassist Red Kelly went home to the Pacific Northwest. He settled in Olympia, the capital of the state of Washington, and bought a bar where he and his friends could play a little jazz.

As state elections began to be discussed in 1976, Red and his cronies started a joke that grew into a grand put-on. Red decided to run for Governor. The ridiculousness of the idea spurred everyone's imagination, and before long they had made up a whole slate of candidates, chosen from regular customers, employees, friends, and family. Red said,

"There was a guy who was completely blotto who was in the joint when we bought it, sitting at the bar. We ran him for Lieutenant Governor."

"Bunko" Bob Kelley (no relation) ran for Attorney General, saying,

"Attorneys have done a bum job, so why not elect a non-attorney to foul things up?"

Red's mother-in-law, Lucy Griswold, ran for Secretary of State under the name "Fast Lucy." She said, "I'm going to give this state something it's never had; a Secretary of State who can type."

Red's pianist Jack Percival ran for Treasurer, promising to open up the vault "so everybody can see their money at work." Ruthie "Boom Boom" McInnis, one of Red's waitresses, ran for State Auditor.

Red's platform promised "to heal the continental divide," and to build "a giant Sindrome outside of Chehalis, where everybody can use it." He promised to improve the economy of the state, warning:

"Unemployment isn't working!"

The candidates formed the OWL Party (Out With Logic, On With Lunacy) and having filed the proper papers, appeared on the ballot. The regular politicians were furious, but the voters were delighted.

"Everybody we ran came in third," said Red.

"Boom Boom" was the biggest vote-getter, racking up over 40,000 votes.

chapter 23

Good Lines

This chapter is a collection of jazz musicians' pithy remarks, bon mots, etc., that have been remembered and repeated. Many musicians have a way with words. One of the best was Eddie Condon. He once inquired of a lady at a theater party, "Is that a hat or a threat you're wearing?"

On arriving at another party at an East Side town house that was decorated in an overwhelmingly modern style, Condon said to the host, "Quite a place, isn't it? Do you suppose anyone lives here?"

His most famous line was tossed off in reference to some criticism, which was actually rather complimentary of his work, written by French jazz critic Hugues Panassié. Eddie said, "I don't see why we need a Frenchman to come over here and tell us how to play American music. I wouldn't think of going to France and telling him how to jump on a grape." (For more Condon stories, see Chapter 29.)

Boomie Richman was also quick with a good line. While he was with the Tommy Dorsey orchestra they played the state fair in Reading, Pennsylvania, in 1945. On the bill was "Sharkey the Seal." His trainer put him through a large variety of tricks on each show, winding up the act with Sharkey playing "The Bells of St. Mary's" with his flippers on a large glockenspiel. He always got a big hand. Boomie wasn't impressed. He said to section mate Sid Cooper, "That's easy! The names of the note are on the bars!"

Boomie once complained about the difficulty of finding a good reed. "This last box of reeds I bought was so bad," he said, "that it squeaked in my pocket!"

Benny Goodman's band had been traveling continuously on a long series of one-nighters. At a roadside diner Art Rollini and Dave Tough climbed onto adjoining stools. Tough said to the waitress, "Bring me a cup of black coffee, so I can stay awake for the meal."

A young trombonist who admired Jack Teagarden's playing was hanging around the bandstand one night. As Jack prepared his slide, his admirer noticed he was using Wildroot Cream Oil instead of cold cream to lubricate the sleeves. Asked why he preferred the hair oil, Jack replied, "It gives me a fuzzy tone."

Benny Carter, asked about his experiences while following the irresistible urge to form a band of his own, remarked, "That sweet smell of failure."

Ed Berger heard the acceptance speech made by Carter when he accepted a posthumous award to Fletcher Henderson from the New Jersey Jazz Society's Hall of Fame. Benny said, "I'm happy to accept this award for Fletcher. Now I've just got to figure out how to get it to him without hand carrying it!"

Merv Gold polished his good lines and slipped them into conversation wherever they fit. He was carrying his trombone case down Broadway one day when he met a friend. Merv explained, "I've just been up to Juilliard to get my money back."

Trumpeter Burt Collins asked Merv, "How can I lose thirty-five years' worth of chops in two days off?"
Merv answered, "I lose my chops during an eight-bar rest!"

Merv was called to play a film date. The only note on his part was a single G-natural. When the date was over, Merv told the contractor, "Call me if you ever need G-sharp. It's one of my best notes!"

John Leone went into the pit at the Majestic Theater one night and came right back out again.

"There's a dead mouse under my chair!" he said. "What should I do?"
"Play taps," said Merv.

Dale Kirkland was sitting next to Merv in a trombone section. While warming up, Dale asked Merv, "What kind of mouthpiece are you using?" "It's a Buick," said Merv.

Merv often repeated the line Jack Benny once used on his radio show during an excruciating violin solo. Jack paused and mused, "If this isn't a Strad, I'm out fifty bucks!"

Jimmy Knepper drove up to a toll booth where a sign declared, "Cars 60 cents." He handed the toll collector a dollar bill and a dime. The collector asked, "What's this?"

"It's an intelligence test," said Jimmy.

Red Mitchell overheard a remark made by Jim Hall to a young musician they were playing with who seemed to feel obligated to fill every measure with as many notes as he could. Jim told him, "Don't just *do* something, *stand there!*"

Jimmy Dorsey listened to the way a new member of his band played one of his arrangements and told him, "Kid, you've got a perfect ear. No hole in it."

Lew Gluckin was on a job with trumpeter Red Clemson. He saw a lady come up to the bandstand and ask Red, "Can you play 'Beyond the Sea'?" Red shook his head. "Lady, he said, "I have enough trouble with the B-flat!"
Another customer asked Red if the band had anything slow.
Red said, "How about January and February?"

When Don Ellis had a band that featured arrangements in time signatures like 9/4 and 27/16, someone remarked, "The only tune they play in 4/4 is *Take Five!*"

Joe Puma was called to substitute for the regular guitarist at a rehearsal of Chuck Israels's National Jazz Ensemble. Chuck was rehearsing one of his own arrangements, which involved several changes of meter. Joe inspected his part and the time signatures marked 5/4, 3/8, 7/8, etc. He asked Chuck, "What are these, hat sizes?"

Puma dropped in at a small New York Club where Jim Raney was working. The club wasn't doing much business. As in all New York nightclubs, there was a fire department sign on the wall. It declared: "OCCUPANCY OF THESE PREMISES BY OVER 116 IS UNLAWFUL." Jimmy penciled neatly underneath: "AND UNLIKELY."

Wally Besser had booked a bar mitzvah party for a customer who asked for some jazz, so he hired Jack Wilkins and Milt Hinton. The guests were happy with the music, but there was the inevitable request for "just one Hora." Getting a nod from Milt, Wally started with *Hava Nagilah* and segued into several other traditional Jewish melodies before ending the set. When they finished, Milt wiped his brow and smiled. "Man, *Hava Nagilah* was cool," he said, "but you did the whole schmeer. When you do *my* gig, you're gonna have to play *Shortnin' Bread!*"

Arthur Godfrey had a group of jazz musicians as regulars on his daytime radio show. One day, after announcing that Johnny Mince would play a solo on the next song, he added, "And this is a song you wrote yourself, isn't it, John?"
"No," said John, "I tried to, but I just couldn't think of it."

When Karl Kiffe was playing drums with the Les and Larry Elgart band, the brothers were trying to get Karl to adapt to the band's style. At one point, Larry told him, "When the band starts to swing, I want you to play more on the ride cymbal."
Karl replied, "When the band starts to swing, will you please raise your hand?"

At a meeting of jazz musicians at Local 802 where the subject of grants and public funding had been raised, Pepper Adams prefaced his remarks with: "I'm all in favor of getting Grant's for jazz musicians. Or any other good brand of Scotch."

Marty Napoleon was leading a steady job with a small jazz combo. One night Lew Gluckin had something else to do and sent Bernie Privin in to sub on trumpet. Lew forgot to tell Bernie they were wearing sport jackets and straight ties. Bernie showed up wearing a tuxedo.

"Don't worry about it," said Marty. "You can be the leader tonight."

"Nothing doing," said Bernie. "If I was the leader, do you think I would have hired you guys?"

Joe Bennett ran afoul of Privin's acid tongue on one of his first jobs in the trombone section of a New York big band. Finding a solo marked on his part, he stood up and took what he considered to be a respectably hot chorus. Joe hadn't met Bernie yet, and didn't know his reputation for barbed insults. He quickly learned. As Joe sat down, he heard a steely voice behind him say:

"What a burnt offering that was!"

Privin countered friendly greetings like, "How are you, Bernie?" with curt rejoinders like, "Compared to what?" When a friend asked, "How's your wife?" Bernie said, "She's not exactly what I had in mind." Bernie sent Derek Smith a postcard from Russia with a picture of the Kremlin. Bernie's message was: "Here's the money I owe you."

Mel Davis tells of a trumpet player who had a question about phrasing a certain passage at a recording date. He asked Jimmy Maxwell, the lead man, "How are you going to play this?" Jimmy gave him a benign smile. "Beautifully," he said.

One night in Birdland, Frank Rehak was leaning against a pillar, sipping a beer and listening to the Basie band. He had recently shaved off a beard he'd worn for years. A young woman walked by, took a second look, and said tentatively, "Frank . . . ?" He looked at her, did a double take of his own, and said, "Oh, I didn't recognize you without my beard!"

Eubie Blake had a string of romantic alliances that began in his early youth, continued through both his marriages, and extended into his nineties. Al Rose asked him when he was ninety-seven, "How old do you have to be before the sex drive goes?"

Eubie answered, "You'll have to ask somebody older than me."

When someone marveled at his longevity, Eubie commented with a shrug, "If I'd known I was going to live this long, I'd have taken better care of myself!"

Specs Powell joined the staff orchestra at CBS on drums. Someone asked him the difference between a drummer and a percussionist. "Oh, about three hundred dollars a week," answered Specs.

Georgia Gibbs was bugging her drummer, Stan Levy, about the way he was reading the drum parts on her arrangements. She kept telling him, "Watch my foot, I'll give it to you." Or, "Watch my elbow for this accent," or "watch my hand, I'll cue you."

On one show she blanked out on the lyric of a song. Panicked, she turned around and whispered to Stan, "What are the words?" Stan mouthed the answer silently, "Watch my lips!"

Percy Heath, enjoying international success as the bassist with the Modern Jazz Quartet, decided he could afford the five hundred dollars it would cost for the split-rail fence he'd always wanted around his colonial house in Springfield Gardens, Queens. After the fence was installed Percy left for a tour of Europe with the MJQ.

Returning home a few weeks later, he stopped to admire his new fence and noticed something odd. All along the fence under the bottom rail ran a neat little pile of sawdust. Closer inspection revealed that the rails were infested with termites.

Percy picked up his suitcase and headed for the house.

"Five hundred dollars!" he said with a shake of his head. "Well, *bon appetit!*"

Bobby Hackett was offering one of his trumpets for sale. "It's a good buy," he said. "In the upper register it's absolutely brand new!"

Passing through Canadian customs with his luggage, Hackett was stopped by a customs officer, who pointed to his trumpet case.

"Is that a musical instrument?" asked the officer.

"Sometimes," admitted Bobby.

As Erroll Garner's manager, Martha Glaser, was preparing him for an overseas tour, she made an appointment for him to receive a smallpox shot. Erroll balked.

"The shots are required by the government," she told him. "Besides, you could get smallpox without them."

Erroll was unconvinced. "So how come you send me to places where I can get sick?"

Paul Desmond loved puns, word play, and spoonerisms. Marian Mc-Partland asked Paul about this reputation for dating beautiful fashion models. Paul said: "They'll go out for a while with a cat who's scuffling, but they always seem to end up marrying some manufacturer from the Bronx. This is the way the world ends, not with a whim, but a banker."

At the time that the sale of a certain Rembrandt made the front page of the *New York Times* because of the unprecedented sale price, Desmond made up this story:

Buster Keaton lived in a luxurious mansion in Beverly Hills. Deciding that he needed to economize, he put the house up for sale. It was worth a great deal of money, and there were few people in the world in a position to buy it, but he did get a call from Aristotle Onassis, who was looking for a California home. Onassis made an appointment to inspect the premises, and one morning was spotted by a news photographer while looking over the Keaton house. And in the paper the next day was the picture, captioned, "Aristotle Contemplating the Home of Buster." ↆ

After many years of traveling with the Dave Brubeck Quartet, Paul chose a title for the book he never wrote: "How Many of You Are There in the Quartet?"

A patron at a dance asked Woody Herman if the band could play some Jewish music. Woody said, "We have some arrangements by Al Cohn."

Woody and Jim Raney were walking up Seventh Avenue in New York when they met Artie Shaw and a beautiful woman he was escorting. "Hi, Woody," said Artie. "What are you up to these days?"

"Well, the band is in town for a couple of dates," said Woody.

Shaw, who had retired early from the band business, looked surprised. "Oh, do you still have a band?"

"Well, said Woody, "some guys dig ditches; I have a band. It's what I do."

At a rehearsal for a Dick Sudhalter jazz concert, Dick told the band to remove the hold mark from the last dotted half note on one arrangement. Everyone but the venerable Vic Dickenson marked their part. George Masso, Vic's section mate, asked, "Shall I mark your part for you, Vic?"

"No," sighed Vic wearily, "I wasn't going to hold that note very long anyway."

Don Leight was sitting next to Leon Merian in the trumpet section of a band rehearsing in Ringle's studios in the old Strand Theater building. Leon was a powerful trumpet player and had a tendency to play lead no matter which chair he was sitting in. At one point Don told Leon he was playing too loud. Leon pointed to the music. "It's marked *forte*," he said. "Leon," said Don, "You're playing *fifty!*"

On another occasion, Leon told Don, "I wish I could play in a section with four Leon Merians!" "Yeah, said Don, "but you'd all be trying to cut each other." "That's okay," said Leon, "I can play better than all of them!"

Ziggy Schatz was working in a trumpet section with Al Porcino. During a brass chorus the finger hook on Al's horn suddenly came unsoldered. His right hand flew sharply into his face, bloodying his nose. During the next rest, as Al sat there wiping off the blood, he looked at Ziggy and announced slowly, "No-pressure system."

While the Sauter-Finegan band was playing somewhere in Kansas, a guy came up beside the trombone section and asked, "When are you going to play something we can dance to?"

Sonny Russo took his mouthpiece from his lips and shouted to them, "When are you going to dance something we can play to?"

Jack Teagarden returned to Chicago after a job on the West Coast. He told a friend, "I wouldn't like California even if the weather was good."

Hampton Hawes passed along a lesson in humility taught by a New York State trooper.

By 1950 I was recording and beginning to appear in the jazz polls, but I haven't had much faith in polls since Jimmy Garrison told me how he had been stopped for speeding on the New York State Thruway. His wife got indignant and said to the cop, "You can't give him a ticket, he's the fifth best bass player in the United States."

And the cop answered, "Lady, the only difference from now on is he's going to be the fifth best bass player in the United States with a moving violation." ↷

When Eddie Miller was with Bob Crosby and the Bobcats, he checked into a hotel signing his name "Mr. & Mrs. Eddie Miller." The hotel clerk asked, "Is Mrs. Miller with you?" Eddie said, "She'll be coming in late tonight." The clerk wondered, "How will I know her?" "It'll be difficult," said Eddie. "She works for the FBI. Sometimes she's a tall blonde, and sometimes she's a short redhead."

Gene Lees asked Art Farmer about his twin brother Addison. "How do you tell *yourselves* apart?" Without a trace of a smile, Art replied, "When I get up in the morning I pick up the bass, and if I can't play it, I must be Art."

Bill Schremp, interviewing arranger George Handy, referred to George at one point as having become "rich and famous." George denied having ever seen enough money at one time to ever be mistaken for rich. Later in the interview, Schremp said, "So you now have become famous, if not rich."

George replied, "This is our secret, though."

Willie Ruff's stepbrother, Buddy-Boy Pruitt, went backstage after a concert by the Mitchell-Ruff Duo at the University of North Alabama in Florence, near Ruff's home town. Pruitt joined the crowd of well-wishers congratulating the musicians.

"Willie Henry," he said when he got to Ruff, "I never did know what you does for a living. But you sure does it."

Cannonball Adderly told Nat Hentoff: "A young tenor player was complaining to me that Coleman Hawkins made him nervous. Man, I told him Hawkins was *supposed* to make him nervous! Hawkins has been making other sax players nervous for forty years!"

Jerry Bruno, playing bass with Bob Rosengarden's band one night, noticed that Bob kept making a beckoning gesture at him. He pulled the strings harder, and Bob still repeated the gesture. "You want it louder?" asked Jerry.

"No, better!" said Bob.

Lou Gatti was the drummer at a wedding reception in New Jersey. During the first set the guests were paying more attention to the bar and buffet than to the band, so the leader said, "As long as nobody's on the floor we don't need to play dance medleys. We may as well enjoy ourselves. Let's stay with one tune for a while and everybody blow a couple of choruses."

The tenor player slammed down his horn in disgust. "Man, I came here to play a club date," he said. "I don't want to play any fucking jazz!"

Shelly Manne gave an interviewer his definition of jazz musicians: "We never play anything the same way once."

When Buddy Rich checked into a hospital, the admitting nurse who filled out his admission form asked if he was allergic to anything. "Country and Western music," said Buddy.

Bob Brookmeyer's father was being rushed to the hospital after a paralyzing stroke that eventually ended his life. As he lay on an ambulance stretcher in the entry to the emergency room, the admitting nurse plodded through an interminable amount of formalities and paper work. Finally, she leaned solicitously over the stretcher and asked, "And now, Mr. Brookmeyer, what are you in here for?"

Mr. Brookmeyer, barely able to speak, croaked, "Burglary."

Reedman Hawky Cogan ordered dinner at Joe Harbor's Bar one evening and then realized he was sitting next to Dizzy Gillespie. After they had chatted for a few minutes, Boris Malina stopped by Hawky's table on his way out. Boris started a conversation in Yiddish, and a few courtesies passed back and forth in that language as Dizzy looked on. Just as Boris left, the waiter arrived with Hawky's order, the chef's specialty, smothered pork chops. Dizzy eyed the chops, then looked appraisingly at Hawky. "You must be one of them *jive* Jews!"

Bill Rohdin was traveling with Maynard Ferguson's band somewhere in the Midwest. Maynard had chartered a couple of Cessna airplanes to get the band and its equipment to a job, and they hit some stormy weather that was really tossing the band's small plane around. Maynard stood up and announced, "I'm going to sleep, but if you see Glenn Miller, please wake me."

At the memorial service for bassist Al Hall, Jimmy Butts told the congregation about his departed friend:

Al noticed when I started adding things to my repertoire. When I started singing, he would call, "Here comes Jimmy Butts, the singer," when I walked in to a club where he was playing. Then, when I started dancing, it was, "Here comes Jimmy Butts, the dancer." One time he called out, "Here comes Jimmy Butts, the singer, dancer, comedian, emcee."

I said, what about Jimmy Butts, the bass player? He replied, "I said, Jimmy Butts, the singer, dancer, comedian, emcee!"

So I picked up his bass, played a few bars of a Jimmy Blanton solo, and said, "How about that?" Al counted again on his fingers. "I said, Jimmy Butts, the singer, dancer, comedian, emcee!"

A little while after that I was at a big party. Al was playing in the band, but he really had eyes to join his friends at the party, so when he saw me, he said, "Say, Jimmy Butts, are you going to come up and play a little?"

I looked at him and said, "I'm Jimmy Butts, the singer, dancer, comedian, emcee!" ↴

On being nominated for but denied a Pulitzer Prize at age sixty, Duke Ellington commented to the inquiring reporters: "I guess the good Lord didn't want me to become famous too young."

James Shacter tells of an unusual interview with pianist Ralph Sutton:

After the concert in Pocatello, Idaho, a local jockey came backstage with a tape recorder to interview the musicians. Ralph says the man turned out to be a know-it-all and asked the usual questions, such as, "How old were you when you started piano lessons?" The conversation then went something like this:

"You call yourselves the World's Greatest Jazzband?"

"Yes," Ralph replied.

"Isn't that a bit pretentious?" the d.j. asked.

"Oh, I don't know," said Ralph. "After all, a name is meant to describe something that group does or can do. In our case, we do it better than anyone else in the world."

"I see," said the d.j.

"Now, we *did* have another name for the band," Ralph went on, "but we decided not to use it."

"What was that?" asked the d.j.

"Well," Ralph said, "we *were* going to call ourselves the Sheep Fuckers, but we decided not to."

Ralph never saw a tape recorder turned off so quickly. ↴

That name, "The World's Greatest Jazzband," was always causing trouble. At a country club in Oklahoma City, a lady asked if they were what their name declared. Bud Freeman said they were.

"Then you must be Benny Goodman."

"Yes, I am."

"But I thought you were dead!"

"Yes, I am," said Bud, and walked away.

Bernie Glow was acknowledged for many years by most other trumpet players as the best lead man in New York. Besides his superior musicianship, his sunny nature was greatly appreciated by the musicians he played with. On a studio date one day, one of his section mates was wondering aloud why a certain contractor didn't call him any more.

"I hope I haven't offended him somehow."

Bernie told him, "I never worry about that sort of thing. I figure, if they don't want the best, then the hell with them!"

"Boy," said his friend, "I wish I could feel that way."

"No, you can't feel that way," smiled Bernie, "you're not the best!"

Bill Berry was on Woody Herman's Herd in 1957, when the music business was in a period of sparse demand for jazz bands. They played a lot of debutante balls and weddings, rarely appearing in a jazz club. Bill dubbed that band "The Un-Herd."

Berry once needed a bass player for a last-minute job he had booked and couldn't find anyone in Southern California who wasn't busy. After calling everyone he could think of, he begged Ray Brown to bail him out. Ray agreed to do him the favor. When Ray showed up at the club, the owner was amazed. He asked Berry, "Isn't that Ray Brown?"

Bill shrugged helplessly. "I couldn't get anyone else!"

Bernie Fleischer was on the road with the Baja Marimba Band in the late 1960s. They stayed in an Akron, Ohio, hotel where Stan Kenton's band was also staying:

> After the job that night, we all got together in someone's room for a nightcap. On the radio a disk jockey was playing some Woody Herman records. We couldn't decide which of Woody's herds we were listening to, so we decide to try to identify the drummer as a clue to the year the records were made. "It's not Don Lamond," someone said. "Is it Shelly Manne, or Jake Hanna?" Lee Katzman listened for a minute and said, "It must be Shelly, 'cause Jake don't jam like that!"

Pepper Adams describes an afternoon he spent with Thelonious Monk:

One time he and Doug Watkins and I are hanging out together, and he had a test pressing of a solo album that he had made. None of us had heard it before, so we went to Doug's and played it on his phonograph. We were sitting there listening to it. Monk looks up and says, "That's a good record. You could give that to your grandmother."

I said, "You couldn't give it to my grandmother. She's a Bud Powell fan." And he just kind of glared at me and then went back to listening to the music again. I don't think he understood joking very much. 🎵

Pete Barbutti is a comedian who makes musicians laugh because, a musician himself, he understands their special humor. One of his best routines is of a cool musician whose instrument is a broom. Exuding hipness at every pore, Pete takes out his broom and announces that he will play *Tenderly*. Then, with great artistic sensitivity, he sweeps the broom across the microphone in the recognizable pattern of the melody while the band plays a lush accompaniment. On the second chorus he sticks a cup mute in the broom.

One night at a club in Indiana, Pete began this routine but couldn't find his broom. He sent the whole band on a broom hunt. One of the musicians found an industrial vacuum cleaner in a closet and brought it to the bandstand to see how Pete would react. Pete inspected it with disdain, "No, man, I don't play Fender broom."

Red Kelly made a sign for the bandstand at his Tacoma nightclub, "Go someplace else and get discovered, and then come here."

Monty Budwig's wife Arlette came up with a motto that might look good on a line of T-shirts: "So many drummers, so little time."

Bill Vaccaro was a successful lead trumpeter in New York for many years. When work got slow he began fixing up apartment houses and reselling them, and eventually found himself out of music and in the construction business. Bill Moriarty asked him if he found his new work satisfying.

"Yes," said Vaccaro. "I nail up a wall, and tomorrow it's still there. It's not like a high F."

When Dave McKenna reached the point in his life that often comes to those who love large quantities of food and drink, his doctor gave him strict orders to lay off rich foods and alcohol. Dave listened glumly, and afterwards he told Zoot Sims's wife Louise, "I suppose if I do what he says I'll live longer. But, how will I know for sure?"

English jazz saxophonist and clubowner Ronnie Scott was well known for his sense of humor. At his club, Ronnie loved to lay funny lines on his audience. When the audience was small, he would announce the opening tune, "Tea for One." If the audience was unresponsive, he'd suggest they join hands and try to contact the living. Or he might tell them, "You've just made a happy man very old."

During an interview in London, Dexter Gordon jokingly accused Ronnie Scott of playing "all that free shit." Scott denied it: "I don't play free. I play very *cheaply*, but I don't play free."

Brew toured in the south of Sweden with Rolf Ericson, Lars Gullin and pianist Lars Sjösten. In the small village of Hultsfred they rehearsed in the afternoon. On one tune the drummer had a problem with the tempo, and Brew was not happy. After dinner, they went back, and the drummer began to hammer some nails in the stage floor so the bass drum wouldn't slide. Brew called across the stage, "That's right! Now you've got it! That's the right tempo!"

Brew's last recording was taped at the Stampen Club in Stockholm in 1971. An announcement he made was included on the Storyville album, *No More Brew*. Over the clamor of background conversation at the tables, Brew says: "We'd like to ask your indulgence once again, now. Probably the audience has turned over, and nobody's listening anyway. But if I said 'motherfucker,' probably everybody would hear it."

Evidently nobody heard it. There is no response from the audience, which continues to chatter. Brew resignedly announces the next tune and continues to play for his "listeners."

Herb Gardner tells about a cornet player who, during a rendition of Louis Armstrong's "Dippermouth Blues," was attempting to play what Louis had played on the original recording, with limited success. There is a break on the record during which someone shouts, "Oh, play that thing!" When Herb's struggling cornet player made that break, someone in the band shouted, "Oh learn that thing!"

Joe Pellicane remembered a New Year's Eve with Georgie Auld's band. After midnight, the band took a break. In the men's lounge Joe ran into the band's baritone saxist, Serge Chaloff. Joe said, "Serge, Happy New Year." Serge replied, "I'm hip."

Jack Sheldon wrote the beginning of what he calls the Hollywood Blues: "Woke up this mornin' and both my cars were gone . . ."

One bandstand wit declared: There are three kinds of musicians. Those that can count, and those that can't.

On a gig, guitarists Joe Beck and John Abercrombie were talking about food. John said, "I'm on the Atkins diet now." "Really?" said Joe. "Yeah," said John, "the Chet Atkins diet. I just pick."

Joe Beck played a studio date on which the conductor soon revealed an extremely high level of incompetence. Sitting at the drum set behind Joe, Grady Tate muttered, "This cat couldn't conduct if they wrapped him in copper wire!"

Joe Temperley remembered a gig with Woody Herman's band, playing a one-nighter at Notre Dame. The band was tired from traveling, and wasn't having one of its better nights. At one point during the evening, Woody stopped and sniffed the air suspiciously. "Something's burning," he said. Sal Nistico muttered to Joe, "It ain't the band!"

At Bourbon Street, a jazz club in Toronto, Barney Kessel finished a set and stood, holding his guitar, while chatting with some fans in the audience. A lady said, I love your guitar . . . it has such a beautiful tone."
Barney laid the guitar down on his chair and asked the lady,
"How does it sound now?"

Bobby Shankin attended the Red Rodney memorial service at St. Peter's Church in New York. Before going in, he stood out in front and chatted with several friends who had congregated on the sidewalk. As they stood there, they saw Gene Bertoncini approaching, walking with a lovely young woman who he evidently had just met. Gene led her over to Bobby and said, "Bob, I'm glad to see you. Will you please tell this young lady how I earn my living?" Bob told her, "Well, he's one of the great jazz guitarists of all time. And I have no idea how he earns his living!"

At a jazz club in Peekskill, Carmen Leggio got his tenor out of its case and twisted his mouthpiece onto the neck, then discovered that the good reed he'd been using for several weeks had come to the end of its road. He reluctantly tossed it aside and put on a new one. As he tightened his ligature and got ready to play, he looked at the new reed and said, "This is like going on a blind date."

At a rehearsal of Bill Whited's band in the Local 802 Club Room, Leggio told Ronnie Zito, "I've got call waiting now. I sit by the phone and wait for a call!"

When Joe Bushkin was asked, "How've you been feeling?" he said, "Well, I wasn't sleeping so well there for a while, so I saw my doctor and he gave me some pills. I took one, and I had a dream about Buddy Rich! I called the doctor back the next morning and told him I wasn't taking any more of his damn pills!"

During the last years of his life, in Florida, jazz saxophonist Allen Eager sometimes listed himself as Allen Reluctant.

Bob Millikan was sitting in the trumpet section of the Dick Meldonian–Sonny Igoe band at a rehearsal in New Jersey. He had just finished playing lead on a couple of lip-busting arrangements. Meldonian asked from the front of the band, "What number would you like me to call, Bob?" Bob rubbed his lip and answered, "911!"

On a gig with the Meldonian–Igoe band, the comedian Charlie Callas was on the bill. Charlie was a drummer before he became a stand-up comic, and he likes to sit in whenever the opportunity pre-sents itself. Sonny stepped aside and let Charlie take over his drums as Dick called the next tune. During the number, Sonny's understanding of that arrangement was sorely missed. When the end mercifully came, there was a moment of silence. Then trumpeter Charlie Camilleri announced, "Better than Mickey Rooney, not as good as Mel Tormé!"

Manny, of Manny's Music on West 48th Street, used to throw a party at his country club every year for some of the recording musicians who frequented his store. They would take a golf lesson before the match, and would look good off the first tee, but by the last hole everyone would be playing a pretty raggedy game. One year Clark Terry was in a foursome with Milt Hinton, Osie Johnson, and Tyree Glenn. On one drive, Osie's ball went into the woods. He went after it and was gone a long time. As the other three golfers proceeded up the fairway, they heard crashing noises in the woods and went to see what was up. Through the trees they spotted Osie, thrashing away at his ball, which was in a terrible lie. Tyree sneaked up behind him as Osie whiffed again, and whispered, "That's twelve, muthafucka!"

Oscar Peterson and his trio operated a music school for a while in Toronto. When the trio, with Ray Brown and Ed Thigpen, appeared at a local jazz room, Bernie Black, one of Peterson's students, was hired as the intermission pianist. One night, as Black stepped to the piano for his first set, a customer said to him, "Mr. Peterson, I love your playing. I have all of your records. I came all the way from northern Ontario to hear you." Ray Brown, sitting at a nearby table, called out, "Wait'll you hear the relief trio!"

Sheila Jordan received the 2004 Lil Hardin Armstrong Jazz Heritage Award at the International Association of Jazz Educators conference in New York. She participated in a panel called "Singing for Our Supper: Vocalists in the Jazz Marketplace." Jordan quipped: "For most of my career I've been singing for snacks."

Tim Ouimette, flying from Kennedy airport shortly after the 9/11 disaster, knew that security would be tight, but he was surprised to have his bags looked through by three different agents on the way to the plane. Just before boarding, another suspicious agent pointed the trumpet bag Tim was carrying and demanded, "Is there anything sharp in there?" "Yeah," replied Tim, "a trumpet!"

When the New Jersey Jazz Society gave their Pee Wee Russell Award to Ruby Braff, Terry Ripmaster, president of the Society, called Ruby to arrange for the presentation. He waited until 11 a.m. to call, in consideration of the hours that jazz musicians work, but discovered he hadn't waited long enough. Ruby, obviously aroused from sleep, answered the phone grouchily: "Don't you know this is midnight for me?" On another day, Ruby was awakened at 10 a.m. by the ringing of his doorbell. He shuffled to the door and asked grumpily, "Who is it?" A voice answered, "It's the Jehovah's Witnesses." Ruby shouted, "The only witness I want to hear at ten o'clock in the morning is Sam Butera!"

Don Robertson, the drummer and editor emeritus of the Jersey Jazz Society newsletter, was approached at a concert by a lady who said, "I want to know how old Dick Hyman is." Never wanting to get into personal details, he fended her off with: "Old Dick Hyman is fine."

When Richard Nixon finished his term as Eisenhower's vice president, he was a frequent guest of Johnny Carson's on the *Tonight Show*. In those days it was still a New York gig. One night, the band played a number that featured Clark Terry, one of the few black NBC staff musicians. Carson mistakenly introduced Clark to Nixon as "Terry Klein." Clark quipped, "Please don't call me that . . . I won't be able to play golf *anywhere!*"

Herb Gardner thinks he knows why the Democrats lost the 2004 presidential election. "They sent rock bands to the swing states!"

chapter 24

Nicknames

The private names that jazz musicians give each other sometimes become well known to their public, but the logic behind a name is not always evident. Some nicknames were invented by childhood friends and lasted a lifetime. The most common of these are descriptive, or in-reverse descriptive. Fats Waller was fat, Shorty Baker short, and Chubby Jackson chubby, but Tiny Kahn was huge and Pee Wee Russell was tall.

Names like Slim (Bulee Gaillard), Brick (Jacob Fleagle), Rusty (Lyle Dedrick), Red (Keith Mitchell), Whitey (Gordon Mitchell), Dizzy (John Birks Gillespie), Specs (Gordon Powell), Cleanhead (Eddie Vinson), and Dodo (Michael Marmarosa) are fairly self-explanatory, as are home-town labels like Tex (Herschel Evans), Kansas (Carl Fields), Bama (Carl Warwick), and Philly (Joe Jones). Names like Satchelmouth or Gate-mouth (Louis Armstrong), Nappy (Hilton Lamare), Jughead (Gene Ammons), Foots (Walter Thomas), Shadow (Rossiere Wilson), Big-Eye (Louis Nelson), and Bags (Milt Jackson) came from the friendly tradition of humorous insults that exaggerate physical characteristics. In the black culture, light skin pigmentation was sometimes called red, hence Henry "Red" Allen, George "Red" Callender, and Red Young, as Lester Young was known in his youth.

Animal names often arose from a resemblance, actual or figurative: Lion (William Smith), Bunny (Roland Berigan), Frog (Ben Webster), Cootie (Charles Williams), Skeeter (Clifton Best), Pony (Norwood Poindexter), Mutt (Tom Carey), Mousie (Elmer Alexander), Cat (William Alonzo Anderson), Tiger (George Haynes), Hoss (Walter Page), Mule (Major Holley), Monk (William Montgomery), Honeybear (Gene Sedric), and Rabbit (Johnny Hodges). But Al Porcino's nickname "Porky" is just a loose translation of his surname, and Joseph "Sharkey" Bonano was named for a fighter, Tom Sharkey.

Wilbur Clayton's mother nicknamed him "Buck," an allusion to his American Indian ancestors. Later, his colleagues called him Cat-Eye because of his unusual blue-green eyes.

Joseph Manone was "winged" in a streetcar accident in New Orleans when he was a boy. The accident cost him an arm and gave him his name, Wingy.

William Randolph Cole was called "Colesy" by his football buddies in school. This was slurred to "Cozy."

Eli Thompson's father bought him a sweater with the word "Lucky" on the front, not realizing that he'd given his son a new name that would replace the one with which he had christened him.

As a young man in New Orleans, Ed Garland was a fancy dresser, and so was a local sport named Montudie. His friends jokingly called him by the other man's name so frequently that he became known to the jazz world as Montudie Garland.

George Brunies became interested in numerology, and he was told by an expert that the letters in his name added up to an unpropitious number. He was advised he could improve the situation by dropping two letters from his name. From then on he spelled it "Georg Brunis," creating an endless problem for the proofreaders who worked for jazz magazines.

Meade Lewis and his childhood friends used to invent games taken from a cartoon strip called Alphonse and Gaston, in which references were made to the Duke of Luxembourg. Meade took his name, which was shortened to "Lux" by his playmates.

Jimmy McPartland earned the nickname "Major Hoople" among his younger colleagues with his attempts to one-up them with good-natured flummery. And Billy Walker was renamed Billy Bang by schoolmates who perceived his likeness to that cartoon character.

Otto Hardwick (who pronounced his name Oh-toe, which his friends changed to "Toby") renamed a few of Ellington's musicians. He called Freddie Jenkins "Posey" because of his showmanship. He also used comic strips as source material: from *Popeye* he took "Jeep" for Johnny Hodges and "Swee' Pea" for Billy Strayhorn. (Hodges had another nickname, "Rabbit," allegedly because of his liking for lettuce and tomato sandwiches.)

When Hardwick was on Elmer Snowden's band with Roy Eldridge, he gave Roy the highly appropriate sobriquet "Little Jazz."

Sonny Greer told how Barney Bigard was named "Creole" by the Ellington band:

Once when we were down south and in a bus on our way back to our Pullman car after a job, we stopped at a greasy spoon to get something to eat. Duke sent Bigard and Wellman Braud in, because they looked practically white. They were in there a long time before the door banged open and Barney came out shouting, "I'm Creole! I'm Creole!" The owner of the place was right behind him, waving and shouting back, "I don't care how old you are, you can't eat in here!" 🖊

Leon Berry picked up his nickname from bandleader Billy Stewart, who called him "Chu-Chin-Chow" because he though Berry's moustache made him look Chinese. His friends later shorted the name to "Chu."

Smack is a street word for heroin, but heroin had nothing to do with the reason Fletcher Henderson had that nickname. He picked it up when he was in school. He was reputed to make smacking noises with his lips while sleeping, and since his roommate was named Mack, they became "Mack and Smack."

In street parlance, a person who went crazy was said to have "flipped his wig." A "flip" was also a person who gave way to irrational outbursts of anger. Because of Flip Phillips's crowd-pleasing solos with Jazz at the Philharmonic tours, many people assumed his name had arisen from the way he played, but it really came from a shortening of his surname. He was christened Joseph Edward Filipelli.

Panama Francis didn't come from Panama. He came to New York from Florida as David Albert Francis, wearing a stylish Panama hat which he wore during his first rehearsal with Roy Eldridge's band. Joe Glaser, Roy's manager, was expecting Sid Catlett to be hired, but Roy had heard Francis playing with Billy Hicks and his Sizzling Six, had liked him, and hired him. When Glaser said, "Who's that on drums?" Roy couldn't remember his name. He looked at his hat and said,

"Oh, that's Panama!"

The musicians in Roy's band assumed that was his name.

"I was too scared to tell them my real name was David," said Panama.

Benny Goodman was called "The Ray" by his musicians because of the stare with which he would fix anyone who had evoked his displeasure. He was at various times called "B.G.," "Pops," "The King," "The Ego," and "The Old Man." Dave Tough called him "Benny Badman" and Jess Stacy called him "Shirley Temple."

Eddie "Lockjaw" Davis didn't get his name from his tenacious saxophone embouchure, as has been reported elsewhere. For some reason, record producer Bobby Shad decided to name the original tunes Davis played on his first record date after various diseases. The one titled *Lockjaw* became a minor hit, and the word was then used on promotional posters to identify Eddie.

Mildred Bailey had her own special names for everybody. She named Big Crosby "The Groaner," and was the one who began calling Paul Whiteman "Pops."

Edward Ellington was renamed in his early teens:

> Just before I went to high school and before my voice broke, I got my nickname, Duke. I had a chum, Edgar McEntree, a rather fancy guy who liked to dress well. He was socially uphill and a pretty good, popular fellow all around, with parties and that sort of thing. I think he felt that in order for me to be eligible for his constant companionship I should have a title. So he named me Duke. 🎵

There are conflicting stories about the origin of Count Basie's name. The first version is John Hammond's:

> It was the announcer at WHB [in Kansas City] who dubbed Basie "Count" because, as he pointed out, there was an Earl Hines, a King Oliver, a Duke Ellington, and Bill Basie deserved to join the royalty of jazz. 🎵

Basie said that when he first moved to Kansas City, he thought the name up himself:

I decided to name myself the Count. I knew about King Oliver, and I also knew that Paul Whiteman was called the King of Jazz. Duke Ellington was also getting to be one of the biggest new names in Harlem and also on records and the radio, and Earl Hines and Baron Lee were also important names. So I decided that I would be one of the biggest new names; and I actually had some little fancy business cards printed up to announce it.

"COUNT BASIE. Beware the Count is Here." 𝅘𝅥

Eddie Durham had a different story to tell:

I named Basie "The Count." That's when they started to call him "Count," from then on. Benny Moten used to say, "Oh, that guy ain't no 'count." So I wrote a tune called *The Count* and gave it to Benny to play. Everybody would laugh, you know. Basie didn't know what it was all about, that Benny had kept saying Basie wasn't no 'count. Because he'd say, "Basie, play this for me, man, I can't read that." And Basie'd sit down and play that little part and a little bit more and then he'd get up and he's gone. Benny'd say, "Where is that guy? He ain't no account!" And that was the expression always. That's why I named that tune *The Count*. 𝅘𝅥

Lester Young made up names for many of his friends, and everyone used them. He called Count Basie "The Holy Main" (shortened by the band to "Holy") because he was the main man, the one from whom the work and the paycheck came. (His later band called him "Chief.") Lester called Harry Edison "Sweets," partly because of his lyrical solos and partly because of his devilish nature. He called Earle Warren "Smiley," and Herschel Evans "Tex." Of course, Lester always gave these nicknames the prefix "Lady." He might say, "Now, Lady Tex, sing me a song."

Lester was responsible for the knighting of Sir Charles Thompson. There were three employees at Café Society with the name Charles Thompson, and to straighten things out Lester started using "Sir Charles" to identify the pianist.

"Motherfucker" was used by Lester as an all-purpose modifier. With such constant use, it became an almost gentle term, but Lester occasionally restored its bite. When annoyed by Birdland's midget master of ceremonies Pee Wee Marquette, Lester dismissed him with a contemptuous:

"Get out of my face, you half-a-motherfucker!"

The most famous nickname that Lester bestowed on anyone was "Lady Day" for Billie Holiday. She returned the courtesy by naming him "The President." Billie tells the story:

Mom and I doubled up with laughter hearing Lester tell how dangerous it was for a young man living alone in a New York hotel. And when he said, "Duchess, can I move in with you?" there was only one answer. Mom gave him a room and he moved in with us.

Lester was the first to call Mom "Duchess"—and it turned out to be the title she carried to her grave. Lester and I will probably be buried, too, still wearing the names we hung on each other after he came to live with us.

Back at the Log Cabin the other girls used to try and mock me by calling me "Lady," because they thought I thought I was just too damn grand to take the damn customers' money off the tables. [It was customary in some clubs for female entertainers to raise their skirts and pick up tip money with their labia. Ed.] But the name Lady stuck long after everybody had forgotten where it had come from. Lester took it and coupled it with the Day out of Holiday and called me "Lady Day."

When it came to a name for Lester, I always felt he was the greatest, so his name had to be the greatest. In this country, kings or counts or dukes don't amount to nothing. The greatest man around then was Franklin D. Roosevelt, and he was the President. So I started calling him The President. It got shortened to Prez, but it still means what it was meant to mean—the top man in this country. 🖘

The Jay McShann band was on its way to play a job at the University of Nebraska. As they passed a farm, the car Charlie Parker was riding in hit a chicken that ran across the road. McShann said:

Charlie told the driver, "Man, go back, you hit that yardbird." They want back, and Charlie jumped out and got the chicken. When they got to Lincoln, he asked the lady who ran the boarding house where we were staying to cook it for dinner. 🖘

After that, the other musicians began calling Charlie "Yardbird" or "Yard" or "Bird."

When Henry Coker nicknamed Sonny Cohn "Buttercup," the rest of the Basie band had shortened it to "Butter." But Quentin Jackson's light complexion and rotund figure, combined with his warm trombone sound and sunny disposition, had already earned him the same nickname. To avoid confusion between the two Butters, Basie's musicians called Jackson "Grand Beurre" and Cohn "Petit Beurre." Later they shifted to calling Sonny "Cup," the other half of "Buttercup."

Eugene Young was called "Snooky" ever since he was given that name by childhood playmates. Harry Edison added another, "Rabbit," an allusion to the fact that Snooky had sired three children.

Cozy Cole called everyone "Face," meaning he didn't remember your name, but your face was familiar. If he also remembered the instrument you played, then he called you "Bass Face," "Sax Face," etc. For the same purpose, Benny Goodman fell back on the all-purpose "Pops." Milt Hinton used "Judge," and Lionel Hampton used "Gates" the same way. As a result all three men found that people called them by their favorite all-purpose names.

When young Jack Sims joined the Kenny Baker band in California, someone had lettered hep nicknames on the front of each music stand. The one on Jack's stand said, "Zoot," and it stuck. His was the only one that did. Zoot's name became such a household word in the jazz community that everyone laughed when they heard that Zoot had called his friend Nick Travis one morning, identified himself to the sleepy trumpet player, and received the fuddled reply, "Zoot who?" Sims was delighted when the creators of the Muppets named their sax-playing Muppet "Zoot." He said, "I'm the only one they named a Muppet after!"

On Woody Herman's Four Brothers band the musicians gave each other the names of movie stars that they resembled. Serge Chaloff was Hurd Hatfield, Earl Swope was Sonny Tufts, Ollie Wilson was Henry Fonda. Zoot said,

"I had two names. I was Charles Bickford in the morning and Joseph Cotton at night."

Claude Thornhill (dubbed "Moonface" by Louis Prima) was unhappy with people who mispronounced his last name. O. B. Masingill said:

He'd been called "Claude Thornton" and even "Claude Toenail" in the past. So, when asked his name, he would reply with a straight face, "Wurmpth Furdber." I don't know where he got that from, but we had a guy who painted our names or nicknames on our music stand, and he did a little one to stand on the piano which said "Wurmpth."

Slim Gaillard invented a lot of nonsense words that he sprinkled liberally throughout his songs and conversation. "Roonie" and "voutie" seem to be basic forms from which sprang words like "o-voutie," "o-roonie," "vouse-o-roonie-mo," "reetie-voutie," etc. When announcing the names of musicians working with him, Slim would add so many vouties and roonies that the names became nearly undecipherable. On the record *Slim's Jam*, Charlie Parker became "Charlie Yardbird-o-roonie" and Dizzy Gillespie became "Sdazz MacSkibbons-vouse-o-roonie." Once, on a radio broadcast, Slim encountered Mickey Rooney.

"Hello, Mickey-roonie," he said. "What's your last name?"

Connie Kay was born Conrad Kirnon. He had no intention of changing his name until he worked at Birdland, where Pee Wee Marquette, the half-size master of ceremonies, always had trouble pronouncing it. Since Pee Wee couldn't seem to get his mouth around "Connie Kirnon," Connie finally told him,

"Just say 'Connie K.'"

Marquette announced it that way from then on, and Connie just went along with it.

Mel Lewis became known as "The Tailor" because Terry Gibbs always called him that. There was speculation that the reference was symbolic, because Mel "stitched" the rhythm together so skillfully. Asked if this were true, Terry replied,

"No. Have you looked at the way he walks? He looks like my tailor!"

Julian Adderley's friends in Florida nicknamed him "Cannibal" when he was a teen-ager, because of his appetite. The name was eventually slurred into "Cannonball," an even more apt description.

Elmer Alexander was known as "Mousie" since childhood. Al Cohn was proud of the new name he invented for him: Mou Sie Tongue.

Kenny Davern dubbed record producer Gus Statiris "Yellowfeather." Asked to explain, Kenny said:

> You know the cat in the cartoon that chases the canary? And when you ask the cat, "Did you eat the canary?" the cat looks innocent and says "Oh, Nooo!" But if you look close at the corner of the cat's mouth, you see a little yellow feather.

Jimmy Rowles gave George Mraz his nickname. George, a remarkably talented bass player, was born in Czechoslovakia. Jimmy said his bass playing was "*baaad!*" (meaning good, in the vernacular). So he named George "Bounce," because that's what a bad check does, "and George is a *baad* Czech!"

Barney Kessel once found a Chicago restaurant named Barney Kessel's. He went in and had dinner, during which he asked the waitress, "Who's Barney Kessel?" She pointed to the man behind the cash register, so when Barney went to pay his check, he pulled out his identification and showed it to the owner. "You and I seem to have the same name," he said. The owner eyed Barney's papers, and then reached into the bowl of peppermints on the counter. He handed one to Barney and said, "It's on the house, kid."

chapter 25

Louis Armstrong

Louis Armstrong transformed jazz. He played with a strength and inventiveness that illuminated every jazz musician that heard his music. Louis was able to do things on the trumpet that had previously been considered impossible. His tone and range and phrasing became criteria by which other jazz musicians measured themselves. He established the basic vocabulary of jazz phrases, and his work became the foundation of every jazz musician who followed him.

An incident on Armstrong's first trip on a Mississippi riverboat with Fate Marable's band brought him to an important decision:

> David Jones starved himself the whole summer we worked on the *St. Paul.* He saved every nickel and sent all his money to a farm down South where employees and relatives were raising cotton for him and getting away with as much of his money as they could, since he was not there to look after his own interests. Every day he would eat an apple instead of a good hot meal. What was the result? The boll weevils ate all of his cotton before the season was over. He did not even have a chance to go down and look his farm over before a telegram came saying everything had been shot to hell. After that David Jones used to stand at the boat rail during every intermission looking down at the water and thinking about all the jack he had lost. I often said to Fate Marable:
>
> "Fate, keep an eye on David Jones. He's liable to jump in the water most any minute."
>
> This incident taught me never to deprive my stomach. I'll probably never be rich, but I will be a fat man. ↲

Baby Dodds played drums with Armstrong in King Oliver's band in Chicago. Dodds described the excitement that band caused among Chicago musicians:

Not all the people came to the Lincoln Gardens to dance. Some of the white musicians came to hear our band. Benny Goodman, Jess Stacy, Frank Teschemacher, Dave Tough, Bud Freeman, and Ben Pollack used to come to listen. George Wettling came when he was still in knee pants.

One of the most frequent visitors at the Gardens was Paul Whiteman. His band was playing at the Granada at Cottage Grove and Sixty-seventh. They got off before we did and every night the whole band would come rushing in there like mad. They had tuxedos on, and on the cuffs of their sleeves they'd jot down different notes we played. Joe Oliver did one peculiar thing which kept a lot of them guessing. He would cut the titles off the numbers, so no one could come up and look at the number to get it for his own outfit. Sometimes they asked Joe what a certain number was called and he would say anything that came into his mind. That's how some of the numbers got different names. Fellows working in other bands would give the numbers the names Joe gave them, and it was all wrong. ⬥

Many said King Oliver hired Armstrong because he wanted to keep the young wonder subordinate to himself, but Louis denied such stories, saying that he was grateful to Oliver for taking him under his wing. Barney Bigard recalled an early challenge to Armstrong in Chicago:

Joe Oliver had sent for Louis to come up from New Orleans to play second trumpet in his band, just like he sent for me, but Louis really won the people where they worked at the Lincoln Gardens, or Royal Gardens as it became later. But Joe had never really let Louis go for himself.

What really started Joe into giving Louis his own chorus, and this is what Joe Oliver told me, was that one night they were playing when this guy Johnny Dunn walked in who was cracked up to be a hell of a trumpet man in those days. Johnny Dunn was with a big show and the people were clamoring to hear what he would play. He walked on to the stand and said to Louis, "Boy! Give me that horn. You don't know how to do." That made Joe Oliver real angry and he told Louis, "Go get him." Louis blew like the devil. Blew him out of the place. They looked for Johnny Dunn when Louis finished but he had skipped out. They never found him in there again. So that's when Joe started to turn Louis loose by himself. ⬥

Lil Armstrong tells a similar story, with a slightly different cast of characters:

Word was getting around that Louis was a good trumpet player. So, one night Freddie Keppard came in to hear us. The bandstand was down low and Freddie stood there by the bandstand and he listened a while, and then he said to Louis, "Boy, let me have your trumpet." So, Louis looked at me and I bowed my head, so Louis gave him the trumpet. So, Freddie, he blew—oh, he blew and he blew and he blew and then the people gave him a nice hand. Then he handed the trumpet back to Louis. And I said, "Now, get him, get him!" Oooh, never in my life have I heard such trumpet playing! If you want to hear Louis play, just hear him play when he's angry. Boy, he blew and people started standing up on top of tables and chairs screaming, and Freddie eased out real slowly. Nobody ever asked Louis for his trumpet again! ♩

Keppard seems to have been the trumpet player to beat. Oliver had established his own reputation in New Orleans in a confrontation with Keppard. Richard M. Jones recalled:

Freddy Keppard was playin' in a spot across the street and was drawin' all the crowds. I was sittin' at the piano, and Joe Oliver came over to me and commanded in a nervous, harsh voice, "Get in B-flat." I did, and Joe walked out on the sidewalk, lifted his horn to his lips, and blew the most beautiful stuff I have ever heard. People started pouring out of the other spots along the street to see who was blowing all that horn. Before long, our place was full and Joe came in smiling, and said, "Now, that _____ won't bother me no more." From then on, our place was full every night. ♩

Doc Cheatham was working at the Dreamland ballroom in Chicago when Armstrong was the featured soloist at the Vendome with Erskine Tate. He went to hear Louis every day and knew all his routines, so he felt safe in accepting the job when Louis asked him to substitute for him one night:

I don't think Louis told Erskine Tate that he was going to be out and he was sending someone. I sat there when the band came in and no one spoke to me at all. I sat there and sat there and finally I got my horn out and got in the pit. They were rehearsing. Everybody looked and wondered what the hell, who was this guy? I felt very embarrassed. ♩

The only problem arose when the band played *Poor Little Rich Girl,* Louis's feature number of the week.

When Louis was there, the minute that spotlight hit Louis on *Poor Little Rich Girl*, the people were screaming so much you couldn't hear what he was playing half the time. So when the spotlight hit me, I jumped up and started playing, and the house screamed and screamed. After a while you could hear the diminishing of the screams. Came right down to nothing, and I'm up there playing like a fool. Well, I'll tell you, it took me years to get over that. I did the best I could with it. I didn't do a lousy job, but I was no Louis Armstrong. ⇃

Nobody was. Harry Edison described the incredulity of other trumpet players:

Some of the symphony musicians thought he played a freak horn to get those high notes. Some trumpet players used to make the hole smaller with chewing gum to play higher, but then they couldn't play low. Pops was getting all *over* his horn, playing high *and* low. Anyway, the symphony musicians [in Columbus, Ohio] went to the first show at the Palace Theater, and he showed them his horn and mouthpiece, and even let them blow the horn. It was not the horn, but the man behind it.

As I was standing in the wings, Louis announced that he was going to play *Tiger Rag*. Since some of the audience still thought he played a trick horn, he had a local trumpet player come up and play it first. Then the band started out, and I never heard a man blow like that in my life! He hit two hundred high Cs, and they counted them as he went around the stage, and he ended on a high F! ⇃

Taft Jordan had heard similar rumors around Norfolk, Virginia, that Armstrong was playing a special kind of trumpet that gave him such ease in the upper register. When Louis came to Norfolk, all the trumpet players in town were there:

One of them asked him, "May I see your horn?"
"Yeah," Pops said, and handed it to him.
"Mind if I blow it?"
"Right," Pops said. "Got your mouthpiece?"
So the guy put his mouthpiece in and sounded C on Pops's horn and C on his own. He ran the scale on his, and he ran the scale on Pops's. It was all the same. It was no trick horn. It was just the man, the difference of the man. ⇃

Fletcher Henderson offered Louis a job with his band. He told about Armstrong's first rehearsal:

Truthfully, I didn't expect him to accept the offer, and I was very surprised when he came to New York and joined us.

The band at first was inclined to be a bit reserved toward the new arrival and there seemed to be a little tension in the air. At rehearsal he was perplexed by the trumpet part I gave him to a new arrange-ment of a medley of beautiful Irish waltzes. Now, those parts were well marked with all the dynamics of the music, and at one point the orchestration was indicated as *fff* with a diminuendo down to *pp*.

The band followed these notations and was playing very softly, while Louis still played his part at full volume. I stopped the band and said, "Louis, you are not following the arrangement."

Louis objected, saying, "I'm reading everything on this sheet." I said, "But Louis, how about that pp?" and Louis broke us all up by replying, "Oh, I thought that meant 'pound plenty.' " There was no tension after that.

There were a lot of serious musicians in that wonderful orchestra of mine, and they were a little too stiff at first for Louis's taste. Fi-nally, a fight developed between the trombonist and the bass player, and they had their coats off and were really going after each other before I quieted them, and this eased everything for Louis. For the first time he said,

"Oh, I'm gonna like this band." ♪

Rex Stewart was impressed with Louis when he heard him in New York:

I said that no individual ever came to town and carved everybody, but there was one exception—Louis Armstrong. He was so tough on trumpet that nobody dared challenge him. Come to think of it, I don't remember ever seeing him at a session. He didn't come to us—we had to go to him. I shall never forget the scrambling to get to one tiny window backstage at Roseland Ballroom, just to catch Satchmo putting the "heat to the beat" with Fletcher Henderson. ♪

Roy Eldridge was unaware of Louis Armstrong's playing when he was learning the trumpet. He shaped his style from hearing Rex Stewart and Red Nichols. He said, "When Lips Page heard me play, he asked me, 'How come you playin' like an ofay?'" When Roy finally heard Armstrong's records, he was intrigued. The two trumpet players finally met in Harlem:

I first met Louis when I was working at Small's. He used to come down to hear me. He'd tell me, "Little Jazz, you gonna be all right." He gave me some salve, that salve that he used to put on his lip. I put that shit on my lip, and I couldn't play for a week! It was good for him, but it didn't work for me *no* kind of way.

I hadn't heard him in person until he played at the Lafayette. I went to hear him, 'cause everybody was talking about him. By this time I kind of had my feathers up, 'cause I was just mowing 'em down left and right. I caught the first show, and I said, "Sheeeit! Is this what they been shouting about? Let me get on out of here!" And I started to go, but then I said, "Wait a minute, this is his first show." I put myself in his position. "Suppose he hung out last night, and his chops ain't cool? I better stay and catch the next show." I know about that trumpet. It can be a devil; it's a bad fellow.

So I stayed the second show, and it got a little better. There was always a sad picture at the Lafayette in those days, but I got high and sat through that until the show come on again.

The next show is when he played this "Chinatown." The rhythm section was chuggin' on him, baby, and it just kept on building. He started down here and went to F, up there, then to A out of the staff, then to the C and the D, and those cats was whippin' him, didn't let up one bit! They got just as intense as he did, See, that's what's suppose to be! When he hit that note on the end, everybody jumped up, and I looked, and *I* was standing up! I said, "Shit, what's goin' on? I got to stay for another show!"

I stayed through four shows, and then I went out and bought the record! I was getting jobs, but I wasn't as popular as I was after I learned how to play "Chinatown." I got so indoctrinated with Louis that for a while I was goin' around tryin' to talk like him.   ↳

Roy developed his own style of playing and eventually abandoned most of the devices he learned from Louis. He was a great competitor and wanted to take Louis on. He said:

Joe Glaser signed both me and Hot Lips Page, but I swear he did it to keep us under wraps and away from Louis, who was having a little lip trouble then. The one time Louis and I did get together [at the Metropolitan Opera House Jam Session in 1944 for *Esquire* magazine] I was ready, but again they kept me away from him. And Louis knew I was getting' to him, too. Just as something was about to happen, he started playing the National Anthem, and that was it!   ↳

Louis smoked "muggles" all his life, but he was rarely given any trouble about it. Most of the enforcement officers liked Louis and his music, and his manager Joe Glaser could usually fix any legal problems that arose before too much damage was done. Louis couldn't see why he should stop doing something that made him feel happy just because it had been made illegal by some squares who didn't know any better. It was as if the government had outlawed the possession of his favorite herbal laxative, Swiss Kriss, which he also used daily.

Many of Louis's fans knew he got high, and they often devised ways to please him. Budd Johnson told about a surprise he found waiting on the bandstand in St. Louis when he was working with Armstrong's big band:

> When I looked on the music rack, all of the racks were filled with reefers. I say to myself, "What the devil is this?"
>
> Louis came out after he had finished warming up. Here walks up six little guys all dressed alike. They walked up to the bandstand and said,
>
> "Louis Armstrong! Pops!"
>
> "Yeah, man, what's happenin' there?"
>
> "We want to present you with this."
>
> And they held their arms out, and it was a great big joint rolled in the form of a baseball bat. It must have been about a foot long. And they had taken a fountain pen and punched holes in it to read,
>
> "TO THE KING OF THE VIPERS from the Vipers Club of St. Louis, Mo."
>
> You know, back in those days, it was not illegal to smoke pot. I mean, we smoked pot all over the bandstand. I asked Louis,
>
> "What are we gonna do with this, man?"
>
> "We're gonna smoke a little bit of it every day, and then we're gonna have Mezz for dessert."
>
> Mezz Mezzrow used to mail Louis marijuana, everywhere we went.
>
> So we were all sitting up on the bandstand playing and all I could see was just images. I couldn't make out nobody's face, I was so high. But I felt all right. A lady walked up and said,
>
> "My, my, they all look so tired and sleepy, but the music is good." ↱

Armstrong had been to a little late-night gathering in a speakeasy. It was in one of the toughest parts of lower Harlem on a pitch-dark street. As he stepped out onto the street, two young men jumped him from behind. One held a knife at his throat and the other said, "Okay, give us your loot, Daddy." Louis looked at them. Flashing the smile, he said in that deep, gravelly voice, "Now listen here, fellas, you can't do that to Pops, 'cause I have to go downtown to make one of those good ole ones today at the record studio, and I can't blow my horn . . ." The two muggers jumped back and pleaded, "Oh, Pops, we didn't know it was you. We're sorry, man." Louis gave them a brief lecture and some money, and went on his way.

Barney Bigard played clarinet with the Louis Armstrong All-Stars. He remembered Louis's distaste for layoffs:

> He never believed in vacations. "Oh, Pops. If I take a vacation, my lips will go down," he used to say. Once in later years when my friend Joe Darensbourg was with the band, Joe told me that they actually took a two-week vacation. Joe went home and was having a great time lying out in the sun by his pool, and the phone rang. It was the office. "You have to come back to work. Louis is getting bored just sitting around so we have fixed up some college dates right quick," they said. Can you believe that? But that's how Louis was. He was never happy sitting around. ↯

Joe Darensbourg replaced Bigard when he left the All-Stars. Joe was on the band when Louis made one of his biggest hit records:

> We made *Hello Dolly* in New York in December 1963 before starting out on tour again. We had a lead sheet, Billy Kyle wrote some backgrounds for Trummy and me, we made the record and completely forgot about it—didn't play it again. About three weeks later we wound up in San Juan, Puerto Rico, around Christmas, and while we were there *Hello Dolly* started making the charts in America. The office called and told the road manager to get Louis to start playing *Hello Dolly* if he wasn't already doing it. We'd all forgot it. Bob, the band boy, had lost the lead sheet, so Louis says,
> "Any of you guys remember this damn tune?" Billy could only remember some parts, so we had to run all around San Juan trying to find the single. Couldn't find it, so they had to fly one out of New York to us and we listened to it. Then we started playing it and the very first time Louis did it on stage in Hotel San Juan he had to take about eight curtain calls, so he knew right then he had a hit. ↯

When Marty Napoleon replaced Billy Kyle with the All-Stars he didn't get a chance to talk to Louis before the concert to find out what was expected of him. He saw that everyone was using plenty of showmanship, so when Louis gave him a solo piano chorus Marty gave it the hard sell. While building up to a climax he raised his eyebrows and gave the audience a big toothy smile as he bobbed up and down while vigorously kneading the keys. He got a good hand and thought he'd done what the job required, but when Louis walked over to the piano to take a fresh white handkerchief from the pile he kept there, he leaned over to Marty as he patted his forehead dry.

"Say, look here, Pops," he whispered in his gravelly voice, "I do all the eye-rollin' on this band!"

Bobby Hackett was a lifelong admirer and friend of Armstrong. He spoke of his idol:

> He was a saint. He was the softest touch in the world. Whenever I went into his dressing room at Basin Street, or someplace like that, it would be full of broken-down musicians and show-biz types looking for a buck. It finally got so that Joe Glaser, who managed Pops most of his life, put a twenty-dollar lid on each handout. Even so, I think he helped support hundreds of people. It was one of his greatest pleasures.

Louis loved jokes and banter. He wrote jolly letters to all his friends, examples of which have been reproduced in books about him. He usually signed himself "Red beans and ricely yours," or "Swiss Krissly yours." (The latter referred to an herbal laxative, Swiss Kriss, that was part of Armstrong's daily regimen.) Gus Statiris remembered riding around New York with a disk jockey who was rolling Swiss Kriss into cigarette paper and smoking it. He asked him why, and the jockey said,

"Louis Armstrong told me this was some good shit!"

Two of Louis's best lines were given in answer to an interviewer's question:

"Mr. Armstrong, what is your definition of jazz?"

"Jazz is what I play for a living."

And when asked if jazz was folk music, Armstrong replied,

"Man, all music is folk music. You ain't never heard no horse sing a song, have you?"

Darensbourg told of Louis's comment when Doc Pugh, his valet, passed away:

> Somebody said they'd heard Doc had died and asked Louis what was wrong with him. Louis looked at them with a kinda sad face and finally he says,

"What was wrong with Doc? Man, when you die, *everything* is wrong with you!" ↴

Al Stewart was sitting in Armstrong's dressing room one night. Louis was in his usual offstage costume: green boxer shorts, slippers, and a white handkerchief knotted on his head as a cap. He sat at his dressing table under a bare 100-watt bulb pecking away on a portable typewriter. Joe Bushkin poked his head in the door and said, "Pops, haven't you finished your book yet?" Louis rumbled, "Aw, man, no! I got six hundred pages done and I'm only up to 1929!"

Marty Napoleon was visiting Louis and his wife Lucille at their home. As Lucille was showing him through the house, Marty noticed the bathroom fixtures. The faucets were in the shape of golden swans. Marty said,

"We have those same fixtures in our bathroom! But, tell me, Lucille, how do you keep them from tarnishing?"

Lucille looked surprised.

"Marty," she said, "that's solid gold, baby."

"Oh," said Marty.

Lucille was on the road with Louis during one Christmas season:

I got a little small Christmas tree and I got all the decorations for it, and set it up in the hotel room while Louis was at work. I didn't say anything to him about it. So when he came in about three o'clock, this tree was up with the blinking lights, you know? So we talked around a while; I gave him his Christmas present—had all the Christmas presents under the tree, and gave him his, and those that I had for a few special friends in the band.

We finally went to bed. And Louis was still laying up in the bed watching the tree; his eyes just like a baby's eyes would watch something. So I finally asked him—I said, "Well, I'll turn the lights out now on the tree." He said, "No, don't turn them out. I have to just keep looking at it." He said, "You know, that's the first tree I ever had."

Well, I hadn't realized that, you know? Louis was forty years old, and it seems to me that in forty years a person would have at least one tree. I was all swollen up inside when he told me that. We were to leave the next day for Kansas City. I figured Christmas is over; today's the 26th now; I'll leave the tree. So Louis said, "No, don't leave the tree; take the tree with you." And he had me take that tree on those one-nighters. Before I even unpacked a bag I had to set that tree up, his Christmas tree. And I've had one for him every year. Louis hasn't been home too often for Christmas, but whenever he has been home, he's had a tree the length of the room.

I kept that first little tree until way after New Year's, putting it up every night and taking it down every morning, in a dozen hotels. And when I did take it down for its last time, Louis wanted me to mail it home. It was a real tree, not an artificial one, and I had to convince him—I really had to convince him—that the tree would dry up. ⟳

Toward the end of Armstrong's life, Clark Terry was delegated to sound him out about being given an honorary degree:

He was still in good spirits, but his limbs were very frail and he was very thin. He'd lost lots of weight. It was about three and a half weeks before his demise. He called me in and asked how I was.

"I'm fine, Pops. Aside from just the pleasure of coming by to see you and be inspired and get my batteries charged again, I'm on a special mission. Harvard University wants to offer you an honorary doctor's degree."

He said, "The hell with them, Daddy. Where were they forty years ago when I needed them?" ⟳

chapter 26

Bessie Smith

Bessie Smith, the Empress of the Blues, was appreciated by the jazz musicians of her day, and she used a number of them on her recordings. One of them was Louis Armstrong, who said:

Bessie Smith was a very quiet woman—didn't bother nobody. But, God, don't mess with her. She had a quick temper. Made a lot of money, though. A cat came up to her one day, wanted change for a thousand-dollar bill. Trying to see if she had it. Bessie said, "Yeah." She just raised up the front of her dress and there was a carpenter's apron and she just pulled that change out of it. That was her bank. ☍

Herman Autrey worked with Bessie at a Philadelphia theater in 1928.

Bessie was married to a detective, Jack Gee. He was a tough man, you know. Jack told me this story, that Bessie used to lay there in bed with a butcher knife telling him, "When you go to sleep I'm going to kill you!" (Laughs) And Jack would be laying there with his .45 in his hand, and say "You start over here, I'm going to blow your brains out." She says, "You go to sleep and start snoring, I'm going to kill you, I'm going to stick you with the knife, man."

I said, "Well, Jack, how can you sleep?"

He says, "Ah, she ain't going to do it."

Bessie was darn near six foot, and big, and strong, had great big arms, you know, she looked like she could pick Jack Gee up by the collar with one hand. And Jack Gee wasn't a little man. But oh, Bessie, what a nice person. ☍

Chris Albertson wrote of Bessie's appearance at a party given in New York by writer and jazz aficionado Carl Van Vechten. Wrapped in a white ermine coat, Bessie arrived at the Van Vechten apartment with her accompanist, Porter Grainger, and her niece and companion, Ruby Walker:

She breezed past the welcoming party and into the room beyond. Trailing behind her, Ruby wore a mink coat which belonged to Bessie and was far too big for her.

Ignoring a chorus of salutatory "Oh, Miss Smiths," Bessie, cold sober at this point, did not come to a halt until someone mentioned a drink. Van Vechten, radiating the pleasure of a celebrity hunter who has at last captured his prey of the moment, beamed, "How about a lovely, lovely dry martini?"

"Whaaat—a dry martini?" bellowed Bessie. "Ain't you got some whiskey, man? That'll be the only way I'll touch it. I don't know about no dry martinis, nor wet ones either."

"Of course," said Van Vechten. "I think we can conjure up something you like," he purred, and disappeared to fulfill the request.

Soon Grainger and Bessie, drink in hand, were marched toward the piano. Mumbling something about her throat being dry, Bessie gulped her drink down and handed her empty glass to Van Vechten. Someone asked her what she was going to sing. "Don't you worry about it," she said. "My piano player knows."

She sang six or seven numbers, each one followed by enthusiastic applause and usually preceded by her request for "another one of these." Each time she handed Van Vechten her empty glass, he refilled it eagerly. Only Ruby and Grainger knew what effect the refills were having on Bessie.

"This is it," announced Bessie as she went into her final number. She was feeling her liquor at this point, and her two companions were watching her closely, knowing it wouldn't take much to set her off.

As soon as the last number was finished, Grainger walked over to Ruby, momentarily shedding his genteel demeanor: "Let's get her out of here quick, before she shows her ass." Draping the ermine over her shoulders, they fell into position on either side of Bessie and began what they hoped would be a graceful exit.

All went well until an effusive woman stopped them a few steps from the front door. It was Bessie's hostess, Fania Marinoff Van Vechten.

"Miss Smith," she said, throwing her arms around Bessie's massive neck and pulling it forward, "you're not leaving without kissing me goodbye."

That was all Bessie needed.

"Get the fuck away from me!" she roared, thrusting her arms forward and knocking the woman to the floor. "I ain't never *heard* of such shit!"

In the silence that followed, Bessie stood in the middle of the foyer, ready to take on the whole crowd.

Grainger was the first to move. Gently he took one of Bessie's arms and told Ruby to take the other. Followed by the horrified stares of the guests, the two of them escorted the Empress out the door and down the richly carpeted hall to the elevator. Van Vechten, having helped his indignant wife to her feet, followed close behind.

"It's all right, Miss Smith," he said softly, trailing behind the threesome in the hall. "You were magnificent tonight."

They had reached the elevator before Bessie realized that she was actually being led away. She threw her arms in the air, almost knocking Ruby and Grainger to the floor, and started shouting again—"What the fuck are y'all pullin' me all over the damn place for?"

When the elevator door opened she stopped shouting, raised her head high, marched past the startled operator, and sank to the floor in the corner of the car.

"I don't care if she dies," said Grainger as he sighed and straightened the tam on his head. 🎵

Albertson described Bessie's style of dealing with management:

Bessie ended 1936 with a week at the Apollo. During the week Frank Schiffman made the mistake of refusing Bessie an advance. She stormed out of his office and into the crowded lobby of the theater, threw her two hundred pounds on the floor, and treated the startled patrons to a performance they had not paid for. Lying on her back, she pounded her heels and fists furiously into the floor, and hollered in a voice that could be heard clear across 125th Street:

"I'm the star of the show, I'm Bessie Smith, and these fuckin' bastards won't let me have my money."

It wasn't long before she got it. 🎵

Garbled reporting of the circumstances of Bessie's death in 1937 led to the development of a legend that will not die. One capsule history declares:

Her tragic death occurred when she was turned away from a segregated hospital after an automobile crash: she died from loss of blood while being sped to one that admitted Negroes. 🎵

George Hoefer gives a more complete account:

Early on Sunday morning, September 26, 1937, Bessie was riding in a car bound for Memphis. Near Coahoma, Mississippi, the car piled into a panel truck, parked on the side of the road, and overturned. Bessie sustained an arm injury. It was reported that her arm was almost severed from her body. She also suffered bruises about her face and head, and internal injuries.

There were many conflicting stories of what happened after the accident. Some of these have undoubtedly been exaggerated because of the racial issues involved. Piecing together the various reports, however, the following appears to be reasonable.

The accident took place on the outskirts of Coahoma, a town too small to have a hospital. The closest town of any size was Clarksdale, Mississippi, a few miles away. A prominent Memphis surgeon came upon the accident a few minutes after the crash. An ambulance had already been ordered, but the doctor could see that Bessie was in danger of bleeding to death. He was attempting to put her into the back of his car (she weighed about two hundred pounds at the time), when another car rammed into the back of his car, wrecking it completely. Five minutes later, the ambulance arrived and rushed Bessie to the Negro ward of the G. T. Thomas Hospital in Clarksdale, where one of the town's best surgeons amputated her arm. She died fifteen minutes past noon that same day. The doctors reported that her death was probably due more to her internal injuries than to the loss of blood. ⤶

chapter 27

Bix Beiderbecke

Bix Beiderbecke played the cornet with a lovely vibrant sound. Eddie Condon described it as "like a girl saying yes." Bix taught himself the instrument by playing along with records, and he developed an original conception of tone and phrasing at a time when nearly every other jazz musician was under the spell of Louis Armstrong. Bix lived in Chicago while Armstrong was playing there, heard Louis and loved his playing, but he went his own way and took a number of young admirers along with him.

Max Kaminsky was one of the younger generation of brass players who fell in love with Bix's music. He tells of the passion that possessed him:

A few months after I first heard Bix play, I was working down at the Cape for the summer, and one Sunday night on the train going back to the Cape, I met Howie Freeman, a drummer from Boston, who immediately showed me a brand new recording he had just bought of Bix's "Singing the Blues" and "Clarinet Marmalade."

"Howie, old pal," I croaked in a voice hoarse with almost unbearable longing, 'let me buy it from you." I peeled dollar after dollar from my thin wad, but Howie wouldn't part with the record at any price. By the time the train pulled into my station I had turned from an ordinarily sane, responsible young man into a demon. After I had gathered up my belongings with sneaky casualness, I turned to say goodbye to Howie, and in the next second I snatched the record out of Howie's hand and raced off the train with it. And that night when I sat in the little room in my boardinghouse playing the record over and over, my only thought was, "It was *worth* it."

Remorse did begin to set in a day or so later, and Howie did eventually forgive me. "I know how it is," he said, But in time I became so ashamed of my action that I hated to think of it.

Another musician, one of the most talented jazz trombonists around, recently told me of a similar incident. He was around fifteen when he heard his first Teagarden record on a jukebox in an ice cream parlor, and he went so wild that he seized a chair, smashed the glass front of the jukebox, snatched the record and fled before anyone knew what was happening. He was from a well-to-do family, with no more excuse or explanation for his behavior than I had.　🎵

Many stories were told about Beiderbecke's pivot tooth. Sudhalter and Evans write:

As a boy, wrestling with a friend on the front lawn, Bix had been thrown to the ground and had broken one of his front teeth. A Davenport dentist fashioned a removable false tooth, slotted at the sides to fit neatly into place. It might never had bothered Bix again, save for his habit of playing with it, removing it and slotting it back in when at all nervous. It had eventually become loose in his mouth, so that a cough or sudden jerk of his head might dislodge it.　🎵

Eddie Condon describes Bix's ensuing dental problems:

He was having the usual trouble with his pivot tooth; it was in front, upstairs, and it frequently dropped out, leaving Bix unable to blow a note. Wherever he worked it was customary to see the boys in the band down on the floor, looking for Bix's tooth.

Once in Cincinnati at five o'clock in the morning while driving over a snow-covered street in a 1922 Essex with Wild Bill Davison and Carl Clove, Bix shouted, "Stop the car!" There was no speakeasy in sight. "What's the matter?" Davison asked. "I've lost my tooth," Bix said.

They got out and carefully examined the fresh snow. After a long search Davison sighted a tiny hole; in it he found the tooth, quietly working its way down to the road. Bix restored it to his mouth and they went on to The Hole in the Wall, where they played every morning for pork chop sandwiches and gin. It was natural for Bix not to get the tooth permanently fastened; he couldn't be bothered going to the dentist. ↳

Hoagy Carmichael also remembered Bix's tooth:

The last time I had seen him his pivot tooth fell out when he leaned out of the hotel window to yell "goodnight" down at me. We searched for it frantically with matches burning our fingers—so he could play that night.

"No tooth, no music." ↳

Beiderbecke was interested in music and alcohol, and little else. His indifference to clothes often presented a problem when jobs turned up that required tidiness. Condon helped outfit him for a job in Indiana:

He ran into some of Jean Goldkette's boys while he was at the Rendezvous. They were playing a prom date at Indiana University; Bix had a strong following there, led by a piano-playing student named Hoagy Carmichael. He was asked to go down and play the date with the band. He turned up at the Allerton House in the usual dilemma—no tuxedo. Jim [Condon, Eddie's brother] and I put him together: Jim's jacket and trousers and shirt, my studs and tie. For good measure and the cool spring nights we gave him a topcoat and a hat. A few days later he returned and brought us the borrowed articles. There was a tuxedo, complete with studs, tie, and shirt. But the tuxedo was not Jim's, the shirt was not his, and the studs and tie were not mine. The topcoat and hat were also different from those we had given him.

"Did you have a good time?" we asked politely.

"I don't know," Bix said. ↳

Mezz Mezzrow was one of the musicians with Bix at a summer job at Hudson Lake, Indiana. Mezz describes an afternoon's adventure there with Bix and Pee Wee Russell:

Bix nearly got run over by a locomotive. Long after the sun came up we ran out of corn, and Bix, with a tricky look in his eyes, called me and Pee Wee aside, along with a couple of the other guys. "I just remembered," he whispered, "that I got a spare gallon buried up on the hill, and if we sneak over there without these other lushes, there'll be enough to go around." We crept out Indian-file, with Bix leading the way like an old frontier scout.

Down the path we followed him across some fields, then over a railroad track and a high fence topped with barbed wire. Sure enough, he dug out a jug, handed it to Pee Wee, and started back. But as we were hopping the fence Pee Wee got stuck on the wire and just hung there, squealing for help and hugging the jug for dear life. If he let go of that crock he could have pulled himself loose, but not Pee Wee—what's a guy's hide compared to a gallon of corn? By this time Bix, having staggered down to the railroad tracks, found he had a lot of sand between his toes, so he sat down on the rail and yanked his shoes off to empty them. Just then we saw a fast train coming round the bend. All of us began screaming at Bix to get the hell out of there, but he thought we were just kidding him and he threw stones at us. That train wasn't more than a hundred feet away when he finally woke up to what was happening. Then he just rolled off the track and tumbled down the bank head first, traveling so fast he didn't have time to snatch his shoes off the rail. Those funky oxfords got clipped in half as neatly as if they'd been chopped with a meat-cleaver.

"That just goes to show you," Bix told us, "it's dangerous for a man to take his shoes off. First time I took those things off in weeks and you see what the hell happens. It just ain't safe to undress."

Condon told of a car that entered the lives of Bix and Pee Wee at Hudson Lake:

The only commodity kept in sufficient stock was a local whisky, purchased in large quantities for five dollars a gallon from three old-maid hillbillies who lived five miles away. Barefoot in a cabin with a brother, they were all past sixty and asked no questions.

Bix and Pee Wee were without a car. It bothered them; they couldn't visit the old maids when they wanted to. One day, having received some pay, they went to LaPorte to buy an automobile. There were several secondhand Model-T Fords available, but Bix had notions of grandeur. He found a 1916 Buick which could be had for eighty dollars.

"This is it," Bix said to Pee Wee. "Wait until the guys see us with this. We won't have to ride with them any more, they'll be begging to ride with us." Pee Wee was dubious, but he agreed.

They drove back to the lake and hid the car in a side road. Just before starting time that night they sneaked off, got into it and drove to the pavilion. As they reached the entrance and caught the attention of the boys on the stand the motor stopped. It refused to start; the owners had to push it to the cottage. Next day they got it going and decided to visit the old maids. They got to the cabin, bought a jug, and started back. Halfway home the Buick went dead. They had to find a farmer and hire him to tow it by horse to a garage.

It never ran again. It had a fine mirror and the owners used that while shaving. Ten years later Pee Wee was driving to the coast with the Louis Prima band; he detoured to reminisce at Hudson Lake and found the cottage. The car was still in the backyard on its wheels, but groggy with rust.

"I own half of that," he said. 🎵

Sudhalter and Evans describe a heroic effort made by Bix to get to a job with Paul Whiteman during a tour in Oklahoma:

It was 6:45 a.m., the morning after the concert in Tulsa. Roy Bargy, shivering with a small knot of musicians on the platform waiting to board the train to Ponca City, Oklahoma, was surprised to see a cab pull up and Bix step out. "He got out and looked at the boys as if to say, 'This time, I made it.' Being no doubt more than a little punchy at that ungodly hour, he walked right onto and through this darkened train and into another one on the next track facing exactly the other way, but also due to leave at seven. When we boarded our train a few minutes later, nobody noticed that Bix wasn't with us. I guess we assumed he was in the men's room or sleeping somewhere." 🎵

Bix was sleeping all right, but on a train headed the wrong way. When he woke and discovered his error he got off at the next station, and found that there were no trains due that would be of any help. He was too far away to make the job by rented car, but a filling station attendant knew of someone nearby who owned a biplane. Izzy Friedman, traveling with the Whiteman entourage on the right train, takes up the story from there:

He sent a telegram to Paul—it was delivered while we were on the train—saying he was going to fly and would certainly be there in time for the concert. When we got into Ponca City, quite a few of us made a beeline out to the airport, such as it was—it looked as though it had until very recently been just another cornfield—to witness his arrival.

Pretty soon this reconverted "Jenny," 1919 vintage, appears out of a deep blue sky, circles and makes a very good landing. We all rushed up to the plane, an open cockpit job, as Bix and the pilot climbed out. As they both hit the ground, Bix put his arms around the guy and shouted to us. "He's the best damned pilot in the world!" And with that the pilot took two steps toward us and fell flat on his face. He was so loaded we had to support him to our cars and take them both to the hotel. He and Bix had been taking alternate sips of corn mash up there, and while Bix was able to hold it, the pilot didn't awaken until seven that evening. ⇂

Pee Wee Russell commented on Beiderbecke's impractical good nature:

Bix couldn't say no. He couldn't say no to anybody. I remember one Victor date we did. Bix was working in the Whiteman band at the time. He had hired me for the date but rather than hurt anybody's feelings he also hired Jimmy Dorsey and Benny Goodman and Tommy Dorsey and everybody.

Every time somebody would walk into the door at Plunkett's, the bar we hung out at, Bix would say, "Gee, what am I going to do?" So he'd go up to the guy and hire him for the date. He didn't want to hurt anybody's feelings. So he went way over his budget and we had to scrape up cab fare to get back from the date. ⇂

Jack Teagarden spent a strange evening with Bix when they were in New York in 1931. Jack said:

He wanted to go down to the Bellevue morgue. I figure it's the most gruesome morgue in the world, because it's where they hold unidentified bodies as long as they can. We went down there and he gave the night caretaker a five-dollar bill to take us through. After the first couple of cases I was doing pretty good, it hadn't bothered me too bad. But Bix was starting to get sick, so we left, and that was all that was said about it.

Years later I asked his brother if he could piece anything together out of it, because I thought Bix had had a premonition. He said, "No, we're in the mortuary business and he just wanted to see the biggest one." ↯

Bix died young. George Hoefer tells a touching story from his last days:

His last weeks were spent in the apartment of a bass player named George Kraslow, out in Sunnyside, Queens. Kraslow recalls that many times through that period Bix would pick up his cornet, no matter what time it was, and play for himself. The tenants in the building would mention to Kraslow that they had been awakened at two or three in the morning by the lovely music emanating from his apartment. They would also make a point to add,

"Please don't mention we said anything as we don't want him reprimanded and would hate for him to stop." ↯

Dick Cathcart recorded a tribute to Bix Beiderbecke in 1959. The Warner Brothers album was titled *Bix MCMLIX. Down Beat* magazine reported a comment that someone overheard in a record store: "Who the hell is Bix McMlix?"

In 1984, Laurie Frink was playing lead trumpet with a band that had photocopies of some of the arrangements from the old Paul Whiteman band. On one chart there was a jazz chorus indicated for the trumpet player sitting next to Laurie. A couple of measures before that chorus she found a reminder on her part that had been penciled there long ago:

"Wake up Bix."

One night at the old Red Blazer, a club on West 46th Street in New York that featured traditional jazz, Vince Giordano informed the audience that it was Bix Beiderbecke's birthday. "If he were alive today," said Vince, "he would be ninety-two years old. And he'd be playing here on Thursday nights."

chapter 28

Thomas "Fats" Waller

Fats Waller refused to repress his rollicking sense of humor just because he happened to be one of the best jazz pianists around New York. His appealing personality made it possible for him to shift his musical venue from barrooms and dance halls to recordings, theater dates, and Hollywood films. Had he been a better businessman, he could have been one of the highest paid entertainers and songwriters in the country. But he lived for the moment, and tried to fill every moment with good times.

Waller was an easy man to work for. He hired good musicians and encouraged them to enjoy their work. Maurice Waller describes Fats's method of encouragement:

> My father had a unique system to reward inventiveness in improvisation. Pop kept two bottles of gin on a table during the rehearsals. One bottle was for himself or anyone who happened to be visiting. The other bottle was the "encourager," as he called it. When one of the band excelled in an improvisational section, Dad would stop the rehearsal, pour him a healthy shot of gin, and the two of them would toast each other. If you wanted to drink at rehearsal, you had to shine. 𝄇

Herman Autrey told of a theater engagement in Washington, D.C., that he played with Waller's band. While standing in the alley behind the theater between shows one day, Fats was approached by a kid who asked to be let in to see the show.

> What's your name?" asked Fats. "Where do you live? Tell all your friends that live on your block that I said to come down here Thursday and see the show."

On the appointed day a mob of kids showed up at the stage door. Fats sent his valet out to buy enough candy to stuff them all. When the theater manager objected to the number of freebies, Fats threatened to pull the band out of the theater. He told the kids, "Follow me," and walked into the theater. The kids jammed the house, and there was no room for the regular customers.

Fats did a good show for them and they went home happy. The theater manager didn't get happy until the following day. For the rest of the week, the mothers, fathers, grandparents, uncles and aunts of the kids who got in free came to see Fats, to find out for themselves if he was as wonderful as the kids said. ♪

Waller's band was playing in West Virginia one night when a madam closed her house and brought all her girls to hear the music. Autrey said she asked for a certain tune:

Fats said, "I'm very sorry. We don't have that tune."

"You recorded it."

"Well, no, I don't think so."

"Don't tell me, I have it in my joint on the jukebox."

"Hey, fellows, did we record this?" The guys don't remember. Fats told his valet, "Go out and look for this." The guy came back with the record. We took it in the dressing room and played it on his machine. Fats said,

"Well, I'll be damned! We did make it, didn't we?" We had to learn it all over again and go out and play it for the ladies. ♪

Fats attended a big party honoring Duke Ellington that was held in a basement club in Harlem. The jazz elite were invited, and Fats and Willie "The Lion" Smith were alternately giving the piano a workout. The party got so raucous that the police raided the joint. When he head police whistles, The Lion ran out the back door and climbed a tree, hiding in the lowest branches. As he listened for sounds of pursuit, he heard Fats's voice from a branch above him:

"What's up? A bull after you, man?"

Smith couldn't imagine how a man of Waller's girth had made it out the door and up the tree ahead of him.

Waller composed songs as easily as he improvised jazz choruses, and he often sold his work cheap. Charles Fox writes:

For the first few years [of their marriage] Waller and his wife were often very short of money, and his attempts at raising funds often took a sadly uneconomical turn. Once, for instance, he offered to sell an entire folio of his manuscripts to the Q.R.S. Company for as little as ten dollars, but luckily for him the proposal was rejected. On another occasion he tried to persuade Don Redman to buy every song he had for the same amount. Several years later he actually sold his rights in *Ain't Misbehavin'*, *Black and Blue*, and seventeen other songs to a well-known music publisher for a total of $500.

There was also the time when he spent an evening with Fletcher Henderson and a group of the musicians from Henderson's band and they all went into a hamburger bar. Fats quickly gobbled down nine hamburgers and then confessed that he had no money. His proposition was simple. If Fletcher would pay the bill, Fats, in return, would present him with nine tunes. The bandleader accepted this offer, so Waller immediately sent out for manuscript paper and within a very short time had roughed out a set of tunes that included *Top and Bottom* (later called *Henderson Stomp*), *Thundering Stomp* (better known as *Hot Mustard*), *Variety Stomp*, *St. Louis Shuffle*, and *Whiteman Stomp*.

Henderson, however, very properly insisted upon paying Fats ten dollars for each composition, instead of the hamburgers which the pianists had demanded. But this practice of trying to rob himself was one that Waller kept up throughout a large part of his life; because of it a great many of his compositions have been published under the names of other men. ↳

Gangsters were often attracted to musicians, though they sometimes had an odd way of expressing their appreciation. Maurice Waller and Anthony Calabrese tell of Fats Waller's adventure with the big boss:

Waller, playing solo piano at the Hotel Sherman in Chicago around 1925, noticed a group of tough looking guys in evening clothes in his audience. When he slipped out for a bite to eat, someone shoved a revolver into his stomach and ordered him into a car. He was driven to East Cicero to what looked like a fancy saloon. It was Al Capone's headquarters, and the boys had brought Fats to play a surprise birthday party for the gangster.

Frightened, Fats began to play with something less than his usual gusto, but when he saw the enthusiastic response from Scarface and his buddies, he swung into high gear. Capone kept him there for three days, shoving hundred dollar bills into his pocket with each request, and then returned him to Chicago several thousand dollars richer. ⟩

Ed Kirkeby describes the eating habits that gave Waller his girth and his nickname:

Charlie "Fat Man" Turner used to engage in monumental eating bouts with Fats and Gene Sedric, whose build gained him the affectionate title of "Honey Bear." Charlie remembers that, whereas he himself would eat with regularity, Fats would go for long hours with little food and then suddenly lower the boom on his stomach with a gigantic spread. This habit gave him the edge on these "chomping contests." It wasn't uncommon for him to consume fifteen hot dogs at a sitting.

One time in Providence, Rhode Island, Fats ordered steaks, one for "Fat Man" and two for himself. When they arrived, the looked so huge Charlie asked if they were elephant steaks. But Fats went at them, and it seemed to Turner that the waitress had hardly had time to get back to the kitchen when Fats was calling for another order of the same size and quantity.

Even more impressive was his performance at Charleston, South Carolina. This was at a church affair where food was sold to enrich church funds. As the band played the last note of the evening, Fats dashed off the stand and over to the food counter, buying outright a twenty-pound fresh ham. Fancying some gravy, he also bought the pan the ham was in, a carving knife, and a gallon of mustard.

Earl "Fatha" Hines also tells a tale about the man's capacity for food. One evening in Washington, D.C., a joyous reunion took place in a night club dressing room. The busboy arrived, bearing a tray of six hamburgers and twelve bottles of beer. "Why, Fats, this is fine!" exclaimed the hungry Earl, whom Fats called his Jug Brother. Fats looked up quickly and said,

"Oh yeah, Earl; if you want some too, you'll sure have to wait 'til we get some more. This little snack is just for me!" ⟩

Joe Thomas also reported on Waller's prowess at the table. The band was traveling to a job in Atlantic City, and Fats had the bus driver pull over to a roadside hamburger stand:

He says, "You guys order what you want." So we ordered. I had two
to three hamburgers. I think we all had two or three apiece. A pretty
big band, around 12 or 13 people. When nobody wanted any more,
she had around 25 hamburgers left on the grill. She says, "What am
I going to do with these?" Fats says, "Just put them in a bag, baby, I'll
take them." On the way to Atlantic City he ate 25 hamburgers and
drank his whisky.

We get to Atlantic City, and he says, "Come on, Joe, hang out with
me." So we get to this place, a nice little restaurant, very clean. Fats
knew everybody. He went right back to the kitchen. "Say, where's the
chef?" He says to the chef, "Give me three chickens. You can fry
them. Might have some baked. Bake me one. And give me three or
four steaks with all the fillin's." The chef is not surprised. We sit
down at a table. Here comes the waitress and she set up the table.
Dig it. Three chickens, three steaks, hot rolls, potatoes, salad. But
she don't know Fats Waller. Says, "Where are the rest of the people?"
He says, "Nobody but me out here." He sat there and ate it all. 🏵

Waller was a fan of John Kirby's group at the Onyx Club. When he was
introduced to Kirby's pianist, Billy Kyle, he told him he'd heard the
group's record of *Rehearsin' for a Nervous Breakdown* while he was in
England.

"That modulation you play from A-flat to F was simply terrific!" said
Fats, patting Kyle on the back. "Where did you get that one from, man?"

"I took it off a record of yours," said Kyle.

After a servicemen's fund-raiser in Milwaukee where Fats had appeared along with Dmitri Mitropolous, Fats was having a late snack at a
Chinese restaurant with some friends and was joined by Cab Calloway,
who was in town for a theater date. When the talk turned to Mitropolous
and the Minneapolis Symphony Orchestra, Cab said, "Some day I'm
going to get up there in front of a hundred men, and I'll lead them
through one of those big symphonies!"

Fats looked up from his plate and said, "When you do that, and you
get to Beethoven's Fifth, you goin' to give it an upbeat or a downbeat?"

When shooting the movie *Stormy Weather,* Waller had a scene that
called for him to open a door and discover the prostrate villain that Bill

Robinson had just punched on the chin. The script read, "Show surprise, facially and vocally." Fats opened the door, inspected the unconscious villain, looked at the camera impishly and improvised his classic line,

"One never know, do one?"

chapter 29

Eddie Condon

Eddie Condon was one of the group of young musicians who developed what became known as the Chicago style of jazz. In addition to playing banjo and guitar, he became an organizer of record dates, producer of jazz concerts, and a saloonkeeper. His two main interests in life besides his family were to hang around the music he loved and to stay loaded. He had a quick wit and a ready tongue. When asked what he thought of jazz as an art form, he was disdainful: "Canning peaches is an art form!"

Condon was at a party where a phonograph was playing an Eddy Duchin record. One of the guests said, "Don't you adore Eddy Duchin, Mr. Condon? He really makes the piano talk, doesn't he?" Condon said, "He certainly does. And what the piano says is, 'Please take your clumsy hands off me.'"

Condon dropped another barb on an ex-employer:

Red Nichols thought he played like Bix, but the similarity stopped the minute he opened his horn case. ⤶

Joe Marsala had the band at John Popkin's Hickory House on 52nd Street in New York for nearly ten years. Condon was his guitar player, but he spent a lot of his time at the bar. Marsala said:

After we had been at the Hickory House about a year, Jack Gold-man [the partner Popkin later bought out] said to me one night,

"I can't understand how people like this jazz music. There's one guy over there who must really love it. He's been in here every night." I told him,

"Jack, that's Eddie Condon. You've been paying him a salary." ⟍

Condon later moved to Nick's in the Village. All the musicians who played there did their drinking across the street at Julius's bar. They knew that this infuriated Nick, but he charged more for a drink than they did at Julius's. Condon was a sociable man who could hold his liquor; these are excellent qualifications for a nightclub operator. Eddie and the manager of Julius's, Pete Pesci, got their heads together and decided that what Eddie needed was a place of his own. They opened the first "Eddie Condon's" on West 3rd Street.

Pesci, who controlled the purse strings, was known as "Ivan the Terrible" to Condon's musicians. The name probably originated with Eddie himself. He had special names for many of the regulars, including "Flush Gordon" for the men's room attendant. Condon said that his club's policy was, "We don't throw anybody in, and we don't throw anybody out."

In 1961, after losing the 3rd Street lease to New York University, Condon and Pesci moved the club to the Hotel Sutton on East 56th Street, where it lasted until 1967. After Condon's death, Red Balaban's club on West 54th Street bore Eddie's name from 1975 until corporate construction in the neighborhood gobbled up the building ten years later.

Max Jones recounted some of Condon's remarks on music and whisky:

He cared little for bop, or anything beyond it in a way-out direction. In the early days of his first club on West 3rd Street, opened with the help of his publicist and friend Ernie Anderson, there was the oft-quoted occasion when a waiter dropped a tray of plates and cutlery. Eddie looked up from his drink and ordered: "None of that progressive jazz in here."

When he launched Condon's in December of 1945 and a reporter asked him the capacity of the club, Eddie replied, "Oh, about 200 cases." I don't suppose he repeated that crack, or his recom-

mended hangover cure—"Take the juice of two quarts of whisky"—
but other people did. ↯

Condon was once invited by a friend to have shashlik and kasha at a
Middle-Eastern restaurant. Eddie declined, saying, "The aftertaste of for-
eign food spoils the clean, pure flavor of gin for hours."

Eddie thought of himself as a rhythm section player, and would almost
never take a solo. (The one exception to this rule that has come to light
is mentioned in Chapter 17.) He once said, when asked why he didn't
take solos,

"I've spent fifteen years working up an answer to that question, and it
now practically in final form."

Eddie played the unamplified four-string guitar he called his "pork
chop" so unobtrusively that some people suspected he was a mediocre
musician, but on his records where the sound has been enhanced by
modern technology, Eddie can be heard playing fine rhythm parts. Wild
Bill Davison said:

> Ed was always there with the right chord and he knew what the hell
> he was doing. On bus rides or on train rides, when I was with Ed,
> he'd get his guitar out; you should hear some of the gorgeous
> chords he played.
>
> Ed drank a lot, you know, and if Ed was drinking, he would have a
> habit of doing such strange things. We had set tempos for every-
> thing we did—a fast song was a fast song—and sometimes Ed would
> come up and play the fast ones slow and the slow ones fast. It would
> throw you for a loop sometimes. ↯

When Condon opened his own nightclub he spent a lot of time chatting with his customers, building his clientele. Sometimes the guitarist
was a little puzzled by his fans. After praising him to the skies, one en-
thusiast sent him back to the stand with the admonition, "Now, go up
there and play me some real hot trumpet!" Eddie said,

"Please don't expect me to be at my peak. I've been having a little
trouble with my embouchure."

Wild Bill Davison talked about the hobby that the musicians developed between sets at Condon's West 3rd Street club:

> We had model trains in the basement and we built a whole railway
> down there. The whole band was in on that one. Some guys were

building box cars and we had tracks running all over the basement at Condon's, through the walls and all around.

Condon was a determined drinker, though his friend Dick Gehman insisted he was not a drunk. Gehman wrote in 1952:

Condon drinks anywhere from thirty to forty one-ounce shots of whisky per night, virtually every blessed night of the week, every single week of the year. Many nights he drinks more. Cumulatively, the total he consumes on heavier-drinking nights certainly balances those infrequent periods when he drinks nothing at all. He generally goes on the wagon for about two weeks out of each year in order to get in condition for a life-insurance examination, or, as he explains, "To give the beater a chance to resume its unnatural rhythm."

It should now be made clear that Eddie Condon is not a drunk. A drunk is a man who slobbers, falls down, sings, leaves his overcoat in bars, calls old girls, and fails to show up for work the next day. Nor is Condon an alcoholic. An alcoholic is a man who absolutely must have a drink first thing the next day.

For the first two fifths, or quarts, of every evening, Condon gives the impression that he has been drinking lemonade prepared by a stingy housewife. His neatly oiled hair is never out of place (some of his old friends call him "Slick," his boyhood nickname). His youthful face—he is forty-six, but looks to be in his early thirties—never glows unnaturally and is unlined and unflecked by those bluish spots and veins and sickly green blotches that mark the dedicated rummy. His quiet suits appear to have come from the cleaner an hour or two previously, his shoes are never without a sheen, his shirts exhibit no stains and no raveled sleeves, and his ever-present bow tie (he has nearly a hundred, and wears no other kind) might have been sewed into position by the manufacturer.

Moreover, his voice does not become thick, nor do the words in his sentences become mysteriously transposed. He essays no tap dances or demonstrations of strength, and he sings only when trying to recall some old tune, such as "It's Tulip Time in Holland," for another musician who can't remember it. A man of decent reserve, he does not attempt to kiss his friends. It may be that Condon is not the heaviest drinker at large in the nation today; New York's Third Avenue is crammed with bars full of men who could stay with him, and the alky ward at Bellevue is the home of several souls whose record for consumption is much higher. But if a trophy ever were to be awarded for the title of Best-Behaved Free-Style Drinker, the small guitarist could claim several legs. No matter how much he puts away, he apparently undergoes no personality change.

In the liner notes for one of his record albums, Condon noted that "a Mr. Dewar from somewhere in the British Isles was also in the studio at the time, very welcome indeed, although exhausted at the end of the ceremony."

Phyllis Condon, Eddie's wife, once became more than usually concerned about his drinking. She typed up a ghoulish list of musician friends who had died of liver trouble and handed it to Eddie without a word. He studied it. "There's a drummer missing," he announced, and handed it back.

Condon's sense of humor didn't leave him even when he was seriously ill. Arnold Benson told of a hospital stay in the late 1930s:

Eddie wound up in the hospital, deathly ill with acute pancreatitis. He was too sick to take food orally, and intravenous feeding wasn't possible. The doctor suggested getting some nourishment into Eddie through the only route available. Eddie didn't want any part of the endeavor; he said it lacked dignity. The doctor tried some primitive psychology.

"It'll make you feel better," the doctor said. "It'll be like having a drink."

That worked. As Eddie was rolling over, he turned his head. "See what the boys in the back room will have," he said.

During the same illness, he was given a blood transfusion. He said, "This must be Fats Waller's blood. I'm getting high."

At the first Newport Jazz Festival, held at Newport's Tennis Club, one of the local patricians asked Condon what he thought of the spectacle. Condon inspected the mob of jazz fans that filled the genteel old landmark and told him, "It's the end of tennis."

Condon walked into a friend's suite at the Warwick Hotel in New York, where he noticed a fake fireplace with artificial logs and the illusion of a fire created by red cellophane in front of a light bulb. Condon said to his friend, "It's cold in here. Could you please throw another bulb on the fire?"

When asked by an interviewer to describe the difference between the music his band played and modern jazz, Condon replied, "They flat their fifths. We consume ours."

When Condon's band staggered from the plane that brought them to England for a tour, they were met by the combined bands of Humphrey Lyttelton, Mick Mulligan, Chris Barber, and Beryl Bryden, who jammed *At the Jazz Band Ball* in a style reminiscent of the very earliest recorded examples of the King Oliver band. Condon looked around and inquired, "Where are the dinosaurs?"

Condon's marathon drinking during his visit to England in 1957 made newspaper copy on both sides of the Atlantic. His entourage included his partner and publicist, Ernie Anderson, and his buddy Dick Gehman, the co-author of one of his books. Max Jones describes their arrival at a London hotel:

It was still quite early and the man at Reception asked Eddie if he would like to breakfast. Being ignorant of the rules, he enquired if it was possible to get whisky for breakfast.

"In an English hotel, Sir, a guest can get alcoholic refreshment at any hour of the day or night," he was informed. The bandleader turned a bleary eye in Gehman's direction. "Dick," he announced, "I'm taking out papers."

This was the prelude to an alleged press reception in Condon's rooms which seared itself on my memory, as indeed did the tour itself.

While the leader reclined gratefully on his bed, fully dressed and with hat tilted forward on his head, right-hand man Anderson offered refreshment to anyone willing. After a check, he lifted the phone and ordered, "Half a dozen large whiskeys, please." The recumbent figure muttered, "Add half a dozen large doctors." Members of the press began to be admitted, and more drinks were dispensed. One or two brave souls attempted questions, such as why Eddie took no solos.

"I don't play solos for a reason; I don't know enough about the guitar," was one muffled response. Pressed further, he opened his eyes and declared,

"I'm a saloon keeper, not a guitar player."

A worried daily with a deadline to meet asked if Mr. Condon would object to answering questions from a sitting position. Peering from under his brim, Eddie promised to do his best. "But I'm not really an athlete." ↳

In Bristol, England, Condon made the rounds of the local jazz clubs until very late on a Saturday night. His attempts to sleep it off the next morning were made difficult by the bells of a dozen churches near his hotel. Condon moaned to his roommate Dick Gehman, "Could you please get Norvo to take a nap?"

Al Rose describes a surprising discovery he made at the Downtowner Motor Inn in Masassas, Virginia, during a jazz festival in that city. Condon's room was between Rose's and that of tenorman Bob Greene:

I'd gotten a full hour of shut-eye when a sudden loud and eerie noise set me rigidly upright in bed. I deduced that someone had broken into Condon's room and was in the process of pulling his fingernails out.

I immediately put on my bathrobe and charged out into the frigid night to rescue our little friend from the demented attackers. Once outside, I noted that Bob Greene, too, had emerged from his room. We faced each other in front of Condon's door and I tried the knob. No dice. Bob knocked. The painful groans and screeches continued unabated. I stepped back, preparatory to charging the door with the intent of breaking it down. Just as I was about to make my initial lunge, we saw Phyllis, Eddie's wife, coming our way down the walk and carrying what looked like an overnight bag.

"Good morning, boys," she greeted us, reacting not a tittle to the howls and screams we knew she couldn't help hearing. "Trouble getting to sleep?"

"Eddie's in trouble!" Bob shouted excitedly. Phyllis had her room key out. "No," she said calmly. "He's all right. He's just singing. He sings in his sleep." Phyllis explained that she was the one who always checked them in at hotels. Without telling Eddie, she always rented an extra room so she could get some sleep, too. Then, early in the morning, she would join him in his room and he would never know the difference. ↰

chapter 30

Pee Wee Russell

As Pee Wee Russell played, he twisted his lanky body and his long, rubbery face into wonderful expressions of struggle, near-defeat, and astonished victory. A shy man, he mumbled and twisted uncomfortably when speaking, but if you paid close attention, you discovered that he was a very determined individualist.

Pee Wee spent a number of years of his life so thoroughly soaked in alcohol that his memory of them was blurred when serious health problems finally forced him to give up drinking. As he sat between sets at a Boston jazz club, a man and woman came over and greeted him warmly. He looked at them with a pleasant, blank inquiry.

"Pee Wee, don't you remember us?" said the woman. "You stayed at our house for six months while you were working in St. Louis!"

Pee Wee smiled uncomfortably and gave a helpless shrug. "If you say so," he said.

Condon and O'Neill tell of Pee Wee's loss of memory on another occasion:

Joe Rushton once loaned Pee Wee Russell his clarinet when Pee Wee broke his on a job in Chicago. Pee Wee was sometimes forgetful and when the job in Chicago was over he took the clarinet back with him to New York. Later, when Joe found out about it, he got on his motorcycle and drove nonstop from Chicago to New York. Pee Wee was playing at Nick's at the time and when Joe got there he was on the stand taking a solo. Joe walked right up to the bandstand and yanked the clarinet out of Pee Wee's permanently trembling hands. He said simply, "Pee Wee, that wasn't very nice." Joe walked out, got on his cycle, and scooted right back to Chicago. ⤷

Smith and Guttridge describe young Pee Wee's arrival in Houston, Texas, to join Peck Kelley's band:

The composition of Peck's Bad Boys was never stable beyond a few months. Departures and arrivals continued to mark the organization's progress. That the musical output remained high in quality was due chiefly to Kelley's shrewdness in selecting replacements. Not only did he bar mediocrity, he sought originality and was able to distinguish it from mere novelty.

One of the most original artists ever to perform under the supervision of Kelley or anyone else stepped off the train in Houston station and glanced nervously around. He wasn't all that far from his home town of St. Louis, but sixteen-year-old Charles "Pee Wee" Russell was already homesick. For comfort he reached into the pocket of his brand new suit and fingered the telegram which had enticed him from his chair in Herbert Berger's Cordova Hotel Orchestra.

He straightened his derby and gazed anxiously at his new spats. Then he felt someone else staring at him. He looked up. Peck Kelley was studying him with disbelief. After terse introductions they got in a car and drove off. For some minutes the journey was painful. Peck's lips didn't move but his eyes were asking, *What the hell is this?*

The purpose of Pee Wee's freshly bought finery had been to impress, certainly. But the reaction of his new boss was not the one he had expected. Peck clearly needed swift reassurance. Pee Wee gave it. He took off his derby and without a word flung it through the window. Then he looked at Peck—and relaxed. Peck was grinning. ⤷

James Shacter tells the story of Pee Wee and a St. Louis physician named Hub Pruett, a friend of jazz musicians:

Pruett's basement den featured a piano, a tape recorder, a mammoth collection of tapes and records, and even a record press.

Also in the den was—and is—a battered old sofa that has a unique name. Pruett had brought Pee Wee Russell home with him early one morning after hearing his old friend play in a local club. "We went downstairs and started winging the music around," Pruett says. "About ten or eleven o'clock, I remembered that my son was playing in a football game that day. I told Pee Wee I was going over to the high school. I got a blanket for him and laid him on the sofa.

"I hadn't seen my wife all that time. She had been asleep when we got home, and I never even let her know that Pee Wee was there. I went to the football game, and during the first quarter I got a call over the P.A. system to phone my home. Emergency. I called, and my wife told me, 'For goodness sake, come home right away. There's a dead man in the basement. He's lying there with his hands folded, and I'm scared to death.' I told her she was wrong, but I said I'd come home anyhow. I knew it was Pee Wee, of course, but knowing Pee Wee, he could have kicked off. He looked half dead most of the time anyway.

"I rushed home and ran downstairs, and there he lay. I shook him a little, and Pee Wee mumbled, 'Mmmmm, bourbon and seltzer.' From then on all the boys called the sofa 'Pee Wee's coffin.' " ◢

Many jam sessions took place at the Evanston, Illinois, home of attorney and pianist Squirrel Ashcraft. Herb Sanford mentioned one that Pee Wee attended:

There was the night Squirrel excused himself early, retiring at 3:00 a.m. because he had an important appointment at 9:00 a.m. The music carried on until daylight. Pee Wee started for home, stopping at a milk wagon, as was his custom, to buy a bottle of milk. The driver was out of sight, making deliveries. As Bill Priestly tells it,

"Pee Wee, who had no change and was not going to leave a bill, got tired of waiting and took a bottle. Of course, the driver returned at this moment, yelled blue murder, and Pee Wee ended up in the pokey. When Squirrel came out of his meeting, he got the S.O.S. and found that the judge before whom Pee Wee would come to trial was a good friend and a jazz buff who particularly admired Pee Wee's playing. So it was in the bag, but rigged as follows: the judge was very stern with Pee Wee, who was shivering in a disheveled tuxedo and in need of a shave, and finally dismissed Pee Wee with a suspended sentence and the grim admonition: 'Mr. Russell, never let me hear of you touching milk again as long as you live!' " ◢

Arnold Shaw writes of Eddie Condon's efforts to keep Pee Wee straight while working with him at the Onyx:

The gimmick was to keep the clarinetist from leaving the club between sets. It did not prevent Pee Wee from imbibing. Only an alley separated the Onyx from Reilly's bar. A window in the men's room of the Onyx opened on the alley. And Reilly's bar had a back door opening on the alley. Russell's countergimmick was to take off the moment another member of the combo embarked on several improvisatory choruses. Through the window, across the alley, into Reilly's, down a double—and he was back in time to join the ensemble.

Charles Edward Smith tells about an erroneous report of Pee Wee's demise:

Once, when Pee Wee was playing gigs in the hinterlands of New England, he was lost track of, so far as his colleagues in New York were concerned. Somehow a rumor started that he had broken a leg or was dying and finally, as rumors will, this one had Pee Wee at death's door in no time at all. Around Plunkett's, the speakeasy under the El, listed in the phone book as the Trombone Club in honor of Tommy Dorsey's fine, upstanding bar bill, the boys were trying to think of all the nice things they'd forgotten to say when Pee Wee was around. Unaware of this morbid turn of events but, like Ulysses, having gone through a series of unforeseen crises, Pee Wee walked into Plunkett's with an eye for the bar, and was caught up short by the expressions on his friends' faces. Everyone looked frightened and, for a split second, no one spoke. Then Pee Wee said, "What's wrong? What's going on here?"

"You're supposed to be dead!" There was shock and accusation in the tone of voice.

Then it all came out. How Pee Wee was supposed to have been ill or something and had passed away. All his friends had been pitching in to buy flowers. Well, that was that. They spent the money in Plunkett's instead.

Art Hodes had the pleasure of putting Pee Wee on educational television:

When the opportunity arose for me to do educational TV in Chicago, Bob Kaiser (director) and I decided on having Russell and

Jimmy McPartland as guest artists. That was a funny show. Maybe you saw it. Bob cracked up. He was in the sound room and both Jimmy and Pee Wee had mikes around their collars. The conversation went something like this:

"Pee Wee, how about you changing places with me?"

Pee Wee liked to stand next to the piano. Some wag remarked the it gave him something to lean on. May be true; but he also liked to hear the chords a piano man was laying down. Anyway, Russell was happy where he was and said so. I still don't know why Jimmy wanted to change but he did.

"I'll give you five dollars."

All he got was a mutter.

A bit later Pee Wee discovered the bartender. Now that was a prop Kaiser had inserted. There was a bar and a life size photo of a bartender but no booze. But just seeing him made Pee Wee go into his act.

"Hey, bartender, I mean you; come over here."

Bob K. finally had to shut off the mike. All through the show Russell would look over in that direction and seemingly he couldn't help himself. Automatically he'd call out "Mr. Bartender."

Pee Wee took up painting late in life, and was as original with the brush as he was with his clarinet. Kym Bonython in Adelaide, Australia, owned one of Pee Wee's paintings until it, along with his record collection and the rest of his belongings, was destroyed in a bushfire in 1983. Having been in the art gallery business, Bonython had gone to Russell's New York apartment in 1965 to look at his paintings. When he asked, "How much for a painting like this?" Pee Wee replied "Twenty-five hundred dollars." Bonython said that was a bit higher than he had intended to go. Pee Wee came back instantly, "How about four hundred?"

Another prospective customer once asked Pee Wee why his paintings were so expensive. Pee Wee replied, "Well, you know, they're all hand made."

chapter 31

Duke Ellington and His Orchestra

Edward Kennedy Ellington was a complex, fascinating man who cast a large shadow across the music world. Even though several books have been written about him, including his own autobiography, he remains elusive. He accepted the sobriquet "Duke" while in his teens, and began creating for himself a persona of elegance and suavity (with a touch of the put-on) that he refined throughout his seventy-five years, a lifetime filled with tremendous musical productivity.

Fond of flowery phrases and romantic gestures, Ellington bore himself with the utmost self-assurance, yet he observed more personal superstitions than a minor-league ballplayer. James Lincoln Collier writes:

> He would not wear certain colors; he would not give or receive gifts of shoes, which suggested that the recipient would use them to walk away; he was afraid of drafts and kept the windows around him closed at all times; he was frightened of flying and refused to do it until the demands of travel forced him into planes; and he subjected himself to many similar taboos. Ellington was hardly the first person to be superstitious, but his collection of taboos make a richer array than most people possess. It is difficult to find an explanation for them. ↱

Patricia Willard asked Juan Tizol about Ellington's superstitions. Tizol said:

> Duke used to say never come in his dressing room eating peanuts or something like that. And if you dropped a button—he would never like to see a button that somebody dropped on the stage or in his dressing room. He didn't like that. ↱

Willard had personal experience with Ellington's superstitions:

I know once he had put all the telegrams he received at an opening around his mirror, some of them from very famous people. When the engagement was over and he was packing up his stuff and the valet was packing his clothes I started to take the telegrams down. He said, "No, don't touch those. Leave them there."

I asked why.

"It's bad luck to take down your opening night telegrams."

The last twenty-five years of his life that I knew him, he never had a watch and wouldn't wear one, but yet he always wanted to know what time it was. ❦

Louis Bellson recalled:

Duke and Strayhorn were full of superstitions. Nobody was supposed to wear anything with yellow in it. Nobody was supposed to button a shirt all the way down the front. Nobody was supposed to whistle in the dressing room. ❦

Rex Stewart remembered Ellington's displeasure with missing buttons:

I have often seen him abruptly stride off stage to change after a button fell off. During that period when I was with the band, some lucky fellow would be the proud possessor of an Ellington suit or jacket, as Duke would not wear a garment after it lost a button. ❦

Lawrence Brown had to deal with Duke's superstitions when he first joined the band:

I didn't play with the band at first, because I was the thirteenth man. There was so much superstition. Oh, no, not thirteen men! I had to wait for the fourteenth man, Otto Hardwick, for about six weeks. And didn't get paid until I played my first job. ❦

Derek Jewell told of the unusual talismans that Ellington carried:

Photographer Ian Yeomans was constructing a magazine feature on what men carried in their pockets. So he asked Duke, unforewarned, to turn out his. There wasn't much in them, in fact, but in his hip pocket was a wad of crumpled dollar bills, each one wrapped around a St. Christopher medal and other religious emblems.

"People send them to me," he said. "This is their way of showing that they know my feelings. I never like to be without them." ⭰

Duke dressed with great flair, especially onstage. His manner before an audience breathed the elegance and dignity of the finest concert halls long before he actually appeared in them. Even when the stage machinery failed him at the Club Zanzibar in New York, he never lost his aplomb. That show opened with the band backlit with blue floodlights as they played a moaning opener, and then a spotlight would pick up Duke, in white tails at a white grand piano, being lowered from the ceiling by four steel cables. One night something went wrong with the cables and two of them stopped moving while the other two continued to descend. Duke remained calm and elegant as the piano tilted. He hooked a leg around the piano bench, grabbed the high side of the piano with one hand and held on until the stage crew got him down safely.

Duke loved the company of women, and had a number of stock lines with which he charmed them. He'd say,

"I can tell that you're an angel; I can see the reflection from your halo shining on the ceiling." Or,

"My, but you make that dress look lovely!"

When he spotted a female to whom he hadn't been introduced, he would usually say,

"Whose little girl are you?"

He automatically dispensed his suave flattery on every woman in his presence, and usually found it quite effective.

Duke's band was booked on a concert tour with Louis Armstrong. Louis's vocalist at the time was Big Maybelle, the blues singer, whose physical proportions did not belie her name. Harold Baker said that when Duke first encountered Maybelle backstage he automatically raised his eyebrows, turned on his 1000-watt smile, and murmured,

"Well! And whose little girl are you?"

Maybelle snapped back indignantly in her stevedore's voice,

"What the fuck you mean, whose *little* girl am I?"

The whole band nearly died laughing as Duke graciously backpedaled and moved on to chat with someone else.

Early in Ellington's career, composer Percy Grainger told him that he heard the influence of Frederick Delius in his writing. Grainger undoubtedly intended it as a compliment, but Duke didn't look happy. Later, a friend of Duke's told him that all great composers have been influenced by other composers. Duke replied, "It's not that. I just never heard of Frederick Delius before."

When an earnest interviewer asked Joe Nanton if he considered Ellington a genius, Nanton replied, "I don't know about that, but Jesus, he can eat!"

Derek Jewell made notes on Ellington's appetite during the 1940s:

With the amount of energy he expended, he needed fuel, and these were the years of Ellington the gourmand rather than the gourmet. Many descriptions of typical Ellington menus exist from this period, revealing, so often, a man whose virtuous resolution to keep his weight down collapsed in stages so that he ended up eating three or four separate meals in succession.

Maybe he started well, with breakfast cereal and black tea, proclaiming that this would be enough. Then, viewing companions carving at steaks, he would add, straight-faced, a plain steak. Several minutes might elapse before the will to resist finally disintegrated. A second steak, onions, French fries, salad, with a Maine lobster on the side might next appear. Then fruit and cheese, and, with coffee, a specially concocted Ellington dessert, for which he was renowned; chocolate cake, custard, ice cream, jelly, apple sauce, and whipped cream. He adored ham and eggs, so that might be added as an afterthought, with pancakes and syrup, of course.

The after-afterthought would be a resumption of the diet: cereal and black tea to finish with. ↡

Ellington's orchestra was as much his instrument as was the piano. Duke hired musicians who had individual sounds and styles in order to have their unique musical qualities for his compositions and orchestrations. His musicians also had unique personalities. Preferring to adapt to the idiosyncrasies of his musicians rather than trying to modify them, Duke ran his band with a loose hand. He didn't reprimand anyone for coming to work late; he simply started the job with whoever showed up, adjusting the music to fit the size of the band. He would wait to call arrangements that required the whole ensemble until everyone was there.

He rarely fired anyone. When he wanted to replace a musician, Duke would just make him so uncomfortable that he'd leave. One of his ways of making a man uncomfortable was to hire a better player to sit beside him and duplicate his part. He even did this with bass players and drummers. If a musician's drinking interfered with his playing, Duke might give him a solo and keep calling for chorus after chorus until the pressure and hard work sobered him up a little.

His manipulations didn't always work. When Ben Webster drank too much before a California concert, Duke announced that Ben would play a feature on "Body and Soul," which was Coleman Hawkins's tour de force. Ben stood up and glared at Duke. "Play it yourself, you sonofabitch!" he said, and walked offstage. Ben was fearsome when drinking, and quite unmanageable, even by Duke.

Cat Anderson described the beginning of a misunderstanding on the Ellington band that lasted for years:

> The band used to play Mary Lou Williams's arrangement of *Blue Skies*. It wasn't just a trumpet feature then. There was a chorus of tenor by Al Sears, a release by Claude Jones, and Rex Stewart used to play the ending. We were at the theater in Canton, Ohio, when Rex didn't show. After listening to it all week—and I'm a great listener to anything good, especially on trumpet—I knew his solo. So when Duke asked if anybody wanted to play it, and nobody volunteered, he said, "What about the new trumpet player?" I told him I'd try, and after the other solos I came down front and played it an octave higher. When I ended up on a double C, and the people were applauding, Duke said, "Good, we'll keep it just like that." As luck would have it, Rex came in the stage door as I was blasting away. He didn't speak to me for fifteen years. ⤻

Buck Clayton ran across the Ellingtonians when they passed through Los Angeles:

> I'll never forget one day when I happened to be in a restaurant in the Dunbar. Most of Duke's guys were in there too and they were all listening to the jukebox. It was the first time since leaving the East that they had heard their recording of *It Don't Mean a Thing If It Ain't Got That Swing*, and that restaurant was swinging like crazy. So much rhythm I'd never heard, as guys were beating on tables, instrument cases, or anything else that they could beat on with knives,

forks, rolled up newspapers or anything they could find to make rhythm. It was absolutely crazy. I found out one more thing about Duke's band being in a restaurant. If there is fifteen musicians that enter a restaurant they take up fifteen tables as everybody takes a table for himself. I never knew why, but everybody wanted and got his own table. 🎵

Barney Bigard discusses Ellington's first drummer, Sonny Greer:

The only thing that bugged me about his playing was that you could be taking a solo and everything was going just nice, he would be giving just the right beat, and then someone he knew would walk in the place and he'd spy them and start to waving his arms to say hello. The beat would be gone right in the middle of your solo. But you couldn't get mad with him. That's just the way he was, always friendly to people. 🎵

Dizzy Gillespie got a different impression of Greer during the month he worked with Ellington in 1944 at the Capitol Theater in New York:

I was there because Ray Nance had union card trouble. I looked at the music, and I couldn't play it! None of them, not Rex or nobody, would give me any help. So I used to sit there each time the curtain came down and I'd play and play to myself. And one day Sonny Greer, he comes up to me and he says, "Hey, *nigger*. What you doin' there practicin' all the time when you s'posed to be restin'?" So I look him straight down the eye and I say, "Hey, *old man!* What you doin' sleepin' behind them drums when you s'posed to be playin'?"

Of course I was full of shit in those days. Still am, baby. But Sonny, umm, he was getting to be real mean by then.

I made a record with Duke later, kind of accidental. I just happened along one day with my horn and we blew and they taped it and they put it out. And when I got no money, I mentioned it, very gently, to Duke, and he smiled and he says, "Well, Diz, I can't pay you what you're really worth." Whee, was that a cunning, elegant man! So I smile and I says, "Don't give it no mind, Duke. Just so long as you *pay* me!" And maybe a year later, he did. 🎵

Johnny Hodges's distinctive alto saxophone playing was a basic ingredient of the Ellington sound for many years. Derek Jewell writes:

Hodges insisted that he be paid on a daily basis, explaining to a questioner on one occasion:

"I don't trust myself or anyone else. When I was pickin' cotton I used to get paid at the end of every day. I want to owe nothin' to anyone and have nothin' owed to me either."

The cotton-picking reference was doubtless metaphorical.

When Ellington decided to add a tenor saxophone to his band, Ben Webster was the one he had in mind. Duke said later, "I had a yen for Ben." But Ben was working for Cab Calloway. Milt Hinton tells how Duke managed to get him:

He always wanted to play with Duke. But there was no way. He would make his desires known that he wanted to play with Duke, and Duke being the very clever man that he was, told Ben, "I would love to have you in the band, but Cab's is my brother band and I can't take anybody out of his band. *But*, if you didn't have a job I'd have to give you one."

This started the chemistry in Ben and he started saving up his money. About six months later we hit Cleveland, Ohio, and Duke was going to play the Jeffrey Tavern in Chicago, so Ben put in his notice with Cab. Ben left and went to Chicago with no job. He went on the corners and told Duke, "Well, I'm unemployed." And Duke hired him.

"Ben Webster was one of the strongest musicians I ever knew," said George Avakian. "Ben and I were listening to somebody, standing at the old Birdland bar, and for the third time since midnight I said, 'Ben, I really have to get home.' Ben looked me in the eye, said 'Uh-uh!' and picked me up, turned me sideways and held me over his head! But he was a gentleman . . . the moment I said 'I'll stay,' he set me down gently and picked up all the change that had fallen out of my pockets."

Dave Frishberg remembered his first night with Ben Webster's group at the Shalimar in Los Angeles. Ben was at the microphone introducing the next song, "Danny Boy," and he turned to Dave at the piano and said, "Reminisce." Dave said, "What?" and Ben repeated, "Reminisce." "What are you talking about?" asked Dave. Webster explained, "When I'm talking to the people, you reminisce behind me." Dave understood, and began to play nostalgic melodies as Ben spoke to the audience.

After Webster moved to Denmark, he often played in Oslo. During his stays there, bassist Bjorn Pedersen was assigned the job of making sure Ben got to the job on time. If Ben had stayed up drinking the night before, he was often difficult (and dangerous) to wake. Bjorn had the key to Ben's hotel room, and when the great saxophonist failed to answer his knock one afternoon, Bjorn quietly unlocked the door and stepped into the darkened room. He felt his way to the window, intending to raise the blind a crack, but it slipped from his fingers and spun to the top of the window with a loud flutter. Sunlight flooded in onto the bed, and Webster sat bolt upright, blinking in the blinding light. He shouted, "Who opened up my coffin?"

Duke's most distinctive female vocalist was Ivie Anderson. Juan Tizol spoke of the health problem that finally caused her to leave the band:

> Ivie Anderson, we got her in Chicago. She was suffering from asthma, you know? She had it so bad she would have to go out on the street to get some air because she couldn't hardly breathe, but she could be feeling bad on the stage and go out there and sing, and you couldn't tell she had asthma. She was terrific. ↳

There was criticism of Cootie Williams when he left Ellington in 1940 to join Benny Goodman's band. Many fans felt Cootie was being disloyal to Duke. Cootie set the record straight:

> When Benny Goodman wanted me, I told Duke, and he said, "Let me handle everything. Let me see how much I can get for you. You deserve to make some money."
>
> So he did—he handled the contract. And when I left, I said, "You have my job open when the contract is up?" and he said, "Your chair's always open."
>
> When my contract with Benny Goodman was up in 1941, I asked Duke for my job back, and he told me, "You're too big for the job. You're bigger than you think you are. Go on your own."
>
> So I did. I organized a big band, and for a while things were bad, but in 1943 I made two hundred and fifty thousand dollars. ↳

Quentin "Butter" Jackson inherited Tyree Glenn's chair in Duke's trombone section. Tyree was road weary and wanted to go home. He talked it over with Duke. There was the problem of finding a replacement who could play the plunger mute solos in the style originated by Joe Nanton. Quentin said:

The next night I came to work and here's this mute and plunger in front of my chair, and I said, "Oh, no!" Duke said, "Tyree told me you could play anything. He said you could do this." And do you know that night he called *Transblucency* on me? He called *Turquoise Cloud* and all those things on me. I didn't even need to read the music because I'd heard every note Tyree played on those parts, and I went out there and played it. 🎵

When Taft Jordan left Ellington he originally had intended just to take a vacation for a few weeks from Duke's grueling road schedule. Other work turned up in New York, so he kept putting off his return to the band. Before he realized it he'd been gone for two years. Ellington dropped in at the Club Savannah one night to hear Lucille Dixon's band, and saw Taft in the trumpet section. As he walked up to say hello to Lucille, he called to Taft, "Are you still on vacation?"

Taft said he enjoyed his four years with Duke, but they wore him out:

When I left Duke, I was so tired I slept almost a whole year. I'd had too much road. For a long time I actually slept two or three times a day, and not cat naps, but for two or three hours. I hadn't realized how tired I was while I was out there. 🎵

Paul Gonsalves, Duke's star tenor player after 1950, was a liberal user of alcohol, among other things. When a critic deplored Gonsalves's condition on the bandstand one night, Ellington defended him, claiming that Paul was a war veteran who had served in the South Pacific where he had contracted malaria. Jimmy Jones described some incidents involving Gonsalves:

Paul fell down on the stand at the Sands in Las Vegas, and he was sober as a judge that night. Just fell off his chair. He stood up and held his horn up to let everybody know he was all right. And Duke walked to the mike and said, "Isn't that amazing? This man doesn't even drink!" And we broke up. Another time, in Italy with Ella Fitzgerald and Duke Ellington, I'm conducting the band from the piano and I could see Paul to my left. He was feeling pretty good that night. They were televising this thing. I could see the leg coming off of Paul's chair, but I'm watching Ella out in front. Paul began to lean over. He fell on the floor. When he got up, he looked out to the audience and said, "Ssh, don't tell nobody!" The television cameras were all over the stage and Ella Fitzgerald had to stop singing because the audience broke up laughing.

There was one time when in Basin Street East, you know they had a high bandstand there. Paul didn't come back from 3rd Avenue where that little bar was where they'd take intermission. So Duke was playing with four saxophones, and I asked Strayhorn,

"Doesn't it bother Duke?" And Strayhorn says,

"Duke doesn't know that he's not there." ↯

Gonsalves fell so deeply asleep on the bandstand at a Chicago concert that his lookout man, bassist Jimmy Woode, was just barely able to nudge him awake in time for his solo on *Take the A Train*. "Paul, you're on!" Still asleep, he stumbled to his feet and got out to the solo microphone on automatic pilot. Ray Nance had just finished his violin chorus. Paul came fully awake to hear the audience applauding Nance. Thinking he must have already played his solo, Paul took a bow and returned to his seat.

When Gonsalves's habits created a problem, Ellington handled it in his own way. Shooting some pictures of Duke at an Ellington record date, photographer Ted Williams observed this scene:

The band tried several takes on a tune. Paul Gonsalves kept botching it. Duke, in the control booth, pushed the talk-back switch on the console and said, "Paul Gonsalves. You're wanted on the telephone in the hall." Gonsalves left the studio, and Duke called to the other musicians, "Lock that door!" And then he kicked off a tempo, and Duke got his take. ↯

There were a couple of times when Duke had two bass players. Billy Taylor, Sr., was on the band when Duke discovered Jimmy Blanton, the young virtuoso who revolutionized jazz bass playing. Duke had to have him, but couldn't bring himself to fire Taylor. The two bassists played side by side until Taylor finally threw in the towel on a job in Boston, walking off the bandstand one night in the middle of the job. He said, "I'm not going to stand up there next to that young boy playing all that bass and be embarrassed."

After Blanton's untimely death Duke hired Junior Raglin. He found that his new bassist would often overdo his drinking and miss the job, so he hired Al Lucas as well, hoping to have at least one sober bassist on the bandstand. Lucas and Raglin promptly became drinking buddies. Duke said, "I'm paying two bass players and neither one of them are here!"

Duke solved a similar problem in Chicago when Sam Woodyard failed to show up for a week at the Blue Note. Duke hired a local drummer to replace him. When Sam finally came to work, Duke had him set up alongside the other drummer and they both played. Sam messed around with the time just enough to cause the local drummer to resign, and Duke had the band back the way he had originally wanted it.

Clark Terry spoke of Duke's persuasive way of extracting good performances from his musicians:

He had a way of getting things out of you that you didn't realize you had in you. Let me give you an example. We were doing an album called "A Drum Is a Woman," and Duke came to me and said, "Clark, I want you to play Buddy Bolden for me on this album."

I said, "Maestro, I don't know who the hell Buddy Bolden is!" Duke said, "Oh, sure, you know Buddy Bolden. Buddy Bolden was suave, handsome, and a debonair cat who the ladies loved. Aw, he was so fantastic! He was fabulous! He was always sought after. He had the biggest, fattest trumpet sound in town. He bent notes to the nth degree. He used to tune up in New Orleans and break glasses in Algiers! He was great with diminisheds. When he played a diminished, he bent those notes, man, like you've never heard them before!"

By this time Duke had me psyched out! He finished by saying, "As a matter of fact, you are Buddy Bolden!" So I thought I was Buddy Bolden.

Duke said, "Play Buddy Bolden for me on this record date."

I played and at the conclusion of the session, Duke came up to me and put his arms around my shoulders and said, "That was Buddy Bolden." ⤵

Grover Mitchell described the state of affairs on Duke's band when he joined it:

I had only been working with him for about a week. The first night or two everybody had gotten on the bandstand and had really roared. But the next two, three, or four nights, maybe there would be five or six of us on the bandstand, and eight or ten guys walking around out in the audience talking to people, or at the bar. One night we were on the bandstand and a waiter came up and told Jimmy Hamilton that his steak was ready. He stepped off the band-stand and started cuttin' into a steak.

Later I says to Duke, "Man, how can you put up with this?" And he told me,

"Look, let me tell you something. I live for the nights that this band is great. I don't worry about nights like what you're worrying about. If you pay attention to these people, they will drive you crazy. They're not going to drive me crazy." ⬧

Major Holley was an Ellingtonian who got overlooked by the historians:

I worked for Duke for over eleven months solid, although for some reason Stanley Dance never mentioned that fact in any of his books on Duke. For eleven months I was in that band, but I never did get paid! No sir, I'd draw an advance from time to time, I had to live, but I never did get paid. I'd go to Duke whenever I had the chance and ask him about my money. Duke would smile. He could charm a snake out of a hole. Without fail he would ask my advice on some bass passage in his latest composition, or some such. But I'd ignore that and ask for my money. And Duke would just glide to his feet— everything he did was in rhythm, you know—and was away. Oh, he was an oblique character, was Duke, but what a charmer, and what a musical genius. It was his manager, of course, who was tilting the machine. Duke never worried himself about money, either his own or anyone else's. I had to take him to the Union in the end before I got paid. ⬧

Lee Young once got a chance to play with the Ellington band. Ben Webster (Frog) and Jimmy Blanton (Bear) engineered it:

Duke was opening at the Trianon Ballroom the same night we were opening at Billy Berg's. So Frog and Bear called me and said,

"Sonny Greer is not gonna make it tonight. You better come on and open with us."

I told them it was my opening night, that my name was out front, Lee and Lester Young. I told Billy Berg, "I'm gonna go play with Duke tonight. You'll have to get another drummer."

"What do you mean? You're the leader!"

"I don't care. I may not ever get a chance again in my life to play with Duke, and I'm not gonna give this up."

I had signed a contract with the man, but Billy Berg was very fond of me.

"You've got to be the craziest man in the world. How can you be the leader of the band and not make your opening?"

"There's no need talking about it. I'm going to play with Duke tonight."

Luckily, when I came back the next night, I still had a job. ❧

Charlie Barnet loved Ellington's music, and tried to get his band to emulate Duke's sound. Duke told about Barnet's fealty:

Charlie Barnet has always been a wonderful friend to me. If he heard we had a layoff in his territory, during those times when his band was not organized and working, he would call my agent and say, "I want Duke's band to play a party for me." Actually, it would be a party for us, for there was no set order of playing—just play when we felt like it. And then, between "sets," we would join the party and ball it up like guests of honor.

One night, at one of these parties, he had signs posted up in the lobby of the country club where we were supposed to be working. They read: *No Requests. No Melancholy Baby. No Anything but Duke Ellington.* He had an electric board fixed backstage, and he sat at it himself and blended the lights to fit the mood of the music. ❧

In the late 1950s and early 1960s there were still a few ballrooms around the country that had become popular during the glory days of the big bands. And during the spring prom season, there was still quite a bit of work for name bands at colleges. But most of the swing era bandleaders who still had name recognition had broken up their bands. When a few gigs came up, they relied on a few New York contractors to put together enough musicians with big band experience to cover the bookings.

Steve Little was often available and took jobs several times with different bandleaders, and one of the nights would always be at the ballroom in Hershey, Pennsylvania. He turned up there with so many different bands that the manager of the ballroom began to think he had been hired locally. He told the bandleaders, "Don't bring that drummer in here any more! My customers don't want some local guy filling in . . . they want the real New York players!"

Then Duke Ellington asked Steve to join his band, and sure enough, one of their first gigs was the ballroom in Hershey. The manager took one look at Steve and went through the roof. "It's that same guy again! Get him out of here!" It took Duke a while to convince him that Steve was a regular member of his band.

Milt Bernhart achieved fame as a trombonist on the Stan Kenton band in the late 1940s, and had a long career in movie and television orchestras in California. In the 1960s, Milt was thrilled to be on a movie call with the Ellington band. For some reason, Duke had gone to California without his trombone section, and had hired Murray McEachern, Vern Friley, George Roberts, and Milt to replace them. The rest of that famous band was intact for the date. Sitting among them, Milt said he thought he'd died and gone to heaven.

The movie was *Assault on the Queen*. On the first day, Duke walked into the studio and placed on each music stand a single eight-bar line of music that he had written. They ran it down once, and then Duke asked the editor how much music was needed for the scene they were doing. "Five minutes," he was told. "Okay," said Duke, "let's do it." Milt described the scene:

> I looked down into those famous baggy eyes and asked, "Pardon me, Duke. What'll we play besides the eight bars we've got?" His eyebrows went up a fraction and he said, "You'll know." That was the end of the questioning period. It was time to play. And we did. Everything worked out as if directed by some unseen hand. We only did it once . . . that's all that was necessary. Duke believed it, and therefore, it had to be. That's as good as things ever got for me. ⑂

Paul Kondziela played bass with Ellington for a while in the late 1960s. One night during a bass-piano duet, Duke hit one of those dissonant chords that were his specialty. Paul, who had studied at Berklee for several years, leaned over Duke's shoulder, looked at his hands on the keyboard, and said, "Ah, double diminished!" Duke spun around and replied, "Oh, is that what it is?"

Leonard Feather tells a story that sums up Ellington's effect on other musicians:

He has withheld his throne from the grasp of thirty years of pretenders, imitated but inimitable. What he has done in those thirty years was best summed up one evening at the Opera House in San Francisco by André Previn, a musician who was not born when the Cotton Club era began.

"You know," he said, "Stan Kenton can stand in front of a thousand fiddles and a thousand brass and make a dramatic gesture, and every studio arranger can nod his head and say, 'Oh, yes, that's done like this.' But Duke merely lifts his finger, three horns make a sound, and I don't know what it is!" ♪

chapter 32

Benny Goodman

Benny Goodman has probably generated more anecdotes than any other musician. He was a superior instrumentalist and an extremely successful bandleader. He was also absent-minded, inscrutable, ruthless, and often infuriating. His eccentricities on and off the bandstand gave the musicians who worked for him abundant material for backstage stories. This sampling of them begins with a story told by Gene Lees:

In the early 1930s, Artie Shaw and Benny Goodman sat together in the same New York studio sax section, before either of them was famous. Shaw always had his nose in a book during breaks. Goodman asked him what he was reading and Shaw showed him: Thorstein Veblen's *Theory of the Leisure Class*.

Thereafter Benny would greet Artie at work each day with "How ya doin', J.B.?" and when they parted, "See ya later, J.B." Shaw was not going to give him the satisfaction of asking him what it meant, but finally curiosity got the better of him.

"All right, Benny, what does J.B. stand for?"

"George Bernard," Benny said with a satisfied smile. ♪

Leonard Feather and Jack Tracy collected several choice Goodman anecdotes:

One of the best known Goodman stories, recalled by Peggy Lee, concerns the time when he and Peggy jumped into a taxicab outside the RCA Building. Awaiting instructions, the driver remained motionless while Benny just sat there quietly for several minutes. Finally the driver said, "Well, buddy?" Benny looked up with a start, said: "Ah, how much is that?" and fished for his wallet as he started to get out of the cab. ↴

One habit for which Benny is well remembered by former sidemen was his tendency to borrow clarinet reeds from members of his sax section. One night, after Goodman had borrowed Vido Musso's last clarinet reed, he called a tune called *Bach Goes to Town*, the only number that featured a five-clarinet passage.

"I can't play it, Benny," said Musso.

"Why not?"

"No reed."

"Then," said Goodman with an air of finality, "fake it!" ↴

André Previn: One day a few years ago Benny came to hear my trio at the Roundtable in New York. He wanted us to record with him, and he said he'd like us to be at his house in Connecticut for rehearsal. "It's going to be a busy day," he said, "so I'd like you to be there at nine in the morning."

"But Benny," I said, "we work here at the Roundtable until four in the morning."

Benny had a perfect solution for that. He suggested, "You be sure to go home right after the job tonight."

During rehearsal we had a lot of trouble, because it was a bitterly cold day and our fingers were practically numb. Helen Ward, who was Benny's original vocalist years ago, was back with him for this record date, and she finally said:

"Benny, you know what the trouble is? It's just horribly cold in here."

"You know," said Benny, "you're absolutely right." And he promptly put on a warm woolen sweater and resumed rehearsing. ↴

Carlos Gastel: When Harry James and Ziggy Elman were both in Benny's band, Benny of course was impressed with both of them. This, however, left poor Chris Griffin with nothing to do but play in the section—no solos. Finally Chris told Leonard Vannerson, the road manager, that he was turning in his notice.

Well, after the job that night, Leonard was riding with Benny in Goodman's car and didn't know how to tell him about Chris, because Benny liked Griffin a great deal. So they pulled up to a diner and Leonard said, "Benny, Chris just gave me his notice." Benny didn't say anything, just kept quiet and walked into the diner. He ordered some scrambled eggs.

When they came, he took the ketchup bottle and the top fell off, right in the middle of the eggs. Well, Benny was so preoccupied he ate all around the bottle top, without moving it. Finally there's nothing left of the eggs but the part that's under the top.

They get back in the car and Leonard starts driving again, and now it's about five o'clock in the morning. A farmer's milk truck pulls out of a side road abruptly and the car ran right into it. Leonard jams on the brakes, there's milk all over the street, the horse that was pulling the wagon is making an awful racket, and the farmer is screaming. Finally Benny broke his long silence. He said, "Now what did Chris want to do a thing like that for?"

John Hammond had a long association with Goodman and was influential in the hiring of many of the key members of his band. He always tried to broaden Goodman's awareness of other talented jazz players. When Count Basie's band was in New York at Roseland, and Goodman was at the Hotel Pennsylvania at the same time, Hammond thought it was time for some introductions:

About a week after the Roseland opening I arranged to take Basie, Lester [Young], Walter [Page], Jo [Jones], and Buck [Clayton] down to the Black Cat [in Greenwich Village]. And because Benny also closed at one o'clock I persuaded him to join us. I wanted Bill's rhythm section to hear Freddie [Green] and—always thinking, always thinking—I wanted Benny to hear Lester.

I was sitting with Benny as Lester's first notes floated our way. He turned to me and said, "My God, John, that's the most wonderful tone I've ever heard. That's just the way I play tenor"—meaning the sound he'd tried to achieve in the days he played tenor as a sideman with Al Goodman and other studio bands.

It was quite a night. Benny had brought his clarinet, so he sat in. Basie took over at the piano and Jo on drums, but Frank Clarke [cousin of Kenny Clarke, the house drummer] remained on bass and, of course, Freddie Green continued to play guitar. Goodman played so beautifully that everyone in the room was overwhelmed. Lester had brought along a metal clarinet, an instrument much less expensive and not so tonally rich as the wooden clarinet most players use. Lester did not have much clarinet technique, but he did have the same intimate sound and sense of phrasing he had on the saxophone. After Lester played a while Benny handed Lester his clarinet. "Here," he said, "take mine"—meaning, keep it. Goodman could get as many clarinets as he wanted; still, it was an extraordinary gesture, a tribute to Lester's playing, an indication that if Benny cared he could be very generous.

Following a tip from Mary Lou Williams, Hammond found Charlie Christian in Oklahoma and convinced Goodman to use money from his *Old Gold Show* budget to fly him to California for an audition. Goodman was opening at the Victor Hugo restaurant in Beverly Hills and recording at Columbia's West Coast studios during the day. Hammond said:

In the middle of the first afternoon session Charlie Christian walked in wearing a large hat, his purple shirt and yellow shoes, lugging an amplifier and his guitar case. Benny took one look, his eyes steely behind those glasses, and went back to business at hand.

The moment the session ended Benny prepared to leave, paying no further attention to Charlie. "Won't you at least listen?" I begged him. "He's come all the way from Oklahoma to play for you."

"John, I've got things on my mind," Benny said impatiently. He paused, glanced at Charlie, and agreed. "Okay," he said, "chord me on 'Tea for Two'."

Charlie never had a chance to plug in his amplifier. Benny, of course, was not impressed and the audition ended.

I left with Artie Bernstein, who was Benny's bass at that time. Charlie Christian left with Fletcher [Henderson] and Lionel [Hampton] for a hotel in the Watts section of Los Angeles, a city as segregated in those days as any in the Deep South. I told Charlie to meet me in the kitchen of the Victor Hugo at eight-thirty, the time Goodman was to conclude his first set.

While Benny was having dinner, Artie and I carried Charlie Christian's amplifier into the restaurant and set it up on the bandstand, where it would be ready when the moment came. The Goodman Quintet at that time included Fletcher on piano, Lionel on vibraphone, Nick Fatool on drums, Artie Bernstein, and Benny. When the time came for them to play, Charlie Christian, still wearing his only costume, appeared through the kitchen door. Goodman watched Charlie approach the bandstand, looked around the room until he spotted me, and zapped me with the famous Goodman "ray." But before the opening night audience there was nothing he could do but go along at least for one tune. He chose "Rose Room," a standard familiar to Goodman audiences, though one he assumed Charlie would not know. This would be Benny's revenge for my interference.

I am reasonably certain Christian had never heard "Rose Room" before, because it was a West Coast song not in the repertoire of most black bands. No matter. Charlie had ears like antennae. All he had to do was to hear the melody and chord structure once and he was ready to play twenty-five choruses, each more inventive than the last. Which is what happened. Benny would play a chorus or two, Lionel would answer him, and their talent would inspire Charlie to greater improvisations of his own. Before long the crowd was screaming with amazement. "Rose Room" continued for more than three-quarters of an hour and Goodman received an ovation unlike any even he had had before. No one present will ever forget it, least of all Benny. ↳

On a bus ride to Chicago with the Goodman band, Jimmy Maxwell had a portable phonograph in his seat, and was listening to a Duke Ellington record when Goodman came by and asked, "Why are you listening to that?" Jimmy replied, "Because it's the best band in the world!" Goodman fired him on the spot. That night, Jimmy went to a Chicago club to sit in. Goodman and his road manager walked in, looking for a replacement trumpet player. It was dark, and Goodman couldn't see who was playing, but he liked what he heard and told his road manager to hire the guy. So Jimmy was back in the Goodman band the next day.

Maxwell was Goodman's lead trumpet player for many years:

It was the surprise of my life when I left Benny's band. Benny had me so buffaloed I didn't think anybody would hire me. Within a week of quitting the band it seemed like everybody in the country offered. Basie offered me a job! I said, "Why didn't you ever ask me before, for God's sake?" He said, "I couldn't afford to pay you." And I said, "You've offered me $100 a week more than Benny was paying me!" Woody Herman, everybody offered me jobs, but I was determined to stay in town. ↳

Charlie Barnet tells another Goodman story, from a bandleader's view-
point:

> Benny Goodman was at the Paramount Theatre and in the middle
> of a long run, thanks to the fact that he had a super picture on the
> bill with him. Benny wanted to take a rest for several days, and the
> theater agreed if he could get guest bandleaders to front the band
> during his absence. I took the job on for three or four days, and be-
> tween the 400 Club and the Paramount I was really working hard.
> The first show at the theater went on at 10:30 in the morning and I
> didn't finish at the 400 till 2:00 at night. For my help, Benny gave me
> a Dunhill lighter that someone had given him, but he had the en-
> graving changed to make it look as though it were a present *from*
> him. If he had been genuinely sick, I would have done the job
> for nothing, as I have done for other bandleaders who became ill,
> but he just didn't feel like working, and I thought the lighter was a
> poor reward for what I'd gone through. Benny was probably
> getting $10,000 a week or better then. His own brother clued me in
> on the Dunhill lighter scam. Besides which, the damn thing never
> worked. ↳

Jess Stacy was probably Goodman's favorite piano player, but he found
life more pleasant on the Bob Crosby band:

> The Crosby band was a fun band. Benny Goodman was really a
> taskmaster. With Benny, perfection was just around the corner. He
> was hell on intonation, too. Between each set he had me pounding
> A's on the piano so the saxes and trumpets could be perfectly in
> tune. When I went with the Bob Crosby band I had the habit of
> pounding A's between sets. Bob looked at me and said,
>   "If you keep pounding that A, I'm going to give you your five
> years' notice." ↳

When Stacy left Goodman, Fletcher Henderson replaced him for a few
months before Johnny Guarnieri was hired. Guarnieri said:

> When I first joined Benny, he called me "Fletcher" for three
> months before he could remember my name. And he told me I was
> the worst piano player he'd had since Frankie Froeba. He didn't like
> my so-called "imitating" other pianists.
>   Both Lionel Hampton and Charlie Christian would tell me,
> "Don't let Benny scare you, you're a piano player, Johnny—and you

swing." As a matter of fact, Lionel and Charlie were the only two guys in the band who would talk to me when I joined. All the other guys were "big shots" and I wasn't.   🎵

Jerry Jerome took Bud Freeman's place when Bud left Goodman:

When Benny hired me, he said sort of in passing, "Incidentally, Pops, do you play anything else?," and, trying to make myself sound more valuable to him, I said, "Yeah, I play the bass clarinet." And I didn't. I'd never put one together. He said, "That's good, because we're going to record *Bach Goes to Town* next week." I said, "Benny, I just sold my bass clarinet!" He said, "That's okay, you can use mine."

Benny hands me the bass clarinet, and I want to Joe Allard, the teacher I worked with for a while, and said, "For god's sake show me how to put this thing together!" He went over the part with me and showed me what to do, and I walked into the studio, cocky as hell, and played it like nothing. From that point on, the only time Benny would ever play this when we were traveling was if he saw I hadn't taken the bass clarinet out of the case. Then he would call it up and make me scramble. There were only two tunes in the whole book that used clarinets, *Big John Special* and *Bach Goes to Town.*

I'd been with the band a week, and near the end of the evening, Benny said, "We're rehearsing tomorrow at two o'clock." I said I couldn't make it.

"Why not?"

"My grandfather passed away, and I'm going to the funeral in Plainfield, New Jersey."

"Oh, that's too bad." A little later, he leaned over while playing and said,

"Hey, Pops, can you get out of that thing?"

Benny had a peculiar way of engaging in conversations. He rarely contributed first-hand knowledge. He'd listen and glean information, and pass it on. We were touring out in the Pacific Northwest. Leonard Vannerson picked up a newspaper, and was reading the headlines:

"NAZIS DROP 4000 PARATROOPS BEHIND ENEMY LINES."

He said it looked like Hitler would take over the world with his new technique. Benny said, "Impossible." Later he went back where Charlie Christian was sitting. Charlie had just joined the band, and was sitting by himself in the back of the bus.

"Hey, Charlie, how you doin', Pops?"

"Solid, solid."

"You know what the Nazis did today? They dropped four thousand paratroops behind the lines. Blitzkrieg."

"They did?"

"Yeah."

Charlie nodded. "Solid," he said.

I was particularly fond of Benny. We always maintained a relationship. Benny liked to stay in contact with me, because he liked to ask, "Who's around? Who's good?" I recommended Warren Vaché to him, and Derek Smith, people like that.

It was always a pleasure to have lunch with him. We'd go to the Century Club. Yes, he paid for the lunch. He had to, there, because he had to sign for it. But other than that, Benny rarely paid for a lunch.

He invited Arthur Rollini and myself and Hymie [Schertzer] to dinner at the Russian Bear in Detroit, just a block down the side alley from the Fox Theater. When we were just about finished, and were eating dessert, he said,

"Oh, my God, I forgot I've got to put a reed on my clarinet. Schertz, take care of it, and I'll catch you later on."

And that was the end of it, of course. Benny always used to stick the guys. And he never bought a cigarette. He wouldn't even ask. He'd make a scissor motion with his fingers, looking around for somebody to put a cigarette in there. ↶

Goodman looked at the back row of the band one night and asked Vido Musso, "Who's the new trumpet player?" Vido said, "Benny, that's your brother, Irving!" Benny said, "Oh. Well tell him to stop chewing that gum."

Zoot Sims went on the road with Goodman when he was nineteen. When they got back to California the band was used in the movie *Sweet and Lowdown*. Several of the musicians, including Zoot, were replaced by actors for the filming, but Zoot played when the soundtrack was recorded. He often told the story of Benny and the apple:

We used to have a lunch break, and I brought this big, beautiful apple and put it on my stand. Benny had a habit of grabbing your cigarettes, or anything, and I saw him looking at that apple. I said, "Oh, oh. There goes my apple." I had a solo coming up. So Benny grabbed my apple, I stood up and took my solo, and it's the longest solo I ever had with Benny Goodman in my life. He kept signaling "one more" until he finished the whole apple. Then he said, "That's enough." 🕱

A sideman was chafing under Benny Goodman's disapproval. Benny kept switching the parts around, and had taken a solo away from this musician and had given it to someone else. Goodman's stares unnerved him, and he was miserably unhappy at the end of each night's work. Finally he decided the money wasn't worth it. He burst into Benny's dressing room after the job and announced,

"That's it, Benny! I can't take this anymore! I'm quitting!"

He turned and stalked out, slamming the door behind him. Benny looked perplexedly at his manager.

"Who *was* that?" he asked.

Benny Goodman once phoned George Simon, editor of *Metronome* magazine, and said, "Whenever I call your house I'm always embarrassed if your wife answers, because I never can remember her name. What *is* her name, Bob?"

Pianist Dave Frishberg met Goodman on a job with Gene Krupa's quartet (with Eddie Wasserman and Dave Perlman) at the Metropole in New York:

Must have been 1962. Benny walked in and the place went crazy. We were on the bandstand, just having finished an hour-and-fifteen-minute set. I looked at Gene and his face was white. He said, "It's the King of Swing, and he's got his horn. I don't believe this. Here he comes."

Benny walked up on the stand and began to try out reeds. He stared off into space and tootled and fluttered up and down the scale. This went on for long minutes. Meanwhile Jack Waldorf had herded dozens—hundreds!—of passersby into the club, and he had them chanting, "Benny! Benny!" Some were hollering out years—like "1936!" The camera girl, standing down by the bar, snapped a picture and hurried downstairs to make prints, promising autographs of Goodman and Krupa.

Benny was finally ready. He said, "Brushes, Gene." Gene obediently picked up the brushes and flashed a big smile, but I could see he was in a cold fury. Then Benny turned to me and said, "*Sweet Lorraine*, in G. Give me a little introduction." I complied, and Benny entered in F. He waved me out and continued without piano accompaniment.

He stayed on the stand for about an hour. The camera girl was going into a second printing. Then, abruptly, he packed up his horn and descended, demanding safe escort through the crowd, and he was gone into the night. He hadn't signed one picture.

Krupa was drenched with two shows' worth of perspiration, but he sat patiently on the steps of the bandstand and signed dozens of photos. He was writing personal notes on each one, asking each customer, "Who shall I inscribe this to?" Later in the dressing room he said to us, "I was glad to sign this picture. This will be in a lot of homes, believe me. Did you get a load of this?"

We inspected the picture then. And there was Benny with his horn in his mouth, perched on a stool with his legs spread wide. His fly was open.

"Buttons!" Gene said. "Buttons! That suit's probably from about 1940." ⇃

Jerry Jerome and some of the other saxophonists on the road with the Goodman band discovered a store that sold toy parachutes that could be blown into the air from small paper tubes. They bought a bunch of them, and on the bandstand at an outdoor job, they began blowing the little parachutes into the air behind Benny while he was playing a solo. As the audience began laughing and pointing, Benny turned around and whispered to Jerry, "Is my fly open?"

Goodman was well known for his absent–mindedness, especially when it came to the names of his side musicians. On one concert, Benny had been especially ornery during the sound check, and during the concert the musicians didn't feel like helping him out when he began to fumble the introductions. So Goodman just began inventing names. When he came to Michael Moore, he said, "And on bass we have Major Holley." Michael calmly grabbed a microphone and said, "And, ladies and gentlemen, how about a big hand for Woody Herman on the clarinet!"

At another concert, Goodman was bringing on Carrie Smith to sing the old Bessie Smith tune, "Give Me a Pigfoot and a Bottle of Beer." He announced, "Here's someone I know you're going to enjoy. Please welcome Carrie . . . Grant!"

Goodman's band appeared on the Ed Sullivan show during the early 1950s. Teddy Wilson was on the band, but for some reason wasn't available that day. Bernie Leighton was hired to fill in. Ed Sullivan had a little extra time, so he called Benny over after the band played a number and said, "Who's in the band, Benny?" Terry Gibbs, who was born Julius Gubenko, said:

> Benny never called me Terry Gibbs—he always called me Gubenko. He loved the name Gubenko. I didn't mind. So he's introducing the band, he looks at me and he really wants to say Terry Gibbs but he couldn't figure it. He said, "Gubenko," and he laughed a little bit. My mother loved it, she got to hear the name Gubenko.
>
> And then he mentioned the other guys and he says, "On piano—." And he looks at this strange piano player he never saw before and he said, "On piano, Teddy Wilson." Now, we in the band had to look around to see who it was. We didn't believe it. Make up a name! Schwartz, call him anything! But he called him Teddy Wilson on national television! ♪

Gibbs once asked Goodman what trumpet players on his band he had liked the best. Benny said, "Oh, Chris Griffin and Doug Mettome, I guess." Terry asked, "What about Harry James?" Benny thought a moment. "Harry? No, he was never on my band."

Bandleader Bob January used to be Eubie Blake's piano tuner. Eubie told him that he once was featured on a concert with Benny Goodman, and they did a duet on Eubie's famous "Memories of You." While they were playing, Benny looked around at Eubie and muttered, "You're playing the wrong chords!"

When Benny took his band to Russia in 1962 he engendered enough strife with his musicians and with Russian officialdom to fill half a book, which the editor has already done elsewhere. When Zoot Sims returned to the States from that infamous tour, he was asked what it was like playing with Benny in Russia. Zoot answered, "Every gig with Benny is like playing in Russia."

In the early 1950s Alfonso Tomaino was studying clarinet at his teacher's apartment on 58th Street when the telephone rang. The French-American teacher, Mr. Duqués, asked Alfonso to answer the phone. "Eef eet ees Bay-nee Goodman, tell 'eem I no here." It indeed was Goodman on the phone, and Alfonso gave the instructed reply. Goodman said, "Tell him Benny Goodman called." The same scenario occurred during a lesson a few weeks later. Curious, Alfonso asked Mr. Duqués why he wouldn't speak to Goodman. He replied, " 'e ees a pain een de nak. 'e send 'ees chauffeur over eere and 'e want me to go to 'otel Pierre to play duets." Alfonso asked, "What's so annoying about that?" Mr. Duqués replied, " 'e no pay me!"

A year or so before Goodman's death, Loren Schoenberg was working at Benny's New York apartment, helping him organize his archives. Loren's pulse raced when he saw the shelves of arrangements from all of Benny's bands and record dates down through the years. Many were by Loren's favorite arrangers, and some had never been recorded. He asked Benny if he could Xerox some of them for his rehearsal band to play, and Benny said he could. Loren immediately began making Benny's Xerox machine hum.

Evidently Benny decided Loren had copied enough arrangements, but instead of saying anything about it, he just stopped buying paper for his Xerox machine. Loren regularly made out various checks to cover office and business expenses for Benny to sign, but the one to re-order Xerox paper was always "overlooked." When Benny needed a copy of a document from time to time, he'd send Loren down to a copying store and pay a quarter a copy rather than restock his own machine.

When Benny was putting together his last band, the time came when he needed sixty copies of an itinerary. Loren mentioned the extravagance of paying twenty-five cents per copy, hoping Benny would decide that the time had come to reorder a supply of Xerox paper. Instead, Benny went to the Yellow Pages and then to the telephone, where he had a long conversation that Loren couldn't hear.

The next day when he arrived at Benny's apartment, Loren saw a police car blocking traffic for a large delivery van on the street outside. Going up in the elevator, he noticed the padding that had been hung on the car walls. Shortly after he started his day's work the doorman called to announce that Mr. Goodman's delivery was on its way up. Loren opened the door and several deliverymen wheeled in what looked like three hospital trolleys covered with sheets. They were followed by an aggressive but courteous young salesman, who proceeded to unveil the delivery: three brand new Xerox machines. He began describing the virtues of the different models to Benny.

Benny, looking at the first machine, pulled out the itinerary he wanted copied.

"Can it make twenty copies of this?" he inquired in a tone of voice that indicated mild interest. No sooner said than done. The salesman popped it into the machine and handed Benny his twenty copies a few seconds later.

"And, what about that one?" mused Benny, pointing to machine number two.

"This has all the features of the first model, plus reducing, enlarging, printing on both sides and collating," said the salesman.

"Ah, let me see how it does twenty copies of this," he said, handing over the original of the itinerary. He soon had another twenty copies.

"And, ah, how about the third one?" Benny asked.

"This one will do everything, including print in color, make the coffee and answer the phone," said the salesman. (Or something very much to that effect.)

"Ah, let me see how it does twenty copies of this," said Benny, and got another twenty copies of his itinerary.

Benny then put his sixty copies under his arm, gave Loren a big stage wink and walked out, leaving Loren to get rid of the salesman and his three machines with promises that Mr. Goodman would "think it over."

When Lynn Roberts was singing with one of the later editions of the Benny Goodman band, she told about a flight they were making to a gig somewhere. As the band boarded the plane, Benny tried to strike up a conversation with a young lady sitting next to him. Getting little response from her, Benny said, "I guess you don't know who I am. I'm the King of Swing." The young lady looked at him and inquired, "What's swing?"

chapter 33

Coleman Hawkins and Lester Young

Coleman Hawkins practically invented the jazz tenor saxophone and set the mold for a generation of reed players that followed him. Known as "the father of the tenor saxophone," his contemporaries called him "Bean," because of his knowledge of chords and the masterful inventions he played on them. He was one of the few giants of the swing era to respond favorably to the innovations of the young bebop players.

Eddie Barefield remembered working with Hawkins in New York:

> He never liked to look back at things. We used to do an arrangement on the "St. Louis Blues." In rehearsal Hawk said, "We'll play it with an old ragtime feeling, a corny feeling, and everybody take a ragtime solo." When they got to his solo, he just went on and played. I said, "Hawk, why don't you play one of them old Fletcher Henderson slap-tongue solos that you used to play?" He says, "I never played like that. I never played anything like that." I said, "Okay, I'll bring you a record tomorrow." And I brought "Dicty Blues," where he was slap-tongueing. He said, "No, man, that wasn't me. I don't want to hear that." ↴

Stanley Dance reconstructed a bit of bandroom badinage between Hawkins and his associates:

> Almost every night, between sets, wherever Hawkins happened to be playing, the length of his career became the subject for discussion or argument. The talk may at first sound unkind, even malicious, but with familiarity the outlines of a kind of game emerged, the object being to prove Hawkins older than he really was. The players did not expect to win. Their pleasure rather lay in seeing how he will extricate himself from the traps they set or how their arguments will be refuted. Two notably talented players of this game are Sonny Stitt and Roy Eldridge. The latter, in fact, through long association, had come to regard himself as Hawkins's straight man.

"Yeah?" someone would say. "Then how about the time when you were working with Mamie Smith?"

"That was somebody else using my name," Hawkins replied with crushing finality.

"I can remember you, a grown man, playing with Fletcher Henderson when I was still a child," says a swing-era veteran.

"I don't think," he says airily, "that I ever was a child!" ⚡

At the Heublein Lounge in Hartford, Connecticut, an eight-year-old girl insisted on getting the autograph of Hawkins—and only his:

How is it, Roy," Hawkins asked Roy Eldridge afterwards, "that all your fans are *old* people? They come in here with canes and crutches. They must be anywhere from fifty-eight to a hundred-and-eight. But my fans are all young, from eight to fifty-eight years old!"

"That little girl thought you were Santa Claus," said drummer Eddie Locke.

"Is that so? Well, who's got more fans than Santa Claus?" ⚡

Rex Stewart recalled Hawkins's preoccupation with youth and age:

As far back as I can remember, he would kid Jimmy [Harrison] or Don [Redman] about how much older they were than he, and this was in the twenties, mind you. As recently as the forties, in the war years, when I ran into Hawk in Chicago, he was still at it, bemoaning the fact that his mean old draft board had reclassified him as 1-A. Then, pulling out a draft card that gave his age as thirty-five (the draft limit at that time), he continued to rave on, cussing out General Louis Hershey, the draft board, and himself for being unfortunate enough to be so young. Roy Eldridge looked at me, and I looked at Roy, both of us thinking the same thought—who's he kidding? Then John Kirby said,

"Damn, Bean, if you keep getting younger, you'll have to start wearing diapers again!" ⚡

Hawkins enjoyed keeping his friends off-balance. Stanley Dance told of an early Jazz at the Philharmonic tour on which several of the musicians, unaccustomed to flying, were extremely uneasy about being up in a plane:

The plane took off uneventfully. No sooner were safety belts unloosed, however, than Hawkins was on his feet, slowly pacing the aisle, his head behind an opened tabloid, the big black headlines of which proclaimed the number dead in a catastrophic air crash. ↴

A fierce competitor at jam sessions, Hawkins loved to hear what every other saxophonist was doing. He quickly absorbed what he heard. "Once I play with you, I've got you," he said. He rarely had a good word for anyone else's playing, but he never gloated. He said,

"Some of my biggest moments have been in jam sessions, but I don't want to talk about them. There were always other people involved."

One jam session that gave Hawkins a workout happened in Kansas City in 1934. Mary Lou Williams said:

The word went around that Hawkins was in the Cherry Blossom, and within about half an hour there were Lester Young, Ben Webster, Herschel Evans, Herman Walder, and one or two unknown tenors piling into the club to blow. Bean didn't know the KC tenor men were so terrific, and he couldn't get himself together though he played all morning. I happened to be nodding that night, and around four a.m. I awoke to hear someone pecking on my screen.

I opened the window on Ben Webster. He was saying, "Get up, pussycat, we're jammin' and all the pianists are tired out now. Hawkins has got his shirt off and is still blowing. You got to come down." Sure enough, when we got there, Hawkins was in his singlet, taking turns with the KC men. It seems he had run into something he didn't expect.

The Henderson band was playing in St. Louis that evening, and Bean knew he ought to be on the way. But he kept trying to blow something to beat Ben and Herschel and Lester. When at last he gave up, he got straight in his car and drove to St. Louis. I heard he'd just bought a new Cadillac and that he burnt it out trying to make the job on time. ↴

From later reports, it seems that Hawkins tended to drive that way all the time. He once complained that it was a shame to put a speed limit of sixty miles per hour on these nice modern highways. He said he couldn't stay awake when driving so slow.

Whatever Hawkins's problems might have been at that Kansas City jam session, he remained a formidable opponent at cutting contests. After a sojourn in Europe, Hawk returned to New York in 1939 and began hanging around Nightsy Johnson's uptown musicians' club to hear what the other tenor players were doing. After listening for several nights he came in with his horn while Lester Young was playing behind Billie Holiday. Rex Stewart said:

> When Billie finished, she announced to the house that it had been a pleasure to have had the world's greatest tenor saxophone backing her up—Lester Young.
>
> You could have heard a pin drop after that remark, but the Hawk ignored it, turning to the piano player and saying "Play me a few choruses of—." I've forgotten the name of the tune, but I do recall that the tempo Hawk set was almost unbelievable, it was so fast. And he had the tune all to himself.
>
> Then he sauntered to the bar, had a big drink, and waited to see how the cats would follow this avalanche of virtuosity. For some reason, nobody felt like blowing at the moment. So Coleman picked up where he had left off, this time with a ballad, in which he proceeded to demonstrate the various ways the tune could be embellished, finishing up with an incredible cadenza, to thundering applause. He then gallantly started toying with "Honeysuckle Rose," motioning for Chu and Don Byas to join him, which they did.
>
> Lester sat on the sidelines, drinking with Lady Day, and I must say that he kept his cool. ↲

Instead of accepting Hawkins as his model, Lester Young was attracted to the lighter tone that Frank Trumbauer produced on the C-melody saxophone. Young's sound and style of phrasing on the tenor sax started a school of playing that provided a valid alternative to the more robust Hawkins sound. Eddie Barefield played Lester his first Trumbauer records:

> Clarence Johnson, a piano player, got a job up in Bismarck, North Dakota, for the winter at the Spencer Hotel. In the annex where we lived was Lester Young's father and his family band. Lester Young's little brother Lee, he wasn't big enough to play then. But they'd dress him in a tuxedo and he would conduct the band. Irma, his sister, was on saxophone and his mother played the piano and his father played tenor sax. Lester was playing alto.

One day I heard a knock on the door while I was playing records in my room. I hadn't met him then. He opened the door and said, "I'm Lester Young. I hear that little saxophone. Who is that playing saxophone?" I said, "Frankie Trumbauer." He said, "Well, do you mind if I listen?" So he came in and we met, and he started to borrow these records. ↯

When Buddy Tate made a tour with Nina Mae McKinney's revue, he met Lester:

We stayed at a hotel in Tulsa, Oklahoma. In the lobby was a big baby grand, and musicians would come in and jam. Somebody told me, "King Oliver's here, upstairs. They just come in this morning. They got Red Young with them." They called Lester "Red" then, you know.

I hadn't seen him since he had switched to tenor, but I'd heard about him, because he had made quite a reputation. So I says, "Well, I'm going to really see if this cat plays like everybody say."

I found out what his room number was and went upstairs. He was laying up there with some corn pads, two on this toe, two on this one. And it was hot. Didn't have no air conditioning then, you know. Windows all up and everything. It was about nine-thirty, ten o'clock in the morning. We didn't go to bed, we just went on down there and started jamming.

So I says, "Lester, you remember me?"

"Oh, yeah. Tate." He didn't call me "Lady Tate" then. He says, "What are you doing here?" So I told him, and says, "We're jamming downstairs. Would you like to join in?"

"Oh, yes." Any time there was a jam session, man, he was ready.

In ten minutes he was dressed and came down there, and I wish you could have heard him then. I never heard anybody play tenor like that in my life!

He sounded just a little bit different from an alto. He sounded between an alto and a C-melody. But ideas? He made them! He was swinging like mad. So then everybody just stopped. Couldn't nobody play. He says, "Look, somebody else play something." We says, "Man, what can we play?" All these saxophone players started putting their horns in the bag. They say, "Tate, you went and got him. You play something." I said, "There ain't a damn thing I can play." He says, "Man, I like the way you play. Come on and play." So I went and played some more. ↯

Jerry Jerome remembered the delicious shock of hearing Lester for the first time:

Lester had a sound like a French horn. Sort of a deadish, unreedy horn sound. It was magnificent! And the lousiest tenor saxophone you'd ever want to look at. It was a Pan-American, with rubber bands, glue, chewing gum—and he just sat there blowing wonderful stuff. He was my idol. ↳

Around 1939, in front of Milt Gabler's Commodore Music Shop, Bud Freeman ran into Lester and asked, "Would you come in and hear a trio album I just made?" Lester accompanied him inside, and Bud played the recording of *Three Little Words* he had made with Jess Stacy and George Wettling. Lester wanted to hear it a second time. Bud didn't see Lester again until 1946, when again they met of 52nd Street. Lester's first words were, "That *Three Little Words* was a bitch!"

The Basie band was touring the Deep South. A party after one job was so good that several band members, including Lester Young and Budd Johnson, missed the band bus when it left for the next town. They found the local bus station and tried to get on a public transportation bus that was going in the right direction, but were prevented from doing so by a bus driver who refused to let them board. Johnson decided persuasion was necessary. He showed the driver the pistol he was carrying, and the driver decided there was some room in the back that they could use. They walked silently past a busful of nervous white passengers and took their seats. As the bus pulled away, Lester clapped his hands with delight and cried, "Shoot your pistol, baby! Shoot your pistol!"

Buddy Tate was with Count Basie when Lester was taken into the army:

Your draft board would send you a notice to report. Well, Lester kept getting the notices all right, but we were out on the road at the time, and sometimes the mail would miss you at one location, and you could always say, "I never got it." Lester kept getting these draft notices and he kept throwing them away.

Well, one night we were playing this dance and there was this fellow hanging around the bandstand. Real nice fellow. We talked, and he was interested in the tour, and Lester hit it off with him. Every break, Lester was standing around talking to this guy. Well, came the last break of the evening, and this guy pulls out his wallet and shows Lester he's an FBI agent! Seems they's sent him around to check up on Lester for not showing up for the draft. He was real nice about it, but there it was.

Prez said afterwards it was a near thing. He was getting along with the guy so well he was about to suggest they step out the back door for a joint when the guy pulled out his I.D.! Lester was gone in the morning.

Lester invented his own language, substituting imaginative imagery for common words. It took some getting used to. Jo Jones was one of the few people that could carry on long conversations with Lester. Some of Lester's words came into common use among musicians, like "gray" for a white person and "Oxford gray" for a Negro.

When the keys on his saxophone got bent on a Jazz at the Philharmonic tour, Lester want to amateur repairman Flip Phillips for help. "Lady Flip," he said, "my people won't play!" His saxophone keys were his "people."

When Sadik Hakim became Lester's pianist, it took him several months to learn to understand him:

The police he called "Bob Crosbys." If something was a real drag, he called it a "von Hangman." His most famous expression, "I feel a draft," could mean that he detected racial discrimination, or that he felt bad since you wouldn't drink and smoke with him. Reefer he called "Ettuce." The bridge of a tune he'd called a "George Washington." When we hit a new town and Prez would go looking for an old girlfriend, he'd say he was going to see a "wayback."

John Collins worked for Lester in the 1940s:

Prez was a very earthy man. He could say things that would really hit home. They weren't very intellectual, but he had mother wit. No one could express himself like Lester.

Lester would quit the job if it didn't suit him. Money or no money. He was a very proud man and had funny ways. You could just hurt his feelings, and he would just walk off and quit.

You had to know him for him to open up to you. Actually, he was very shy every way but musically. He was very outgoing musically.

Prez didn't know chords, but he had an innate sense. He had an ear that was just terrific. He would make an intro by himself and he would run some of the most intricate patterns. You would think that he knew the chords. And I would ask him, "Now, do you know what chords you're playing?" He said, "No." He would just hear them. I could play any progressions and he could play it right away, but he didn't know any chord. ↱

One night in Birdland a jazz critic was complimenting Lester for letting the members of his quintet have so much solo space. Lester squeezed his eyes together and smiled. He whispered,

"Yes, Prez has to let his kiddies play, so when it comes time for Prez to play, his kiddies don't be stepping on Prez's toes!"

In those days jazz drummers were beginning to use the bass drum for accents rather than steady rhythm. Lester preferred the style of drumming he grew up with.

"No bombs," he told his drummers, "Just chink-ty-boom for Prez."

Lester went to a jazz club to hear some friends play. He didn't bring his saxophone. He just wanted to listen. He intentionally sat in a dark part of the room, hoping not to be recognized, but someone noticed him, and he heard them whispering, "Wow, that's Lester Young!" "Maybe we can get him to sit in!" Lester leaned over to the table and whispered, "I don't dig being dug while I'm digging."

Lester called a piano player who lived in Chicago and offered him a job in New York. When he mentioned the low wages, the pianist said, "Prez, I'd love to make the gig with you, but I can't afford to live in New York on that kind of bread." Lester chided him, "Baby, you got to save up to be able to make these out of town gigs!"

At one of the first jazz festivals in Newport, Ruby Braff saw Lester one afternoon, sitting alone in the sun on a folding chair, not far from the festival stage. Ruby was horrified to see that Lester was publicly smoking a joint.

"Prez, what in the world are you doing?" cried Ruby.

"Where are we?" countered Lester.

"What do you mean, where are we! We're at the Newport Jazz Festival!" Lester half-closed his eyes and took another puff.

"Then, let us be festive!"

Junior Mance has pleasant memories of working in Lester's quintet:

He wasn't like a bandleader. He hung out with all of us. He was so down to earth. When we came to New York, we lived at the Marden

Hotel on 44th Street. Nothing but musicians lived there. Harold West lived there, Bird lived there. A lot of people. There were times when Prez would take off with Norman Granz for three or four weeks to go to Europe, and Prez would support us. He would leave money for us to make it until he got back, and wouldn't let us pay him back. Playing with him, he was very generous with the solos, because he said, "We might be playing somewhere where they might not like me, but they might like somebody else's playing." On the road he'd knock on our door every day to find out how we were. We'd go on long walks. He never talked about music. We never rehearsed. We just played. ↱

During the early days of live television, Trigger Alpert used to play a CBS show on Saturday mornings. One week, the featured artist was Lester Young, who played with the house quartet: Trigger, Hank Jones, Sonny Igoe, and Chuck Wayne. On the opening number, "Lester Leaps In," the director decided to take advantage of Lester's visual uniqueness. Lester always wore a pork-pie hat, wore his hair long, and while he played he held his instrument out to his right, almost like a flutist. The director had Lester stand facing away from the camera. The idea was for him to slowly turn around during the number, to be in full view by the end of the first chorus. But once Lester started playing, he never did turn around. Before the second number, after a lot of whispers of "turn around, Lester!" they finally got his face on camera.

Jesse Drakes played trumpet with Lester's quintet for several years:

There were a lot of people who said Prez should not have me or Roy Haynes or that type of player around him because we didn't fit. There was an interview once with Prez on a broadcast. They said, "Well, people say you got a bebop band now. Are you playing bebop?" Prez says, "No, I don't play bebop, but the kids that play with me play bebop." That's where that whole thing started.

Playing with him was an education—an education I never seemed to learn. Prez always had something that puzzled me and once I thought I had it figured out, he'd come and play it another way, and I'd go home and think about it again.

He never went into a restaurant to eat. I used to bring food to his room. He thought people were looking at him. But then, when you see a gentleman in a big black pork pie hat, long black coat down to his ankles, hair hanging down almost to his shoulders—people are going to look at you! ↱

At a Jazz at the Philharmonic concert in Sweden, Lester was one of the featured soloists. While Norman Granz was onstage giving him a big buildup, Pres was having some trouble backstage. He couldn't seem to get the top off of a bottle of local gin. As Granz went on about how Young was one of the greatest influences on modern jazz, Pres struggled unsuccessfully with the gin bottle. Finally, the Swedish drummer Bert Dahlander took the bottle from Pres, seized it firmly, and yanked off the top. Pres gave him an admiring look and crooned, "Oh, you Viking!"

Lester Young's influence on the younger generation of tenor players was tremendous. Hawkins was admired by them, but it was Lester's sound, swing, and melodic conception that they took as their model. Criticized for playing too much like Lester, Brew Moore was emphatic in his response: "Anybody who *doesn't* play like Prez is *wrong!*"

chapter 34

Art Tatum and His Children

Though handicapped by the loss of all sight in one eye and nearly all in the other, Art Tatum had complete command of the piano. Harmonically he was years ahead of his contemporaries. It seemed inconceivable that his work would ever lose the respect of the jazz world, but there were a few years during the bebop revolution when critics down-rated him because he hadn't "progressed." He simply continued to play in the breathtaking style that he had invented and mastered.

A resurgent interest in Tatum restored him to his rightful place in the jazz pantheon not long after Norman Granz had the imagination and daring to record and release eleven LPs of Tatum's solo playing.

Pianists in Tatum's day literally quailed before him. He made it a practice never to sit down at the piano until all the other pianists in the house had played. None of them would play after him, and he wanted to hear what they were all doing.

Teddy Wilson was a great admirer of Tatum:

That man had the most phenomenal musical gifts I've ever heard. He was miraculous. It's like someone hitting a home run every time he picks up a bat. We became such fast friends that I was allowed to interrupt him anytime he was playing at the house parties in Toledo we used to make every night. When I asked him, he would stop and replay a passage very slowly, showing me the fingering on some of those runs of his. You just couldn't figure them out by ear at the tempo he played them. 🎵

Count Basie was traveling with Benny Moten's band and arrived all un-suspecting in Toledo:

We stopped off there and went into a bar where you could get sandwiches and cigarettes and candy and things like that, and they had a good piano in there. That's the part I will never forget, be-cause I made the mistake of sitting down at that piano, and that's when I got my personal introduction to a keyboard monster by the name of Art Tatum.

I don't know why I sat down at that piano. We were all in there to get a little taste and a little snack, and the piano was there. But it was just sitting there. It wasn't bothering anybody. I just don't know what made me do what I went and did. I went over there and started bothering that piano. That was just asking for trouble, and that's just exactly what I got. Because somebody went out and found Art.

That was his *hangout.* He was just off somewhere waiting for some-body to come in there and start messing with that piano. Someone dumb enough to do something like that, somebody like Basie in there showing off because there were a couple of good-looking girls in the place or something like that. Oh, boy. They brought him in there, and I can still see him and that way he had of walking on his toes with his head kind of tilted.

I'm pretty sure I had already heard a lot of tales about old Art. But when I went over there and hopped on that innocent-looking piano, I didn't have any idea I was on his stomping ground.

"I could have told you," one of the girls at the bar said.

"Why didn't you, baby? Why didn't you?" 🎵

Eddie Barefield also knew Tatum when he lived in Ohio:

In Toledo, Tatum had started making a little money, and he bought a new Ford. He had a chauffeur. We was up to one of the after-hours spots one night and drinking a little of this lightning, and looked around, and Art was missing. We went out, and he had gone down and gotten into the Ford and drove it right straight into a lamppost! He was sitting up there in the Ford. He couldn't get out of it. He was juiced. Finally we got him out of the car, and he had the car towed away and had it fixed. But he was like that, he was very independent. He didn't like for anybody to help him across the street or anything. He played good pool, played pinochle, because he could see close. ↳

Milt Hinton played cards with Tatum at the Three Deuces in Chicago:

Art used to put a big light behind him so he could see his cards, and he'd drop a card and we'd call whatever cards we played, and he would play his card. ↳

Sadik Hakim remembered hearing Charlie Parker play with Tatum in Chicago:

After his gig in the Loop, Tatum would come down to a club on the South Side, drinking beer after beer and playing for five or six hours. All the piano players in the city would be there. I remember Bird telling me then, "I wish I could play like Tatum's right hand." ↳

Tatum caused quite a stir when he arrived on the New York jazz scene. The Rhythm Club was where the top Harlem jazzmen spent their free time, and was the best place to drop a new reputation onto the grapevine. Roy Eldridge said:

When Art first came here, I was working at Smalls, and me and Jo Jones carried him down to the Rhythm Club and we played two tunes before we cut him loose. Fats was playin' pool, and Fletcher and them was playin' cards. All of a sudden, boom, we all dropped out and let Art go. Boy, you could hear a rat piss on cotton! That sumbitch tore that Rhythm Club up!

I laugh at these cats that say, "Well, I finally got a decent piano." He played *any* of those pianos: he'd play it if it only had four keys on it! ↳

After a performance with the New York Philharmonic one night, trombonist Jack Satterfield grabbed a cab and rushed down to the Famous
Door on 52nd Street to hear Tatum. He didn't bother to change his
clothes, and arriving at the nightclub dressed in tails, he made quite an
impression on the headwaiter. He was given the best table in the house,
right in front of Tatum's piano. Jack sat there happily until closing time,
drinking and listening to the music. Then he paid his check and headed
for the door. On the way out, the headwaiter clasped his hand and said,

"Don't forget the Maitre D'."

Jack shook his hand fervently.

"I'll *never* forget you!" he said, and walked out.

Arnold Shaw remembered seeing Tatum frequently at Hansen's drug-
store, a vaudevillians' hangout at the corner of Seventh Avenue and 51st
Street in New York:

> Tatum always took a seat at the L-shaped counter, not at the tables
> in the rear. When the counter was crowded, he would ask someone
> to drop a handful of coins on the marble top. Then, as people
> stared in astonishment, he would demonstrate the acuteness of his
> hearing by identifying each coin on the counter. ♪

Gene Rodgers gave an illustration of Tatum's remarkable memory:

> When I met Art again in Los Angeles in the early forties, we'd go
> around to the little after-hours rooms when we had finished work.
> One of those times, I discovered what a memory he had. We were
> standing at a bar talking, and his man came up and said, "Hey, Mr.
> Great Art Tatum, I bet you don't know who I am." Art said, "I'm with
> friends. Don't bother me now," and this guy went on, "I'll bet the
> great Mr. Art Tatum fifty dollars he don't know who I am."
>
> I could tell Art was getting annoyed, but all he said was, "I know
> who you are, so why don't you go away and leave us alone?"
>
> I said I'd take half the bet, and another man standing with us took
> the rest, and Art said, "Your name is Such-and-Such and the last time
> I met you was on such-and-such a day in such-and-such a year at the
> Three Deuces on Fifty-second Street in New York City, and you were
> just as rude then as you are now."
>
> We each won our twenty-five dollars. ♪

Tatum loved to use his musical skill to confound his friends. Jimmy
Witherspoon remembered an encounter with him:

> One day I'll never forget, we were down at Mike Jackson's, a bar on
> Central Avenue, and Tatum was drinking a beer.
>
> "Would you like to sing one?" he asked.
>
> "Yeah," I said.
>
> "What key?"
>
> "Put it in B-flat."
>
> He started in B-flat, but after that he went to every key in the lad-
> der, and I didn't know what key he was in. Jay [McShann] had told
> me what he would do, so I paid no attention to Art and his chord
> structures, kept my mind on B-flat, and sang right through.
>
> "Spoon," he said, hitting me on the shoulder and laughing,
> "nobody in the world can do that. I put you through so many
> keys."
>
> He had a sense of mischief and loved to do things like that.

John Collins had many adventures with Tatum while working with his
trio:

> Art Tatum loved piano players. We were working together in New
> York at Café Society Downtown. During the intermission we would
> drive uptown. We had two hours off. We would go up to the Holly-
> wood Club to listen to the Beetle—these are stride piano players—
> or whoever was there. Marlow Morris. We would go up there
> between shows and we'd have the chauffeur drive us back down to
> finish.
>
> That was the first time I really was aware that Scott Joplin's widow
> was alive. They had this after hours spot. All Art said was, "John,
> we're going to Scott Joplin's wife." She had a nice apartment, and
> we'd go up there and he'd buy drinks and he would play. She was
> blind.
>
> There was a guy there, I think he was a little effeminate, that lived
> there. He was a bartender or something, and he played piano. He
> was a traditionalist. The pure chords, you know, one, three, five
> chords. Art would upset him so badly sometimes. Art would tell me,
> "Say, watch, John. Watch what I'm going to do."

So he would start playing *Danny Boy*. This was one of the guy's favorite tunes. He'd start playing it and then about four bars in, he'd hit one of these outrageous chords and this guy would say, "Art, you boob, you don't even know the chords."

And Art would die. He would just laugh, you know. Had a tremendous sense of humor. ⇟

Tatum was an inspiration for many blind musicians, since he accomplished more than any sighted musician of his time. Tatum and Al Hibbler, the blind singer, were good friends. They were riding in the back seat of Slam Stewart's car one night after the Tatum Trio's job at the Streets of Paris in Los Angeles. They had invited Al to come with them to a session at Lovejoy's. Art and Al began talking about driving. Stewart recalled:

Art would say to Al, "Oh, I can drive better than you, man. You can't drive no car." And the same, vice versa, Al would holler over to Art that he could drive better. Art hollered out, "Stop the car, Slam, I'm going to show this cat who's the better driver." I pulled over and stopped the car, and Art said to Al, "Here's your chance to drive the car."

So Al backed down. "Well, man, you know I can't drive." And Art said, "Well, I can drive. Let me get over to the wheel." I started the car up for Art and let him get behind the wheel, and do you know that Art drove at least a block down the street? Fortunately there wasn't much traffic. ⇟

Another pianist inspired by Tatum was George Shearing. Some of George's friends set him up for a joke one night as they left Birdland. They got into a car to go somewhere, and as George heard the motor start he also heard the driver's voice and recognized Al Hibbler. George jumped right out of the car.

An interviewer asked Shearing if he'd been blind all his life. "Not yet," replied George. George once announced a tune as "On a Clear Day, I Still Can't See a Thing." And he mentioned his CDs which were on sale in the lobby. "Remember, profits from these sales will go to help the blind. Not many of the blind, mind you."

Stan Shaw met George Shearing on a job at the Three Deuces on 52nd Street:

In talking to George I found out that he lived in Queens and was liv-ing on the same subway line as I was. He asked me if I would be kind enough to escort him home at night, and it really wasn't a great big deal. The subway entrance to the Queens line was on 53rd Street and 5th Avenue and at that point it is the deepest subway station, where the east-west line starts to descend to go underneath the East River.

In the daytime they had an escalator that came up. It was a long way down and they had a flight of stairs that had to be two or three hundred steps and they were not in any sort of uniformity. There would be eight steps and then a landing, then it'd be 17 steps and then a landing, then it'd be 12 steps, and so forth. The first night I took George home he walked down very gingerly. He took hold of the handrail and came down the steps gradually as I told him where each landing was, and he'd feel where the next step was.

The next night we got to the top of the stairs, George grabs the handrail and says, "Come on, I'll race you to the bottom!" He went down those steps like he was shot out of a cannon. He had the whole thing memorized, how far the landings were, and he beat me to the bottom of the stairs! Unbelievable!

At a party being given at the Lincoln Center Library by Oxford Univer-sity Press to announce the publication of Marian McPartland's book *All in Good Time*, Shearing was introduced and graciously consented to play a couple of tunes. Later Marian saw George and his wife working their way toward the exit, and called to him on the microphone: "It was wonderful of you to come and play for us, George. I can't thank you enough."

George waved a hand and smiled devilishly. "Then send up someone who can," he said, and disappeared into the elevator.

Before playing at the memorial service for Gerry Mulligan at St. Peter's Church, George Shearing mentioned Gerry's use of contrapuntal improvisations in his jazz quartet, and likened them to the lines of J. S. Bach. George then went on to wonder at the large amount of music Bach was able to produce, considering the number of children he sired. "Mrs. Bach had her hands full," George said, "with so many mouths to feed. When she sent the children off to school every day, she used to make a parcel of food for each one. And that's how we got the term 'Bach's lunches.'"

George loves word play. On another concert, he used the term "endless love," and then gave his definition: "Endless love is a tennis match between me and Ray Charles."

Lennie Tristano, who lost his sight during childhood, spent a lot of time during his formative years practicing the figures on Tatum's records. Tristano made recordings of his own that changed the shape of jazz, and he appeared in New York nightclubs for a few years in the late 1940s and early '50s with an innovative jazz group before concentrating exclusively on teaching.

One afternoon Lennie became a student himself. He talked Billy Bauer, his guitar player, into teaching him to drive. After learning where all the controls were, Lennie put Billy's car in gear and started off, with Billy navigating.

"I think maybe you should steer a little more to the right," Billy would offer, as Lennie, delightedly following Billy's instructions, slowly piloted the car down a suburban street. Later, Bauer said, "He wasn't a very good pupil."

Eddie Thompson, the blind English pianist, once played a gig at the old Birdland. As he felt his way into the tiny back dressing room, Eddie heard a voice say, "Watch out for the saxophone on that table." Eddie quipped, "Why, is it loaded?" "No," said the voice, "but the guy who owns it is." The voice and the saxophone belonged to Stan Getz.

Another sightless musician inspired by Tatum's example was Roland Kirk. He had such acute hearing that he could recognize friends by the sound of their footsteps. He thrived on learning to do things for himself and refused assistance as much as possible. Asked where he found the odd reed instruments that he called a manzello and a stritch, which he played in addition to his tenor saxophone, he said, "Oh, I was feelin' around the basement of a friend's music store, and I ran across these things and wondered how they would sound."

The image of Kirk exploring a music store by touch is an appealing one.

Ronnie Scott presented Kirk a number of times at his London jazz club:

I don't know how he did what he did. He knew who you were *immediately*, one word. I went to his house in New York, hadn't seen him for two years. I just said hello. We got raided one time he was here. We didn't have a proper club license. Members only club, but it didn't work that way, it was impossible to function. So we just ignored it. And we got raided.

Roland was doing that pennywhistle thing. He distributed about a hundred pennywhistles to the audience, and everyone was blowing like mad. It was like a madhouse. About twenty plain-clothes men and women came in. And no one took a bit of notice. Just went on blowing, like an aviary. Roland couldn't see what was happening, of course, just thundered on.

All this law trying to get names and addresses. Policeman says to me, "Go up and tell him to stop." I said, "*You* go up and tell him to stop." ↄ

chapter 35

Joe Venuti

Aside from being one of the best jazz violinists to ever pass our way, Joe Venuti was the jazz world's most famous prankster. His fondness for jokes and his habit of acting on impulse made him a legendary figure. Joe became the talk of 52nd Street for the way he dealt with an annoying drunk who was bending his ear at the bar of the Onyx Club. While standing there feigning interest in the conversation, Joe urinated on the drunk's leg.

Joe preferred more elaborate jokes. On Paul Whiteman's band a fellow musician like to take a hot bath after the job every night. Joe filled the unsuspecting victim's hotel room bathtub with hot water and a case of Jell-O powder. The gelatin set quite satisfactorily, and everyone had a good laugh.

One of Venuti's most famous inspirations involved Wingy Manone, the one-armed trumpet player:

Joe Venuti sent me a birthday present one year, in a big box, wrapped up fancy. After I spent fifteen minutes gettin the box unwrapped, I found he had sent me one cufflink. That was twelve years ago, and I'm still waitin' for the other one.

The best gag Joe ever played on me happened in New York, though. Joe and me, and his wife, Sally, got on the subway one afternoon on our way to a theater date. The train was so crowded we had to stand by the door. After we got on they tried to shut the door on our car, and it wouldn't shut.

The train didn't start, and everybody was wondering what the trouble was. Finally the conductor had to push his way through the crowd to see what's the matter.

When he got to the door he found my bad [prosthetic] arm was stuck between the sliding doors, and they wouldn't go shut. Man, I couldn't feel nothin' in that arm, I didn't even know it was caught in the door.

But the conductor hollered at me for holding up traffic for twenty minutes. Boy, I was so embarrassed, I wanted to run off that train and hide. And Joe was standin' there, laughin' like hell. He was the one who had stuck my arm in the door.   ↳

Joe Venuti and Tommy Dorsey worked together in radio studio bands. Bill Priestley recalled a New Year's Eve broadcast:

The leader made the unwise move of angering Tommy and Venuti at rehearsal. So they sneaked back to the studio before anyone returned for the program, and in the big stand-up chimes inserted a piece of paper, rolled up in the bottom of each pipe, so that, when released, the paper expanded and deadened the note completely. The result was that, when the old year went out, the leader signaled for the chimes and got "tick—tick," a little louder—"TICK," really hard blow, but no note—and finally the chimes player, realizing he'd been had and the leader having a change of life, gave a full golf swing on the last note, which overturned the whole chimes set. It sounded like they were taking the annual inventory at Hammacher Schlemmer's.   ↳

The often-told story about Venuti hiring thirty-seven bass fiddle play-

ers and having them meet one Saturday at 8:00 p.m. at the corner of
52nd Street and Broadway with their instruments is slightly inaccurate.
The details were corrected by Milt Hinton:

> It was in Hollywood, California. And it was tuba players. He went
> through the union book and called up all these tuba players and
> told them he had a gig for them and to be at Sunset and Vine, and
> he sat around and watched all them guys show up. Of course the
> union took it to him and had him pay for it; it was a great joke and
> he paid for it. But when he played Chicago, about twenty-six bass
> players decided to show up for fun. So that's how that story got out,
> but they planned it for a little publicity stunt. He bought all the guys
> a drink and bought them a double so it cost him a couple of hun-
> dred bucks for that. ♪

In 1974, Gene Lees asked Venuti about the tuba players:

> He told them to meet him at Hollywood and Vine, and watched
> the chaotic scene from the twelfth floor of the Taft Hotel with
> Jack Bregman of the publishing firm of Bregman, Vocco, and
> Conn.
>   "The joke was on me, though," Joe said. "They took me to the
> union and I had to pay ten bucks a man. Two weeks later, Jack Breg-
> man said 'Call them again and I'll pay the fine.' But I said, 'No
> chance!'" ♪

Lees researched some other Venuti stories that had become legend:

> In 1936, Joe and his twelve-piece band were hired to work in Fort
> Worth opposite the Paul Whiteman band in a huge theater-
> restaurant called the Casa Manana, as part of the Texas Frontier
> Centennial. The extravaganza was a Billy Rose production, with
> chorus girls, a revolving stage a block long, and a lagoon with a jet
> spray of water to separate the proscenium and the audience. Rose
> had suggested two bands be used; Whiteman had suggested Venuti.
> At some points both bands played together. In his biography of
> Whiteman titled *Pops*, Thomas A. DeLong wrote, "The Whiteman
> bandstand was placed opposite the smaller platform holding Venuti

and his players. As the open-air theater was generally dark, Paul decided to use a lighted baton so that both bands could see him directing them when they played together."

Joe thought this was a bit much. (Whiteman was a notoriously inept conductor.) DeLong said he got a broomstick with a flashlight attached to the end; Joe said it was a fishing pole with a huge lightbulb on its end. He came onstage in long underwear, carrying this "baton." "It lit up the whole arena," Joe said. "Billy Rose came back and said, 'What do you think I'm running here, a circus?'

"I said, 'That's exactly what you're running.' But they couldn't fire me, because I owed Paul five thousand dollars."

The King of Jazz was playing at the Roxy in New York. It opened May 2, 1930. Whiteman's band was combined with the Roxy Symphony to form an orchestra of 130 musicians. As always, the *Rhapsody in Blue* was to be featured, with Gershwin playing the piano part. Concertmaster Kurt Dieterle was to lead the orchestra as it came up out of the pit, and then Whiteman would appear.

What Joe said he did may have been at the opening night dress rehearsal. By now you should know that Joe had a conspicuous intolerance for anything that smacked of bombast.

Joe said, "We had no fanfare or tympani roll to open the curtain. There was a big tuba note.

"George Gershwin was a good friend of mine, and I thought I ought to come up with something special for the occasion.

"So I put five pounds of flour in the tuba. We had blue full-dress suits, and all of a sudden as the curtain went up, the tuba player blew that note and they became white full-dress suits. We looked like snowmen. Paul came out and said, 'Pardon me, where are we?' We had to close the scrim and get ourselves dusted off, and then we played."

Charles Thompson tells of another Venuti put-on aimed at Whiteman:

Whiteman was very fond of the violin and at every performance played a chorus of *My Wonderful One*—much to the annoyance of the rest of the band and particularly their top solo violin, jazz great Joe Venuti. Says Bing [Crosby], "Joe always teased Pops about his intonation and as Pops never practiced, it was somewhat suspect. At one matinee, as Whiteman concluded his solo and was taking a bow, Joe stepped out from the band, shook Pops by the hand, took his violin, salted it from a huge salt shaker—and proceeded to eat it!"

Venuti was once hired by a Philadelphia madam to play for her girls one night after the customers had left. Her only stipulation was that he had to play without any clothes other than a top hat. Joe carried off the job with great aplomb.

Barry Ulanov told a Venuti story:

Joe, a first-rate golfer, was a natural companion for Bing [Crosby], off and on the golf course. When his luck was bad, he let loose the largest string of Italian curses ever heard west of Sicily. One particularly luckless afternoon, after finding that the curses didn't relieve his injured pride, Joe took the club he was using, broke it over his knee, and tossed it into a water hole. The caddy laughed. Joe followed the first club with all the rest and tossed in his golf bag too. The caddy bent over with laughter. Joe bent over, too, grabbed the kid by the middle, and threw him into the water. Bing, who was with him, couldn't stop laughing either, so Joe grabbed him, and in he went, too. [W.C. Fields used this bit in one of his movies. Ed.] ↷

Arnold Brilhart worked with Venuti at the Pennsylvania Hotel on the Roger Wolfe Kahn band. Arnold and several other musicians started making paper airplanes during intermissions. Venuti topped them by constructing one about ten feet long, out of cardboard. He got three waiters and a busboy to help him carry it out of the back room, across the dance floor and out onto a high balcony. When they launched the plane, it took a screaming dive right into a traffic cop on Seventh Avenue. The furious cop came up and arrested everyone in the band.

Accordionist Tommy Gumina told this one:

Irving Edelman once played bass for Joe Venuti. Joe drove him nuts with one gag he played on him. He started putting a little bag of sand in Irving's bass every night, and the instrument gradually kept getting heavier and heavier. Irving went up to Venuti one night and told him he was going to quit, because all that heavy Italian food and wine they'd have after work each night was getting him so out of shape he could barely carry his bass anymore. Joe finally had to explain the gag or lose a bass player. ↷

Sudhalter and Evans write:

In later years [Red] Nichols told a curious story about the fate of the small upright piano he and Bix had in the room at the Pasadena. A frequent visitor was Joe Venuti, jazz violinist and notorious gagster.

"Venuti," said Red, "wondered aloud one day what the 'predominant key' of the piano was. I told him I thought it was 'C,' but he disagreed. He said if all the keys were hit at once, how could you tell which key would dominate?"

Venuti announced he knew a way to find out, and that as of that moment he was taking bets on it. The whole issue sounded intriguing enough so that every musician to whom he mentioned it during the next few days offered to place a five-dollar bet on it. The decision would be made in Red's room at the end of the week.

Came the day, and a number of colleagues, Bix included, assembled in the room. Venuti, abetted by a couple of the more muscular among them, carried the upright over to the window, lifted it, and before the horrified Nichols could object, dropped it into the alley.

"It landed with an enormous crash, with snapping of piano wires and whatnot, but there was no hint of any pitch," said Red.

Joe went around the room, returning $5 to each investor. Nichols, stunned, kept asking why on earth he'd done it, and who was going to pay for the ruined piano.

"What the hell are you crying about, Redhead?" said the violinist. "I gave you your $5 back, didn't I?"

The last Joe Venuti story comes from the summer of 1978, when Joe was enjoying a resurgence in his career as a new generation discovered his playing. Nick Brignola went to hear him in a club in Schenectady. He said that Joe, in good spirits that evening, announced,

"Ladies and gentlemen, I'm gonna do something that I don't usually do. I'm gonna take a few requests." A woman cried out, "Play 'Feelings.'"

"'Feelin's'?" Joe responded. "'Feelin's'! Why, that's the worst goddam song I ever heard! That's it, no more requests. You had your chance."

He played "Sweet Georgia Brown."

chapter 36

Tommy Dorsey

Tommy Dorsey was a tough man to work for, but his high musical standards and good salaries always attracted excellent musicians and
arrangers. Dorsey had a formidable temper and a ready pair of fists. He
frequently fought with his brother Jimmy, especially when they were co-
leaders of the Dorsey Brothers Orchestra. When Tommy broke up the
partnership and set out on his own, part of his drive to succeed reportedly came from his desire to have a better band than Jimmy's.

Tommy's primary concern was musicianship. Once, when he needed a
trumpet player, he asked his band for suggestions. A musician said, "How
about so-and-so? He's a nice guy."

"Nice guys are a dime a dozen!" snapped Tommy. "Get me a prick that
can play!"

When Tommy found a musician he wanted, money was secondary.
Willie Smith was leading Jimmy Lunceford's saxophone section, and
Dorsey decided to woo him onto his band. He drove out to the Larch-
mont, New York, casino that Lunceford had built and gave Smith a lift
back to New York City after the job. When they stopped at Smith's address, Dorsey pulled out a checkbook and signed his name to a check.

"You see where it says *Pay to the order of*? Put down whatever amount
you want."

Smith declined the offer because he couldn't bring himself to break
faith with the Lunceford band, which had developed a strong espirit de
corps even though they weren't making any money.

Frank Rehak found himself in an excellent position as Jimmy Dorsey's
featured trombone soloist:

I stayed with Jimmy Dorsey for about three years. I quit the band the first night, because they went overtime and I missed my train back to Long Island. He gave me a raise the next day and I stayed on.

My instructions from Jimmy were, "Anything you can do to make Tommy mad, go ahead and do it. If you can play something that's so wild that he can't play it, I'll love you for it."

We'd get on these radio shows, and Jimmy would just cut me loose and let me do whatever I wanted. I would get a call from Tommy every three or four months, and he'd say, "What are you playing with that guy for? Why don't you come with my band?" I'd say, "Why would I want to come with your band? I'll never get anything to play, and I'll never make any money." And he'd say, "But you'd be getting a free lesson from me every time I picked up my horn."

So I would use that, of course, against Jimmy; I'd go down and say, "Jimmy, guess what? The old Grey Fox called me last night."

"Oh, man, how much is it going to cost me this time?"

"You'd better tack on another $25." ⤶

In the 1930s, Arnold Brilhart used to play golf with Tommy Dorsey. He said there was one guy Tommy couldn't seem to beat, so he had a friend who was handy with tools make a special driver for him. It was hollow, and had a little spring-loaded door in front. When a golf ball was hit with it, the door would open and the club head would swallow the ball. Tommy would tee off with the trick club, pretend to be watching his ball fly straight down the fairway, and then would walk to within an easy chip to the green. A lever on his club handle would eject the ball where he wanted it.

Herb Sanford tells of an impromptu surprise party T.D. gave Johnny Mercer and his wife Ginger at a club where the band was playing:

Tommy, visiting at their table, learned it was Johnny's birthday. Later in the evening the band played *Happy Birthday* and Tommy sent a large birthday cake to the Mercers' table. "When I cut into it," says Johnny, "it turned out to be full of lead sheets of my flop songs, which amused Tommy greatly and also pleased Ginger and me." ⤶

Pee Wee Erwin once got separated from T.D.'s band in Pennsylvania:

After the Easton job I was in my room medicating [an infection on] my hands, and the bus left without me. The band was 200 miles away before my absence was discovered. Since I didn't have anything else to do, I went to bed, and I had logged eight hours of sleep by the time Tommy called from Pittsburgh.

He said, "Look, you have to make the job tonight, so go out to the airport and wait for the airplane I'm sending for you." Following his instructions and disregarding the rain that was coming down in buckets, Roberta and I went out to the airport and waited. Finally, during the brief let-up in the storm, a Beechcraft came out of the clouds and landed. The pilot taxied up to the apron and motioned us aboard. We climbed in, and he immediately took off into the storm again, headed for Pittsburgh. He told us he had flown over from Floyd Bennett Field and the storm was everywhere.

We made it to Pittsburgh all right. The only trouble was that when we got there everything was completely closed in and we couldn't land. The pilot decided to try Ohio, but conditions there weren't any better. "I'll turn around and head back to Pennsylvania," the pilot told us finally, "and see if we can set down any place."

Luckily, on the way back conditions around Harrisburg improved enough for us to land, so we got off the plane and caught a train for Pittsburgh, arriving around 12:30 a.m.—or just about a half-hour before Tommy's job finished. He told me later that the plane and pilot had cost him $400, and I still never made the job. ❧

Tommy Dorsey's favorite drummer was super-soloist Buddy Rich, who got his start at the Hickory House with Joe Marsala. Several other musicians started with Marsala and then went with Tommy, including Dave Tough, Joe Bushkin, and Carmen Mastren. When Rich left him, Marsala sent Dorsey a telegram: DEAR TOMMY, HOW ABOUT GIVING ME A JOB IN YOUR BAND SO I CAN PLAY WITH MINE?

Tommy had strict rules about punctuality and exacted fines from anyone he caught arriving late for work. Once Joe Bushkin had to pay up:

The fine was that you had to buy booze for the whole band, which cost a lot of bread. Now Buddy Rich was late for the first set nearly every night. But Tommy wasn't there and nobody ever finked on him.

As it happened I was always on time, except about twice. Once I was terribly late and that was when I had a fight with Buddy Rich.

When I appeared Tommy stopped the band and said, "You used to play with us."

Well, I was late and I had the wrong uniform on. It was Tuesday, after the Monday off, and we changed to the light suits. But I hadn't been home all night and I woke up somewhere uptown of course, so I was wearing the wrong uniform. I was happy to buy the booze.

Anyway, he called the waiter over and made it pretty tough. George Arus and Chuck Peterson drank Canadian Club: a bottle of that. Somebody else had a bottle, and so on. A case of Coca-Cola and, finally, a bottle of wine for Buddy Rich.

"Cancel the wine," I said. Tommy wanted to know why and I told him, "Not for that cat. He was late every night when you weren't there. I refuse to buy him wine. Let him pay off first."

The waiter arrived with all the bottles and the wine was there. So I sent it back. Afterwards, Buddy and I went out in the park and beat the shit out of each other. Well, it was a fighting band.

Dorsey came out and tried to stop the fight, which I wouldn't have minded because I was getting the worst of it. But he wasn't worried about us.

"Take the jackets off," he shouted. "The jackets! We got another set to play!" ↟

Rich told about continuing to work for Tommy Dorsey with a temporary handicap:

I only had one arm for a while. We'd just gotten off the bus in Dayton, Ohio. I never could sleep when we arrived anywhere and so I went and played some handball, and I tripped and broke my left arm in three places. It was put in a cast and I had a sling made to match my band uniform. I played with my right hand and used my foot as a left hand. Solos, too. I never missed a day for the three months the cast stayed on. ↟

Rich and Dorsey were temperamentally too much alike to stay together for long, but when Buddy finally left, Dorsey found himself dissatisfied with most other drummers. Oddly, the one besides Rich who pleased him the most was Dave Tough, whose playing couldn't have been more different. No technician, Tough avoided taking solos, preferring to concentrate on swinging the band.

In the early 1950s Tommy, the "Sentimental Gentleman of Swing," was playing a couple of weeks at the Pennsylvania Hotel and was audi-

tioning drummers. The guy who had the job hadn't had much of a
chance to play, since Dorsey was calling nearly every drummer in New
York to come down and sit in for a set. The word was around town that
nobody was going to satisfy him unless they were another Buddy Rich,
so when Frank Isola's phone rang one morning, he wasn't too excited
by the call.

"Frank! It was Tommy's manager. "Come down to the Pennsylvania
tonight! Tommy wants to hear you play!"

Frank thought a minute, and then drawled softly, "Aaah, thanks, but
tell Tommy I'm not in a sentimental mood."

Jo Stafford was singing with the Pied Pipers when Dorsey made some
impulsive personnel changes:

> One night in Texas, half of the band got fired. Tommy was in one
> of his drinking phases, and he was pretty well smashed. He had al-
> most a concert arrangement on *Sleepy Lagoon*. There's a part where
> he had to go up to a real high note. And this note just splashed all
> over the stage. He stopped the band about three times. On the
> fourth try it started getting to the players. They started giggling. The
> whole saxophone section started, and then it's like the measles; it
> spreads. Tommy turned and said, "You're fired, and you're fired,
> and you're fired." He fired about half the band. They all got up and
> picked up their horns and left. I can still see it. Freddy Stulce walked
> by the Pipers and said to us, "See you later." We played the rest of
> the night with about half a band.   ♪

Young Terry Gibbs was thrilled when T.D. hired him. He was to join
the band in California. In deference to his mother, who didn't trust airplanes, Terry got Dorsey's manager to send him train tickets. After one
night with the band Terry realized that he had made a mistake. In New
York he had been working infrequently but playing jazz all the time with
his friends. On Dorsey's band there was little opportunity to solo, and
Terry wasn't interested in playing dance music. He gave the manager his
notice. Dorsey wasn't pleased when he heard about it:

> I'd heard about Tommy having a terrible temper, so I'm standing
> there talking with one or two of the guys and he comes over to me.

"Hey, shithead."

He called everybody shithead. I turned around and held my guard, 'cause I knew he'd hit you first and then talk to you. He was like nine feet tall compared to me.

"Did you just quit my band?"

I tried to explain.

He says, "Nobody quits. You're fired."

I says, "Well, if you fire me you gotta pay my way home."

He says, "No, you quit. You pay your own way home." ⟍

Dorsey made Terry sit out his two weeks' notice. He didn't let him play, so Terry sat on the bandstand turning pages for the bass player. The band took pity on him and let him play on the last set every night, after Dorsey had gone home.

chapter 37

Lionel Hampton

Lionel Hampton's band provided exposure for scores of talented young musicians. Hamp always paid low salaries, so his turnover was high, but with one of the few bands to survive the demise of the Big Band Era, Hampton was a magnet for young jazz musicians all over the country. They would usually put in enough time to establish professional credentials and would then jump to the next opportunity that presented itself.

A showman himself, Hamp always encouraged showmanship in his musicians. When Quincy Jones joined his trumpet section in 1950, he said, "I soon saw which way the wind was blowing. The first solo he gave me, I played the best jazz chorus I could play. He didn't point to me again for quite a while, and in the meantime I saw that everybody who got solos was juggling and dancing. The next solo he gave me, I shucked a little, and after that I got more solos."

Hamp's band was making a swing through several cities in eastern

Canada, with a one-nighter in Buffalo on the way up and another on the way back. At the first gig in Buffalo the ballroom was packed, with people jammed against the front of the stage in a solid mass.

Hamp was delighted when an alto player who had just joined the band came down front to play his solo, jumped up on the footlight cover, and "walked the rail" while playing, exaggerating his movements as if he were balanced on a tightrope. At the climax of his solo he turned around and fell backwards into the tightly packed crowd. In a self-protective reflex, the people put their hands up and caught him, pushing back onto the stage. He continued playing furiously through it all, and was a great sensation.

Hampton had a habit of stealing the best bits of showmanship that his sidemen invented. On the return trip to Buffalo, at the same ballroom, Hampton made his move. During a number where the alto man was playing clarinet, Hamp grabbed his saxophone from its stand and jumped up on the footlight rail. He began a rhythmic riff on one note while imitating the alto man's balancing act, and the crowd began to applaud.

At the climax, Hampton turned his back and fell backwards into the crowd. But, since the band had appeared there fairly recently, the turnout wasn't as heavy as it had been the first time, so there was room enough for the people who saw Hamp falling to step quickly out of the way. Instead of being pushed back onto the stage, Hamp fell flat on his back on the floor. The band laughed so hard they could barely continue playing while Hampton abashedly climbed back onto the stage.

One night during the Canadian tour Hampton got mad at trombonist Jimmy Cleveland about something. By the end of the job Hamp was in a towering rage. When the bus started rolling toward the next town everyone including Cleve was pillowed against a window trying to get a little sleep, but Hamp was pacing the aisle and ranting beside Cleveland's seat. Cleve kept pretending to be asleep, but Hamp wouldn't give it up. He said to the bus driver, "Stop the bus! Stop the bus! I want you to put this man off right here! He's fired!"

"Aw, Hamp," said the driver. "I can't do that. It's the middle of the night, it's ten degrees outside, we're in the middle of nowhere in Canada!"

"I don't care!" said Hampton. "I want this man off the bus! Stop the bus right now!"

The road manager explained that they had all come into the country on a single work permit, and they would all have to leave together.

"I don't care. This man is fired, and I want him off my bus!"

The bus driver wouldn't stop, which made Hamp even madder. He got right up into the seat with Cleveland, leaned over him and began yelling into his "sleeping" face, enumerating his personal deficiencies. With his eyes still closed, Cleve reached up into the ditty bag he was using for a pillow and pulled out a big shiny pistol, which he put between Hamp's face and his own.

Hampton quickly sat down in his own seat, and was "asleep" within five seconds. He never said anything more about firing Cleve.

Dinah Washington sang with Hampton before she broke through as a single act. Lionel kept promising her recordings, but when the band went into the studio Hamp rarely got around to doing any of Dinah's numbers. After one broken promise, Dinah partially drowned her anger with a fifth of gin and went to work that night carrying quite a load, as well as an old pistol with no firing pin that someone had sold her. She laughed all the way through "The Man I Love," because the musicians kept whispering, "Sing it, Miss Gin." When Hampton called her on the carpet after the show, Dinah lit into him for breaking his promise. Arnett Cobb described the scene:

> Hamp told her, "Kiss my ass." She went upstairs and got her pistol and come back down and said, "You told me to kiss your ass," and put that gun right over the top of his nose, and Hamp's hair turned green. I ain't never seen anybody's hair turn green. I'm right there!
>
> You know, Hamp didn't come out of that dressing room until Gladys [his wife and manager] came back. When Hamp told her what had happened, she terminated Dinah's contract, that she had for ten years for $75 a week. Dinah had an offer to do a Broadway show for $350 and couldn't make it because of that contract. She didn't know it could have been broken. But she broke it for herself right there. She broke it with that pistol, and it wouldn't even fire!

Jimmy Cara worked with Hampton for a short time. Later, Jimmy was playing with the Sammy Kaye Orchestra in Washington's Aero-Space museum for President Reagan's inaugural ball. He heard that Hampton's band was playing on the other side of the building, and Jimmy and a few other musicians from Kaye's band walked over to see Hamp. He hugged them and then, looking at the S K initials on their red band jackets, inquired, "Aaah, who you with now? Stan Kenton?"

Milt Hinton played a concert with Louis Armstrong in Washington, D.C., on a barge on the banks of the Potomac. The bands of Lionel Hampton and Illinois Jacquet were also to be on the program:

We unloaded our suitcases and instruments and moved everything over to the barge. By the time we'd changed into our tuxedos, it was six-thirty. Jacquet should have gone at six, but he still hadn't arrived. To make matters worse, Hamp hadn't either.

Standing backstage, we could sense the audience was getting restless. Every couple of minutes they'd start applauding and chanting, "Start the show," and "We want music."

About fifteen minutes later one of the producers went to Frenchy [Armstrong's road manager] and asked if Louis wouldn't go on first. Louis was a star, but he didn't care about billing or protocol. He was usually understanding and cooperative.

So we went out and started playing. After waiting so long the audience gave us an unbelievable reception. They applauded every solo and when we finished a tune they'd stand and cheer for a couple of minutes.

We played about an hour and then took our bows. But the people wouldn't let us off the stage. They screamed for encores and we kept doing them. Louis knew there was no act to follow us. And he was content to stay out there and keep everyone happy until help arrived. Finally, during our fifth or sixth encore, we saw a bus pull up and unload. As soon as Louis knew it was Jacquet's band, he told us, "This time when we end, walk off and stay off."

As soon as we finished, we headed for the dressing rooms and changed. Then we packed up our instruments and hung around backstage talking to some of the guys from Jacquet's band.

Trying to follow a performer like Louis really put Jacquet in a difficult position. To make matters worse, the audience knew he'd been scheduled to play first and had kept them waiting. so when he came out on stage, he got a lukewarm reception.

Jacquet had eight or nine good musicians with him. They started with a couple of standards, but there was no response. They even featured the drummer, but that didn't seem to rouse the audience either. Then Jacquet must've figured he had nothing to lose, so he called "Flying Home," the tune he'd made famous with Hamp's band.

It took a couple of minutes before the audience recognized the tune and started to react. By then Jacquet was soloing and he gave it everything he had, building, honking, screaming, and dancing. All the moves, chorus after chorus. By the time he finished, he had the audience in the palm of his hand, the same way Louis had them an hour before.

The audience screamed for an encore and Jacquet did another couple of chorus of "Flying Home." But right in the middle, Hamp's bus pulled up. Hearing someone else play a tune he was known for and seeing the fantastic audience reaction must've made him furious. Everyone backstage saw what was going on and knew Hamp would want to somehow outdo Jacquet. Louis was watching and he got interested too. I remember we were set to get on the bus, but Louis turned to a couple of us and said, "Wait, we have to see this."

Jacquet finished and after the stage got set up, Hamp came out. He began with "Midnight Sun," one of his famous ballads. But after Louis's performance and Jacquet's finale, the audience was in no mood for it. He did "Hamp's Boogie Woogie," and a couple more numbers. He even played drums and sang, but he still didn't get much of a reaction.

I was standing in the wings with Louis and a couple of other guys and we could see how hard he was working. But time was running out. He looked frustrated and desperate and he finally called "Flying Home."

The band started playing but there wasn't much response from the audience. Hamp wouldn't give up. He put everything he had into his solo, starting out soft, then building to a crescendo. When he finished, sweat was dripping off every part of him, and a handful of people cheered.

I guess Hamp sensed he was making some headway with the crowd. So while the band continued, he went back to Monk Montgomery, who was playing Fender bass, and told him, "Gates, you jump in the river on the next chorus. I'll give you an extra ten."

Monk must've agreed because when the band got to the next crescendo and Hamp raised his mallets, Monk jumped over the railing. The audience went crazy.

The band kept playing and a few minutes later Monk came out on stage soaking wet. Hamp walked over to him and said, "Another ten if you do it again."

Monk made it back to his bass and played another chorus. Then when the band came to the same crescendo and Hamp raised his hands, he went over the side again.

By this time the people were in a frenzy and Hamp knew he'd accomplished what he'd set out to do. Louis turned to us and said, "Start up the bus. We can go now."

chapter 38

Charlie Parker

Charlie Parker upset the jazz world with the beauty and inventiveness of his playing, in the same way Louis Armstrong had upset it twenty-five years earlier. Like Armstrong, Parker added a whole new set of melodic phrases to the standard jazz vocabulary. As Lennie Tristano remarked when Parker died,

"He could sue almost everybody who's made a record in the last ten years."

Al Cohn tried to explain the impact that Parker had on his contemporaries:

> The thing about Charlie Parker was that he was such a giant, he was so much better than everybody else. It's not like there was this guy, and that guy. There was everybody else, and then there was Charlie! You could take his solos, if you would put them down on paper and analyze them, they really had substance, creativity, the way he used changes. There wasn't anybody else doing that then. He was a great influence musically, but a terrible influence in other ways. 🎵

Parker didn't spring full blown into the world as the master musician he was to become. Bird tells it in his own words:

> I'd learned the scale and learned how to play two tunes in a certain key, the key of G for the saxophone, you know, F concert. I'd learned the first eight bars of *Lazy River* and I knew the complete tune of *Honeysuckle Rose*. I didn't ever stop to think about any different kind of keys or nothing like that. So I took my horn out to a joint where the guys, a bunch of fellows I'd seen around, were, and the first thing they started playing was *Body and Soul*. So I go to playing my *Honeysuckle Rose* and they laughed me off the bandstand, laughed at me so hard I had to leave the club. 🎵

Jo Jones was on the bandstand that night. He gave the final blow by pulling his top cymbal off its stand and tossing it at young Parker's feet, "giving him the gong," as was done on Major Bowe's radio *Amateur Hour*. Eddie Barefield was one of the musicians who joined in the laughter:

> I was in Kansas City when he first came out to play. He sounded so bad that we wouldn't let him play. He went down to Oklahoma and stayed about six months with Buster Smith, who really taught him a lot about his playing. And he came back and just washed everybody out. ⤵

Parker established his reputation in Kansas City, but that town had passed its prime as an entertainment center with the fading of Tom Pendergast's political regime. Charlie wanted to know what was going on in Chicago. Having no money, he jumped a freight train.

Art Blakey remembered Parker in Chicago:

> The man was hoboing, got off the train in Chicago and went over to hear Earl Hines. Walked into the dressing room, said, "Can I look at your horn?" Looked at the horn, hadn't even cleaned himself up yet, just played. Saxophone player named "Goon," played with Earl Hines, said, "What!" Went and got him a clean shirt, gave him a horn and pushed him out on that stage. ⤵

Kansas Fields told the same story, but placed Goon Gardner with the King Kolax band at the time, not Hines.

Sadik Hakim, whose name was then Argonne Thornton, met Parker in Chicago and began dropping by to hear him play at a job he had found at the Rum-Boogie Club:

> Bird was never there for rehearsals. He always came about two or three minutes before the show hit. He'd look at the third alto part, glance at his lead part, and when the curtain came up, Bird was playing that music like he owned it, plus adding things to the part.
>
> One night Jimmy Dorsey was playing at the Sherman Hotel in the Loop, and he came down to hear Bird. Bird's bandleader knew what was happening. He called "Cherokee," which featured Bird. Bird, of course, played like a man possessed. Jimmy Dorsey came back to the dressing room, introduced himself, and said to Bird, "Here, man, you need this much more than I do," and gave Bird his brand new

padless Selmer. I was with Bird the next day when he put it in pawn. I begged him not to. His own horn was a wreck, held together with tape, gummed paper, etc. This didn't matter to him. ↱

Parker joined Jay McShann's band and came to New York with him. McShann recalled those days:

It came time for Bird to blow his solo, and you know, he used to have bad feet. His feet would hurt him. And so he started out to the mike, but his shoes were off and he was in his stocking feet. And I kept wondering what the people was laughing about. He was in his stocking feet and his big toe was showing. ↱

Jimmy Forrest was Parker's roommate on the Jay McShann band:

At the time, in 1940, if you paid fifteen dollars for a sports shirt, that was a pretty good shirt. I was fortunate enough to have saved some money, and I bought three of them. Fifteen dollars each. That's a lot of bread, especially when you're only making seven a night, you dig? So I bought the three shirts and I brought them back to the hotel room and said, "Hey, Bird, look what I got." Bird said, "Which one is mine?" (laughter)

He was such a personable guy you had to give it to him, you couldn't refuse. ↱

McShann remonstrated with Parker about being the worst dressed man in his band. Parker said,

"Hootie, would you like it if I came to the bandstand looking like a doctor, and played like a doctor?"

McShann clearly was more interested in his playing. He spoke of Parker's effect on the New York musicians when he arrived in town:

Ben Webster went down and told all the saxophone players down on 52nd Street. He said,

"All you guys who think that you can play saxophone, you'd better go up there. There's this little saxophone player up there with Jay McShann's band. All you guys better go up there and go to school."

Ben told us that he would hide. He didn't want nobody to see him up there. After he told the rest of the guys down on the Street, he said he'd come by and they'd run into each other, hidin' from each other! ↱

Earl Hines wanted Parker and two other men from McShann's band. "You know I'll get them," he told Jay. "Why don't we just sit down and talk this thing over. How much money do they owe you?" He offered to pay McShann what they owed him if he'd let them go. McShann agreed, and Hines paid him off, saying, "I don't think you know how to handle this guy Charlie Parker. You're all a bunch of kids. I'm going to take him and make a man out of him." McShann said:

> The next time I saw Earl Hines he said, "Come get this madman! Listen, this guy owes everybody in the band and every loan shark in town!" ↱

Parker's addiction to heroin, which had developed when he was seventeen, created most of his financial problems during his life. Although he was able to function better than most users, his habit increased his tendency to ignore time schedules on jobs. It forced him to put a higher priority on finding a supply of narcotics than on obligations to his employers and his sidemusicians, and it ate up whatever money he made, even when his price increased considerably during his years as a star soloist. He showed a friend the veins on his arm one day and said ruefully, "This is my Cadillac," and hold out the other arm, "and this is my house."

Billy Eckstine met Parker on Hines's band:

> He used to miss as many shows as he would make. Half the time we couldn't find Bird; he'd be sitting up somewhere sleeping. So he often missed the first shows, and Earl used to fine him blind. You know, fine him every time he looked at him. Bird would miss the show, Earl would fine him.
>
> So one time we were working the Paradise Theatre in Detroit, and Bird says, "I ain't gonna miss no more. I'm going to stay in the theater all night to make sure I'm here."
>
> We answered, "Okay. That's your business. Just make the show, huh?"
>
> Sure enough, we come to work the next morning, we got on the stand—no Bird. As usual. We think, "So, he said he was going to make the show and he didn't make it."
>
> This is the gospel truth. We played the whole show, the curtains closed, and we're coming off the band cart, when all of a sudden we

hear a noise. We look under the stand, and here comes Bird out from underneath. He had been under there asleep through the entire show! ⸙

One of the delightful features of Parker's improvised choruses was his ability to extract quotes from various musical sources and artfully weave them into his own lines, always fitting them imaginatively to the chord structure of the tune on which he was improvising. He was interested in every kind of music. The quotes he used during an evening's performance might be extracted from Stravinsky, Mantovani, Bo Diddley, Guy Lombardo, television commercials, or any other music that he might have been listening to. Idrees Sulieman remembered Parker's listening habits:

Kenny Drew would come up and listen to records and my wife and I would get in bed and go to sleep. Dizzy and Bird used to also come by one or two o'clock at night. I had a lot of Stravinsky records and I wouldn't like for Bird to come by, because he would never leave. I could never get him out. He'd say, "I'll stay here." He would play what he heard from the records on the jam session nights.

One day Miles and I were playing out of this clarinet book, and it's very hard struggling, trying to play. Bird was just sitting there listening. Later, we'd go to the show and Bird was playing all those exercises we were trying to play.

At a jam session at Small's Paradise, there was this tenor player who had just bought his tenor a few days before. Came up on the stand and didn't know anything. He was playing this one lick; that's all he knew. The musicians were just rolling, but Bird was sitting there like he was really listening.

Somebody said, "Come on, Bird." Bird said, "I hear what he's trying to do." The next set Bird went up on the stage and played what the cat was trying to do, but he *played* it! ⸙

Earl Hines cited an example of Parker's phenomenal memory:

The remarkable thing about Charlie, he had such an advanced mind that when we rehearsed an arrangement that no one had seen before, we'd run it down once or twice, or whatever time we had to run it down, and we'd put it away. We decide to play it that night, everybody got the music but Charlie; he's sittin' over there on the end with his tenor, I'd say, "Look, Charlie, when you goin' to get the tune out?"

He says, "I know that."

"I mean that new number."

"I know it."

And sure enough, he knew the arrangement backwards. ↳

Cliff Smalls, Hines's arranger, confirms the story:

> Although Charlie played tenor all the time he was with the band, it sounded like he was still playing alto, because he'd always have an alto style.
>
> Now Earl had two tremendous books—a society book and a book for regular gigs, one-nighters. Charlie used to sit on this book, with all those reed choruses and everything in, all the time. Everybody else got their music out, but he was sitting on his! He'd remember it all. When we got a new tune, he might look at it a couple of nights, but after that it wouldn't come out of his book anymore. ↳

Eddie Barefield worked with Parker in a band at the Apollo Theater in New York:

> I was playing tenor and Bird was playing third. And they had a juggler who had music, but it was "Tico-Tico," and he wanted it at a very rapid speed. It was so fast the first man couldn't play it. Bird said, "Play it over for me a couple of times." The guy played it over for him slowly, and then he started playing it, and he played it for the rest of the week. It got faster and faster, and the faster it got, the more improvisations he put on it. It was just like taking a saxophone lesson listening to him play this. He was a marvelous musician. ↳

When Jay McShann got out of the army in 1944, he heard that Parker was working with Ben Webster on 52nd Street:

> Ben says, "Well, he works here, but he plays down the street!" They'd take intermission and Bird would take his horn down across the street and blow with the cats over here. Then if he gets carried away and he likes it, he'll stay there, you know. He don't come back to his gig. ↳

Frank Socolow was playing tenor at the Famous Door when Bird came to the Street:

He would come in, when I was with Bill Harris, and grab my horn and sit in one set on tenor, sound beautiful, and then run back and do his own gig on alto. ↱

When Sadik Hakim became a member of the house rhythm section at the Onyx Club on 52nd Street, Parker was in the band:

Bird was always late. Mike Weston, the owner, would be frowning as Bird came in late, but after a couple of Bird's choruses he'd be smiling. One night Bird was very, very late. He came in while Ben Webster was drinking at the bar; the rest of us were trioing. Bird picked up Ben's tenor and said, "Cherokee." He played that tenor like he owned it, and Ben was shook. He just kept saying, "Give me another double." The thing about this was that nobody could get a sound out of Ben's tenor but Ben himself, due to the thickness of the reed, etc. I saw many great tenor players try—Prez, Buddy Tate, Ike Quebec; no good. ↱

Hakim saw an even more impressive display of Parker's virtuosity in Chicago:

When I was with Prez we had a week off before a gig in Chicago, so I went out ahead of time to hear Bird and Miles. The saxophonist who had the house band at the club Bird was at was named Eddie Wiggins. Wiggins had a long line of reed instruments up on the bandstand—clarinet, flute, bassoon, alto, tenor, English horn. Bird came in early for once; no one else in his band was there. He had left his horn in the club. Now Bird had very good connections in Chicago, but this time he apparently forgot to pay them. He opened his horn case to find all the keys torn off or broken.
Without blinking an eye, Bird asked Wiggins if he could play the first set with Wiggins's group. Then he proceeded to play all those instruments, a few choruses on each one, even the bassoon. I was dumbfounded. Bird never ceased to amaze me. And Bird is the only person who knew me before I became a Muslim and changed my name, who never, after I told him my new name, called me anything but Sadik Hakim. ↱

Dizzy Gillespie remembered the exciting days of musical invention in New York during the forties:

During the war years when apartments were scarce, as they still are, my wife and I found a place which was comfortable. In order to avoid any complaints about noise, I did all my practicing in a studio and refrained from any trumpet cadenzas in the evening. Three in the morning the doorbell rang, and I opened it as far as the latch chain permitted. There was Bird, horn in hand, and he says,

"Let me in, Diz, I've got it; you must hear this thing I've worked out."

I had been putting down Bird's solos on paper, which is something Bird never had the patience for himself.

"Not now," I said. "Later, man, tomorrow."

"No," Bird cried, "I won't remember it tomorrow; it's in my head now; let me in please."

From the other room, my wife yelled, "Throw him out," and I obediently slammed the door in Bird's face. Parker then took his horn to his mouth and played the tune in the hallway. I grabbed pencil and paper and took it down from the other side of the door. ⮑

Just before Parker suffered the breakdown that put him in Camarillo State Hospital in California, he and Dizzy Gillespie were on Slim Gaillard's 1945 record date that included the famous "Slim's Jam." Jack McVea was also on that date:

I was working at a club in San Diego and my wife told me to call this number. I called and Slim Gaillard was on the phone. He said, "Jack, can I get you to come up here and make a date with me?" I said, "Yeah." He said, "We'll send you a round trip plane ticket." It was made in L.A. on my day off. We didn't rehearse anything. The guy working the dials says, "Slim, what should I do?" He said, "You sit behind there and turn the dials on when I tell you to, and that's it." Slim told the man, "Turn the thing on." And he went to talking.

Bird came in and there were no reeds in his case, not one. No reed on his horn; he was loaded, too. I use plastic reeds on my tenor, but I did have some cane reeds in my case. He picked through the cane reeds and said, "I'll take this one." He took my razor blade and shaved it and put it on the horn; didn't even try it. You heard the solos. He did that just before we started. ⮑

On the record, Gaillard improvised dialogue that introduced each musician. When he addresses Parker as "Charlie Yardbird-O'Rooney" and asks if he has his horn with him, Charlie says, "Got my horn, and I want to blow some, but I'm having a little reed trouble." "Haven't got a reed?" says Gaillard. "Well, MacVouty's got a reed. He can trim it down a little." Until McVea told his story, this was considered to be one of Gaillard's humorous exaggerations.

Frank Morgan met Parker when he was a boy, and renewed the friendship in California:

Charlie Parker came out to California again in 1951 and we spent a lot of time together. Bird never said too much, but he would talk to me sometimes, usually when I was playing. He would say things like, "take your time" or "breathe deeply" or "don't let the rhythm section scare you." You have to realize that being around Bird was always an experience. I was amazed at his level of intelligence. I remember seeing him talking with nuclear physicists at a party and they were scratching their heads. Now I have no way of validating what Bird was saying but it sure sounded good. It makes you wonder when this saxophonist had time to know about things of that nature.

On another occasion we were at a party with a bunch of very wealthy people, and we were playing away when Bird suddenly stopped and said, "I think we would all relax more if we took our clothes off!" So at Bird's suggestion, everyone took off their clothes. [Laughs] ♪

Jackie McLean was occasionally called to fill in for Parker on a job:

That was one of the biggest musical honors of my life, when Bird asked me. I played for him a couple of times. And when the gig was over he paid me, and that was an honor too, because I wasn't playing for money. I hadn't even thought of it when he asked me. I never asked him how much was the gig, and I didn't ask him at the end of the gig. I was just hanging around when he came over, you know, to ride up town with him, and he called everybody one at a time, and then he called me and he said, "put your hand out," and he started counting, putting dollar bills in my hand. When he got to eighteen, I still had my hand out and he said, "Well damn, Jackie, take your hand back sometime." So I took fifteen dollars and gave him three dollars back. That was a lot of money for me then. ♪

Sometimes when he was short of cash, Parker would walk up to McLean, put his hand in Jackie's pocket, and take out whatever money was there.

The first time he did that, I had six dollars, and he took four and asked me if I could make it on a deuce, and one of my friends who was with me cracked up. I said, yeah, I could make out on a deuce. The next time I saw him, he reached into my pocket and I was broke, and I thought to myself, "Well, this cat's going to be in for a surprise this time." But he was putting something in. He put ten dollars into my pocket. That's the kind of guy he was. He used to do that to a lot of musicians. Freddie Redd is another person he played that pocket game with. When he reached into your pocket you didn't know whether you were going to blow or whether you were going to cop.

Bob Reisner booked Parker whenever he was available for his jam sessions at the Open Door in Greenwich Village:

One evening things were swinging. People were drifting in, and Parker had them glued to their seats. No one danced, just drinking in the sound. Then it was intermission. Bird was walking around smiling, shaking hands, checking with me on business details. Suddenly I heard music from the bandstand. Usually we put on the juke box for fifteen minutes till the band went back on, but now I saw two men, one with a guitar and one singing—cornball junk, tourist stuff, phoney jive. I could hear slight groans from the audience. I went over to the stand.

"Gentlemen," I said, "you're excellent but not for this audience. Get out."

They glared at me. "Man, don't bug us in the middle of our number."

"I'm manager here," I said.

"Charlie Parker hired us," they countered.

"Are you sure?"

"Ask him."

I walked away. Bird would never hire those clowns.

"Charlie, you didn't hire those guys on the stand."

"Yes, I did," he said.

"The audience is reacting unfavorably, and I'm throwing those idiots off."

"If they leave, I leave," he said, and I was stymied.

I knew that Bird's taste in music was catholic, that he dug classical music, and he always turned on the radio in a car to listen to pop music and even hillbilly; but this stuff was really bad. I just sulked. After a few moments he came over to me, put his arm on my shoulder, and said, "You fool, you just don't understand business. We're full up. These cats are so bad that some of the audience will leave. We need a turnover." ↱

Pepper Adams recalled Bird's feelings about being idolized by the jazz world:

He said, "You know, it's nice that people like what you're doing, but sometimes it's something that makes *me* feel funny." he said, "One day going to the gig I'm looking for a handkerchief so I can wipe off my sweat. I couldn't find a clean handkerchief. There was this red bandanna that somebody had give to me so I figured that's gonna work, so I put it in my pocket. I'm playing the gig, and pull it out from my pocket, and wipe the sweat off my brow. About fifteen people in the front row say, 'Hey, look, Bird got a red bandanna! We gotta get one!' You know, that's dumb!" ↱

Parker, at the end of his short life, during which he had inhaled, imbibed, ingested, and injected monumental quantities of every form of stimulant, euphoric, narcotic, soporific, hypnotic, and hallucinogen known to modern man, went to visit Baroness Pannonica de Koenigswarter at her New York apartment at the onset of his final illness. When his friend Nica saw the condition he was in, she called her doctor. The doctor asked Bird the routine questions as he examined him.

"Do you drink?"

"Sometimes," Charlie answered, with a wink at Nica, "I have a sherry before dinner."

Thirty-three years after Parker's death, during the publicity surrounding the making of Clint Eastwood's movie *Bird*, Red Rodney, who is portrayed in the film, got a call from a representative of a newspaper in Nebraska:

She asked me all about my life, where I was born, why I play the trumpet, what I eat for breakfast. After she got everything she wanted, she said, "Thank you, Mr. Rodney. And, by the way, can you give me Charlie Parker's phone number?" ↴

chapter 39

John Birks Gillespie

Dizzy Gillespie never saw a reason to limit himself to any narrow application of his musical talent; he discovered early in his career that he could entertain the soul, the intellect, the feet, and the funnybone at the same time. Even though his early admirers created a cult of modernity around him, Dizzy established himself as one of the most ecumenical artists in the jazz world.

Although Gillespie and Charlie Parker had a rare musical rapport, Parker didn't understand Dizzy's urge to make his audiences laugh. Privately, Charlie had a good sense of humor, but he felt Dizzy's capers on the bandstand detracted from his artistic dignity. Standing at the bar in Birdland one night, Bird watched Dizzy "cutting the fool" to the delight of his audience. Charlie said with genuine concern, "How can he do that?"

John Coltrane worked with Dizzy, and years later made this comment:

> I don't make a habit of wishing for what I don't have, but I often wish I had a lighter nature. Dizzy has that beautiful gift. I can't say, "Be happy, people." It's something I can't command. But you have to be true to your own nature. ↴

Quentin Jackson remembered Dizzy's playfulness on Cab Calloway's band:

> The trombones were on the left of the bandstand facing the theater and the trumpets would be to the right. Cab would be in front, singing a beautiful ballad. And Tyree [Glenn] and Dizzy would act

like they were playing football. Dizzy would throw a pass and Tyree would act like he was catching it, and as he caught it, Cozy Cole would hit the bass drum a tap, and the people would laugh in the middle of a beautiful ballad. Cab didn't know exactly what was going on. ↯

Billy Eckstine had Dizzy in the trumpet section of his band, and remembered his clowning:

I'd be out on the stage singing, and I used to notice people laughing, or something like that. And then I'd turn around and look back at Diz, and he's just looking straight ahead. Well, all the time that I'm singing, he's doing pantomime to the audience, pointing at me saying that my teeth are false. And he's pointing, saying that I'm a faggot, and that I go with him and all. And when I turn around and look, he's just looking straight up in the air. ↯

For a while during the 1950s Dizzy had a small group that combined bebop with rhythm-and-blues, featuring songs like "School Days" and "You Stole My Wife, You Horse Thief." While singing a simple riff tune called "Hey Pete, Let's Eat Mo' Meat" one night in a Los Angeles club, he noticed two hipsters at a front table making disparaging faces about this un-hip tune. After the vocal, Dizzy put his trumpet to his lips and played three of the most brilliant, explosive, difficult choruses ever played by any trumpet player. When he finished, he leaned over to the hipsters and said pointedly, "Seeee?"

Then he went right back to singing, "Hey Pete, Let's Eat Mo' Meat."

Dizzy developed funny routines as fast as he developed original music. With them he attracted and held audiences that might not have understood everything he was playing. Thus he kept his band working and was free to play what interested him.

Some of his funny ideas developed into classic clowning routines as good as anything ever seen in vaudeville. One of the best was the mock fight he developed with James Moody. After the opening chorus of a tune with both horns playing in unison, Moody and Dizzy would step to the microphone at the same time. They would bump into each other, stop, look at each other, and pantomime a dispute, while the rhythm section continued to play. The following is a free translation of the mimed gestures:

Moody: I'm supposed to solo first.

Dizzy: No, I'm going to play first.

Moody: But I play first on this tune.

Dizzy: It's my band, and I'm going to play first. (Pushes Moody.)

Moody: Don't push me!

Dizzy: I'll push you again if you don't get out of my way!

Moody: Put your hand on me again if you dare!

Dizzy: Get out of my way! (Pushes Moody again.)

At this point Moody reaches quickly into his pocket and keeps his hand there, with an obvious sharp point showing through the material of his pants. Dizzy's eyes pop open in alarm, and he reaches into his own pocket. They crouch warily and circle each other as the tension mounts. Then, simultaneously, they whip their hands from their pockets and spring dangerously at each other—and dance an elegant fox-trot together as the rhythm section plays on.

When Pee Wee Marquette finished announcing an attraction at Birdland, he usually walked off the bandstand leaving the microphone at the height he had adjusted it for himself, about three feet from the floor.

One night, Pee Wee announced, "And now, ladies and gentlemen, Birdland proudly presents, DIZZY GILLESPIE!" and walked away from the microphone. Out came Dizzy on his knees to accept the applause and announce the first tune. The microphone needed no adjustment.

Dizzy often began an evening's program with an apologetic announcement:

> I'm sorry we're a little late getting started this evening, but, you see, we just came from a very, very important show. The Ku Klux Klan and the John Birch Society were giving a benefit for the Catholic Youth Organization and the B'nai B'rith. It was held at the Harlem YMCA. So you can see we're very lucky to be here at all this evening! ⤵

After playing "The Nearness of You," dedicated "to the Lifebuoy Soap Company," Dizzy would accept the audience's applause and then say, "And now, I'd like to introduce the members of the band." He would then formally introduce the bassist to the drummer, the drummer to the pianist, the pianist to the saxophonist, etc., with elaborate bowing and hand shaking all around.

Dizzy's sets often closed this way:

"And now, we'd like to play a very short number."

Dizzy would count off a fast tempo, and the band would play a single, short unison note, and leave the stand.

One night at Birdland, Dizzy and Moody were carrying on a little improvised comedy while the rhythm section played a Latin figure. Chris White was Dizzy's bassist at the time. Chris was also a good comedian, and often joined in the routines, but on this number his job was to play a pedal bass note on the fourth beat of every measure. The chord didn't change throughout the pattern being played by pianist Lalo Schifrin, so Chris had to play the same note on the fourth beat of every bar for about five minutes.

Drummer Rudy Collins and Lalo were free to invent whatever variations they wanted, but the bass note was the anchor and had to stay the same.

The new jokes that Dizzy and Moody came up with that evening delighted Chris. He started adding his own funny remarks behind them, and suddenly realized that Dizzy had stopped clowning and was looking askance at him. Chris knew that he must have skipped a beat. Among the cross-rhythms that Lalo and Rudy were playing, the bass note could have fit anywhere. There was no way to find where it really belonged just by listening.

One thing was certain; Dizzy knew where it belonged. No matter how much he fooled around, Dizzy always kept track of the meter. He kept looking at Chris until the audience began to understand what had happened. They also could see that nobody was going to help Chris out. Chris joined in the laughter, but was still faced with the problem.

He tried moving his note a beat ahead of where he'd been playing it. From Dizzy's expression, he could tell he'd guessed wrong, so he moved it ahead one more beat. Dizzy still stared at him.

There was only one beat left that could be the right one, and Chris pounced on it with relief. Dizzy nodded, and began to set his embouchure. Just as he was about to begin playing, he took the mouthpiece away from his lips again and said to Chris in an intense whisper that carried to the back of the room,

"I give you *one note* to play, and you *fuck it up!*"

This got the laugh Dizzy intended, and he again set his embouchure.

Again, he shook his head and said to himself (and the audience) in utter disbelief, "*one note!*" He managed to milk three or four more laughs out of the situation before he let Chris off the hook and began to play the last chorus.

Stan Free was walking up Broadway with Dizzy Gillespie one day. On an impulse, Dizzy headed into the Howard men's clothing store at 48th Street. "Gimme a raincoat," he said to the sales clerk. "What size?" asked the clerk. Dizzy said, with a look of surprise, "*My* size!"

Percy Heath helped Dizzy fill some idle time on the road with a bit of entertainment:

> We were walking around San Francisco. We had some baskets. Somebody gave us Indian woven baskets out there on the Coast, one of them was shaped like an inverted turban, and the other one looked like a Chinese coolie hat. Dizzy and I put those baskets on with our beards and what not, and we walked into several places. And people didn't know who we were, were wondering what nationality we were, what country. We went into some French place and put people on.

Dizzy was a past master of the put-on. He often enlisted his band members to assist him in a gag. In 1963, dressed in Nigerian robes and an African tarboosh, he arrived at San Francisco's International Airport in the guise of Prince Iwo, with band members Chris White, Kenny Barron, and Rudy Collins, dressed in diplomatically dignified black suits, attending him. They got into a taxi. Patricia Willard said:

> To their cabby they presented a slip of paper bearing the name of a hotel where they held reservations, and proceeded into a violent and extended argument among themselves in pseudo-African double talk all the way there. The driver began to show signs of nervous uneasiness. At the hotel, the passengers looked uncomprehendingly when the fare was quoted. Everybody "Ungawa"-ed. The cabby began raising his voice and pointed to the meter. The passengers got more excited and more confused. In desperation, the man held up eight fingers and slowly counted them to indicate the dollars owed.
>
> "Man, why didn't you say so in the first place?" Diz smiled warmly as he handed him a ten dollar bill and gestured that no change was necessary.

chapter 40

Charles Mingus

Charles Mingus was an accomplished bassist and an imaginative composer. A warm, engaging man when at ease with friends, he could quickly become bellicose and menacing when he felt threatened. He was outspoken about discrimination against blacks and particularly black artists. He displayed high energy and sensitivity, righteous anger, pride, ambition, and an attractive artistic madness, but he often seemed naïve in his confrontations with the music business establishment. Many of the dragons he fought were real; some existed only in his imagination.

His book *Beneath the Underdog* purports to be an autobiography but should not be read for factual content. It is more a dream narrative charting the turmoil that complicated this artist's inner life.

Pepper Adams got a chance to see Mingus's book when it was still in manuscript form:

> I didn't read the *whole* thing, you know. That was enormous. Five big notebooks, typewritten, before they were published. Some of it was very interesting, some was excruciatingly dull, some was highly self-serving, and some was the sexual fantasies and lies he'd been telling for twenty years. And it was basically *those* things that the editor chose to print.
>
> It's a shame, because, properly edited, I think there was the germ of a very, very interesting book there, because Mingus was no fool, although he could certainly do a great imitation at times! ↰

One passage from Mingus's book has appealed to anthologists because of the skillful way it captured Duke Ellington's style of delivery:

> Tizol wants you to play a solo he's written where bowing is required. You raise the solo an octave, where the bass isn't too muddy. He doesn't like that and he comes to the room under the stage where you're practicing at intermission and comments that you're like the

rest of the niggers in the band, you can't read. You ask Juan how he's different from the other niggers and he states that one of the ways he's different is that HE IS WHITE. So you run his ass upstairs.

You leave the rehearsal room, proceed toward the stage with your bass and take your place and at the moment Duke brings down the baton for "A Train" and the curtain of the Apollo Theatre goes up, a yelling, whooping Tizol rushes out and lunges at you with a bolo knife. The rest you remember mostly from Duke's own words in his dressing room as he changes after the show.

"Now, Charles," he says, looking amused, putting Cartier links into the cuffs of his beautiful handmade shirt, "you could have fore-warned me—you left me out of the act entirely! At least you could have let me cue in a few chords as you ran through that Nijinsky rou-tine. I congratulate you on your performance, but why didn't you and Juan inform me about the adagio you planned so that we could score it?

"I must say I never saw a large man so agile—I never so anybody make such tremendous leaps! The gambado over the piano carrying your bass was colossal. When you exited after that I thought, 'That man's really afraid of Juan's knife and at the speed he's going he's probably home in bed by now.' But no, back you came through the same door with your bass still intact. For a moment I was hopeful you'd decided to sit down and play but instead you slashed Juan's chair in two with a fire axe!

"Really, Charles, that's destructive. Everybody knows Juan has a knife but nobody ever took it seriously—he likes to pull it out and show it to people, you understand.

"So I'm afraid, Charles—I've never fired anybody—you'll have to quit my band. I don't need any new problems. Juan's an old prob-lem, I can cope with that, but you seem to have a whole bag of new tricks. I must ask you to be kind enough to give me your notice, Charles."

The charming way he says it, it's like he's paying you a compli-ment. Feeling honored, you shake hands and resign. ⟡

Mingus later commented whimsically, "Mingus's advice to young con-cert performers. First thing you do is check out the acoustics in the hall. And then find the fire axe!"

Juan Tizol remembered the incident somewhat differently:

What really happened, this little piece of music that I wrote for him was nothing that I composed. I got that from a little legit thing from an opera or a symphony or something.

So I asked him about it. He was practicing, I think, downstairs, and I went down there and I showed him, and said, "Try to play this to see what it sounds like on the bass."

He tried and so forth, and he wanted to raise it an octave higher. I said, "I don't want that. If I wanted to write for a cello, I would have wrote for a cello! I want to hear this on the bass."

So apparently he got insulted or something. I said, "Well, go ahead and do what you want. I'm going upstairs to my dressing room."

So he followed me upstairs to tell me, what's this and the other and so forth. I don't know. He raised a lot of hell, so by the time it came for the show, he was still hot and said he was going to kick me in the behind, you know,

"I should kick your behind."

"You're gonna do what?" And he repeated it.

I said, "I'm gonna go upstairs and when I come back, I would like for you to kick me right in the behind."

And I went upstairs, and when I came down he thought I had a knife. He grabbed one of those big pieces of iron that holds curtains and so forth. Carney said, "Watch out, Juan, he's got a piece of iron!"

But he was thinking I had a knife, you know. I didn't have a knife. I used to sometimes carry a knife, because you can never tell. But not all the time. One of the stage hands grabbed him and stopped it.

After the show I was upstairs in my dressing room, and I was so nervous I was crying. And he came up there, and the manager was at the door of my dressing room. He still wanted to keep arguing about it with me. I didn't respond or anything. I stayed right like that in my dressing room, and [Al] Celley was there trying to hold him back. Duke came over and told Celley to throw him out, to give him his two weeks' notice, pay him off and let him go.

So he came back again and said, "Juan, you made me lose my job," and so forth, and I said,

"Well, I can't help it. You started it." That was about the end of it.

That stuff about white folks and niggers, that's ridiculous. I never used words like that. I don't believe I ever used the word "nigger" in my whole life. ↯

Pepper Adams got to see Mingus in action when he visited his apartment one day:

I remember one time when he lived uptown, somewhere around 135th and Lenox, a modern high rise building. He had a beautiful apartment. It was at that time a new complex of quite fancy apartment buildings, with a doorman downstairs, and the telephone service. I arrived downstairs. We were going to do some work, so I had a bag with some manuscript paper in it. I gave my name to the doorman, the doorman calls the apartment and tells Mr. Mingus that Mr. Adams is on his way up.

I take the elevator up, go to his door, the door is cocked open. From inside I could hear Mingus shouting. I went inside. He's on the telephone, talking to the musicians' union, and he's saying, "You white motherfuckers, I'm gonna bring a shotgun down there! I'm gonna blast all you Whities away."

You know, it's all this racial diatribe, and very strong language, screaming at the top of his lungs into the telephone. He says into the phone, "Wait a minute!" And to me, "Cold beer in the refrigerator, Pepper." Then back to the phone, "And another thing, you mother! . . ."

When Herb Mickman was first living in New York, he hunted up Charles Mingus and arranged to study the bass with him. At Herb's first lesson, Mingus growled, "So, the white boy comes to steal the black man's music and make a lot of money!" Herb joked, "No, I just came to steal your music . . . I don't care about the money." Mingus didn't laugh.

Bob Zottola dropped by the Village Vanguard to hear the Mingus band and to visit his friend, Paul Bley. Paul told Mingus that Bob was a good trumpet player, and Mingus immediately said, "Get out your horn and come on up." When the music began, Mingus started a tune and then pointed to Bob, who took a couple of choruses. When he seemed to be about to stop, Mingus yelled, "Blow another!" After a couple more, Bob again tried to stop, but Mingus ordered, "Keep playing!" At Mingus's insistence, Bob played about ten choruses. When he finally stopped, Mingus leaned over and growled, "Bird could have said it in two!"

One Sunday afternoon when Mingus was leading a group at the Village Vanguard, the audience was particularly noisy and inattentive. A couple of tables of patrons right in front of the bandstand seemed com-

pletely oblivious to the music. Their animated conversation was distracting to the musicians and made it difficult for the patrons sitting farther
back to hear. Indignantly, Mingus hauled his bass up to the microphone
and made a few scathing remarks about the noise, but the offending patrons were so wrapped up in their conversation that they heard none of
Mingus's diatribe.

"Okay," said Mingus, "We're not going to fight you anymore. On this
next number, we'll take turns. We'll play four bars, and then you-all talk
four bars. Okay?"

He stomped off a tune, and after the opening chorus Mingus played a
four-bar break and waved the band out. The loud conversation at the
front tables continued. The musicians carefully counted out four measures during the hubbub and then the band took the next four, with the
solo tenor playing as loudly as possible. Another four for the oblivious
talkers, another for the band. As the rest of the audience laughed, Mingus continued grimly with his announced format until the end of the
number. The talkers never knew they had been featured, but they joined
the applause at the end.

One night Horace Parlan was to play with the Mingus band at the Village Vanguard. Mingus entered the club ahead of him carrying several
brown paper packages which he piled at one side of the stage before
starting the first set. The people in the audience were chatting loudly
among themselves, paying little attention to the music. Mingus stopped
the band in the middle of the first number, laid down his bass and
began opening the packages he had brought. He took out a newspaper,
which he gave to Horace to read, and a chess set, which he gave to
Danny Richmond and Booker Ervin. They set up the pieces and began
to play chess as Mingus unwrapped a small television set which he
plugged in, turned on and began watching. These activities finally attracted the audience's interest. They stopped talking and began watching the musicians. When Mingus was satisfied that he had their
attention, he packed up the props and started the music again right
where they had left off.

At another club, in a similar situation, Mingus announced, "As long as
nobody wants to listen, we might as well get something to eat." He had
the waiter bring food to the bandstand, and he and his band sat down
and ate for half an hour instead of playing.

On another evening at the Vanguard, one loud-voiced patron kept talking over the music until Mingus stepped furiously to the microphone and announced, "I'll give a hundred dollars to anyone who'll punch that cat in the mouth!" A young woman at a rear table cried out, "I won't do it for money. I'll do it for *love!*"

chapter 41

Zoot Sims and Al Cohn

Like most saxophone players of his generation, Zoot Sims was influenced by Lester Young's playing, but he didn't imitate him. He developed his own style, with equal parts of lyricism and swing. He loved to play and was always ready for the next jam session.

When he first came to New York, Zoot went to sessions at a place on 48th Street called the Red Door. One night, a little loaded on wine, he became so disgusted with the way he was playing that he slammed his horn into its case, dropped it on the floor, and kicked it all the way down the stairs to the street. Then he fell down the same flight of stairs after his horn.

Word traveled fast on the jazz scene. When Zoot showed up at the Onyx Club the next evening and asked Brew Moore if he could borrow his horn and sit in, Brew was reluctant. Zoot assured Brew he'd be careful with his horn, and Brew finally handed it over. Zoot climbed onto the bandstand and had only played a few notes when he lost his balance and fell right into the party of four sitting at the front table. As he fell, he held Brew's tenor high over his head, saving it from any damage. He got up, handed the horn back to Brew, and slunk out the door.

Zoot was rarely at a loss for words. When asked by a fan how he could play so well when he was loaded, Zoot replied,

"I practice when I'm loaded!"

Al Cohn was driving Zoot home from a record date one night. Zoot had downed a few, and was asleep in the back seat. Riding in the front seat with Al was A&R man Jack Lewis. Jack had a cast in one eye that limited his vision, and Al wore a prosthetic replacement for an eye he had lost to an infection some years earlier. As they drove along, Zoot roused up and leaned into the front seat between his two friends, examining them alternately.

"What's up, Zoot?" asked Al.

"I just wanted to make sure you guys were keeping both eyes on the road," said Zoot as he lay back down and went to sleep again.

Zoot was sitting in Jim and Andy's with Jim Hall and his wife Jane.

"I'm beat," said Zoot. "I've been recording all day, and I still have to work at the Half Note tonight."

"If you want it, I have a Dexedrine spansule," said Jane. "I use them once in a while when I'm tired. I don't really think they're good for you; they're pretty strong. I usually open one up and pour some of it out."

"Pour some of it out!" said Zoot. "Are you crazy? Don't you know there are people *sleeping* in Europe?"

Zoot, playing a week in a jazz club somewhere out of town, was engaged in conversation by a local fan who tried to talk like a hipster without a firm grasp of the terms. He gave Zoot a nudge and said,

"Hey, man, hip that crazy chick at the bar!"

Zoot replied, "Yeah, I'm dig!"

Zoot worked at a club in the Pacific Northwest with a local rhythm section. The piano player had great command of the keyboard and crowded every measure with notes. Red Kelly described his playing as "busy as a one-legged man in an ass-kicking contest." Zoot played and listened for a while and then asked the pianist, "Hey, man, are you getting paid by the note?"

There was a pianist that worked with Zoot Sims for a while who had a habit of swaying back and forth while he played. Zoot finally said he couldn't play with him anymore. "He made me seasick!"

Zoot said he like the way the Dukes of Dixieland played at the Monterey Jazz Festival one year. Two or three other musicians jumped on him, demanding to know how he possibly could like their music.

"Well, you know me," Zoot said. "I haven't got very good taste."

On Louise Sims's birthday one year, she got a call from Zoot at the office where she worked. At that time they had only been married several months, and were living in a rather small apartment on 69th Street. Zoot said, "I got you the birthday present that every wife is dying to have! When you come home, don't use your key . . . ring the bell." With visions of diamond rings and fur coats floating through her head, Louise hurried home after work and rang their apartment doorbell. Zoot flung the door open to reveal a brand new ping-pong table that was taking up nearly all of the living room. He held up two paddles, and, beaming like a new father, handed her one. "Here," he said, "this one's yours!" Louise realized at that moment that life with Zoot was going to be unusual.

Zoot appeared one noon at Jim and Andy's bar wearing a dark suit, white shirt, and a tie. Zoot's usual daytime costume was corduroy trousers and a baseball jacket.

"Hey, Zoot," someone said, "How come you're all dressed up so early in the afternoon?"

Zoot adjusted his tie and grinned his gap-toothed grin. "I don't know, I woke up this way."

Joe Temperley was hanging out with Zoot Sims during the days when the first U.S. moon landings were taking place. As they watched the news coverage on the TV at the bar where they were having a taste, Zoot shook his head with amazement. "Geez, they're puttin' men on the moon," he said, "and I'm still playin' *Indiana!*"

Zoot took great pride in his little red 1962 Volvo. He bought it from a friend when it was only a year old and kept it for many years. Zoot drove it to a job he was playing with Coleman Hawkins, and Hawk came out to look at it. As Zoot told him what a great car it was, Hawkins started to look inside. He grabbed the door handle on the passenger side and gave it a twist, and the handle came off in his hand. Astonished, Hawk passed the handle to Zoot, who silently stuffed it in his pocket.

When Zoot was away on a long tour one year his wife Louise had the Volvo restored as a surprise. But she said Zoot never got the door handle fixed. He always got in the car first and flipped the door open for her from the inside. The broken handle stayed in the glove compartment as a memento of Hawkins.

Frank Canterino and his sons, Mike and Sonny, operated a jazz club on Hudson Street in New York called the Half Note. The Zoot Sims and Al Cohn quintet was their favorite group. In 1962, just before Zoot left with the Goodman band to tour Russia, Frank's daughter Rosemary threw a party for him at her home.

Rose had a pet rabbit that she kept in her bathtub. She didn't let it run around the house too much because she had smooth wood floors that gave little purchase to the rabbit's feet. He would hop and slip on the polished floor and sometimes crash into things.

Rose decided to play a trick on Zoot, the most formidable imbiber on her guest list of Half Note regulars. She knew that Zoot's drinking had once reached the hallucination stage, forcing him onto the wagon for a short time. She made the rabbit a tiny jacket and a little hat with holes for his ears. Having told the rest of her guests to pretend they didn't see anything, she waited until the party was in full swing and then dressed the rabbit in its hat and coat, smuggled it out of the bathroom and put it under the piano.

The rabbit began to explore the room. It hopped out across the floor, slipped, scrabbled, and crashed into the wall before disappearing around the corner. Zoot's eyes widened. He looked around at the rest of the guests, who showed no reaction.

"What's the matter, Zoot?" asked Rose.

Zoot put down his glass, looked straight ahead and muttered, "Nothing!"

On a Canadian television show that Oscar Peterson used to host, Oscar would play with his trio and sometimes with a guest soloist, and would include interviews with his guests between tunes. When Zoot Sims appeared on the show, Oscar asked him, quite seriously, "What do you see for your instrument for the future? What would you like to see?" Zoot paused thoughtfully, glanced down at the tenor hanging from its neck strap, and replied, "I can get a new lacquer job."

Zoot and Al Cohn often were booked into the Half Note for New Year's Eve. They both would put away quite a few drinks during an ordinary night's work, and on New Year's Eve so many customers bought them rounds that they carried quite an extra load. One year, just before the old year was due to expire, one of the Canterino brothers shouted up to the bandstand, "It's twelve o'clock!" Al nudged Zoot and repeated, "Twelve o'clock!" Zoot stopped the tune they were playing and went right into a swinging version of "Happy Birthday." He took several hot choruses right into the new year without realizing he had the wrong tune.

Al liked funny lines as much as Zoot did, and came up with many good ones. He once defined a gentleman as someone who knows how to play the accordion, and doesn't.

A disheveled man accosted Al at the bus terminal and asked for a dollar to buy a drink. Al started to hand him the money, and then said, "Wait a minute. How do I know you won't spend this on food?"

When Joe Ciavardone complained to Al that the drummer he was working with slowed down when he played with sticks and rushed when he played with brushes, Al immediately suggested, "Tell him to play with one of each!"

In Europe, Al was drinking at a bar with some friends who recommended the local beer.
"Have you tried Elephant Beer?" he was asked.
"No," said Al, "I drink to forget."

When a bartender asked Al, "What'll you have?" Al replied "One too many."

Meeting a friend on the street, Al asked what he'd been doing.
"I'm going back to school," was the reply. "I'm studying Jewish history."
"What would you like to know?" asked Al.

Zoot and Al had dinner together in a restaurant one evening, and when the check came, they both grabbed it. Al said, "Let me get it," and Zoot said, "I'd feel better if you'd let me get it." Al immediately relinquished his hold on the check. "Oh, well," he said, "If it's for your health . . . !"

Al mentioned at Charlie's Tavern one day that he'd just finished an album with 24 mandolin players. Someone asked, "Where did they find that many mandolin players?"

"Well," said Al, "all day today you couldn't get a haircut in Jersey City."

At a jazz festival in Italy, Al joined some of the local musicians in liquid merriment after the concert. When he came downstairs for a late breakfast at the hotel the next morning, he met one of his colleagues.

"How do you feel, Al?"

"Like a million lire."

Al Cohn's father, Dave, was a jazz fan ever since Al was a member of Woody Herman's famous Four Brothers saxophone section. Dave, a fixture for years around the New York jazz scene, walked into a "Jazz at Noon" concert. Bucky Pizzarelli saw him and nudged bassist Frank Tate. "Here comes one of the Four Fathers!"

chapter 42

Miles Davis and John Coltrane

Miles Davis was in the vanguard of modern jazz through several major periods of its development. At the beginning of his career, while jamming with Charlie Parker and the other innovators of the bebop era, he was already finding a sound and style that broke away from Dizzy Gillespie's powerful influence on young trumpet players. Miles was impressed with the sound of men like Freddie Webster and Shorty Baker, and developed a fat, smoky middle-register sound and a sparse style all his own.

Davis grew uncomfortable whenever he felt he was repeating himself, continually changing his groups in search of something new to play. He was very successful in finding and shaping new talent, and in choosing the right combination of music and musicians to take the next interesting step forward.

Miles was one of the first jazz stars since the days of the haughty piano ticklers to refuse to ingratiate his audience. He spoke little onstage, never announced his musicians or the names of the tunes that were played, and often played with his back to the audience and then left the stage while others were soloing. His music was so strong that his listeners accepted it on his terms.

Coleman Hawkins once twitted Miles about his practice of leaving the bandstand after he finished his solo. Miles said,

"I played with you on 52nd Street. What kind of example were you? Sometimes you didn't show up at all!"

In the mid 1950s, when Red Garland was with the Miles Davis quintet, Miles took a weekend gig at a small club in Brooklyn. They were supposed to hit at nine, but Red didn't show until after ten-thirty. The place was packed, and Miles was furious. Red finally walked in, looking upset. He said, "Gimme a drink! You won't believe what happened. I was waiting in the subway at 42nd Street when all of a sudden this cat throws himself in front of a train that was pulling into the station! He falls under the wheels, there's blood all over the place, people are screaming. The cops came, the medics came. It was horrible! The cops started questioning everybody. All the trains stopped running. Nobody was allowed to leave. They kept us there nearly two hours. As soon as the trains started running again, I got over here as quick as I could."

Miles calmed down, and the quintet did two long sets, and everyone was happy. After the gig, Red sat at the bar as Paul Chambers packed up his bass. Miles, Coltrane and Philly Joe Jones had already left. Paul said, "I'll ride back to the city with you on the subway." Red replied, "You don't have to take the subway, man. I'll take you home. I got my car outside."

When Dan Barrett and Howard Alden had a Quintet in the mid-1980s with Frank Tate on bass, Chuck Wilson on reeds, and Jackie Williams on drums, they played a couple of times at the Nice Jazz Festival in France. The outdoor performances were on three different stages. One year Dan and Howard's group was set up on a stage in the ruins of a medieval amphitheater, and a quarter of a mile away Miles Davis's electronic band occupied the enormous Garden stage for an audience of several thousand. The volume of sound coming from the Davis band's stage was so loud that the quintet in the amphitheater was being totally wiped out as they played a quiet version of "920 Special." Frank Tate began laughing, and when asked what was so funny, he said, "I always wanted to play with Miles, and I'm doing it right now!"

Miles enjoyed the unexpected. He took special pleasure in tormenting writers and critics, often making outrageous pronouncements about music, or giving them opinions that were in complete opposition to statements he had made at other times.

While Miles was playing at the Sutherland Lounge in Chicago, Don DeMicheal, at that time a new member of the staff at *Down Beat* magazine, offered to present Davis with the 1960 Critics Poll plaque on the stage during a set. Miles said, "You're not gonna plug that goddamned magazine on *my* bandstand. Give it to me at the bar."

Jimmy Cobb was drumming with Miles's Quintet at the Sutherland:

On the first floor of the hotel there was the reception desk, and right across from the reception desk was a little travel agency. Some time that day they had a short in the wires in the ceiling and it started smoking—it caught fire. The room where we were working was right on the first floor—you could walk directly from the reception desk into the club. And the club was packed! And the firemen were outside the door putting out this fire, and *nobody left!* Smoke was all in the joint and nobody left. And the place was packed! Yeah, Miles was very popular. ↄ

In New York, Joe Goldberg once took a ride with Miles and his wife Frances:

I chanced to be in Miles's white Ferrari when he was driving it up the West Side Highway at about 105 miles per hour. Frances got very frightened and asked him to slow down. Miles said, "I'm in here, too." ↄ

Baroness Pannonica de Koenigswarter-Rothschild was known to the New York press as the Jazz Baroness. The musicians she befriended called her Nica. Her apartment at the Stanhope Hotel in Manhattan became a hangout for a number of great jazz players, notably Thelonious

Monk and Charlie Parker. The Baroness sheltered and cared for Parker there during his final illness.

Hampton Hawes describes a ride with the Baroness in her Bentley:

> Miles was running around town in his sharp Mercedes-Benz. Monk and his wife and Nica and I were driving down 7th Avenue in the Bentley at three or four in the morning—Monk feeling good, turning round to me to say, "Look at me, man, I got me a black bitch *and* a white bitch"—and Miles pulling alongside in the Mercedes, calling through the window in his little hoarse voice cut down by a throat operation, "Want to race?" Nica nodding, then turning to tell us in her prim British tones: "This time I believe I'm going to beat the motherfucker." ⟍

When Paul Chambers was a member of Miles's Quintet he took him to a jam session in his home town, Detroit. At the session Miles was impressed with the young trombonist Curtis Fuller. He told him,

"Any time you want to be in my band, just let me know."

Curtis was thrilled. He tidied up his affairs in Detroit and then packed up and went to New York, where Miles was appearing at the Café Bohemia in Greenwich Village. Curtis arrived at the club carrying his trombone case and a valise. He asked someone at the door to call Paul Chambers outside when the band finished its set.

Paul greeted him warmly and went back inside to find Miles, who was sitting at a table near the bandstand, arguing with a girlfriend. Paul waited for a pause in the argument and got Miles's attention.

"Curtis Fuller is outside," he told him.

"Fuck Curtis Fuller!" said Miles, and went back to his argument.

Curtis didn't join the band, but he did stay in New York, finding other employment without much difficulty. Miles was right about his talent, even if he didn't hire him.

Of the many brilliant musicians Miles did hire, John Coltrane left the strongest personal stamp on his music. In the 1950s Coltrane played with a broad, dark tenor saxophone tone, but he produced a more crystalline sound during his early period with Davis. He developed a personal approach to melody that perfectly complemented Davis's playing. In his later period with Davis and afterward with his own group, Coltrane began pouring an amazing number of notes into each phrase, playing sets of choruses that lasted for over half an hour. Jimmy Cobb talked about Coltrane's long solos:

Coltrane would play all night, and come off in the intermission and go somewhere and play—stand in a corner or something. You know, Miles had to make him stop, because he would play an hour solo himself, and we were only supposed to be on the stand for forty minutes or something. He had incredible chops—he couldn't stop, Miles used to say, "Man, look, why don't you play twenty-seven choruses instead of twenty-eight?" Coltrane would say, "I get involved in this thing and I don't know how to stop." ⑃

Miles once suggested, "Try taking the saxophone out of your mouth."

The third man in Miles's front line at that time was Cannonball Adderley, who said:

Once in a while, Miles might say, "Why did you play so long, man?" and John would say, "It took that long to get it all in." ⑃

Jimmy Cobb had the difficult job of keeping the rhythm alive during Trane's long solos:

We were playing at the Sutherland in Chicago once, when Trane was just finishing one of his thirty-minute solos. I was feeling so tired of playing so long that a drumstick flew out of my hand and whipped by Trane's head, just missing him. When we finished the set, I told him, "I'm sorry, man, it just slipped out of my hand." He said, "I thought you finally threw something at me for playing so long." ⑃

Benny Golson knew Coltrane when they were both growing up in Philadelphia:

Before John joined Miles, he performed with a lot of rhythm-and-blues groups. I saw him walk the bar, stepping over drinks in Philadelphia. I went to see him once at the Ridge Point. We all knew that anybody who worked that club had to walk the bar. You had to play those B-flat chords and honk. As I opened the door, there he was, honking and stepping over the drinks, and I looked right into his face. He looked into mine and stopped, and said, "Oh, no!" and dropped his head. [Laughs] I knew it must have been embarrassing for him. ↵

Gato Barbieri and his wife sent Coltrane a gift from Argentina. A friend worked as a linenkeeper on a freighter that ran between New York and Buenos Aires, and delivered the gift to the United States for them. J. C. Thomas writes:

It was a tenor saxophone case; hand-made from green leather, a silk lining inside, the word TRANE gold-lettered outside, bought and paid for by Gato and his wife, Michelle.

The saxophone case was delivered, but Coltrane didn't know who had sent it, for the Barbieri note read, "From a friend in Buenos Aires."

The following year, the Barbieris moved to Rome. When they discovered that John Coltrane was playing a date in Milan, they came to hear him. They went backstage to meet him, and there, in a corner of the dressing room, they saw the saxophone case they had sent him.

"Oh, you're from Argentina?" Coltrane said, after they were introduced. He pointed at the saxophone case and commented, "Someone from Argentina sent that to me. I use it all the time."

When Barbieri confessed that someone was he, Coltrane thanked him and said, "It's beautiful." Then, his voice humorous but his eyes serious, he asked,

"Do you think you could send me one for my soprano, too?" ↵

John Coltrane's son Ravi was playing at a jazz club in California. Ravi enjoyed Jim Carrey's movies and was excited to see that Carrey was in his audience. "Do you think it would be okay if I went over and met him?" Ravi asked his band. They told him, "Man, he came in to see you. Of course, go on over." So Ravi went over to Carrey's table and introduced himself. Carrey told him, "I'm a big jazz fan. My dad played the tenor sax." Ravi said excitedly, "Really? So did mine!"

chapter 43

Jokes

When musicians run out of stories about each other to tell at band room rap sessions, a favorite pastime is telling jokes. This is a collection of the more printable ones.

Bobby Hackett enjoyed telling this story:

A violinist noticed that his playing had a hypnotic effect on his audiences. They sat motionless, as though they were in a trance. He found he had the same effect on his friends' pets. Dogs and cats would sit spellbound while he played.

Wondering if he could cast the same spell over wild beasts, he went to a jungle clearing in Africa, took out his violin and began to play. A lion, an elephant, and a gorilla charged into the clearing, stopped to listen, and sat mesmerized by the music. Soon the clearing was filled with every kind of ferocious animal, each one listening intently.

Suddenly another lion charged out of the jungle, pounced on the violinist, and killed him instantly. The first lion, bewildered, asked, "Why did you do that?"

The second lion cupped his paw behind his hear. "What?"

Teddy Sommer brought this one back to New York from a road trip:

Deep in the African jungle, a safari was camped for the night. In the darkness, distant drums began a relentless throbbing that continued until dawn. The safari members were disturbed, but the native guide reassured them: "Drums good. When drums stop, very bad."

Every night the drumming continued, and every night the guide reiterated, "Drums good. When drums stop, *very* bad."

Then one night the drums suddenly stopped. The guide looked frightened. "When drums stop, *very, very* bad," he said.

"Why is it bad?" asked a member of the safari.

"Because, when drums stop, bass solo begin!" ♪

At a jazz concert in New Jersey, Lou Carter delighted the musicians backstage with this one:

A bandleader was having a few words with his musicians just before the job.

"Now, listen, you guys. When I say eight o'clock, I want the music to start at eight. I don't want you walking in here at eight!" And the drummer went "Rum-pum" on his snare and bass drum.

"And I want a clean shirt and a clean shave on everyone. I don't want any bums on my band!" And the drummer went "Burr-rum-pum!"

"And when I say a blue jacket, I mean a nice blue blazer. Don't come in here wearing the top half of some worn-out black suit!" And the drummer went "Burrr-rum-pum-crash!"

"And if I find out who's making that noise . . . !" ♪

Not having Clark Terry tell this one robs it of some of its charm. You have to imagine the devilish look in Clark's eyes as he sings each song:

A guy walked into a pet store looking for a Christmas gift for his wife. The storekeeper said he knew exactly what would please her and took a little bird out of a cage. "This is Chet," he said, "and Chet can sing Christmas carols." Seeing the look of disbelief on the customer's face, he proceeded to demonstrate.

"He needs warming up," he said. "Lend me your cigarette lighter."

The man handed over his lighter, and the storekeeper raised Chet's left wing and waved the flame lightly under it. Immediately, Chet sang, "Oh Come, All Ye Faithful."

"That's fantastic!" said the man.

"And listen to this," said the storekeeper, warming Chet's other wing. Chet sang, "O Little Town of Bethlehem."

"Wrap him up!" said the man. "I'll take him!"

When he got home, he greeted his wife:

"Honey, I can't wait until Christmas to show you what I got you. This is fantastic."

He unwrapped Chet's cage and showed the bird to his wife.

"Now, watch this."

He raised Chet's left wing and held him over a Christmas candle that was burning on the mantlepiece. Chet immediately began to sing, "Silent Night." The wife was delighted.

"And that's not all, listen to this!" As Chet's right wing was warmed over the flame, he sang, "Joy to the World."

"Let me try it," cried the wife, seizing the bird. In her eagerness, she held Chet a little too close to the flame. Chet began to sing passionately, "Chet's nuts roasting on an open fire!" 🎵

Art Blakey, the original Jazz Messenger, has been such an advocate of jazz that someone made up this story about him:

Art was driving to an out-of-town job and passed through a village where traffic was completely tied up because of a funeral procession. Since he couldn't get past the cemetery until the service was over, he got out and listened to the eulogy. The minister spoke at length about the virtues of the deceased, and then asked if anyone had anything else to add. After a silence during which nobody spoke up, Art said, "If nobody has anything to say about the departed, I'd like to say a few words about jazz!" 🎵

These stories have been passed around so much that they are unattributable:

A guitarist sat tuning his instrument all through the first set that the band played. Each time the leader pointed to him to take chorus, he would say, "No, man, I'm still tuning up." Half an hour into the job he was still not ready.

"Why do you need so much time for tuning?" asked the leader. "When I went to hear Segovia he played a whole concert and I didn't see him tune up once!"

The guitar player gave a shrug. "Some cats just don't give a damn!" 🎵

A Greek bandleader wasn't happy when his regular drummer sent a young jazz player as a substitute on a traditional dance job. After the first set, he took the youngster aside. "Look, kid," he said, "forget about all that Elvin Jones stuff. Just give me a simple afterbeat on two and five!" 🎵

A club date leader who was primarily a singer held and plucked at a string bass while fronting his band, but knew very little about playing the instrument. One evening his pianist arrived at the job to find the leader holding a little boy by the collar while he angrily cuffed him about the head.

"Why are you hitting the kid?" asked the pianist. The leader said, "The little sonofabitch twisted one of my tuning knobs, and he won't tell me which one!" ♪

A traveling ballet company was doing *Swan Lake* in a small Midwestern city. Just before the first performance, the percussionist got sick and was rushed to the hospital. Emergency phone calls by the contractor finally located the only drummer in town that was available, a jazz drummer who sometimes played at the local vaudeville house. He rushed to the concert hall and into the pit, and the curtain went up, only slightly late.

After the first ballet, the conductor whispered to the contractor, "Get him out of here! We'll play without percussion!" "What's he bugged about?" said the amazed drummer. "I caught everything!" ♪

A vocalist hired a pianist to accompany her at an audition for a night-club job. After listening to a couple of songs, the owner said, "Can you sing 'When Sunny Gets Blue?' It's my favorite song. If you can sing it, you're hired." The singer whispered to her pianist, "I don't know it all the way through." The pianist said, "I know it. Go ahead and start, and I'll prompt you."

Reluctantly, she began: "When Sunny Gets Blue . . ." She looked at the piano player for help, He whispered confidently, "B-flat minor ninth." ♪

A jazz fan walked into a London nightclub just as the band began to play a blues that sounded vaguely familiar. He asked a listener at the bar, "W. C. Handy?"

"Sure, it's just outside to the left of the stairway." ♪

A saxophone player at a charity ball wore out his reed. He removed it from his mouthpiece, tossed it aside, and replaced it with a new one. The discarded reed fell into the cylinder that contained the raffle stubs for the door prize. When a scantily clad young lady drew out the winning stub and handed it to the announcer, he proclaimed, "And the winner is—Rico, Number three!" ♪

Two salesmen were having a drink at a bar. One claimed he was successful because of his ability to relate to anyone. "Whatever their

I.Q., I can talk to them on their own level" His friend wanted a demonstration, so he tapped a stranger on the shoulder.

"Excuse me, what is your I.Q.?"

"It's about 200."

The salesman immediately engaged him in a discussion of nuclear physics.

The next candidate admitted to an I.Q. of 100. The salesman launched into a discussion of politics and ecology with him. Then the man at the end of the bar was asked his I.Q. He said, "Oh, I suppose it's about 34." The salesman said, "What kind of reeds do you use?" ↶

Chick Corea claims to have heard about a hostage situation where some terrorists were holding thirty drummers hostage, and were threatening to release one of them every six hours until their demands were met. ↶

A musician who had spent many years trying to break into the big time was feeling very depressed. He'd been turned down by every record company in the business. Seeking a perverse revenge, he booked a recording studio and told the engineer to record exactly what he would say, then copy it onto a thousand compact discs and send them to all the recording executives in the country. In the vocal booth, when the red light came on, he ranted, "This is a message to all you sycophantic, talent-less bastards who have ignored me all these years. I dedicated my life to writing beautiful, emotive, soul-touching music, and all you idiots do is bin my tapes and sign pretty-boy bands and the Spice Girls. Well, I've taken all I can of your puerile, shallow industry, and it's YOU who've driven me to it! Goodbye, murderers of art!" With that, he pulled out a gun and blew out his brains. The engineer said from the booth, "Okay . . . that's fine for level. Want to go for a take?" ↶

A big band drummer was having time problems. He kept pulling the tempos down, playing slower and slower. The rest of the band urged the leader to get rid of him. The leader talked it over with the drummer, who made frantic efforts to keep the tempos up where they belonged, but he couldn't seem to stop dragging. Even his fills and accents were late. Finally the whole band threatened to quit, and the leader reluctantly fired the guy. The poor guy was so despondent that he went down to the railroad tracks and threw himself behind a train. ↶

A jazz bass player found himself without work. To pay the rent, he took a job with a society trio on a cruise ship. The job required that the bass player and the drummer keep to the society formula, two bass notes to each measure, and a crisp afterbeat on the drums. Whenever the bassist would forget himself and play a few measures of four-four, the leader would whisper, "Stay in two!" "We could swing more if we played in four," complained the bassist to the drummer."

"I know, man, but this is the gig."

After a week of calm weather, the ship ran into a hurricane. Terrible waves dashed the ship about, and it burst a seam. Water began to come in faster than the pumps could get rid of it. The passengers were told to put on their life jackets and prepare to abandon ship. To calm the terrified passengers, the leader of the trio gathered his musicians and began to play. As the passengers climbed into the lifeboats, the ship began to sink. The bassist said to the drummer, "Screw it, man, let's play in four!"

Teddy Sommer remembered that old joke when he was working on a cruise ship in 1980. The old S.S. *France* was refurbished and renamed the S.S. *Norway,* and her maiden voyage in the Caribbean made the front pages because a power failure on board left the ship adrift without engines or electricity for several days. Teddy and Irv Joseph were on board, accompanying Rita Moreno, the star act of the show. After the evening entertainment and a late buffet, Teddy and his wife were in their stateroom watching *Saturday Night Fever* on the ship's closed circuit TV. Suddenly the screen went blank, the lights went out, and the throb of the engines stopped. They could hear the watertight doors automatically closing off the passageway outside.

"What's happening?" said Teddy's wife. "What are we going to do?"

"I'll show you," said Teddy, grabbing the phone. It seemed to be still working, so he dialed Irv Joseph's room.

"Teddy! What happened?" cried Irv.

"I don't know," said Teddy, "But, screw it, let's play in four!"

An old joke has a lady stopping to ask a musician on the street in New York, "Pardon me, can you tell me how to get to Carnegie Hall?"

The musician answers, "Practice!"

During the 1950s, hundreds of New York musicians visited the Local 802 union floor every Wednesday afternoon, looking for work. Many of them completed the rite with a visit to Charlie's Tavern on Seventh Avenue in the old Roseland building. One sunny Wednesday a good part of Charlie's clientele was standing on the sidewalk outside, chatting and saying goodbyes. A studious looking young woman stopped and asked one of the musicians, "Excuse me, can you tell me how to get to Carnegie Hall?"

Everyone standing there knew the joke. The young woman was completely confounded when at least twenty voices replied in delighted unison, "Practice!"

Pete Brush had a similar opportunity when standing outside a midtown department store waiting for his wife. A woman approached carrying a violin case and asked,

"How can I get to Carnegie Hall?"

To his eternal regret, Pete said, "Go uptown to 57th Street and make a left to 7th Avenue."

Acknowledgments

Some of the anecdotes in this book are from personal interviews and conversations. Others have been extracted, with permission, from published works by writers on jazz, from the published interviews and memoirs of musicians, and from the Oral History Collection at Rutgers University. Many of these stories first appeared in my column *The Band Room*, a regular feature of *Allegro*, the monthly journal of New York's Local 802, American Federation of Musicians. I am grateful to John Glasel, the president of Local 802, for providing space for my column, and to all the musicians who have been kind enough to share their stories.

Thanks to Martin Williams and Nat Hentoff, who got me started as a writer for their magazine *The Jazz Review* in 1958. And a large thank you to Gene Lees, who often publishes essays of mine in his *Jazzletter*. Gene has encouraged and educated me as a writer, and recommended me to Sheldon Meyer at Oxford University Press, hence this book. More thanks to Sheldon and his staff for their support with this project.

I am grateful to the Institute of Jazz Studies at Rutgers University in Newark, New Jersey, for letting me rummage through their excellent library, especially the Oral History files. Funded by the National Endowment for the Arts, the Jazz Oral History Project has recorded interviews with scores of jazz musicians, many who are no longer with us. The tapes and transcripts of these interviews reside at the IJS, where, over a year's time, I read or listened to them all.

My regular trips to Rutgers were made pleasant and fruitful by the IJS staff. Dan Morgenstern, the curator, has a prodigious memory that always manages to locate the obscure detail one needs. Don Luck, Ed Berger, John Clement, Vincent Pelote, and Esther Vasquez are ever friendly and helpful, and the background music is exquisite.

A final thank you to my son Dan, who got me interested in computers, and to Barry Kornfeld, who helped me select and understand the computer hardware and software that were so useful in assembling this book.

Following is a list of the authors and publishers who have kindly given me their permission to extract anecdotes from previously published sources:

Albertson, Chris, *Bessie*, Stein and Day, New York. Copyright © 1972. Reprinted by permission of the author.

Armstrong, Louis, *Satchmo, My Life in New Orleans*. Prentice-Hall, Englewood Cliffs, NJ. Copyright © 1954, 1982. Reprinted by permission of the publisher.

Balliett, Whitney, *American Musicians*. Oxford University Press, New York. Copyright © 1986. Reprinted by permission of the author.

Balliett, Whitney, *Such Sweet Thunder*. Bobbs-Merrill, New York. Copyright © 1966. Reprinted by permission of the author.

Barnet, Charlie, with Stanley Dance, *Those Swinging Years: The Autobiography of Charlie Barnet*. Copyright © 1984 by Louisiana State University Press. Reprinted by permission of the author and Louisiana State University Press.

Basie, Count, *Good Morning Blues: the Autobiography of Count Basie, as told to Albert Murray*. Copyright © 1985 by Albert Murray and Count Basie Enterprises, Inc. Reprinted by permission of Random House.

Bechet, Sidney, *Treat it Gentle*. Copyright © 1960 by Twayne Publishers Inc., and Cassell & Co. Ltd. Reprinted by permission of Hill and Wang, a division of Farrar, Straus and Giroux, Inc.

Berger, Morroe, Edward Berger, and James Patrick, *Benny Carter*. Scarecrow Press, Metuchen, N.J. Copyright © 1982. Reprinted by permission of Edward Berger.

Berton, Ralph, *Remembering Bix*. Harper and Row, New York. Copyright © 1974. Reprinted by permission of the author.

Bigard, Barney, *With Louis and Duke*. Reprinted by permission of Macmillan, London. Copyright © 1986.

Blesh, Rudi, *Combo, USA*. Chilton Books. Copyright © 1950 by Rudi Blesh.

Brask, Ole, and Dan Morgenstern, *Jazz People*. Harry N. Abrams, New York. Copyright © 1976. Reprinted by permission of Mr. Morgenstern.

Brunn, H.O., *The Story of the Original Dixieland Jazz Band*. Da Capo Press, New York. Copyright © 1960, 1986. Reprinted by permission of the author.

Callender, Red, and Elaine Cohen, *Unfinished Dream*. Quartet Books, New York. Copyright © 1985. Reprinted by permission of Mr. Callender.

Calloway, Cab, *Minnie the Moocher*. Reprinted by permission of Thomas Crowell Publishers. Copyright © 1976.

Carmichael, Hoagy, with Stephen Longstreet, *Sometimes I Wonder*. Copyright © 1965 by Hoagland Carmichael and Stephen Longstreet. Reprinted by permission of Farrar, Straus and Giroux, Inc.

Carr, Ian, *Miles Davis*. Reprinted by permission of William Morrow and Co., New York. Copyright © 1982.

Chambers, Jack, *Milestones*. William Morrow and Co., New York. Copyright © 1983. Reprinted by permission of the author.

Chilton, John, *Billie's Blues*. Da Capo Press, New York. Copyright © 1975. Reprinted by permission of the author.

Chilton, John, *Stomp off, Let's Go*. Jazz Book Service, London. Copyright © 1983. Reprinted by permission of the author.

Clayton, Buck, *Buck Clayton's Jazz World*. Oxford University Press, New York. Copyright © 1987. Reprinted by permission of the author.

Cole, Maria, *Nat Cole, an Intimate Biography*. Copyright © 1971 by Maria Cole. Reprinted by permission of William Morrow & Co. World rights by permission of the author's agent, Scott Meredith, Inc.

Collier, James Lincoln, *Duke Ellington*. Oxford University Press, New York. Copyright © 1987. Reprinted by permission of the author.

Condon, Eddie, and Richard Gehman, *Eddie Condon's Treasury of Jazz*. Copyright © 1956 by Eddie Condon and Richard Gehman. Used by permission of Doubleday, a division of Bantam, Doubleday, Dell Publishing Group, Inc.

Condon, Eddie, and Hank O'Neal, *The Eddie Condon Scrapbook of Jazz*. St. Martin's Press, New York. Copyright © 1973. Reprinted by permission of Mr. O'Neal.

Condon, Eddie, and Thomas Sugrue, *We Called it Music*. Copyright © 1947, 1962, by Eddie A. Condon. Reprinted by permission of McIntosh and Otis, Inc.

Dance, Stanley, *The World of Count Basie*. Da Capo Press, New York. Copyright © 1980. Reprinted by permission of the author.

Dance, Stanley, *The World of Duke Ellington*. Charles Scribner's Sons, New York. Copyright © 1970. Reprinted by permission of the author.

Dance, Stanley, *The World of Earl Hines*. Charles Scribner's Sons, New York. Copyright © 1977. Reprinted by permission of the author.

Dance, Stanley, *The World of Swing*. Charles Scribner's Sons, New York. Copyright © 1974. Reprinted by permission of the author.

Darensbourg, Joe, *Jazz Odyssey, as told to Peter Vacher*. Copyright © 1987 by Helen Darensbourg and Peter Vacher.

Davis, Francis, *In the Moment*. Oxford University Press, New York. Copyright © 1986. Reprinted by permission of the author.

Doran, James M., *Erroll Garner, the Most Happy Piano*. Scarecrow Press, Metuchen, N.J. Copyright © 1985. Reprinted by permission of the author.

Easton, Carol, *Straight Ahead: The Story of Stan Kenton*. © 1973 by Carol Easton, excerpts used by permission of William Morrow & Co. World rights by permission of the author.

Ellington, Duke, *Music Is My Mistress*. Copyright © 1973 by Duke Ellington. Used by permission of Doubleday, a division of Bantam, Doubleday, Dell Publishing Group, Inc.

Erwin, Pee Wee, with Warren Vaché Sr., *This Horn for Hire*. Scarecrow Press, Metuchen, N.J. Copyright © 1985. By permission of Mr. Vaché.

Feather, Leonard, *Pleasures of Jazz*. Horizon Press, New York. Copyright © 1976. Reprinted by permission of the author.

Feather, Leonard, and Jack Tracy, *Laughter from the Hip*. Horizon Press, New York. Copyright © 1973. Reprinted by permission of Mr. Feather.

Foster, George, *Pops Foster: The Autobiography of a New Orleans Jazzman as Told to Tom Stoddard*. © 1971. Reprinted by permission of University of California Press.

Fox, Charles, *Kings of Jazz 7: Fats Waller*. Reprinted by permission of the author.

Gara, Larry, *The Baby Dodds Story*. Contemporary, Los Angeles. Copyright © 1959. Reprinted by permission of the author.

Giddins, Gary, *Celebrating Bird*. William Morrow, New York. Copyright © 1987. Reprinted by permission of the author.

Giddins, Gary, *Riding on a Blue Note*. Oxford University Press, New York. Copyright © 1981. Reprinted by permission of the author.

Gillespie, Dizzy, *To Be or Not to Bop*. Copyright © 1979 by John Birks Gillespie and Wilmot Alfred Fraser. Used by permission of Doubleday, a division of Bantam, Doubleday, Dell Publishing Group, Inc.

Gitler, Ira, *Jazz Masters of the Forties*. Macmillan, New York. Copyright © 1966. Reprinted by permission of the author.

Gitler, Ira, *Swing to Bop*. Oxford University Press, New York. Copyright © 1985. Reprinted by permission of the author.

Grime, Kitty, *Jazz at Ronnie Scott's*. Photography by Val Wilmer. Copyright © 1979 by Kitty Grime and Val Wilmer. Reprinted by permission of the author.

Hammond, John, with Irving Townsend, *John Hammond on Record*. Copyright © 1977 by John Hammond. Reprinted by permission of Viking Penguin, a division of Penguin Books USA, Inc.

Hawes, Hampton, and Don Asher, *Raise Up Off Me*. Coward, McCann and Geohegan, New York. Copyright © 1974. Reprinted by permission of Mr. Asher.

Hentoff, Nat, *Jazz Is*. Ridge Press/Random House, New York. Copyright © 1976. Reprinted by permission of the author.

Hentoff, Nat, *The Jazz Life*. Dial Press, New York. Copyright © 1961. Reprinted by permission of the author.

Hinton, Milt, and David G. Berger, *Bass Line*. Temple University Press, Philadelphia. Copyright © 1988. Reprinted by permission of the authors and publisher.

Hodes, Art, *Selections from the Gutter*. University of California Press, Berkeley. Reprinted by permission of the author.

Holiday, Billie, with William Dufty, *Lady Sings the Blues*. Copyright © 1956 by Eleanor Fagan and William F. Dufty. Used by permission of Doubleday, a division of Bantam, Doubleday, Dell Publishing Group, Inc.

Jewell, Derek, *DUKE, a Portrait of Duke Ellington*. Reprinted by permission of W.W. Norton & Company, Inc., and Elm Tree Books, London. Copyright © by Derek Jewell.

Jones, Max, *Talking Jazz*. Macmillan, London. Copyright © 1987. Reprinted by permission of the author and publisher.

Kaminsky, Max, *My Life in Jazz*. Harper and Row, New York. Copyright © 1963. Reprinted by permission of the author.

Kirkeby, Ed, *Ain't Misbehavin'*. Dodd, Mead & Co., New York. Copyright © 1966.

Knauss, Zane, *Conversations with Jazz Musicians*. Copyright © 1977. Reprinted by permission of the Gale Research Co., Detroit.

Lees, Gene, *Meet Me at Jim and Andy's*. Oxford University Press, New York. Copyright © 1988. Reprinted by permission of the author.

Leonard, Neil, *Jazz: Myth and Religion*. Oxford University Press, New York. Copyright © 1987. Reprinted by permission of the author.

Lomax, Alan, *Mister Jelly Roll*. Copyright © 1950, 1973 by Alan Lomax. Reprinted by permission of the author.

Manone, Wingy, and Paul Vandervoort, *Trumpet on the Wing*. Copyright 1948 by Wingy Manone and Paul Vandervoort II. Used by permission of Doubleday, a division of Bantam, Doubleday, Dell Publishing Group, Inc.

Mezzrow, Milton "Mezz," and Bernard Wolfe, *Really the Blues*. Copyright © by Milton Mesirow and Delores Wolfe. Reprinted by permission.

Mingus, Charles, *Beneath the Underdog*. Copyright © 1971 by Charles Mingus and Nel King. Reprinted by permission of Viking Penguin, a division of Penguin Books USA, Inc.

Nisenson, Eric, *Round About Midnight*. Copyright © 1982 by Eric Nisenson. Used by permission of Doubleday, a division of Bantam, Doubleday, Dell Publishing Group, Inc.

Pearson, Nathan W., Jr., *Goin' to Kansas City*. Copyright © 1987 by Nathan W. Pearson, Jr. Used by permission of University of Illinois Press.

Reisner, Robert, *Bird: The Legend of Charlie Parker*. Copyright © 1962 by Bob Reisner. Published by arrangement with Carol Publishing Group.

Rollini, Art, *Thirty Years with the Big Bands*. University of Illinois Press. Copyright © 1987. Reprinted by permission of the author.

Rose, Al, *I Remember Jazz*. Louisiana State University Press. Copyright © 1987. Reprinted by permission of the author.

Rusch, Robert D., *Jazz Talk: The Cadence Interviews*. Lyle Stuart, Secaucus, N.J. Copyright © 1984. Reprinted by permission of the author.

Russell, Ross, *Jazz Style in Kansas City and the Southwest*. © 1971 The Regents of the University of California. Reprinted by permission of the University of California Press.

Sanford, Herb, *Tommy and Jimmy: The Dorsey Years*. Copyright © 1972. Reprinted by permission of Crown Publishers.

Shacter, James D., *Piano Man: The Story of Ralph Sutton*. Jaynar Press, Chicago. Copyright © 1975. Reprinted by permission of the author.

Shapiro, Nat, and Nat Hentoff, *Hear Me Talkin' To Ya*. Dover, New York. Copyright © 1955. Reprinted by permission of Mr. Hentoff.

Shapiro, Nat, and Nat Hentoff, *The Jazz Makers*. Rinehart & Co., New York. Copyright © 1957. Reprinted by permission of Mr. Hentoff.

Shaw, Arnold, *The Street That Never Slept*. Copyright © Arnold Shaw, 1971. Reprinted by permission of Ghita M. Shaw.

Smith, Willie "The Lion," *Music on My Mind*. Copyright © 1964 by Willie Smith and George Hoefer. Used by permission of Doubleday, a division of Bantam, Doubleday, Dell Publishing Group, Inc.

Smith, Jay D., and Len Guttridge, *Jack Teagarden: The Story of a Jazz Maverick*.

Reprinted with permission of Macmillan Publishing Co. (London, Cassell Ltd., 1960.)

Spellman, A.B., *Four Lives in the Bebop Business.* Copyright © 1966 by A.B. Spellman. Reprinted by permission of Pantheon Books, a division of Random House, Inc.

Stewart, Rex, *Jazz Masters of the Thirties.* Reprinted by permission of Schirmer Books, a division of Macmillan, Inc. Copyright © 1972 by the Estate of Rex W. Stewart.

Sudhalter, Richard, and Philip Evans, *Bix: Man and Legend.* Macmillan, New York. Copyright © 1974. Reprinted by permission of Mr. Sudhalter.

Taylor, Arthur, *Notes and Tones.* G. P. Putnam's Sons, New York. Copyright © 1977. Reprinted by permission of the author.

Thomas, J.C., *Chasin' the Trane.* Copyright © 1975 by J.C. Thomas. Used by permission of Doubleday, a division of Bantam, Doubleday, Dell Publishing Group, Inc.

Thompson, Charles, *Bing.* David McKay Co., Inc. Copyright © 1976.

Tormé, Mel, *It Wasn't All Velvet.* Copyright © 1988 by Mel Tormé. Reprinted by permission of Viking Penguin, a division of Penguin Books USA, Inc.

Travis, Dempsey J., *An Autobiography of Black Jazz.* Urban Research Institute, Chicago. Copyright © 1983. Reprinted by permission of the author.

Ulanov, Barry, *Handbook of Jazz.* Viking, New York. Copyright © 1957. Reprinted by permission of the author.

Ulanov, Barry, *The Incredible Crosby.* McGraw-Hill, New York. Copyright © 1948. Reprinted by permission of the author.

Voce, Steve, *Woody Herman.* Apollo Press, London. Copyright © 1986. Reprinted by permission of the author.

Waller, Maurice, and Anthony Calabrese, *Fats Waller.* Copyright © 1977 Maurice Waller and Anthony Calabrese. Reprinted by permission of Schirmer Books, a Division of Macmillan, Inc., and by Cassell Ltd., London.

Wilmer, Valerie, *As Serious As Your Life.* Lawrence Hill & Co., Westport, Conn. Copyright © 1980. Reprinted by permission of the author.

Zinsser, William, *Willie and Dwike.* Harper and Row, New York. Copyright © 1984. Reprinted by permission of the author.

Bebop and Beyond magazine, Los Angeles.

Cadence Magazine interviews. Reprinted by permission of Robert D. Rusch. Pepper Adams interview by Gary Karner.

Coda Magazine, Toronto, Ontario. *Claude Thornhill* by Ian Crosbie; interview with Sadik Hakim. Reprinted by permission.

Jazz Journal International, London. Al Haig article by John Shaw; Ed Hubble article by Eric Townley. Reprinted by permission.

Jazzletter, Ojai, California. Reprinted by permission of Gene Lees.

The Jazz Oral History Project. Funded by the National Endowment for the Arts. Reprinted by permission of the Institute for Jazz Studies, Rutgers University, Newark, N.J.

New Yorker magazine. Whitney Balliett article on Louis Bellson. Reprinted by permission of the author.

Life Magazine. Louis Armstrong interview, 1966. Used by permission.

New York Times. "Who Didn't Write 'Tin Roof Blues'" by Arnold Benson. Copyright © 1988 by The New York Times Company. Reprinted by permission.

Park East magazine, New York.

Riverside Record RLP 12-120, liner notes. Extract reprinted by permission of Fantasy Records, Berkeley, Calif.

Index